Monumental Lies

Monumental Lies

Culture Wars and the
Truth about the Past

Robert Bevan

VERSO

London • New York

First published by Verso 2022
© Robert Bevan 2022

1 3 5 7 9 10 8 6 4 2

Verso
UK: 6 Meard Street, London W1F 0EG
US: 388 Atlantic Avenue, Brooklyn, NY 11217
versobooks.com

Verso is the imprint of New Left Books

ISBN-13: 978-1-83976-187-4
ISBN-13: 978-1-83976-190-4 (US EBK)
ISBN-13: 978-1-83976-189-8 (UK EBK)

British Library Cataloguing in Publication Data
A catalogue record for this book is available from the British Library

Library of Congress Cataloging-in-Publication Data
A catalog record for this book is available from the Library of Congress

Typeset in Sabon by MJ & N Gavan, Truro, Cornwall
Printed and bound by CPI Group (UK) Ltd, Croydon, CR0 4YY

For Agnes
For all the library books

Contents

Introduction

The ideal subject of totalitarian rule is not the convinced Nazi or the convinced Communist but people for whom the distinction between fact and fiction (i.e., the reality of experience) and the distinction between true and false (i.e., the standards of thought) no longer exist.

– Hannah Arendt, *The Origins of Totalitarianism*[1]

If we read a city carefully enough, it will tell us about our past. Just like a book on a library shelf or a document in an archive box, monuments, architecture, and cities are evidence of history. What's more, the city's constituent elements are *material* evidence – actual physical traces of past events as well as witnesses to previous ways of thinking. Embedded within them are politics, economics, and values that may be very different from ours but which are still having their effect today. As Hannah Arendt observed: 'The reality and reliability of the human world rest primarily on the fact that we are surrounded by things more permanent than the activity by which they were produced.'[2]

So when our cities are reshaped as fantasies about the past, when monuments and statues tell lies about who or what events deserve immortalisation, the historical record is being manipulated. When we are told, falsely, that certain architectural styles are alien to our culture or that people naturally prefer to live among their own kind, the reliability of the world is called into question. Our streets and squares are not the morally neutral, inert assemblages of brick and stone they pretend to be. Even absences can be telling. We need only look around us and see – or rather not see – the memorials to female achievement, the Black experience, or LGBTQ+ lives. For those with the power and money to place a likeness on a pedestal, monuments are more often a tool to obscure the real facts of history, to shape a chosen narrative, to invent nationalist and civic traditions, and to enforce imagined communities that extend only to those deemed to belong.[3]

This book is about the truths and lies that our built environment embodies, whether at the scale of a figure on a plinth or an entire city: From *Judensau,* the co-mingled stone images of Jews and pigs used as anti-Semitic grotesques on medieval churches, to digitally made copies of ancient temple arches intended to replace originals obliterated by Islamic State/Da'esh; from the use of city planning to purposefully segregate on racialised grounds or separate a suburban mother from the wider world, to the attempts to stop minarets appearing on the skylines of Western cities.

The chapters that follow are, for the most part, about the historic built environment rather than contemporary architecture, and they focus on the public realm rather than the interior world of the museum and how these institutions interpret their troublesome holdings. But the focus is not simply the internal machinations of the heritage world (although the failures of a politicised UNESCO and the dangerous 'military–heritage complex' emerging are discussed). Instead, it is about the facts and narratives of architectural history and how they are used and misused. Often this historic environment is portrayed as superficial heritage rather than serious history. As someone who works in the heritage world daily, this can be an uncomfortable distinction, but it is vital to be aware of it. Heritage can indeed be simply historical facts filtered through 'mythology, ideology, nationalism, local pride, romantic ideas or just plain marketing.'[4] Heritage's politically conservative, superficial side was eviscerated in David Lowenthal's 1985 classic *The Past Is a Foreign Country* and in Robert Hewison's *The Heritage Industry: Britain in a Climate of Decline* published two years later. Sympathetic accounts of heritage on the Left are few, and it is one of the great cultural tragedies of the past half century that the Left has ceded the heritage narrative to conservatives.[5]

William Morris and his Society for the Preservation of Ancient Buildings, the National Trust, and the creation of National Parks are among the many preservation initiatives that have their roots in a socialist resistance to capitalist spoliation and not nostalgic Little Englandism and country house tours. Today's Left has forgotten its own history and now treats all heritage with suspicion. Given the way heritage has been used as a form of Tory entryism into the cultural sphere, this is hardly surprising. Still, it would be a fine thing if the Left could reclaim the symbolic high ground when it comes to heritage and preservation, because heritage and the past constantly come back to bite us.

When Lowenthal and Hewison were writing in the 1980s, the impact of neoliberalism on culture was beginning to make its effects felt. The term 'culture war' has often been ascribed to Pat Buchanan who at the 1992 Republican Convention called for a war for the soul of America: 'It is a cultural war, as critical to the kind of nation we will one day be as was the Cold War itself.'[6] Buchanan's attack was on Black rights, gay liberation, and feminism, and it happened in the wake of the 1991 Los Angeles riots that erupted after the dismissal of charges against LAPD officers for the savage beating of Rodney King. Buchanan's was a law and order message that dismissed the 'mob' and supported military intervention in a city still substantially segregated in places (a racial separation enforced over the previous decades by everyone from local chapters of the KKK and the American Nazi Party to redlining estate agents and federal agencies): 'And as they took back the streets of LA, block by block, so we must take back our cities, and take back our culture, and take back our country,' instructed Buchanan.

But culture wars have a longer history, from the nineteenth-century German concept of the *Kulturkampf* through to the liberation struggles of the 1960s and '70s. The 1980s and '90s version often took the form of accusations of 'political correctness' that aimed (as they do today) to stymie progress on social justice and if possible reverse its gains. In '80s Britain, the tabloids were full of invented stories about loony Left London councils banning words such as 'blackboard' and 'manhole,' stories given support by a Tory central government in the face of challenges by municipal socialism and the trade unions which by then had become successful vehicles for promoting equality. In the United States, proxy weapons in the '80s and '90s ranged from the Parental Advisory stickers on rap records and federal funding for art museums displaying the fetish photographs of Robert Mapplethorpe, to the war on drugs and abortion rights. In the subsequent context of the war on terror and its othering of entire peoples and religions, the culture wars ratcheted up further and have escalated again in the wake of the 2008 global financial crash, a crisis of capitalism, and austerity policies that sets one against another in a scrabble for resources. Anxieties have intensified beyond previous hotspots.

So we are not so much in the middle of a brand-new culture war as deep within the latest campaign in a cultural conflict that has been underway for decades and which is blowing hot once more. On the one hand, there is a post– 9/11 fearfulness of the other, a neoliberal land grab of the public realm, and the rise in nationalism and nativism, and on the other, the Black, feminist, decolonialist, and queer critiques of the monumental canon that are having some success in changing the conversation. Historic places and commemorative landscapes have each been contested over and again down the centuries, but there is a renewed ferocity to these twenty-first-century disagreements and this time around, architecture and heritage are on the front line.

This is reflected in a new period of memorial mania, a statuary arms race characterised by an astonishing proliferation of hasty public monuments to everything from B-list celebrities (who are not always even dead) to nationalist causes. At the same time, activists are demanding not just more and better statues but the toppling of stone and bronze street corner killers that have been used to whitewash reputations and justify the stolen fortunes of entire continents. Its critics regard this iconoclastic demand as a literal no-platforming, an element of cancel culture, or a form of grievance archaeology. It is not. This is simply the consequence of lies about the past finally being called to account and a demand that the commemorative environment of the present reflect larger truths.

In Eastern Europe after the fall of the Soviet Union, and in New World nations built on indigenous land, the culture wars have been more directly framed as history and memory wars. In the former Eastern Bloc, populists collaborate with emboldened churches on eradicating the legacy of communism and putting the traditional family centre stage. In Australia, their main focus is on narratives of colonisation and dispossession; in the United States on the legacy of slavery.

In Britain, where the Conservative government's offensive against multiculturalism ratcheted up under David Cameron and then intensified under Boris Johnson, race and empire are core concerns but anxieties range much wider. Johnson's administration has threatened the independence of major museums and university education in ways that would make a Polish or Hungarian populist proud. He has set about putting his placemen (and they are more usually men) in the BBC and other cultural institutions and ensured that equality ministers and government rights bodies spend more time attacking the very concept of systemic racism and the dignity of trans people than on protecting minorities. The small fortune Johnson has spent, post-Brexit, on Union Jack flags is just the icing on his poisonous cultural cake. A similar process is underway in countries such as France where, as the 2022 national election approached, the Macron government conjured the phantom of *Islamo-gauchisme* intent on assailing L'Hexagone from its mythical 'no-go' ghettoes.

Statue wars apart, however, it is in Germany, perhaps, where the culture wars have taken on their most architectonic character. Here, as part of a concerted attempt to rebuild blitzed city centres as historicist pastiche, we are seeing not only the rehabilitation of Classical architecture (for a while entirely tainted by Third Reich associations) but also the rebuilding of long-vanished palaces, churches, and whole quarters of city centres as if Hitler had never happened. These purposely forgetful efforts are often linked to Germany's Right and Far Right such as the Alternative for Germany (AfD).

Modernism's record, which at its utopian best was about building for a more egalitarian post-war world, is under attack by a resurgent and reactionary architectural traditionalism. In the United Kingdom too, Classicism, for a long time a marginal vanity project of Prince Charles and his architectural courtiers, is now, with the assistance of policy outsourced by government to the likes of think tanks such as the Policy Exchange, gaining a sneaky foothold in national planning policy to potentially devastating effect for creativity. Back in the 1980s, the Prince was one of the earliest to drag architecture into the culture wars and his patience seems to be finally paying off. Arguments over beauty and ugliness are the Trojan horse concealing a desire to reimpose conservative historicism while it dismantles the Modernist architecture of the welfare state and public housing in favour of the free market. All this is part of a remaking of our gentrified city centres that prizes spectacle and illusions such as 'pseudo-public space' at the same time as seeking to demolish Modernism's utopianism. It is useful for the Right to demonize Modernism as a style promoted by cosmopolitan elites when they don't want to fund the architectural infrastructure of a welfare state or build social housing; horizontally proportioned windows rather than austerity are then the problem.

In the United States, the culture wars escalated once more following the 2015 murder of nine members of an African American church in Charleston, South Carolina, by a white supremacist obsessed with Confederate symbols. Flags and statues became the focus as Black Americans asserted their rights and dignity in the face of violence. They are rightly unconvinced that such symbols are about Southern heritage rather than hate. And in the aftermath of the murder of George Floyd in May 2020, the Black Lives Matter movement boosted pre-existing calls to topple colonialist statues worldwide.

In Britain, this led to felling of the statue to slave trader Edward Colston in the port of Bristol, while in Belgium there were attacks on statues linked to colonial atrocities in the Belgian Congo. In Australia, where the conservative government had been commemorating the founding narrative of Captain Cook's discovery voyage and the concept of *terra nullius* rather than foregrounding the genocide of Indigenous Australians and the destruction of their material culture by mining companies, statues of Cook became battlegrounds after Floyd's death.

Figurative statues honouring individuals are the most contested sites in these history and heritage-driven culture wars. This is hardly surprising because, more usually honouring power rather than genuine virtue, they are most easily caught out in deliberate, calculated lies. These are also places where meaning and values seem distilled. What we see on plinths and in commemorations from the size of a mountainside to a small plaque are, with rare exceptions, raised to rich, white, and (ostensibly at least) straight men. In Edinburgh there are more statues to dogs than real-life females; in London more figures of animals than named women.[7] Even monuments concerned with the end of slavery are more likely to celebrate white abolitionists rather than the experience of the oppressed.

Antonio Gramsci, imprisoned by Mussolini, wrote about struggles for cultural hegemony and control of the narrative. He differentiated between 'wars of manoeuvre,' that is, attempts to gain control of the state by arms or elections and 'wars of position' that recognize the importance of culture, institutions, and symbols in deciding the ideological agenda for change and the basis of future struggles. Those who control culture use it to propagate norms that become seen as commonsense values that simply aren't questioned.[8] If one accepts his premise, then commemorative environments are clearly used as a weapon in wars of position. Already in 1917, Gramsci was critiquing the changing of street names in Turin in order to immortalize the Savoyard elite road by road: 'Armed with an encyclopedia and an axe,' he wrote, the street naming commission is proceeding with the evisceration of old Turin. Down come the old names, the traditional names of popular Turin that record the fervent life of the old medieval commune ... They are replaced with medal names. The street map is becoming a medal showcase.[9]

What he would have made of the Via Antonio Gramsci in Rome replacing the Fascist Via dei Legionari in 1944 is anyone's guess, still less the later renaming of part of the Via Antonio Gramsci as Piazzale Winston Churchill.

More than being about manipulating historical narratives in the interests of the ruling class, sometimes these monuments are also spatial acts of aggression. Take Confederate statues across the United States: In the period immediately after the Civil War ended in 1865, memorials to the war dead were mostly in cemeteries. It was only after former slaves began to assert their freedom in the Reconstruction era that followed manumission that white supremacists shifted the focus of their monument building from the graveside to the centre of towns and cities, often on the courthouse square. The equestrian generals, obelisks, and mass-produced 'Silent Sentinels' were designed not as acts of mourning and not just as a means to perpetuate the lie that the Civil War had been about state rights rather than to preserve chattel slavery; they aimed to assert control over Jim Crow-era segregated public space and serve as reminders of who could enforce justice and injustices. They were territorial markers. Their aim was oppression. And they were still being completed as late as 1972. The anger among American people of colour that these monuments still stand is entirely understandable.

The dynamic across the Atlantic was very different but in certain ways extraordinarily similar. In Bristol, Britain's chief slaving port in the middle of the eighteenth century, the horrific realities of the Triangular Trade were offshored as much as possible. Here, Edward Colston has been the city's most honoured son, at the centre of Bristol's self-identity as a city made admirable by a legacy of charitable giving. Colston commemorations included not just the city centre bronze of Colston toppled by

0.1 Robert E Lee being craned away from New Orleans in 2017. A number of Confederate monuments were removed following the mass shooting of Black church-goers in Charleston, South Carolina, in 2015 by a white supremacist obsessed with Confederate symbolism.

Black Lives Matter activists in the summer of 2020, or the name of a nearby Colston Hall built on the site of a slavery-fuelled sugar mill, but its cathedral windows and in the many streets, schools, hospitals, and almshouses named in his honour. As recently as 2019, Bristol school children were being shepherded to the cathedral for religious services praising Colston. Yet when Edward Colston died in 1721, it was after a lifetime leading the Atlantic slave trade where he was complicit in the death of many tens of thousands of Africans, branded and shipped in the sickening conditions of the Middle Passage to rape, beatings, mutilation, and an early death on the plantations of the Leeward Islands and the Americas. It's no wonder that Colston has become emblematic of all that is wrong with Britain's manipulative monuments and the country's failure to recognise its brutal colonial history.

As with the Confederate statues, appearances are deceptive here, too. The toppled Colston bronze was not put up by a grieving but thankful citizenry immediately after his death in 1721. It was erected in 1895, more than 170 years later and half a century after the slave trade ended in most of the British Empire. This and other memorials were raised as part of a consciously shaped Cult of Colston promoted by Bristol's merchant elite. While defending the mercantile narrative of the city's imperial history, the cult at that time was not so much about enforcing racial oppression locally as about patrolling class. Colston was a historical figurehead useful in creating a paternalist and cross-class civic narrative in the face of rising industrial unrest and labour organisation. When it came to Colston's own ignoble career it was simply a case of eyes averted. No one wanted to discuss the funding source for Bristol's elegant buildings and its

Getty

0.2 Protestors rolling away the toppled statue of Edward Colston in Bristol in June 2020. The bronze figure was tipped into the nearby harbour which had been a major port in the transatlantic slave trade. The 'drowning' of the statue was considered poetic justice by many. It was retrieved and displayed in a museum.

Christian institutions. Quite rightly, such lies are no longer good enough for the rising generations.

To those concerned with social justice, there is a simple answer to dealing with these false narratives, to these liars we are supposed to look up to in their elevated positions: tear them down. A sincere reckoning with racism and colonialism, runs the argument, means that we should topple its monuments and rename places that honour despicable people and events. Their mere presence, their attempt to assert a particular collective identity and inaccurate and incomplete narrative, effectively serves capitalism, nationalism, white supremacy, misogyny, and heteronormativity.

But, in this, are we giving these objects too much power? Figurative statues are simply the most attention-seeking, the most visible aspects of heritage manipulation, and mostly visible only after their true meaning has been brought back to our attention by diligent activists. There is a danger of a culture war collusion in focusing attention on symbols whose removal creates an illusion of change while systemic injustice, whether against people of colour, women, LGBTQ+, and working-class people continues unaltered. Isn't it mass incarceration rather than a problematic commemorative landscape that's the chief motor of contemporary Jim Crow?[10] Others argue that tackling monuments is a constituent part of the wider, systemic dismantling process.

Certainly this objectionable landscape cannot be left untouched. However, at the same time as needing to create a more equitable physical environment, we have a duty to ensure that we don't forget that the ruling class has been perfectly willing to honour genocidaires such as Cecil Rhodes or Christopher Columbus in our public spaces.

This book dwells less on the objectionable histories of many of these monuments, which have been rehearsed regularly in the press in the past few years, and more on what we should do about them. The answers are not as simple as they might first seem. Before we embark on a new iconoclastic wave, we need to acknowledge the many myths and misunderstandings about why our commemorative landscape is the way it is and about the great iconoclastic episodes of the past – especially those that came at the end of totalitarianism.

A central question is how we go about the task of honest revision in the face of conservatives upholding a deceitful status quo, throwing around accusations of the erasure of history and putting in place bad faith 'retain and explain' polices that are intended to avoid any genuinely meaningful explanation. We need to go about this carefully so that we forge a clearer under-standing of the past while safeguarding evidence of the reality of historical wrongdoing. All manner of evidence is required if we are to successfully smash the mythology of colonialism and empire and have an honest reckoning.

Facts themselves have become entangled in the culture wars. Many worry that we are in a post-truth age where emotion and beliefs have achieved primacy over reality. 'Post-truth' was the Oxford Dictionary's word of the year in 2016. The phenome-non is far older, however. One of a slew of recent books on the subject, Lee McIntyre's *Post-Truth* neatly summarises its lineage drawing largely on the American context.[11] McIntyre goes back to the fake news (a close cousin of post-truth) pamphlets of the French and American Revolutions. Then there were the famously deliberate distortions of William Randolph Hearst's newspapers, including fake drawings of Cuban officers strip-searching American women that allegedly helped bring about the Spanish-American War in 1898. Orwell was still worrying about it in 1949 when *Nineteen Eighty-Four: A Novel* was pub-lished: 'The very concept of objective truth is fading out of the world. Lies will pass into history.'[12] McIntyre sets out the more recent role of Big Tobacco and its PR campaign whose purpose was to deny the authority of modern science. This denial of authority has since become the reactionary's aim whether discussing the climate or vaccinations. Purposefully manufac-turing doubt is the desired product; facts such as climate change become only theories. He charts the rise of new media in fos-tering the phenomenon. This is all on top of the mainstream media's obsession with a 'both sides' approach to coverage that supports false equivalence even where one side's claims have zero basis in fact.

McIntrye argues that post-truth 'amounts to a form of ideological supremacy, where its practitioners are trying to compel someone to believe in something whether there is good evidence for it or not and that is a recipe for political domination.'[13] This is a reformulation of Hannah Arendt's observation that the real totalitarian threat comes not from arguments about what is true and what is false but convincing people that the difference between them doesn't really matter.[14] Fascism, after all, relies on strong emotion and spectacle rather than reality to help secure its hold. Those subject to the lies *feel* that they are accepting them freely. While it can be too easy to blame the media, especially new media, for false beliefs and conspiracy theories, the dangers are real. As Timothy Snyder wrote in the *New York Times*:

> Post-truth is pre-Fascism, and Trump has been our post-truth president ... If we lose the institutions that produce facts that are pertinent to us, then we tend to wallow in attractive abstractions and fictions. Post-truth wears away the rule of law and invites a regime of myth.[15]

On the face of it, architecture should be immune from such 'post-truth' forces because there would appear to be no more indisputable evidence of the form of the present and shape of the past than a weighty and long-standing building. The very physicality of architecture, its relative longevity, gives the impression of certainty, a 'what you see is what you get' lack of complication. 'Reality,' Philip K Dick reminds us, 'is that which, when you stop believing in it, doesn't go away.'[16]

This makes the architectural a useful dupe for those wishing to manipulate the present by misusing the past, especially because the outward impassivity of non-figurative structures is particularly effective in disguising its ideological content. In a context where anti-cosmopolitans are on the offensive, the foolish belief that this townscape is disinterested makes its manipulation an effective weapon against the truth. The architectural and commemorative environment thus has a much-underestimated role in fostering and cementing falsehoods about history. It is a tool that renders these falsehoods physical, making them harder to refute. Arendt's test of reliability becomes undermined.

Strangely, the culture warriors of the Right regularly focus on postmodernism as the source of what they see as a decay in conservative values. This is partly because they regard class politics as a spent force and see the main challenge to their cultural hegemony (some have read their Gramsci too) as the identity-based politics of contemporary social justice activists who are, it's true, often substantially informed by postmodern theory in their understanding and tactics.

Postmodernism has indeed been a problem but, I argue, for the Left and for the primacy of facts and historical materialism because as a theoretical framework, postmodernism sought to undermine foundational concepts fostered since the Enlightenment. As a set of ideas its academic interest may have peaked, but it still exerts a pernicious effect. And while it may have enriched our analytical tools and widened the terms of enquiry in favour of the overlooked of history, it has also contributed to an erosion of objectivity and historical truth that it sees as naïve and totalising. Postmodernism and its linguistic turn attacked the very possibility of a scientific history based on the rigorous investigation of primary sources. Culture and history become concepts that lack a universal, explanatory power and were reduced to a series of experience-derived, separate, overlapping, and competing narratives that are true only to particular groups of people. Alternative facts.

In architecture, this has meant more than the adoption of Po-Mo as a cheeky style willing to juice the material accumulation of design history in a blender, or being in thrall to a data-driven but values-free parametricism particularly suited to the spectacle of late capitalism; it has also undermined the evidentiary and archival role of the built historical record. Essential concepts that have been valued for more than a century and promoted by the likes of Socialist William Morris, such as 'authenticity' in conservation and reconstruction that demands intellectual honesty in being able to visibly separate new work from old, are being hastily abandoned. Previously precise terms such as 'reconstruction' or 'restoration' are being used without their old precision and are being undermined by potentially useful but ethically fraught and unregulated technologies such as digital copies that offer a superficial faux authenticity. Authenticity is a word in danger of being rendered meaningless by brand market-eers but which is too important to lose to such slipperiness.

The rot starts at the top. In UNESCO's case, this is a conse-quence of not just postmodern thinking about heritage, but of political convenience, misjudged attempts at post-conflict recon-struction and reconciliation, and a desire to resist iconoclasts such as Da'esh. The role of selective architectural destruction in shaping social constructs such as the nation-state or repressing and othering ethnic groups was central to my 2006 book *The Destruction of Memory: Architecture at War.*[17] It focused upon the targeting of architecture, heritage, and monuments in armed conflicts, particularly (but not only) those characterised by com-peting identities where cultural destruction was an aspect of ethnic cleansing and genocide. However, such dynamics and the manipulations of a contested historical record exist too in the reconstructions immediately following a war and under the longer peace that follows.

In some ways *Monumental Lies* is a companion piece to that earlier volume, in others it revises its earlier optimism about, for example, the role of the international community in properly protecting cultural heritage. Whereas the notion of rebuilding the Bamiyan Buddhas was once deemed unacceptable fakery by UNESCO, the organisation has since embraced rebuilding copies – Mostar Bridge, for instance – with the new span hastily declared a World Heritage Site, a designation only possible by jumping through hoops to ensure the facsimile made it past UNESCO's own strict authenticity criterion. Then in 2015,

UNESCO declared that war-ravaged Palmyra would be rebuilt without even having examined the damage. Failures in trials at The Hague, myths of reconciliation through memorialisation, and the destructive and genocidal campaign by Da'esh have also seen the worrying shift to heritage professionals becoming embedded in Western military decision-making. The British government can boast about setting up a cultural protection unit in its army and funding heritage safeguarding measures in Yemen through the British Council at the same time as it sells weapons to Saudi Arabia that are used to annihilate that same heritage.

We have more data about the world, more measurements, more images of it, than ever before in history, but we live in a time when verifiable facts are trashed as fake, as unreliable along with the expertise that identifies them. But the verifiable facts about history are vital and authentic built fabric can absolutely evidence the past, to the point where the architectural can be a crucial witness to dark events: The slum and the palace, the public health clinic or private art gallery, all are architectural archaeology revealing how we live, how society is organised, and what larger forces are at work in the world. Yet in the post–Floyd phase of statue toppling, various commentators have claimed that statues are not even history. This simply will not do; the evidence supporting the historical record is not only words on a page but also material artefacts. Leon Trotsky might seem an unlikely source of design wisdom, but he was an astute cultural observer and understood the role of architecture as a record of history. He wrote that the Renaissance

> only begins when the new social class, already culturally satiated, feels itself strong enough to come out from under the yoke of the Gothic arch, to look at Gothic art and on all that preceded it as material for its own disposal.[18]

This is more than an elegant metaphor; he believed that architecture above all the arts revealed the dialectical processes of the arc of history. This book places historical materialism and evidence at its core rather than the more unreliable and problematic idea of memory.

It also questions the degree to which changing the built environment genuinely alters our lives and values. There are many determinist illusions, 'cause and effect' expectations about the impact of monuments and of iconoclasm – or indeed architecture and architectural style more generally – on us and our politics and societies. Winston Churchill's oft-repeated remark that 'we shape our buildings, and afterwards our buildings shape us' is, in truth, a problematic over-simplification. He made the claim in a 1943 speech calling for the bombed-out House of Commons to be restored to its pre-war appearance.[19] There is an underlying thread of determinism here that architecture and design have heavily invested in and promoted: the belief that design may not simply build more equitable places that positively shape lives (which it can) but will actually *cause* social change rather than simply reflect it. It is a view that not only marginalises the agency of people in driving societal change but peddles myths about our behavioural response to the physical environment that persist to this day. Arguably, these myths continue when we believe that a more progressive and inclusive monumental landscape will itself produce social change. Those calling for the no-plinthing of triggering statues might be buying into the same illusions about the real-world impact of such actions. Offence is not necessarily the same as actual harm.

All this is influenced by identity-based politics and its tactics. Both progressives and reactionaries are weaponizing the built historical record. Identity-based equality struggles have made huge strides over the past half century and more, challenging those in power and their narratives, revealing hidden histories and demanding that past oppressions are recognized and redressed in the present. The 1960s to 1980s in particular saw history wrested from its traditional gatekeepers and democratised with mainstream accounts revised and ordinary working class lives made the legitimate subject of enquiry. The rise of intersectional thinking in recent decades has enriched this

further, although a desire to pressure an economically reductiv-
ist Left to look beyond class, has too-often reduced class issues
to just another identity characteristic rather than a motor of
change.

The Left's identity-based approach has also been mirrored by
dangerous identitarian equivalents on the Right and Far Right
that focus on who belongs and who is other and that use heritage and history for their own regressive purposes. Journalist
and academic Kenan Malik consequently warns of the potential
pitfalls of identity approaches: 'Many on the left now embrace
the idea that one's interests and values are defined primarily by
one's ethnic or cultural or gender identity,' he writes. 'The politics of identity is, however, at root the politics of the reactionary
right. Now, identitarians of the Far Right are seizing upon the
opportunity provided by the left's adoption of identity politics
to legitimise their once-toxic brand.'[20] Racism, for example,
became rebranded as white identity politics by those wishing to
exploit cultural anxieties and foment culture wars.

If the period between the First and Second World Wars was, in
Eric Hobsbawm's coinage, 'the Age of Catastrophe,' then today
might be characterised as an era of 'permanent catastrophe.'
This destabilised context is the perfect soil for identity conflicts
and culture wars. With no economic solutions on the horizon,
the wars become the means by which politicians attempt to
court their constituencies. The Right resists the drive by progressives to transform communities in the name of equality and
diversity, and it doubles down on preserving its own invented
traditions and imagined nationalist communities of long-
standing. The social-democratic Left, unable to offer its own
economic solutions to capitalism's crisis, the long-term decline
of the West, or the climate emergency, has relied instead (when
it suits) on the dynamism of identity-based progress movements to substitute for their economic powerlessness. The focus
then becomes the cultural superstructure rather than material
improvements.

We must tread carefully then when making demands to reshape the built environment and alter the material record of the past. A culture war is not one that progressives should normally choose. Yet however phoney these wars may be in the sense of them being deployed as wedge issues by the Right, the consequences are real; Charlottesville has white supremacists marching by torchlight chanting 'Jews Will Not Replace Us' and London has had fascists *Sieg Heiling* at the Cenotaph on Whitehall. The Right's culture warriors are encouraging their constituency to feel embattled and to create 'last stands' against the so-called 'great replacement' of whites by non-whites, an anti-cosmopolitan binary of 'my culture, my heritage, my identity – or yours.' But while we may not wish to start from here, it is where we are and we cannot back down. The stakes could not be higher.

We need, however, to be able to separate out truths from lies not just online or in news bulletins but in the built environment: the cradle to grave container of our daily lives. We need to look at ways we can layer our monuments and our city that turns sites of honour into sites of shame, that change the meaning of the past without losing altogether the vital evidence of that past from the public realm. Without such an approach, there is the real concern that we, in the name of progress, are paving the way for a dangerous Humpty Dumpty populism where truth, including truth in architecture, is whatever you say it is. Historical truth is not necessarily the absolute or total truth, but it is the closest point we can get to about the facts of the past and this relies on having the best available evidence and an open-minded willingness to test that truth against any newly emerging evidence including that provided by the architectural record. If we fake or destroy that record, how can we ever learn from it or guard it against those who would use an absence of facts against us?

Fundamentally, this book argues that if we can no longer trust the tangible world around us to tell the truth, then we are in real trouble.

Timing and Terminology

This book was commissioned only months before the police murder of George Floyd in Minneapolis in May 2020. In the immediate aftermath of his death, contested heritage moved from being a somewhat arcane debate to a main front in the culture wars. Writing about a subject that is evolving continually even as one writes presents its challenges: Black Lives Matter erupts. Confederate statues are craned away. Colston is hauled from his pedestal in Bristol. Trump is there and then he's gone only for leadership of the reactionary baton to be passed back to Europe where culture wars are now in full swing, not just in the former Eastern Bloc but in countries such as Britain and in France (where, at the time of writing, the Far Right was sniffing at the presidency). Some of the places that I discuss may already have changed once more. I hope I have conveyed the arc and meaning of this ever-shifting experience.

Terminology is also evolving and I have had to make some decisions using terms that groups self-identify with as far as possible. In Britain, for example, Black and Minority Ethnic (BAME) is a bureaucratic catch-all that is now seen as too flattening of different experiences, so I have tended to use terms such as the previously more American 'people of colour.' I have capped Black as is commonly done in the United States. Similarly, the lesbian and gay family and alphabet are ever-evolving. I have stuck with LGBTQ+ or queer.

Political terms are also subject to change or vagueness of definition. What for instance, are the shades between populism, the Right, the Hard Right, the Far Right, and proto- or full-blown Fascism? I have tried to negotiate this as best as I can. In this context, I have tended to use the term 'white supremacy' as it relates to violent groups such as the Proud Boys and various other organised racists and neo-Nazis rather than as part of theoretical framings such as white privilege. I use the (insulting) Arabic term 'Da'esh' rather than ISIS and ISIL that have the effect of legitimising its territorial claims.

I have also sometimes used 'cosmopolitan' and 'multicultural' almost as synonyms while being aware of the potential for multicultural to be seen as problematic in a similar way to BAME for the way that government taxonomy and policies can serve separation and competition rather than bring genuine diversity. Apologies for any infelicities. I know that I will not please everybody.

London. April 2022.

1

Killers on
Every Corner

Spill the blood of continents and it's Portland stone and a plaque
in your honour.
— Charlie Gilmour, *The Independent*, 2016[1]

Visiting Bolzano in the strange Covid summer of 2020, I meet
Hannes Obermair at Bolzano's railway station, high in the
Italian South Tyrol. Hannes is a historian and philosopher in
residence at the local Eurac research institute in what remains
one of the more culturally complex parts of Western Europe.

When the station opened in 1859, the town – Bozen in
German – was still part of the Austro-Hungarian empire and
we set off into town past elaborate edifices that appear worthy
of Vienna's Ringstrasse. Hannes tells me, however, that, suspicious of the cosmopolitanism of Freud's Vienna, Bozen, while
only an hour south of the Brenner Pass, more often looked to
Germany rather than Austria for a 'purer' architectural inspi-
ration. Bolzano's Italian speakers, meanwhile, looked south to
Venice and Rome rather than its immediate multicultural region.
Just before reaching the stuffy Teutonic grandeur of the Hotel
Lauren, Hannes pulls up at a public noticeboard pasted with
posters for CasaPound, the violent neo-Fascist party that at the

time of my visit had seats on the city council. Above its turtle and arrows symbol is the word *Osare!* (To Dare!). With a swift efficient pull Hannes tears one poster down.

Bolzano was annexed by Italy in 1919 when the vast majority of its inhabitants were German speakers. Under Mussolini a forced Italianisation programme was set in train. The German language was supressed and Italians brought in from other parts of the country to work in the expanding factories of the Fascist industrial–military complex and, more importantly, to manipulate the region's demographics. After the 1939 German-Italian South Tyrol Option Agreement, German residents had to either opt for removal to the Reich or stay and be fully Italianized. The war got in the way, though, and Bolzano-Bozen today remains thoroughly bilingual.

Hannes hurries me on through Waltherplatz/Piazza Walther with its 1889 statue of the twelfth-century poet and minstrel Walther von der Vogelweide at its centre. 'He is facing south, a gatekeeper against the Pope,' observes Hannes. On we go past the crouching medieval arcades of an Alpine town and through Piazza Domenicani whose buildings, at first Gothic and Renaissance, become steadily more Fascist as you move west. Eventually, we cross a bridge over a turbulent river. There's a rumble of thunder and gravid clouds ease themselves through the humid air over the nearby mountain ridge. Fat drops of rain spatter the paving. This west bank used to be Gries, a separate spa town among water meadows. But once the Blackshirts took power in 1922, Gries steadily vanished under the grid of Bolzano's Fascist town extension.

At its heart is the Piazza del Tribunale, formerly Piazza Arnaldo Mussolini. Here, in early 1957, construction workers were busy scaling the gently curved façade of Bolzano's financial courts. Being fixed into place were the last three of fifty-seven travertine panels that together formed a 198-square-metre bas-relief across the front of the building, formerly the Casa Littoria, the town's Fascist headquarters. They were completing the largest Fascist artwork in Europe. What on earth were they thinking? This was little more than a decade after Mussolini had

1.1 The former Fascist HQ in Bolzano-Bozen, northern Italy. It is considered the largest surviving Fascist artwork in Europe and was completed years after the end of the war. Other contenders could include the cross above the Valley of the Fallen near Madrid.

been shot and a similarly short time since the occupying Nazis began dismantling Bolzano's concentration camp at war's end in an effort to destroy the evidence of their brutality.

The building was designed by architects Pellizzari, Rossi, and Plattner with the frieze by local artist and Fascist Hans Piffrader. Like a sculpted strip cartoon, the frieze pictorially celebrates Mussolini's achievements, from the 1922 March on Rome, through participation in the Spanish Civil War on the side of Franco, and onwards toward a bright Italian Fascist future. At its centre is Mussolini mounted on his horse – the new Augustus Caesar. It weighs in at ninety-five tons. Why, in 1957, were they putting it up, not taking it down?

Work had stopped on the incomplete HQ in 1943 when the Allies signed an armistice with the Italians and, overnight, Italy's erstwhile fellow Axis powers became her enemies. The final bas-relief panels lay half-forgotten for years on the building's declamatory balcony before it was seen fit to complete the project in now democratic Italy – a still fragile democracy, admittedly.

At the same time as the final panels were being carefully placed, the South Tyrolean Liberation Committee was launching its bombing and assassinations campaign, a terror later backed by Austrian and German neo-Nazis whose aim was secession for the Alpine region. The monument may have been finally completed, but Fascism was not dead. Nor is it still.

It is raining in earnest as Hannes and I stand on the wet cobbles of the piazza looking up at the frieze. Hannes points out the oversized doors fit for a giant race, the oak leaf symbols, and other totalitarian devices. Peering through the locked gates into an internal courtyard, Roman torches can be seen fitted as uplighters. On the frieze above our heads there are the various Fascist party symbols and heroic workers, farmers, and soldiers. Between the legs of Mussolini's horse is the frieze's completion date (the twentieth year of the Fascist era, that is, 1942). Except, as we know, this is not entirely true. Below his mount's belly is the Fascist slogan: *CREDERE, OBBEDIRE, COMBATTERE* – Believe, Obey, Fight.

The building and frieze are just one element in a still unnervingly extensive Fascist townscape that extol the ideological triad of state, party, and the Catholic church, that together created the spaces in which daily totalitarian life was conducted. One edge of the square is today's Corso Italia where the streetlights look like abstracted Roman legionary standards. On it stands the church of Christ the King designed in a Veneto Romanesque style. It has a triple arched loggia entrance whose masonry spells out an M for Mussolini, an arrangement that was the McDonald's golden arches of its day and used across Italy. Oh yes, Hannes assures me, local people would have understood the symbolism of the triple arch – the Duce is ever present, ever watching. Hannes also reckons that the figure of Christ over the door has his hand lifted not so much in benediction as in a hesitant Roman salute.

Nearby is Fascist Bolzano's main avenue, Corso della Libertà, lined with soaring, rectilinear arcades, their scale subordinating the people walking beneath. Interrupting the flow is the Monument to Victory, a triumphal arch that Mussolini had built in

1928. Dedicated to Italy's First World War 'martyrs,' its construction required demolishing a memorial to the Austrian infantry and tens of thousands protested over the border in Innsbruck. There were various attempts to blow it up in the years following. In style it is pure Fascist Classicism with lictorial columns and bronze wolves, lions, axes, and helmeted soldiers. It sits in a park surrounded by still more Fascist buildings. The city's former SS headquarters is down a nearby side street.

The purpose of all this building, all this hubris, was not only to Italianise Bolzano and to signal the party's total control, but also to form the gateway to the glories of Fascist Italy for anyone heading south from Austria. But at war's end, it was not only the frieze was incomplete; so too was much of the new city that had been laid out but not yet built out.

In Bolzano, determining who was a victim and who a perpetrator under Fascism is understandably complicated. There is not a single narrative, argues Hannes. With few exceptions everyone was guilty in some way. To many in Italian Bolzano, the Fascist iconography simply evolved into symbols of Italian local identity, and it is these voices rather than the iconoclasts that triumphed. It was the same across the whole of Italy. The victory arch had its likeness of Mussolini removed and some other minor alterations, but essentially everything stayed the same. So, in 1957, when the Italian president was due to visit Bolzano for a trade fair, local Christian Democrats applied pressure to the regional monuments office to tidy up, completing unfinished buildings in time for his arrival – a massive Fascist frieze included.

In recent decades, what to do about the Monument to Victory, the frieze, and Bolzano's other Fascist monuments began to be debated. In 2010, Hannes and a group of local historians wrote an open letter to the press condemning the monumental status quo. After some local political wrangling, a decision was made to carve a museum out of the basement rooms below the victory arch that would address the history of the two Fascisms, German and Italian: "one monument, one city, two dictatorships." Externally, the arch's triumphalism was to be undercut by a digital sign with red rotating lettering in a ring clasped around one column. Its leg was, effectively, electronically tagged like a criminal. The museum remains the only one in the nation dedicated to examining Italy's Fascist history. Most locals had preferred to ignore the frieze, but with the arch now tagged, the question over what to do about Europe's largest Fascist artwork became unavoidable. Surely something had to be done. To leave it unchanged would be obscene.

'There is nothing in the world more invisible than a monument,' wrote the Austrian philosopher Robert Musil in 1927, musing on the lack of attention given to your average statue by the passing public.[2] And most citizens of Bolzano-Bozen do indeed go about their business without much noticing their frieze. But tell that to the thousands who gathered around Bristol's statue of Edward Colston on a warm Sunday in June 2020. Black Lives Matter (BLM) protestors whooped, air horns blared, and the excited young, mixed crowd chanted 'pull it down!' The graffi-tied Colston was lashed with ropes, his eyes obscured by loops of cord like a blindfold. 'Get him!' shouted one young woman as people hauled on the ropes.

1.2 The statue of Colston was erected in 1895 in 'The Centre', a garden formed over a culverted river in Bristol city centre. It was part of 19th century 'statue-mania' that saw a number of figures honoured in the gardens and nearby. A fund-raising campaign among Bristolians failed and the statue was paid for by the Colston-promoting city elite.

As Colston teetered on his stone plinth, the whooping intensified. Finally, it was happening. He tipped forward, then, with the centre of gravity decisively changed, the metal figure crashed to the paving. A young Black man scrambled onto the empty plinth with a cardboard BLM placard and waves it high in the air. 'I can't breathe!' chorused the crowd, evoking the last words of George Floyd and others before him. Hands are raised in Black power salutes. Half a dozen young men then lift and turn the heavy bronze figure, rolling Colston along the street to the nearby harbour where Bristol ships once sailed to Africa on the first leg of transatlantic slavery's Triangular Trade. You could hear the tinny hollowness of Colston as he scraped across the ground, holes torn in his battered metal torso. Finally, the statue was heaved upright then tipped off the quay, hitting the water below with a splash. Colston was swimming with the fishes and the crowd roared its approval. It was thrilling.

But it had taken the murder of an African American man half a world away to finally topple Colston. George Perry Floyd Jr was killed on 25 May during an arrest in Minneapolis after an officer knelt on his neck for nine minutes and thirty seconds (rather than the popularly recalled and still symbolic eight minutes and forty-six seconds, the length of time one protestor kneeled on the felled Colston). According to National Academy of Sciences statistics, 1 in every 1,000 Black men in the United States can expect to be killed by police.[3] Why this particular death was the final straw in sparking such widespread revolt is complex. No doubt the phone camera images played a crucial role. In any case, it led to global anti-racist protests and the widespread toppling of contested monuments to the champions of slavery, colonialism, and empire, on a scale not previously seen. In the United Kingdom alone, over the following six months, at least seventy monuments were either taken down or their removal was put in train. Places were renamed and the future of hundreds of other commemorations put under review by commissions set up by museums, cities, the Church of England, and the home nations. In the United States, Confederate monuments were the main focus, along with statues of various genocidal conquerors from Christopher Columbus onward.

Floyd's death was a turning point in this new iconoclasm (defined as the desecration or removal of statues) but it was far from being its beginning. Iconoclasm and contested monuments have a history from at least the ancient world onwards. In its contemporary form, however, the issue is not simply about consigning rulers to oblivion or doctrinal differences over graven images, but about issues of representation, of controlling the public conversation and revising historical narratives about identity, place and nation. In short about culture war struggles for control of the past and future in which monuments have become proxies.

In the twenty-first century, the demands for action on symbolic honours given to the dishonourable was rubbing against a Britain already in upheavals about its own identity. In the face of economic decline and waning influence, in an age of globalisation and the aftermath of Brexit, what did it mean to be British? The US has been asking itself similar questions about its identity, as are the countries of a changing Europe and in increasingly diverse settler colonial societies such as Australia. That these monuments to the great and the bad often promulgate historical lies is hardly surprising given that they have almost always been erected in the name of power. They are distorted history but history nonetheless in the accounts of how and why they arrived in our streets and squares. They tell us about the values of the societies that put them up and those of their contemporary defenders and opponents today.

In the footsteps of Gramsci, sociologist Pierre Bourdieu describes such monuments, ceremonials, plaques, and other cultural products as 'symbolic capital,' so that in the built environment, naming and commemoration bring social distinction for some and marginalisation for others. Bourdieu goes further, describing as 'symbolic violence' the ways in which cultural meaning and historical narratives are shaped through commemoration and actions such as the naming of places. These measures are foisted upon us in an attempt to subordinate and to define the powerful's view of the world as the natural order of things. At least until their meaning becomes forgotten and their role in manufacturing consent, their symbolic capital, drains away as they become barely glanced at street furniture.[4]

In Europe, the first secular statues erected in the street were generally to kings and emperors. Common people were occasionally immortalised anonymously, as portraits carved into churches, modelled as angels and the like. Later, the monarchs, their relatives, and courtiers were joined by the newly emerged and rapidly ennobled merchant class, often those who had profited from the slave trade. The Enlightenment saw the commemorative scope widen, if only slightly. Erasmus was still probably unique when a wooden statue to him was erected in 1549 in Rotterdam's Grote Markt –the first commoner to be honoured with a public statue. It was said to be large enough to contain, on special occasions, a small boy spouting Latin as if the statue was speaking. It was replaced first in stone and then, in in bronze by Hendrick de Keyser (designed 1618, cast 1622). His likeness has had a tendency to fall over repeatedly and was buried to hide it from the Nazis during their occupation of the city.

In England, the first recorded statue to a commoner is probably the figure of Robert Clayton (1629–1707), one of a group of working men made good who as philanthropists gave generously to St Thomas and Guy's hospitals. Clayton paid for his own marble statue by Gibbons in 1701/2.[5] Thomas Guy himself appears in a likeness by Pieter Scheemakers and, as recorded on the stone pedestal, the statue was erected in 1737. Sir Robert Geffrye was immortalised slightly earlier in 1723 on the almshouses he built in Shoreditch. Guy, whose statue pedestal depicts the Good Samaritan (a common and problematic comparison), made a fortune from the Atlantic slave trade via the South Sea Company as did Geffrye, who grew rich on trade in gold, slaves, and 'elephants' teeth' (ivory) through the Royal African Company that for many decades had a monopoly on the English slave trade.[6] Robert Clayton was also involved in the slave trade including through his bank, Clayton and Morris.[7]

These profiteers from human misery became mayors and Bank of England governors. Each was knighted.

It was only in the nineteenth century that these implicated merchants and military leaders were regularly joined by doctors, artists, statesmen, scientists, and engineers on public pedestals. Berlin had to wait until 1860 for a trio of civilian 'heroes without swords' on the newly created Platz an der Bauakademie. Even then, civilians sometime had to watch their backs. Edward Jenner, the doctor who discovered the smallpox vaccine, once had a statue in Trafalgar Square, the martial heart of empire with statues to match. It was unveiled in 1858 by Prince Albert, a great supporter of Jenner's pioneering work, on a plinth next to General Sir Charles James Napier. The statue outraged Victorian anti-vaxxers, while the placement of a civilian among the military top brass honoured in the square scandalized the Admiralty. It was shunted out to Kensington Gardens, with indecent haste, two swift months after Albert died in late 1861. Commenting on the move in 1862, the *British Medical Journal* noted of the square's military commemorations that they were there 'because they killed their fellow creatures whereas [Jenner] only saved them.' *Punch* joked:

> England's ingratitude still blots
> The escutcheon of the brave and free; I saved you many million
> > spots,
> And now you grudge one spot for me.[8]

In 2000, then Mayor of London Ken Livingstone suggested that the statue of Napier should be removed from Trafalgar Square, because no one had any idea who he and his fellow soldiers were. The square and the surrounding streets still bristle with violent colonisers and the military, however. Writing in *The Independent* newspaper in 2016, Charles Gilmour called Whitehall a 'Murder Mile.' He suggested that if you slaughter a few innocents, you will be serving life in gaol, but 'spill the blood of continents and it's Portland stone and a plaque in your honour.'[9] Quite.

This is not a phenomenon unique to Britain, of course. The principal colonising nations of Europe – France, Spain, Portugal, Italy, the Netherlands, Belgium – all have their commemorative landscapes celebrating empire, landscapes which expanded rapidly in the late nineteenth century in parallel with the conquered territories. The triumph of the middle class was also being celebrated with figures of its heroes erected at the time alongside commissions from independently minded industrial cities intent on creating their own municipal narratives. The period saw countless likenesses created across the Western world's towns and cities and it became known as a time of 'statue mania.'

France in particular saw a slew of statues to 'great men' appear in its streets – more than 170 in Paris alone between 1870 and the First World War.[10] This bronze and stone assault can be attributed, in part, to the Third Republic's attempts to create cultural distance between itself and the authoritarian Second Empire. Many of the new monuments commemorated figures associated with the French Revolution. In some ways, the appeal to Revolutionary history also disguised the colonial ventures of the expansionist Third Republic, especially in North Africa and Indochina where commercial exploitation went alongside the 'civilizing mission.' This *statuomanie* was decried at the time, sometimes for questionable commemorations or by artists unimpressed with their aesthetic quality. Degas suggested placing small metal fences in parks to stop sculptors 'depositing' their works on the lawns like dog shit.[11]

Almost all those honoured with a plinth were white, straight men. In 2016, the journalist and activist Caroline Criado-Perez spent time trawling through the (now revised) database of Britain's Public Monuments and Sculpture Association to determine how many statues of women existed in the country. Her findings were dispiriting.[12] If you're a woman, she determined, your best chance of becoming a statue is to be a mythical or allegorical figure, a famous virgin, a royal, or nude; just 2.7 percent of all the 925 statues she counted were of female commoners commemorated for their achievements. It is a similar story for Black representation. And but for exceptionally rare funerary monuments such as the 'lesbian-like' couple on the fifteenth-century brass grave marker in the church at Etchingham, East Sussex, queer people are also among those mostly invisible in the commemorative landscape or are remembered only in the negative.

Oscar Wilde could not escape posthumous censure even in sexually liberal Paris.[13] The prominent testicles of the angel Jacob Epstein carved for Wilde's tomb in Père Lachaise Cemetery met opposition from the prudish. The angel balls were eventually hacked off surreptitiously in 1961, by which time the offending articles had developed a shiny patina – the result, it was supposed, of the tomb becoming a pilgrimage site for the gay community. That they were subsequently used as paperweights by the cemetery guardian may be urban myth.[14]

There remains a popular misunderstanding that long-standing statues in the public realm were usually commissioned by the state at national level or were put up by popular acclaim and subscription. In some circumstances this is true, but this was more often not the case. While many are now owned and managed by local or national government and their agencies, in the nineteenth and early twentieth centuries funding came from politically and culturally motivated interest groups or by those such as Robert Clayton and Cecil Rhodes who paid for their own charitable legacy to be honoured. As such, these monuments are more usually representations of partial and private interests rather than the wider public will. Even national heroes such as Lord Nelson couldn't rely on the English to put their hands in their pockets. The memorial committee that chose William Railton's competition-winning column for Trafalgar Square spent some fifteen years unsuccessfully trying to persuade the public to pay for the project. Monuments to the hero of Trafalgar were erected in the provinces and colonies before London. Decades later, the controversial statue to Oliver Cromwell outside the Houses of Parliament was secretly funded and hurriedly erected overnight by former prime minister Lord Rosebery while that to Edward Colston in Bristol was furtively paid for by local politician James Arrowsmith, a leading member of the Anchor

Society, a club devoted to Colston's legacy, after a subscription drive among Bristol citizens conspicuously failed.

In the United States, monuments celebrating national and civic foundation stories were also put up as part of the mania seen elsewhere. These encompassed figures of Puritans, Columbus and others who re-affirmed a settler-colonial claim on the land. However, Confederate commemorations were something different. They were designed not only to glorify the myth of the Lost Cause, the lie that attempts to disguise the South's war to defend chattel slavery as an issue of states' rights, but to intimidate and segregate space along racial lines.[15] This was one of the most comprehensive and widespread programmes of monumental falsehood undertaken, perhaps only matched by Stalin's cynical use of the image of Lenin across the Soviet sphere of influence.

The Reconstruction period in the decade or so following the South's Civil War defeat in 1865 saw Black people make political and educational advances and limited economic gains.[16] By 1870 more than 15 percent of elected officials in the southern states were Black.[17] Opposition from white supremacists was swift and bitter; this was the period when the Ku Klux Klan emerged in its first incarnation. Conflict intensified in the 1890s (and monuments proliferated) after the Populist Party created a successful, if temporary, progressive alliance between freed Blacks and poor rural whites against the planter elite. This was a terrifying prospect to the ruling class of the United States – and not just in the South. Legal and violent measures mounted and were successful in oppressing and disenfranchising Black voters and crushing multiracial solidarity. This consolidated into what were to become the segregationist Jim Crow laws that defined the Black American experience in the twentieth century. The erection of Confederate monuments was intrinsic to this process and reflected its course.

In addition to the Klan, a number of dainty-sounding organisations were formed, such as the United Daughters of the Confederacy (UDC).[18] Initially at least, these women appeared to be responding to the federal government's policy of only setting up war cemeteries to the Union dead while Confederate soldiers' bones were left to be ploughed up on former battle-fields. In the immediate aftermath of the conflict, the women gathered body parts, created Confederate war cemeteries, and erected suitable commemorative monuments therein. Beginning in the 1870s, however, the efforts of these groups shifted from graveside memorials to erecting intimidatory monuments to the Confederacy in the middle of towns and cities across the rapidly segregating South and beyond. Foot soldiers and equestrian officers in stone and bronze were set up to patrol the spaces around them – often in association with the courthouse square, that comforting symbol of smalltown America, the better to demonstrate the power of the law and the threat of discriminatory incarceration. There was a further massive expansion in monument building following the First World War.

Although some of these monuments were substantial and undoubted works of art commissioned by the UDC from leading artists across the country, many others were generic military figures churned out in northern foundries by the hundred. Typically, these 'Silent Sentinels' depict a solitary infantryman at rest, gripping the barrel of a musket, its stock on the ground and could be obtained for $450. Obelisks, meanwhile, a standard funereal marker in cemeteries, becomes a specifically Confederate symbol in the South. Some obelisks were vast, such as the 1924 Jefferson Davis Memorial near Fairview, Kentucky, which, at 107-metres, remains one of the tallest unreinforced concrete structures in the world. Even figurative statues could be giants at ten metres or more – the better to dominate streets, squares, and landscapes.

According to civil rights organisation, the Southern Poverty Law Centre, 1,747 commemorative items still existed on public property in 2019 even after the many removals in the previous few years. These were not, by any stretch of the imagination, primarily monuments to grief and the losses of war. Monuments were raised in states such as Ohio and Massachusetts that were never even part of the Confederacy. 'These statues,' said New Orleans mayor Mitch Landrieu, who was one of the first to

order the removal of monuments dedicated to white supremacy, 'are not just stone and metal. They are not just innocent
remembrances of a benign history. These monuments purposefully celebrate a fictional, sanitized Confederacy, ignoring the
death, ignoring the enslavement and the terror that it actually
stood for.'[19]

Just as African Americans were excluded and othered in public
life, they were also almost invisible in the commemorative environment except where they were to be diminished. Demeaning
statues portraying Black people kneeling, crouching, beseeching,
and thankful below white figures were erected in various places
as commemorations of cooperative 'faithful slaves.'[20] Where,
mayor Landrieu asked, are the commemorations of slave ships,
of slave auction blocks, of lynchings?

Charlottesville's extensive commemorative landscape was
another example of this pattern. Gigantic statues in its down-
town avenues and parks constituted a net of symbolic control
thrown over the city between 1919 and 1924, paid for by local
benefactor Paul Goodloe McIntire who also funded some of
the segregated parks in which the new statues stood. Jackson
Park (now renamed Court Square Park) adjoining the county
courthouse was created by demolishing a small Black quarter
called McKee Row. Confederate flags were waved at the unveil-
ings while thousands of KKK members marched in full regalia,
all under the benevolent eye of Virginia governor Harry Flood
Byrd, who made sure Jim Crow was enforced and successfully
disenfranchised Black voters using poll tax and literacy tests as
crosses were burned and Black men were kidnapped, whipped,
and lynched.

Stone Mountain in Georgia, also commissioned by the
UDC, was the largest of these lying monuments – a Confederate Mount Rushmore. Planning for it began in 1914, with
significant funding coming from the Klan. An initial idea for
a giant bust of Lee grew into a proposal by its first sculptor
Gutzon Borglum for a 1,200-foot-long frieze with Lee, Jackson,
and Jefferson Davis prominent. In 1915, the Second KKK was
founded in a ceremony on the heights of Stone Mountain. The

1.3 Stone Mountain in Georgia is the Confederate version of Mount Rushmore and was a notable site of Klan activity. After a long pause in the work, it was completed in 1972 by the state government in response to the Brown v, The Board of Education verdict that made school segregation unlawful. The surrounding park, which featured a replica plantation has recently seen changes to its Confederate symbolism following BLM protests but the cliff carving remains unchanged.

project then foundered for decades, interrupted by the Great Depression and Second World War until, following the Supreme Court's 1954 decision in *Brown v Board of Education* that made school segregation illegal, defiant anti-integration Confederate monument building resumed. The State of Georgia used $1 million of public money to buy Stone Mountain and ensure the sculpture was restarted with giant equestrian figures across three acres of granite cliff, constructed at a scale where a person could stand within the horses' mouths. The park below once included a replica plantation. Work was completed as late as 1972.[21]

The propaganda campaign for the Lost Cause was carefully crafted by slavery's apologists, including the Southern Historical Association (in its early days), and was not confined to monuments but also encompassed censoring texts books, shaping national historic sites, and cultivating the soft focus image of an easeful Antebellum plantation life of mint juleps on the porch swing. It appeared on Aunt Jemima pancake mix packets and in books and films such as *Gone with the Wind*. This is a problem

that continues today in the interpretation of historic plantation mansions where slave quarters, if they have survived at all,
rarely form part of the visitor experience.

This is partisan heritage rather than accurate history and a
heritage grounded in hate where every period of struggle for
Black emancipation has been matched by a white pushback
using monuments as part of the armoury. Infamously, the 2017
demonstrations against proposed statue removals in Charlottesville by white supremacists including Klan members, Proud
Boys, and neo-Nazis, resulted in the death of Heather Heyer
when she was deliberately rammed by a car. Historian David
Blight concludes that 'As long as America has a politics of race,
it will have a politics of Civil War memory.'[22]

If Confederate statuary perpetuates lies that served to segregate US towns and cities for more than a century, those of the
European colonial powers sought to justify their brutal acquisi-
tiveness and promote national stories of greatness. Bristol's 'Cult
of Colston' has become totemic in this regard, with the man
playing a central role in Bristol's image of itself as a city with an
admirable history of charitable giving. The city's pantheon is an
open space called 'The Centre.' It was created when the River
Frome was culverted in 1893 near its outfall into a harbour that
had brought the city riches on the back of slavery and plantation products such as tobacco and sugar. In the eighteenth
century, one of the very few public commemorative monuments
in Bristol was the 1736 equestrian bronze of William III, the
focal point of Queen's Square, a development laid out to house
Bristol's slavery enriched merchants. But as statue mania reached
its height in the late 1800s – not coincidentally also the height
of empire building – four statues appeared in the city centre in
less than a decade.

The first, in 1887, was a Carrara marble figure of local MP
and merchant prince Samuel Morley who had died the previous year. He had been an active abolitionist and dissenter
when living in London but was best known in Bristol for his
Liberal politics – strong in the city – and as an advocate of the

temperance movement. The second, also in white marble, was raised to Queen Victoria (1888); then five years later, and almost a century after his death, a bronze of arch-conservative thinker and parliamentarian Edmund Burke was put up, paid for by the fabulously wealthy Bristol tobacco merchant W. H. Wills. Burke has sometimes been portrayed, with little evidence, as being anti-slavery. Then in 1895, the next statue arrived. It honoured the slave trader Edward Colston. The plaque on the plinth below declared: 'Erected by Citizens of Bristol As A Memorial of One of the Most Virtuous and Wise Sons of Their City.'

At least 10 million Africans were enslaved, branded with hot irons, and transported across the Atlantic between 1490 and 1879, and it is thought that the 'virtuous and wise' Colston accounted for some 84,000 of those trafficked, of whom some 19,000 died en route. As Tory member of parliament for Bristol, he supported the city's merchants to the point that, by the 1730s, Bristol had outstripped London as the nation's leading slave port. Coffee, sugar, cocoa, cotton, indigo, rum, and other plantation goods were imported and traded, and manufactured items exported to Africa to sell in exchange for slaves. His statue's position of honour, surrounded by public gardens, was far more apparent before the arrival of modern layers of highways and municipal paraphernalia.

And the statue was not the only tribute to the slave trafficker. In addition, the city had a Colston Street and a Colston Avenue, also named for the man in the late nineteenth century, while just up the hill past Victoria is Bristol Cathedral with its prominent Colston memorial window in the north transept. 'GO AND DO GOOD LIKE WISE' runs the quote from the Good Samaritan (Luke 15:37) in the 1890 stained glass. Another memorial window to Colston could be seen at St Mary Redcliffe. There was Colston's Boys' and Colston Girls' schools. There was Colston Place. Each November, Bristol celebrated Colston's birthday. The girls' school held a service in the cathedral in his memory, a ceremony that continued to 2019. At another service, Colston buns were given out to the children. All in addition to his actual effigy reclining on his elaborate tomb at All Saints

Corn Street. Bristol still has its Colston Society, Dolphin Society, Anchor Society, and The Grateful Society that were all founded in the eighteenth century to perpetuate Colston's good name – and their own mercantile interests.

Why the sudden flurry of Colston memorialization some 170 years after his death? What did the erection of his statue within a few years of Burke and Morley mean to Bristol? Surely those promoting the Colston cult knew they were doing wrong – this was half a century after the abolition of the slave trade in the British Empire and two decades after the end of the American Civil War. 'Even by [the] 1780s,' wrote Madge Dresser in her essay on slavery and Bristol's urbanism, there was 'a new self-consciousness about the propriety of the slave trade ... [people] preferred to distance themselves from the Guinea [slave] trade ...'[23]

The monuments, taken together, were a representation of Bristol's elite in the public realm. They were designed to shore up this elite's continued leadership, their civic power, to foster an imagined civic community in the face of rising class conflict, growing trade unionism, and socialist ideas. The 1880s and 1890s had seen a wave of strike actions in Bristol docks and in local industry, where demonstrations were met with state violence including, on Black Friday in 1892, sabre-wielding cavalry as at Peterloo. Morely's statue, it has been said, was set up at one end of Bristol Bridge as a moral lesson greeting the workers who trooped in from the poorer districts each morning.

Everything about the Colston statue is a lie, from the thoughtful pose for a man with a notable lack of empathy to the wording of the plaque below. The panel on the rear of the Colston plinth depicts the miraculous story of one of Colston's stricken slave ships being saved by a dolphin that inserted its body into a hole in the hull, cementing the idea of Colston as a civic saint. Colston's fingernails and hair are (or were) kept at Merchant's Hall like sacred relics. When his body was exhumed in 1843 it was said to be miraculously preserved.

This promotion of Colston's 'virtue' and his philanthropy was not only used to whitewash his own reputation and render him a suitable civic figurehead; it was also a justification by the various elite societies for their own charitable work, which in turn supported their own mythology. In 1884, all the societies combined contributed only 1.5 percent of the money raised in Bristol for the relief of the poor, and even this was distributed in an arbitrary way (echoing Colston's own religious bigotry). Colston's memory was far more effective in perpetuating the interests of the ruling class than actually benefiting the city's slum dwellers.[24] When erected, these monuments were far more about class than race, although racism and the racialisation of peoples was of course, utterly entwined with justifications of slavery and colonialism's civilising mission.

Racial discrimination in Bristol continues. A 2014 report by the Runnymede Trust found that Bristol had the worst inequities based on race of ten cities it looked at, the third worst in terms of educational inequality, and the seventh worst overall of the 348 areas of England and Wales it examined.[25] At the time, more than 100 years since Reverend H J Wilkins had first set down his disquiet about Bristol's 'Cult of Colston' in his biography of the slave trader, Bristol's cult objects remained firmly in place. When Bristol held its Festival of the Sea in 1996, the lack of a mention of slavery led to protests. Colston Hall was long boycotted as a concert venue by anti-racism campaigners, including by local band Massive Attack, who refused to perform there. In Bristol Cathedral, there was only a tiny apologetic notice in the north transept pointing out that some of the nearby graves might be those of slave owners; no proper interpretation of Colston's massive memorial window was provided. 'You as well?' grumped a verger when I asked to be directed to the window during a 2017 visit. 'We have to be careful that people don't put a brick through it,' added a chaplain. 'This is the Victorian corner where they all worked hard,' explained a guide showing visitors around the north transept's memorials to plantation-owning families. In 2019, the still pale, male, stale, and elitist Society of Merchant Venturers went as far as frustrating attempts to replace the Colston statue's plaque with something more accurate, arguing that the wording should 'present another side to the debate'. Perhaps a defense of slavery?

With commemorative gatekeepers repeatedly squandering their chance to do the right thing, it is no wonder that the angry and ignored took matters into their own hands. So finally, in the summer of 2020, after the death of George Floyd on the other side of the Atlantic, ordinary Bristolians did exactly that. No mythical dolphins were on hand to save Colston.

A second focus of dissent in both Britain and South Africa has been the monumental legacy of the deeply unpleasant Cecil Rhodes, who violently exploited southern Africa for its fabulous mineral wealth, set up the British South Africa Company with its paramilitary police that killed thousands in land grabs, and disenfranchised Africans under his rule. In his book *The Cult of Rhodes*, Paul Maylam recounts the myriad ways in which Rhodes is commemorated across southern Africa and England in statues, foundations, plaques, building and place names, a university, the renowned scholarship to Oxford, and most obviously in the toponyms North and South Rhodesia – now Zambia and Zimbabwe. Like Clayton, like Colston, and like the opioid-pushing Sackler family since, Rhodes carefully washed his despicable record with monuments and philanthropy. 'Rhodes desired, and purchased, his own immortality,' notes Maylam.[26]

The Rhodes Must Fall (RMF) movement began in South Africa in March 2015. It focused on a colossal seated figure of Rhodes in the grounds of the University of Cape Town. RMF activist Chumani Mawele explained that shit was thrown at the statue in one protest as a political comment on Apartheid's legacy of ongoing disparities in South Africa such as the lack of sanitation in poor areas. Mawele said that seeing the Rhodes statue, a symbol of white supremacy, pained and angered him daily.[27] There were other demands related to the predominantly white teaching staff. Within a month the university agreed to remove the statue but the movement had already spread to other South African campuses and then internationally, including to England where Rhodes Must Fall Oxford (RMFO) was established.

RMFO focused its attentions on a figure of Cecil Rhodes high above High Street on the Rhodes Building wing of Oriel College, which was built between 1909 and 1911 using a £100,000 bequest from Rhodes who was an Oriel alumnus. The wing, by architect Basil Champneys was fashioned in a historicist Jacobean style with the statue mounted high on the facade between barley-sugar columns and sheltered by a shell canopy. Below his feet is a relief inscription: LARGA: MVNIFICENTIA CAECILII:RHODES, which translates as 'Out of the splendid generosity of Cecil Rhodes.' The building's pediment incorporates Rhodes' coat of arms. This previously long-ignored image, perched high above shoppers and students promptly became one of the most contested monuments in England.

Many accused RMFO of wishing to erase history. However, the movement's arguments, though in some mouths about simple removal of a statue, were, in the main, far more subtle than this: "We believe that statues and symbols matter; they are a means through which communities express their values", RMFO said in a statement. As in Cape Town, this was part of a wider push to decolonise the spaces, the curriculum, and counter university racism. It included: "tackling the plague of colonial iconography...that seeks to whitewash and distort history."[28] Lord Patten, the chancellor of the university, told students who did not like the Rhodes statue that they should consider studying elsewhere.[29]

In December 2015, Oriel College issued a statement after receiving a petition from RMFO, calling for the removal of the figure. It said it was thinking through the complex issues. 'In the absence of any context or explanation,' Oriel conceded, 'it can be seen as an uncritical celebration of a controversial figure, and the colonialism and the oppression of black communities he represents.' A six-month consultation programme was promised, but within weeks a new announcement said the statue would definitively stay. Oriel argued:

The college believes the recent debate has underlined that the continuing presence of these historical artefacts is an important reminder of the complexity of history and of the legacies of colonialism still felt today ... By adding context, we can help draw attention to this history, do justice to the complexity of the debate, and be true to our educational mission.[30]

According to the *Daily Telegraph*, the rapid change of heart was the result of benefactors threatening to withhold £100 million if the statue went.[31] So at Oriel, nothing changed.

In retrospect, the 2015 RMFO debate was an early rumbling in Britain's gathering culture wars, which had turned rapidly more toxic on the announcement of the Brexit referendum. Immigration, national security, and questions of cultural identity, of the need to make Britain great again were serving the nationalist Right well. Having the country's imperial record vigorously questioned by a young generation of 'woke' activists was the last thing the Tories wanted as they prepared to go it alone, promising trade deals across the former empire.

The same weekend as Colston was toppled, however, the heart of imperial London and other British towns and cities including Oxford saw well-supported BLM demonstrations over successive weeks. The Churchill statue outside the Palace of Westminster was graffitied to point out his racism, while one protestor tried to burn the Union flag on the national Cenotaph on Whitehall. The boxing-in of central London monuments, including Churchill, ahead of more BLM demonstrations the following weekend was an opportunity for prime-ministerial outrage ('absurd and shameful'), even though this was a standard precaution taken in advance of marches likely to be large and angry.

Establishment fury at the successful 'no-plinthing' of Colston, at the popular London BLM protests, and at the proposed further removal of monuments announced by Labour councils, meant that in the Summer of 2020, the government set to work stoking fear and invoking nostalgia at the same time as rejecting the very concept of systemic racism. The supposed threat to British history, traditions, and identity was a dog whistle to extreme nationalists and white supremacists. BLM organisers were forced to call off a planned assembly in Hyde Park because of threats from Far Right hate groups. In Bristol a corrosive substance was poured over the statue of Black writer and actor Alfred Fagon, and the headstone of Scipio Africanus, an eighteenth-century enslaved man buried in the city, was vandalised. Biker gangs, hooligan football fan 'firms,' and neo-Nazis gathered to 'protect' cenotaphs. Paul Golding of the white supremacist group Britain First called for followers to 'guard our monuments.' 'Every single man should be in London next Saturday or forever don't call yourself a patriot,' said neo-Fascist leader Tommy Robinson (Stephen Yaxley-Lennon).[32]

There were calls for the statue of Nelson Mandela in Parliament Square to be toppled, for the 'repatriation' of Black Britons and assaults on BLM supporters. Former UK Independence Party organisers set up 'Save Our Statues,' (SOS) defending statues of slavers in an attempt to 'push back against the bullies, shrink the size of handouts to extremists, dismantle loony left legislation and defeat biased local council reviews designed to delete your history.' Its logo is an adaption of UNESCO's temple front symbol. SOS describes itself as a nonpartisan organisation 'which will deploy all legal, education and political domains ... to save our beloved history and culture from intentional destruction, distortion and deterioration.'[33] It sends out bulletins celebrating efforts to resist changes to contested statues, or even plaques that would provide more information about historical figures. The populist SOS soon had the ear of sections of the right-wing media that gave it positive coverage. Columnist Melanie Phillips claimed that a war on Western culture was being waged from within, and she was far from alone. Former UKIP leader Nigel Farage was among those likening statue-topplers to the Taliban, and he predicted race riots would follow.

In an interview with online platform Joe, *Spectator* journalist Douglas Murray argued that Britain had different concerns from America:

> In Britain we are conserving something different. We have our own holy places and holy figures and we are seeing every single

aspect of that assailed ... One of the reasons why some of us were very concerned about the pulling down of statues [is] because we know from history that you start by pulling down statues by mob diktat ... and next you go [to harming] people as they have in Portland Oregon.

The violence Murray was referring to was Antifa resistance to the Proud Boys and other Far Right agitators.[34]

On both sides of the Atlantic, the word 'mob' was thrown around frequently as part of an attempt to discredit anti-racist demands and push backs against police violence by turning the protests into an issue of public order and the protection of private property and to set the white suburbs and countryside against cosmopolitan big cities and their cultural elites. Similar reactions to statue removals were being voiced by the Right in the United States. Speaking below Mount Rushmore, President Trump called the removals a merciless campaign by 'angry mobs' intent on wiping out history and 'sacred memorials' and who were indoctrinating children and unleashing a 'wave of violent crime in our cities.'[35]

Similar debates with varying outcomes were already being had across the former British Empire. After 'No Pride in Genocide' was sprayed across the figure of Captain Cook in Sydney's Hyde Park, then Prime Minister Malcolm Turnbull said it was an act of Stalinist revisionism, describing it as a 'deeply disturbing and totalitarian campaign to not just challenge our history but to deny it and obliterate it.'[36]

As Trump encouraged white supremacists on to the streets and militarised police fanned out, Boris Johnson likewise took to Twitter to falsely claim that British BLM protests had been hijacked by extremists intent on violence and to argue against the removal of any more monuments. 'We cannot now try to edit or censor our past,' argued Johnson.

We cannot pretend to have a different history. The statues in our towns and cities were put up by previous generations. They had different perspectives of right and wrong. But those statues teach us about our past, with all its faults. To tear them down would be to lie about our history.[37]

It was Johnson doing the pretending.

This wasn't a case, as the Tories like to claim, of past com-memorations being judged by present day values. There had been misgivings about slavery even as far back as Colston's lifetime, and the practice was thoroughly reviled by the time the Colston statue came along. Colonialism too had been challenged for centuries in places such as Ireland and India. Rhodes himself, seen as extreme even by the standard of his time, was opposed in Africa through numerous wars and insurgencies ever since the 1890s and also back in Britain. In 1899, for example, eighty-eight Oxford dons signed a petition objecting to the man receiving an honorary degree. G K Chesterton wrote that Rhodes' ideas were the poisonous dregs of Darwinism. In 1930, Evelyn Waugh suggested that a 'very small expenditure on dynamite should be enough to rid us forever of ... the High Street front of Oriel ....' [38] Waugh's criticism was partly about the quality of the architecture, but the disdain was wider.

Nonetheless, amid hysteria about cancel culture, in 2020 the British government set levers in motion to ensure that no more statue removals could happen under its watch. It was the beginning of legislative and other measures aimed at shutting down discussion and gathering decision-making powers on monuments across the country, away from locally elected councillors and into the hands of government ministers. The first salvo was the Desecration of War Memorials Bill introduced to Parliament weeks later, presenting the isolated incident at the Whitehall Cenotaph as an immediate peril to war memorials everywhere that must be crushed. There was no such threat.

Doubling down on Johnson's tweets and ignoring the biographical facts about, and contemporary reaction to figures such as Rhodes, culture secretary Oliver Dowden circulated a letter to public cultural institutions and museums across the country, in which he argued:

History is ridden with moral complexity. Statues and other historical objects were created by generations with different perspectives and understanding of right and wrong. Some represent figures who have said or done things which we may find deeply offensive and would not defend today.[39]

Again, the same false arguments about values having changed with respect to these commemorations. Rather than 'erasing' these objects, he continued, it was better to contextualise or reinterpret them in a way that enables the public to learn about them in their entirety.

At first blush, such explanatory contextualisation might sound a somewhat reasonable compromise (if meaningfully done), but Dowden was not just stating a preferred position; the missive was a threatening letter attempting to shift the long-standing principle of a museum's freedom over content and curation. The approach of publicly funded organisations, Dowden claimed, must now be 'consistent with the government's position.' Hints were dropped about cutting the support they received from the taxpayer. Leading heritage organisations and national museum directors were called to Whitehall to have a strip torn off them. They were told that they were engaged in censorship to 'impose a single, often negative narrative' of British history.[40] Amid a series of politically motivated changes to the boards of national museums, Dowden appointed Trevor Phillips, the controversial former head of the Equality and Human Rights Commission who had previously warned of the formation of Muslim ghettoes in Britain, to a new heritage board. Phillips had recently chartered the statues wars for the Policy Exchange, the right-wing think tank that had an increasing grip on Tory policy. Around the same time, a trustee of the National Maritime Museum did not have his term renewed when he argued for the colonial content of the museum to be reviewed while a trustee of the Science Museum resigned rather than implement the government's 'retain or explain dictat.' If she was suspicious of the policy's purpose, this was entirely understandable.

All this amounted to restrictions on cultural and intellectual freedoms. Kristiana Wrixton, of the UK charity leadership organisation Acevo, said: 'I struggle to see how politicians telling academics and charities which historical facts and research they can talk about publicly is anything but an abuse of power.'[41] Museums Association director Sharon Heal also challenged the government's interference in how museums tell the story of empire and slavery: 'We are particularly concerned that a climate of fear has been created amongst museums and museum staff, especially those working on subjects relating to Britain's imperial past,' she said.[42]

Days after Dowden's letter was sent, a parliamentary debate saw Conservative Sir David Amess taking up the cudgels, arguing not only that statues remain but that more be added. He argued at great length that the lack of women figures in the public realm could be remedied by a statue in central London of recently dead wartime singer Vera Lynn, 'the forces' sweetheart.' A few weeks later the reactionary Common Sense Group of Conservative MPs proposed that all 1,761 recipients of the wartime Victoria Cross and George Cross medals be immortalised with a statue in their place of birth, radically increasing the militarisation of public space. Women's groups were swift to point out that only 11 medal recipients were women and that the idea would only further imbalance the gender inequality in memorials. One Vera Lynn wasn't going to make much of a dent in in that. At the same time, referencing the summer's BLM protests, the government said it was reviewing its prison sentencing policies 'for this type of offending.' It would eventually result in legislation that proposed longer prison sentences for defacing a monument than for rape.

In early 2021 a flurry of additional initiatives were floated. In January, Robert Jenrick, secretary of state for housing, communities and local government, announced his intended planning laws on monuments. 'We should never tolerate criminal acts and mob rule' said Jenrick in a ministerial statement.[43] In England, national planning policy was to be amended specifically to incorporate the 'retain and explain' approach and to frustrate the removal of any 'historic' statue or memorial – whether on the National Heritage List or not. 'Historic' was not defined.[44]

With these moves, the British government was going further even than Trump's Executive Order of the previous June, signed in response to what the President had called censorship by 'the unhinged-left wing mob' attempting to 'vandalize our history, desecrate our monuments, our beautiful monuments, and punish, cancel and persecute anyone who does not conform to their demands.'[45] US removals were already restricted in many states of the former Confederacy which had, over the previous decades, passed laws that aimed to prevent the removal of any Confederate memorials. Trump only reiterated existing federal heritage protection laws; he did not expand them. Even the 2017 Alabama Memorial Preservation Act only applied to monuments more than forty years old and allowed for statues to be moved or altered if new facts about them arose (not that the repugnant facts weren't already well-established). There were no such provisions about new facts or a monument's age in the British policy.

In this new culture war climate where history was being weaponised, even thoroughly middle-class and traditional heritage organisations such as the National Trust were taken to task for commissioning studies looking at connections to slavery on its properties. A similar study by semi-autonomous government body English Heritage published several years earlier about slavery's connections to the country houses in its care had provoked nothing like the same opposition from ministers or the media; it was the culture wars that had changed the context in which the Trust's report was received. Professor Corinne Fowler, director of the National Trust's Colonial Countryside project, countered: 'When you try to interfere with academic freedom in the name of free speech, you're steering the country in a dangerous direction.'[46] Less convincingly but necessary given the Trust's apolitical charitable status, Fowler claimed her work was 'absolutely not political.' Clearly such studies are inevitably political – although that doesn't necessarily undermine their accuracy or worth. Under the name Restore Trust, right-wingers launched an unsuccessful insurgency move to control the National Trust's governing council. The 'anti-woke' candidates it backed included Christian fundamentalist Stephen Green, who has previously lobbied against the criminalisation of marital rape and defended the death penalty for gay people in Uganda.

The same week that Dowden was haranguing museum curators, his dimwit colleague, Education Secretary Gavin Williamson, introduced measures that would appoint a 'free speech champion' while encouraging the suing of universities and cash-strapped student unions by speakers who felt that they had been denied a platform. Williamson's 'evidence' supporting his proposed legislation relied heavily on a flawed 2019 report by the Policy Exchange that, among other points, falsely claimed that feminist Germaine Greer had been denied a platform at a 2015 event at Cardiff University for her views on trans women.

In reality then, the biggest threat to free speech has not been from a phantom cancel culture but rather from ministerial attempts to police what can and cannot be said on campus or at cultural sites and museums. Other skirmishes have ranged from the supposed banning by the BBC of *Rule Britannia* from the Last Night of the Proms at the Royal Albert Hall in 2020 when, in fact, an instrumental-only version had been proposed by the broadcaster because of the risk of choral singing spreading Covid-19, to a label placed beside the 1880 heroic painting in the Royal Collection, *The Defence of Rorke's Drift*, a battle in the Anglo-Zulu war. The label noted: 'This work is connected to colonialism and imperialism.' Whether a label stating the blindingly obvious was of any educational use, its content is uncontestably true.

More serious actions have included new education guidance for schools in 2020 that described anti-capitalism as an 'extreme political stance' that could not be discussed by teachers, effectively preventing any open discussion on the history of industrialisation, colonialisation, and other exploitation and the centuries of resistance. Other Tory members of parliament wanted to add the concept of 'white privilege' and critical race theory to the list of supposedly extremist ideas that could not be discussed, as has been happening in some US jurisdictions. The Conservative Party kneecapped an inquiry into Islamophobia in its own ranks and, post–Floyd, commissioned the much-derided Sewell Report on racial and ethnic disparities that not only rejected the very concept of structural racism but also included tortured arguments stating that the period of Caribbean slavery was 'not only about profit and suffering.'[47]

Government threats did not take long to have an effect. Only weeks after Dowden circulated his museum letter, the director of the Museum of the Home in east London that inhabits a set of almshouses endowed by the same Sir Robert Geffrye who made his fortune through links to the slave trade, revealed that Dowden's funding threat had led to her reversing a decision to relocate and recontextualise the statue of Geffrye, a facsimile from 1912, from above its main door. Likewise, the Corporation of London that oversees the city's financial district announced a reversal of its Tackling Racism taskforce's recommendation to remove statues of slave trade merchants William Beckford and Sir John Cass from its Guildhall after they received their own warning letter from Jenrick. The following autumn, the Corporation announced that the statues would now stay in place with 'plaques or notices placed alongside them, with contextual information about the two men's links to slavery.'[48] One of the richest and most powerful organisations in the country had bowed down before 'retain and explain.' The threats were working, self-censorship being the most effective kind of silencing.

Scenting this new wind, Oriel College changed tack once more on its Rhodes statue. Following the BLM demonstrations, the college has set up another commission to consider the Rhodes legacy, donors, and memorials. When the report eventually made the light of day in the early summer of 2021, it discussed options such as relocating the statue somewhere less prominent, but it did not definitively recommend removal which, it was eventually revealed, had been beyond its terms of reference. Now, citing Dowden's 'retain and explain' policy, the enormously wealthy and venerable college said that obtaining planning permission for its removal would be too costly and too lengthy.

The statue would stay put unchanged. Oriel would instead set up an online 'virtual explanation' explaining the story of Rhodes and increase provision for Black and Minority Ethnic students as if these actions were a binary and the provision was a concession. A small metal plaque at street level was also unexpectedly unveiled, noting that Rhodes was a 'committed British colonialist' whose fortune came through exploitation in Southern Africa. The text lamely states that 'Some of his activities led to great loss of life and attracted criticism in his day and ever since.' A small mealy-mouthed plaque does little to counter the honour still given by Oriel to Rhodes by the presence of the unaltered and elevated statue.

Any true reckoning with the past needs to move beyond oversimplified accounts of colonialism that seek to formulate positive/negative balance sheet evaluating, say, railway building versus army massacres under the British Raj or that weigh bigoted civic philanthropy against mass murder of enslaved Africans. We need to understand the impact of this past on the present world and the lived consequences today of centuries of discrimination,

The establishment's real fears here are not for statues, a song, or a painting's label, but about successful challenges to their partial and self-serving accounts of history. Trivial matters are ruthlessly twisted into enormous symbolic threats to the national story and identity. Far from the Left being engaged in a campaign of censure, it is the Right's practices that are busily shifting the window of acceptable political discourse – the Overton window – as far rightward and as fast as it is able. There is a determination in these Gramscian wars of position to crush the perceived hegemony of the Left in the cultural sector.

When Boris Johnson calls for 'retain and explain' and argues that to tear down statues would be to erase history, we should be aware of the extraordinary hypocrisy at work regarding the British government and the historical record. Remember that during the post-war retreat from empire, the government set about systematically burning or concealing documentation that could evidence British wrongdoing in its colonies including racial and religious discrimination, torture, mass murder, and other atrocities. The smoke from pyres of documents spiralled up from New Delhi and Jerusalem, Nairobi, and Aden, from more than twenty-three countries and territories. Those documents that weren't burned were tipped into the sea or hidden away in the Home Counties. Known as Operation Legacy, the coordinated historical erasure continued into the 1970s, the better to allow the false narrative of the British Empire as benevolent to take hold. Indeed, it continues still with countless documents remaining official secrets and unavailable to historians.[49] In 2013, for example, it was revealed that Ministry of Defence archivists had destroyed 97 percent of its old papers. Many of those that survive remain under lock and key.[50] It was the British government, not activists, that systematically destroyed thousands of the original landing cards of the Windrush generation of Afro-Caribbean immigrants who, under Teresa May's Hostile Environment policy, had been threatened with illegal deportation. The landing cards were important evidence of their right to remain. It was a Tory government that in 2013 revised *Life in the United Kingdom: A Guide for New Residents*, a history booklet for those seeking citizenship, to remove previous references to deaths on slave ships and enslaved people liberating themselves in favour of a narrative of British abolitionists acting on moral grounds. In defiance of the facts, the booklet claims that there was a mostly orderly transition from colonised countries of the empire to independence. References to anti-Semitism and the Holocaust were also removed. Hitler's war aims were described as simply a desire to conquer more land for the German people.[51]

It is governments not cancel culture activists that are busily resisting historical truths, interfering politically in the allocation of research funds for historical projects and in education. Donald Trump's 1776 Commission to encourage 'patriotic education' fell with his administration, but more than a dozen states have put in place laws since outlawing anti-racist, anti-sexist or gay-affirmative lessons in schools. In the post–Trump White House too, Biden staffers has been busily taping back together official records ripped up by Trump and his team.

CR

With such a hypocritical track record, cynical establishments and tamed heritage gatekeepers cannot be trusted to safeguard the truth about the past. The British government's 'retain or explain' policy is just another bad-faith maneuvre in its culture wars.

At the same time, however, we need to caution the many on the Left who deny that monuments are part of history and who argue for a wholesale sweeping away of the existing commemorative landscape. They are misguided. Because, despite all the cynicism and hypocrisy and the state's own record of erasure, monuments *do* help us understand the past. They *are* historical records. How to make sense of them is not straightforward; the myths and misunderstandings about the impact statues have on our lives and on society, about the nature of past iconoclastic waves and the impact such removals have on history are, perhaps, even more widespread, more complex and fraught than the reasons these monuments were put up in the first place.

There is in fact the potential for a good faith 'retain and explain' policy, a policy that turned sites of honour into sites of shame that we can learn from. What this could look like is set out later. But first the lies about the past and bad faith attempts to conceal them are not confined only to statues. We need to look at how these are being perpetrated at the scale of entire cities.

2

Style Wars/ Culture Wars

'What I do not think is sensible is when the avant-garde becomes the establishment.'
    – Prince Charles, *The Private Man, the Public Role,* (1994)[1]

Ursula Friedrich is a tour guide with a difference; she specialises in close, beady readings of Dresden's monuments, readings that are not always popular with the city's elite[2] In theory, Ursula agrees, you can interpret the story of a city through its public art and sculptures, what it chooses to remember or celebrate, what it seeks forgiveness for, and what it chooses to conceal from itself and from the world. Monuments, both purposeful memorials and historic edifices more widely, tell you about the political, economic, and cultural context in which the artworks were commissioned and erected – about the very idea a city has of itself.

The made and remade monuments and cities of Germany are particularly fascinating in this regard. The German language also has usefully specific terms for the categories of its memorials. There is the *Denkmal,* which simply means 'monument,' and the *Ehrenmal,* which is a memorial designed as a positive commemoration of a person or event. And then there is the *Mahnmal*, derived from an old German term for a scar. A Mahnmal can deliberately point to darker, negative events or record sites of shame that administer admonishing warnings from history.

But what happens when monuments are evasive in their attempts to shape the truth or provide an altogether false narrative for a place? What happens when these stone recordings are not even genuine products of their time but are modern installations masquerading as historic artefacts?

Over the last few decades, Dresden has been steadily resurrected from its wartime ruins using an extravagant pastiche Baroque to the point that, as one German commentator acidly observes, the city once celebrated as the 'Florence on the Elbe' has become 'Las Vegas on the Elbe,' a place made entirely tacky by faux historic landmarks and entire streets of repro townhouses and apartment blocks.

Ursula is among the critics. She takes me on a tour, pointing out the obvious power symbols such as Augustus the Strong's crown that serves as a pinnacle to the onion-domed Crown Gate of the Zwinger pleasure gardens. More telling than the crown, she says, is the stern male mask above the gateway clad in a lionskin helm. Clearly the wearer is a fearsome lion killer. But the mask is set amidst allegorical figures of the seasons and abundance. The ensemble is meant as a threat from a monarch to his subjects, argues Ursula: 'Life will be good if you obey. If not, I will hunt you down and kill you.' Over in the Altmarkt, rebuilt by the German Democratic Republic (GDR) following the 1945 firestorm that devastated Dresden, are facades that incorporate subtly propagandistic symbols of peace and plenty: masonry wheatsheaves, vines, and cornucopia. A freshly caught fish carved on a keystone is, to Ursula's mind, not being depicted as ready for the pot but is being handled gently by a boy – a propagandist message of humanity in harmony with nature. This is not, of course, an accurate account of the immediate post-war East given its many privations.

Around the corner on Kreuzstrasse, the brutal values of the Stalinist state in the late 1950s are gently rebuked in bas-reliefs of friendly snails, tortoises, and sunflowers – as opposed to vainglorious lions and eagles. These are by three artists including sculptor Wieland Förster, who was then out of favour with the regime. Close by is the Rathaus, also remodelled following war damage. Here, stone city shields representing Leningrad, Lidice, Dresden, Coventry, Breslau, Florence, Ostrava – all historic places ravaged by war – were installed above the entrance doors. Dresden has placed itself in the middle of these victim cities.

We continue walking and reading as we go – statues, inscriptions, carvings, memorials – and arrive back where we started, in the central Neumarkt. With a thump of a furled umbrella's ferrule on the cobbles and arms flung wide, Ursula takes in the 360-degree view of the city square lined with the prettily rendered facades of its tall houses and businesses, criss-crossed by horse and carriages and supervised by the great stone dome of the Frauenkirche church with its booming bell. Everything you see, the complete historic vista across the square, from the dome to the side streets leading off it, the very cobbles of the square itself, are, bar one sole structure, not genuine historic fabric at all but thin-skinned fake facades, constructed at vast expense over the last few years, sometimes wrecking genuinely historic vaults that survived the Allied inferno in the process. Many of the tourists here are older than the buildings they are looking at. 'This,' declares Ursula Friedrich, 'is all fake news.'

Germany has been engulfed in an architectural culture war since reunification. It has set forward thinkers against traditionalists, democrats against neo-Nazis, stylistic Classicists against Modernists. This is not only affecting Dresden. Across the country, long-vanished urban palaces, streets, and churches are being rebuilt from scratch, whole city quarters of half-timbered gabled townhouses recreated to replace what was lost in the war. This is astonishing in a country where for decades a classical column was entirely *verboten*. Classicism as a style, and architectural traditionalism more widely, had been fatally linked to Hitler and his totalitarian vision which had been translated into ponderous, imperious colonnades and gargantuan parade grounds by the regime's pet architects such as Albert Speer and Paul Ludwig Troost. What's more astonishing and alarming is that many reconstruction initiatives are not the consequence of simple nostalgia but are linked to Right and Far Right figures intent on restoring Germany's identity and pride, abandoning the notion of national responsibility for war crimes, and denying in their rebuilding efforts the fact of Fascism and war altogether. Dresden's homegrown Pegida Party (Patriotic Europeans against Islamisation of the Occident) has gathered tens of thousands on its 'pilgrimage' marches to the new Neumarkt and its reconstructed Frauenkirche.

Stuttgart architecture professor Stephan Trüby has been tracking the rise of what he calls 'right-wing spaces' in Germany for years.[3] He notes the use of terms such as *heimat* and *boden* (homeland and soil/earth) that have Nazi-era resonances. They are indirect enough to be deniable but are recognisable to committed neo-Nazis and an online alt-Right community. This is similar to England and the United States where words such as 'beauty' and entreaties to preserve a distinct European cultural heritage and civilization are often coded dog-whistles to the Hard and Far Right.

Recreating the past through architecture is now being seen across Europe and beyond. Long-destroyed buildings including entire churches, castles, and palaces are being resurrected from the ground up and wholly new ones that never previously existed raised from scratch in backward-looking traditional styles like never before. Why?

In the immediate post-war period, many cities in Germany and elsewhere had seen extensive restoration of key historic cultural landmarks damaged by bombing but, in most places, a consensus emerged on both sides of the Iron Curtain that Modernist city-making was the way forward.[4] In Britain as elsewhere, Modernism was decidedly the architectural language of a peaceful, more equitable Europe, of new clinics and kindergartens, of decent public housing and comprehensive schools, a sunny and secular New Jerusalem. With rare exceptions, traditional architecture was vanquished. That consensus in favour of the new has now broken down amid attempts to bury the very idea of social democracy's post-war settlement.

Some architectural traditionalists are simply sincere nostalgics for past crafts, and styles who don't look at the political consequences of their enthusiasms. But there are too many others whose interventions betray a darker, ideological tone that is now contributing to an atmosphere of an increased hostility to expressions of difference or diversity. Some are on the periphery of organised hate groups and conspiracy theorists that are now venturing into the topics of architecture and urbanism. Almost daily there are posts in traditional architecture groups on Facebook, Twitter, and other platforms, hailing every local triumph over modernity, praising every post-war Polish or Hungarian building demolished or refaced in traditional garb: 'We need that kind of restoration in Bulgaria, so we can finally get rid of our communist past,' offers one typical post celebrating another Modernist structure levelled. 'Architecture is one of the tools used by the elites to control the people,' argues another, 'elites are intent on destroying our traditional societies ... The architect is just the dumb hammer being used to smash our society.'[5]

This is not simply a matter of aesthetic preference – it is nativist and identitarian politics using appeals to architectural tradition, especially the Classical, as a proxy for attacks on cosmopolitanism and pluralism. American neo-Nazis such as Identity Evropa have paraded in front of the 1897 copy of the Parthenon in Nashville to demonstrate their allegiance to a racist Eurocentricism. Dutch radical right populist politician Thierry Baudet calls for a return to tradition, arguing that ugly modern architecture is corrupting society and is the project of a cosmopolitan global elite that is hostile to the nation-state: 'Modernism, multiculturalism and the European project enforce ... a world without a home ... [with] gargantuan tower blocks with satellite dishes directed towards Al Jazeera.'[6] Like English journalist Douglas Murray, Baudet is not religious but regards himself as a 'cultural Christian' and has associations with the likes of the influential philosopher Sir Roger Scruton, Theodore

Dalrymple, and various other figures of the reactionary Right who are sympathetic to nativist and populist cultural policies at the national or European level. There is an attempt here to capture architecture's cultural castle using concepts that mirror, in a distorted way, Gramscian ideas of cultural hegemony. Not so much 'retain and explain' as rewind the clock and obfuscate the truth.

Among the online posts is a long video by English YouTuber Paul Joseph Watson that neatly sums up this perspective. His videos have gained a following with their mash-ups of sneering falsehoods, conspiracy theories, and bravura ignorance of the subject matter. *Why Modern Architecture Sucks* a video post from 2017, is a case in point. It opens with aerial footage of medieval European cities with church spires prominent, the backdrop for a lament for the loss of traditional architecture at the hands of degenerate modernity: 'We are being indoctrinated to accept ugliness as a form of beauty,' snarls Watson. 'Aesthetic ugliness encourages ugly behaviour' and 'Modernist architecture is inherently totalitarian' leading to 'moral decay.' Over images of one of Le Corbusier's Unité blocks, he asserts: 'Radical architects launched a revolution against earlier traditional styles [because] they represented colonialism, racism, slavery ... They were the social justice warriors of their time – aesthetic terrorists.' This is self-evidently utter nonsense. Le Corbusier, for one, was a political reactionary and about as far from being a social justice warrior as you could get.

Watson is sweeping in his dislikes from tower blocks, to Brutalism, to Hi-Tech, to Postmodernist styles – reserving, for some unknown reason, a particular venom for Renzo Piano. Watson claims an elite is using architecture to 'atomize and segregate workers and the lower classes.' Modern architecture has here become the equivalent of the anti-Semitic trope of the rootless cosmopolitan. Preposterously, Watson edits-in a decades-old television interview with Prince Charles to bolster his point about elites, with the heir to the throne cast as a counterweight to elitism: 'What I do not think is sensible,' drawls Charles, 'is when the avant-garde becomes the establishment and that is

what happened.' The Prince's neo-Classical Poundbury development comes up on screen as a 'pocket of resistance.' Excerpts
from Sir Roger Scruton's BBC documentary *Why Beauty Matters*
feature the philosopher speaking from a graffitied service yard to
call Functionalism 'the greatest crime against beauty the world
has ever seen.' Watson may come across as a crackpot, but such
ideas are now infiltrating mainstream government policy.

Let's be absolutely clear here: there is nothing inherently right-
wing about Classicism as a style – or Left about Modernism,
for that matter. Architectural form, the assemblage of bricks
and mortar, concrete and glass, is not per se political; the materials have no agency or values. Instead, architectural style is
politicised by the purposes to which it is put and the motiva-
tions of those doing the shaping. Classicism, historically, has
been used by royalty and republicans, democrats and despots,
while Modernism, despite some close early links to socialist and
utopian agendas, has not been exclusive in its allegiances; the
International Style became the spatial currency of global capitalism, for example. Mussolini for one was happy to make use
of both Modernism and Classicism, and Franco's regime might
be best known for its preference for Escorial-era architectural
austerity but could also countenance Modernism for resorts
that brought in tourists' hard currency or even Andalusia's
Islam-derived architectural tradition in the right circumstances.
Individual architects have worked in various idioms for clients
savoury and unsavoury; Gropius and Mies van der Rohe were
both willing to work for the Nazi Reich.

Later, with the political upheavals of the late 1960s and the
economic crises of the '70s that ushered in neoliberalism, the
grip of top-down, technocratic Modernism began to falter.
Critic Charles Jencks felt he had pinpointed the end of the Modernist project: 'Modern architecture died in St Louis, Missouri
on July 15, 1972, at 3:32 p.m. (or thereabouts).' That was the
date and time when the first homes of the failed fifty-seven-acre
Pruitt-Igoe public housing estate in St. Louis were dynamited
less than twenty years after its slab blocks were constructed.

A 2011 documentary, *The Pruitt-Igoe Myth,* unpicked Jencks' polemic, demonstrating that the estate failed not just because of its Modernist design (which admittedly had problems) but chiefly because of wider, non-architectural forces such as bad tenancy decisions, lack of maintenance, and socio-economic factors such as intense local unemployment and racism that were crucial in causing a downward spiral into violence and decrepitude.

However, is the very architecture of Modernism as well as its ideals rather than these other factors that have taken the blame on thousands of public housing estates since, and which were often built as cheap knock-off versions of the style in the first place. Some of this blame was deserved. But Postmodernist architecture, and postmodernism more generally, has defined itself in opposition to these failings by falsely depicting Modernism as monolithic rather than being made up of multiple strands ranging from the humanism of Alvar Aalto to the brute force of Le Corbusier in city planning mode. More positively, the postmodern brought a new interest in historical architecture, contextualism, the vernacular, and the everyday. Collage and quotation became a norm under one kind of Po-Mo interpretation, often with detached irony. For architect Philip Johnson, who once helped organise an American Fascist gang called the Grey Shirts and designed them a podium for rallies, the entire AT&T skyscraper in Manhattan becomes a giant Chippendale cabinet with a broken pediment.

However, Postmodern architecture's pluralism and interest in historic forms also opened the door for a reactionary Classical revival. These traditionalists did not want to deal in ironic Po-Mo quotes – a capital here, a finial there – but were still building with rigid classical orders in stylistic and often ideological opposition to modernity. With honourable exceptions, these Classicists are a sect that caricatures modern life and Modernist architecture in the most venomous terms, concentrating on Modernism's worst failings rather than its utopian ideals or practical achievements in fields such as public housing.

◌

While Britain, along with the United States, was the home of many of these revived traditionalist theories and theorists, it was in Germany that they began to flourish in practice. Since reunification, they have been reshaping the centres of major cities and small towns, flattening post-war quarters to reconstruct long-vanished pre-war buildings. They are making their appeal to the anti-immigrant Far Right who, as Stephan Trüby also notes, are 'filled with disgust at any kind of metropolitan, multicultural way of life.'⁷ At first, this had particular resonance in the former East Germany, whose industrial base had been asset-stripped by corporate raiders from the West. The population were left living often desperate lives among decaying, gimcrack GDR modernity. They were ripe for reaction.

Yet it is an approach to urbanism and architecture that has also become a notable feature of the former West. And it is accelerating. In Frankfurt am Main, for example, the 1970s Technical Town Hall, built on a war-ravaged section of the medieval Old Town, has been demolished and a fake 'Old Town' has been constructed in its place, all quaint half-timbering (*Fachwerk*) and gables, between the cathedral and the Römberg Square. Dubbed the Dom-Römer-Projekt, it has used public money in a €200 million public–private project for the creation of an upmarket enclave of shops and apartments. The new old quarter is promoted as a faithful recreation of the medieval city, but this is false. The Old Town had already been considerably altered before the war, and the rebuild has been created above a post-war car park and U-Bahn station that results in some very peculiar juxtapositions between faux *Fachwerk* structures and the infrastructure of modern life.

Wandering its narrow streets and pocket-handkerchief squares at the end of the working day, you pass through a fairy tale theme park of souvenir, jewellery, and ceramics shops and milling tourists before arriving at the reimagined Hühnermarkt (Chicken Market) square where glossy professionals are packing café tables laden with bottles of rosé and glasses of fluorescent Aperol spritz. Not just historicist facades but entire galleried inner courtyards have been built. Some of the architectural

2.1 and 2.2 Before and After Images. The Dom-Römer project in Frankfurt is a pastiche recreation of part of the city's Old Town that was blitzed in the Second World War. The Brutalist Technical Town Hall was demolished to make way for it. All the buildings in the second image are new. Some constructions incorporate salvaged architectural elements.

recreations are very well done and are mixed in with interest-ing, contemporary interpretations of medieval forms. In places, genuine carvings rescued from the wartime blitz have been reaffixed to buildings at key corners. Elsewhere, the details are cringeworthy. Modern necessities such as insulation peek out, revealing the true age of buildings.

Local architecture critic Dieter Bartetzko has defended the project, describing the demolished Brutalist town hall as a 'provocative and ignorant *foreign body* in the urban fabric' (my emphasis).[8] The official website for the project talks about pic-turesque courtyards, historic alleys and grand patrician houses bringing a 'special atmosphere' back to the heart of Frankfurt. It argues that this represents the 'heart's desire' of Frankfurt's resi-dents when in fact it has been deeply divisive. But this enclave is not one of working chicken markets or long-operating artisans' workshops hugger-mugger with patrician mansions, nor for that matter is it horse manure and the plague; it is instead a sani-tised dolls' house quarter whose purpose is separating visitors from their euros. All this while genuine medieval survivors such as the rundown Haus Wertheym (1479) diagonally across the Römberg square is in sore need of restoration.

Is this fantasy of the past necessarily problematic? True, unlike some of the splendidly humanist Modernist works of the 1950s found close by, the demolished Technical Town Hall was a leaden affair that related poorly to the surrounding city; it ignored street lines, materials, and scale. True too that the Dom-Römer's new pedestrian streets are human-scale with active frontages and quality materials that, for the most part, tick all the right urban design boxes. But is this sufficient justifi-cation for the conservative, historical language of the buildings themselves which may fool the casual observer about their age? Possibly, although this is not where the chief harm lies.

What troubles most is the meaning behind this expensive exercise, the erasing of genuine history, its clock-reversing denial of the destructive consequences of war, and the ideological aims of the people pursuing it, some of whom have murky agendas. Among the most vocal backers has been Claus Wolfschlag, an author who has made his name attacking anti-Fascists and who regularly appears at events organised by right-wing extremists such as the Danubia Munich Fraternity. He admires totalitarian monuments and has written for Far Right or nationalist titles such as the Austrian weekly newspaper *Zur Zeit* that has defended Hitler, is hostile to minorities, and has called for policies such as the reintroduction of workhouses and the restriction of voting rights. Wolfschlag argued that Dom-Römer 'ends the cult of guilt' represented by the Modernist rebuilding of Germany's cities post-war. He put forward a motion to the city council that kicked off the plans along with local politician-journalist Wolfgang Hübner, formerly active in the Alternative für Deutschland.

In Frankfurt, as elsewhere, the campaigns to reconstruct the centres of German towns and cities to their prewar appearance are too often allied with this kind of politics. There is an agenda among many traditionalist rebuilders that wants to visually deny the record of both National Socialism and several decades of democracy since. These fantasies are ideology in built form that seeks to reconnect with an eternal German *heimat* and its deeply conservative values. Architectural fakes are one of its tools. As Trüby argues, 'the reconstruction architecture in Germany is currently developing into a key medium of authoritarian, ethnic, historical revisionist rights.'[9]

This is not an entirely new debate in Germany, but it is one whose parameters have, over the last decade or so, changed profoundly. The devastation at war's end following aerial carpet bombing that had killed some 600,000 German civilians saw most cities simply get on with rebuilding for the future without examining the recent past. In both East and West Germany, major monuments were reconstructed from their ruins and damaged apartments repaired but the balance of reconstruction in urban areas was generally Modernist. Hannah Arendt, travelling through Germany's ruinscapes, was struck by Germany's seeming inability to face both past and present: 'Amid the ruins, Germans mail each other picture postcards still showing the cathedrals and marketplaces, the public buildings that no longer exist.' She argued that the French and British mourned their comparatively limited monumental losses far more than Germany where entire historic cities had been levelled.[10]

In Munich, unlike in most German cities, it was the traditionalists who narrowly won the key post-war votes which meant that the historic city was largely restored from ruins, using a full photographic record commissioned by the National Socialists ahead of the predicted aerial bombing. Today its inner city has a remarkable homogeneity, an illusion of venerability that in many cases does not extend beyond a thin veneer of old material. Most of its chief Nazi monuments remain in place too. Half a century later, other cities that had once rejected the Munich model are now using traditionalist rebuilds to excise the war and its destructive consequences. The lack of mourning for lost monuments observed by Arendt appears then to have been only a temporary repression. Mourning has surfaced with all its attendant nostalgic politics.

Among the most egregious of these rebuilds is the attempt to recreate the Garrison Church in Potsdam. The eighteenth-century church, with its Baroque tower covered in carvings of guns and swords, was long a primary site for the celebration of Prussian militarism, gatherings of Weimar-era anti-democratic reactionaries and ultra-nationalists, and, infamously, the place where President von Hindenburg shook Hitler's hand marking the Fuhrer's final rise to power. This was a moment commemorated on Third Reich banknotes and when the Garrison Church's carillon was played between features on Goebbels' radio network. The church was bombed in the war, destroying its sculptures of helmeted angels, and its ruins finally demolished by the GDR in 1968.

Right-wingers are determined to resurrect it, and they have received federal funding for their misadventure despite widespread protests. The rebuilding campaign was underway even before reunification. In 1984 Max Klaar, an extreme Right former West German army officer, founded an association that recreated the carillon and he then presented the bells to the city of Potsdam after the Berlin Wall fell. The carillon features dedications to eastern territories that Germany had lost on defeat and to questionable military organisations such as the Kyffhäuser League for war veterans.[11] The Protestant Church supported Klaar's reconstruction plans, complete with all its martial sculptures, only parting from him when he successfully resisted a proposal to substitute the Prussian eagle and sun once at the spire's apex with a reconciliatory (or exculpatory, depending on one's perspective) Cross of Nails from Coventry.[12]

Tourism alone cannot justify this project, nor is there a strong urban design argument that this is an essential repair to the town's overall fabric given its now comparatively marginal location. Historian Paul Nolte, chair of the church's advisory board, has justified the rebuild on the grounds that people now think less intellectually and more visually: 'And because we think visually, the need for reconstructive architecture also arises. We want to remember the past, but not abstractly. But rather in authentic places.'[13] Authentic is a cynical word to use in such circumstances. Construction has started on the Garrison Church's controversial bell tower. In the meantime, gilded details for its exterior, including a golden crown, are displayed in a wire cage by the road, covered in dual carriageway dust.

The Garrison Church may be the most burdened of Potsdam's historical recreations, but it is far from the largest. Between the town and main station entire city blocks are being rebuilt – or, more accurately, reimagined – in a process that has seen GDR-era buildings systematically demolished and Baroque copies put in their place including the former Stadtschloss palace – recreated as the Brandenburg state parliament building in which the AfD has often performed strongly. It is a strange conservation strategy that builds expensive pastiches while there are genuine historic mansions in the town centre in a parlous state. Traditionalist pressure to make this happen included intervention by the Prince of Wales who in 1996 used his Urban Design Taskforce to lobby for reconstruction. 'It can be claimed,' he wrote, 'that the memory of an older, finer Potsdam has never truly been erased, and that it still occupies the hearts and minds of those who live in the city.' The Taskforce's director Brian Hanson called the earlier Communist levelling of the bomb-damaged palace ruins 'ideological' (as if its rebuilding isn't) and called for the retrieving of a 'lost idea.'[14]

Yet the scale of Potsdam's palatial reconstructions, extensive though they are, are entirely overshadowed by the reconstruction of Berlin's own massive Stadtschloss. In a decades long battle for the heart of the capital and for all its bohemian reputation, traditionalists have here too come out on top with the palace now reborn as the Humboldt Forum.

Berlin's Stadtschloss was the 1,200-room Baroque palace of the Prussian royal family, the Hohenzollerns. Badly damaged by wartime bombing, its ruins were removed on the orders of East German leader Walter Ulbricht, who also objected to the palace's militarist connotations. Ulbrecht wanted a 'great square for demonstrations in which the will to rebuild of our people can be expressed.'[15] Only one section of the old palace was preserved – a bay incorporating the balcony from which Karl Liebknecht declared a socialist republic on 9 November 1918. It was relocated to the nearby Council of State building where it still forms an incongruous element of an otherwise modern façade. The royal palace was replaced by the GDR Palast der Republik, which was part peoples' fun palace and part rubber-stamp parliamentary chamber.

Despite its almost Trumpian mirror-clad dictator kitsch, the Palast was beloved by many East Berliners, but like much of GDR culture, it became a casualty of the triumphant reunification steamroller, a machine driven by the West Germans that aimed to level the substance and symbols of East German life and values. The presence of asbestos was used as a justification for its demolition even though the material has been successfully removed from post-war buildings the world over. The push by conservatives was for the recreation from scratch of the Hohenzollern palace facades. It didn't really matter what went on inside as long as the traditional image of the city was reinstated. The head of the Berlin Historical Society at the time favoured a reconstruction approach that would draw a line under any sense of guilt. Instead, she argued that the 'city must be beautiful so that people will be happy and they will not repeat these mistakes.'[16] Backers included the Berlin mayor, the former chancellor turned lobbyist Gerhard Schröder, and other figures in big business. Prussian prince Georg Friedrich also lent his support while simultaneously demanded the return to him of other palaces, paintings, and the imperial crown and sceptre, claims that reignited discussion of his Hohenzollern family's historical relationship to the Nazis. Henry Kissinger and George H W Bush were among other donors.

As finally realised by Italian architect Franco Stella, the €644 million Humboldt Forum is an architectural camel (the proverbial horse designed by committee) splayed out under one giant domed hump. Opening in stages during Covid-ravaged 2021, the 30,000 square-metre Humboldt Forum houses an ethnological museum, an Asian art museum, a city museum for Berlin,

Robert Bevan

2.3 The Humboldt Forum in Berlin is a partial recreation of the bombed Prussian royal palace designed by architect Franco Stella. Shown here, is its clash of historicist and modern facades – both are new.

and space for the Humboldt University across its football field-size floorplates. In an extraordinarily ineffective architectural compromise, three of its facades are historic and the fourth contemporary, a mix and match exercise repeated at close quarters and to worse effect in its inner courtyards and in sections of its interior.

This is not the reconstruction of ruins but beginning again from square one. The faux-Baroque meets corporate office architecture is an aesthetic car crash that feels less like a compromise and more like a case of wanting to have it both ways – attempting to resist charges of fakery why still presenting, overwhelmingly, an image of the old. It is almost as if it is trying to invent a new history, an instant illusion of evolution over time delivered in one quick construction hit.

The strangeness continues inside where some tall gallery spaces have dropped ceilings to accommodate services. This is a common, almost standard feature of uninventive conversions of historic buildings with difficult floor levels, but in this case it has been built-in from scratch, as if the project were actually adapting a tricky historic structure. The reconstruction has also set up a truly bizarre situation where, when viewed from Unter den Linden, you are presented with a double-vision of two balconies: one the original Liebknecht balcony transferred to and surviving on a neighbouring building and then its modern copy incorporated into the freshly resurrected palace.

Objectors to the rebuilding of the palace are unhappy about the loss of the GDR Palast and the ugly juxtapositions that the architectural antics of the Forum has forced on Berlin; they also object to its ideological meaning, the sense that like Munich, it is seeking to erase the past while reviving an illusion of it. Decisions such as reinstating the royalist inscription by Frederick William IV around the base of the recreated 1840s dome which demands that Berliners 'bow down on their knees' and submit to Christianity, and the large golden cross atop seek, critics point out, to reimpose old pre-Fascist and pre-Communist hierarchies on Berlin that deny the reality of today's diverse city. Rabbi Andreas Nachama, who heads the German council for Christian–Jewish cooperation, said that the inscription should be removed, calling it an appropriation of faith and pointing to Frederick William's reactionary rule.[17] The Humboldt name lends a rational gloss to a highly irrational exercise in architectural adventurism. And it is not just the Forum. Bourgeoise villas and office and apartment blocks in period disguise are appearing across the capital. One senses an impatience to move away from the dark periods of the city's past. Self-examination is over.

At least Berlin's reimagined royal palace has not become a rallying point for populists, xenophobes, and worse (or not yet, at least), which cannot be said for Germany's other major exercise in grandiosity – the reconstruction of Dresden's Frauenkirche, first completed in 1743 as a statement of Lutheran bourgeoise power independent of the Saxon state. Today, the church sees itself as having a reconciliation ministry that umbilically connects it to Coventry Cathedral, but it is notably reluctant to address its own Nazi past associations. In embodying and bolstering Dresden's victim status, the recreated church has helped facilitate the intolerance of Pegida, the city's home-grown racist movement dedicated to defending Germany against an Islamic 'great replacement.' Founded by PR consultant and convicted criminal Lutz Bachmann in autumn 2014, Pegida's weekly, anti-immigrant *passeggiata* through the Florence of the Elbe grew from a few hundred adherents to a cast of tens of thousands who regularly descended on the 'fake news' Neumarkt surrounding the church.

Under the Nazis, various Protestant confessions were forcibly united as a National Socialist German Christian church, and the Frauenkirche became a notable symbol of the new politico-religious movement and one of Nazism's most important cathedrals. Swastikas were hung from it, and mass weddings of uniformed Nazis took place inside. This was not too surprising in a city such as Dresden that backed the Nazis hard and early, conducting not one but two book burnings in its squares, burning down its magnificent synagogue, and enthusiastically persecuting its Jewish residents. The church came to symbolise

2.4 and 2.5 The ruins of Dresden's Frauenkirche were left as a war memorial by the GDR government. Following reunification, the church and the surrounding Neumarkt were reconstructed with faux Baroque facades. Every structure in the second image is brand new.

something entirely different after February 1945 when Allied air raids systematically erased the city centre. At first the Frauen-kirche appeared to have survived the onslaught, but its stones had been cooked by the intense heat and two days later, with a great shudder, it crumpled to the ground, another ruin in the field of ruins that was the old city. To some, beauty had been meaninglessly murdered.

In the post-war period, and as funds allowed, the GDR repaired the major public monuments of Dresden, putting them back together piece by piece. Its cathedral, the opera house, the superb art galleries, the Zwinger, the castle – all were exten-sively repaired, usually with little to distinguish new work from old. But it was decided the Frauenkirche would remain a ruin, a war memorial, a poignant void in the skyline. Around the pile of stones that were left, the Neumarkt was first reconstructed on substantially Modernist lines. The void and pile of stones where the church stood became the focus of annual ceremonies marking the 1945 air raids.

Matters took a fresh turn after reunification. In December 1989, Chancellor Kohl used the ruins as the backdrop for his first reunification speech in East Germany. In a neoliberal climate that echoed that of Britain and the United States, tra-ditionalist campaigners were soon arguing for the church to rise once more, suggesting that its recreation would itself be a beacon against war. In 1990 local cultural figures published 'Appeal from Dresden' in favour of reconstruction. The new church was to be topped by a British cross blessed by the Bishop of Coventry, presented to the city by architect Prince Michael of Kent, and made by a descendent of one of the original bomber crews. Money rolled in with fragments of old stone sold as souvenirs. Work started in 1994.

Despite the official focus on peace and mourning, the Far Right soon began to assemble at the construction site. At issue are concepts of innocence and victimhood. Dresden's enthusi-asm for the Nazi cause and its small but important industrial role in producing items including specialist instruments for advanced munitions (using local concentration camp slave labour) has generally been underplayed in the narrative where Dresden is portrayed as a city *entirely* dedicated to culture and beauty which was savagely assassinated.

It is true that the Allied carpet bombing of German cities became increasingly indefensible as the war progressed – not that it had ever been justified. The blanket annihilation of city centres in the hope of hitting peripheral industrial and military targets was an Allied war crime and would not, except in the minds of its most intransigent supporters such as Bomber Harris, do anything to shorten the war. It neither destroyed German morale or assisted the Red Army in its push westwards. However, the fate of Dresden has long been used by neo-Nazis and Holocaust deniers to justify their ideology. Casualty figures for the bombing based on false information were inflated ten times over and used by the likes of David Irving to push the idea of the moral equivalence of the warring parties. It is a narrative that took hold in Dresden in the minds of bourgeoise and extremist alike. The city, and the Frauenkirche particularly, became symbolic of the injustices done to the German people, with an additional layer of resentment against GDR Stalinism, then, finally, an assertion of an East German identity then being bulldozed by Chancellor Kohl and his business cronies. Germany had only properly begun to come to terms with its Nazi past from the 1960s onwards, yet by the 1990s, concerted attempts to end the period of self-reflection were surfacing alongside reunification. Germany's concept of itself, more and more, became that of a united and absolved nation.

The shell of the Frauenkirche was largely completed by 2004. Reconciliation was still the dominant message of the project, but its problematic flipside was also stacking up. From at least the late '90s, the annual night-time *Trauermarsch* (funeral march) to the Frauenkirche's ruins on the anniversary of the Allied bombing began to attract a few dozen marching Nazis from various fringe groups. By 2000, some 500 were taking part and this grew year on year. There were flaming torches, the flags of lost German territories in the East, and banners shouting 'Bombing Terror' and 'It Wasn't War It Was Murder' as the marchers commemorated victims of the 'bombing holocaust'. As the Far Right began to dominate the procession, Dresden's Jewish community refused to participate in the ceremony any longer. February 2005 saw around 6,500 Nazis assemble for the event from across Germany and Europe, and a Nazi 'Alliance against Forgetting' was formed to 'remember' Allied mass extermination. Nazis fixed wreaths to the church construction site fence and handed out leaflets calling Dresden's wartime fate 'genocide'. Anti-Fascist counter-protests also massed in struggles for the control of Dresden's streets.

In 2008, a committee of historians confirmed conclusively that the death toll from the Allied raids had been approximately 20,000–25,000, not the 250,000 or 300,000 figures used by those wishing, by comparison, to diminish the Holocaust. The committee decided that local myths such as Allied planes flying low to machine gun survivors had no basis in fact. But the image of an innocent city of art, full of refugees burned alive by phosphorous bombs (which were not used in the raid), persisted – and well beyond Far Right circles. Dresden's own perpetrator role was ignored.

With the rise of Pegida in 2014, the neo-Nazi (as opposed to more broadly right-wing) element of the gatherings did not disappear; it was instead subsumed in Islamophobic marches to the Frauenkirche made up of tens of thousands of racists, populists, avowed Fascists, as well as those from Dresden's decaying peripheral estates protesting rising rents and their economic circumstances under rule from Berlin. This despite Dresden being a relatively successful East German economic success story. It is Muslims rather than Jews who were now seen as conspiring to usurp Christian Europe. Pegida set up chapters in other European countries, including a short-lived English version, before itself being eclipsed by the rise of the Far Right Alternative for Germany, which then became a mainstream political player. Far from being a memorial against war, a tool for reconciliation and peace, the reconstructed Frauenkirche has become a dropped stone in a murky ideological pool from which extremist ripples have spread.

The church has not helped itself by its own myth-making or lack of full disclosure about its own history. The exhibition in its crypt, for instance, gives no information about its military and political role in Nazi religiosity. The church's website refers to Dresden bishop Hugo Hahn's resistance to Nazification of the Lutheran church and has erected a plaque in his honour, but there are no images here of the swastika banners or Nazi weddings. The crypt, points out Ursula Friedrich, displays a copy of a discredited Nazi-era document about the 1945 raids later used by those wanting to establish moral equivalence between the raids on Dresden and the Holocaust. The document's original title referred, in Goebbels-approved style, to the 'Allied terror raids' and it called the church by its Nazi name (the Dom). The displayed version has been edited to omit these telling phrases. How can there be reconciliation without truth?

These evasions extend to the building itself. Visitors are told that a large percentage of the church uses authentic stones rescued from the ruins. What is actually visible externally, however, is almost entirely new work but for one corner tower and a few blackened stones patched in. The reclaimed stone was mostly unsuitable for facing purposes, and where used it has been largely buried deep within the structure, dispersing and diffusing the material of the now-vanished memorial against war. Even so, less than half the reclaimed stones were used in the new building.

More fundamentally, the war-warning void, the Mahnmal at the centre of Dresden, has vanished. It has been replaced with a fake that attempts to deny the dark reality of the past. This matters more with a symbolic building such as the Frauenkirche than structures that are less burdened by contemporary ideology such as, say, the Zwinger. Not enough care has been taken to understand and explain the Frauenkirche's changing materiality and meaning. As Pegida's night-time marches spread across German cities in 2015, landmarks such as the Brandenburg Gate and Cologne Cathedral and those of the Semperoper in Dresden turned off their floodlights in protest of the movement's intolerance. Those at the Frauenkirche stayed on.

CR

Reconstructing the church alone has been insufficient for those that see Dresden's entire post-war Modernist townscape as a foreign and ugly second destruction, a Communist-era penance that it no longer needs to pay and which can be swept away. The physical reconstruction wave has radiated out from the Frauenkirche across several city blocks. Post-war Dresden has been replaced with fakery. This is not the full restoration of genuinely old but ruined structures but the reinvention of traditional architecture from the ground upwards. These structures are a fantasy of what once existed in the city, often simply decorative facades and front roof slopes concealing concrete structures behind. Before the Second World War, the Neumarkt also had pre-Baroque stepped-gable buildings and nineteenth-century edifices, but the rebuild is entirely in the Baroque or Baroque-inflected style, creating a fiction of Dresden's unified pre-war appearance.

Dresden was not the first reconstructed urban centre – Hildesheim, for instance, has been reconstructing its marketplace in replica since the 1980s – but it has been the most extensive and influential. The Dresden Historical Neumarkt Society is the powerful business organisation behind many changes. It is now turning its attention to the opposite side of the river where it wants to replace GDR social housing with more ersatz recreations. The opaque organisation has opposed *any* contemporary buildings among the faux Baroque confections lining the old town's reinstated street pattern in which it has been involved. The market square and the surrounding new/old streets are filled with tourists rather than locals, who are not the customers for the champagne bars, luxury watch dealers, and Meissen china shops that have sprung up. A passing resemblance to the pre-war city has been recreated, but it is not truly a part of the city as lived by contemporary Dresdeners. There has been no similar investment in the good quality but neglected 1950s public housing blocks in the city centre. Indeed, the last glimpse of these blocks from the Neumarkt is set to be hidden by a reconstruction of the bombed Hotel Stadt Rom.

The dangers of all this fake history are sometimes very obvious. Ursula Friedrich leads us to Sporergasse just off the Neumarkt and an apparently Baroque edifice with a plaque saying it was built in 1695. This is the Triersche Haus. In 1940 it became one of Dresden's Judenhäuser into which the couple of hundred Jews who had not yet been deported to their deaths were crammed, after their own homes had been expropriated. The house was levelled in the 1945 bombing and its Jewish inhabitants killed. They had not stood a chance because Jews were banned from Aryan air raid shelters. The entire street was constructed from scratch as a pastiche in 2016, but the plaque on the reimagined Triersche Haus conceals more than it reveals; merely stating that Jews were killed in the raids but not explaining why they were in this house in the first place. The story between the lines, argues Ursula, 'is that the Allies killed Jews in Europe. No comment. Just that they did it. It creates an equivalence [between the bombing and the Holocaust].'

A similar tale was woven in Jörg Friedrich's *The Blaze*, a 2002 novel in which he refers to the shelters and vaults in which so many died in the 1945 raid as 'execution chambers' and 'crematoria.' It's not that Dresden's modern remakers are themselves Nazis, explains Ursula. And she agrees that there is not a problem with traditional styles per se but with their impetus and meaning and their erasure of the material evidence of history. Reconstructions are being used by the Right and Far Right in their anti-modern, anti-cosmopolitan culture wars. Only one major building in Dresden has been reworked in a way that layers the old and new and that's the old main post office, now apartments, where fragments of the former ruin are layered with modern elements. As Ursula Friedrich pithily concludes: 'Dresden had the chance to be a world centre for truth in architecture but blew it.'

Contrast this with the rebuilding of the city synagogue by Dresden's Jewish community. Its site at the end of the elevated Brühl Terrace was reused but the 2001 building designed by architects Rena Wandel-Hoefer and Wolfgang Lorch does not attempt to recreate Gottfried Semper's octagon, once as integral a part of the city skyline as the Frauenkirche. Instead, the new building is an avowedly contemporary sandstone cube. The congregation was concerned that fake reconstruction would have erased the real history of the original's destruction on Kristallnacht. It rejected nostalgia and the fantasy of recreating a past in which the Nazis had not existed.[18] Unlike the new Frauenkirche, the synagogue was not constructed with funds from big business and has been criticised for its modernity by some locals. It has also been the subject of at least one anti-Semitic attack.

While, in the wake of postmodernism, these traditionalist ideas flourished in Britain amid the cultural and economic climate of Thatcherism, very little classical architecture was actually constructed at that time beyond the occasional pompous country house. Ruins were not generally being resurrected. Yes, British cities were and are often victims of commercially driven 'facadism' where a historic building is demolished behind a wallpaper-thin frontage of old material, leaving the city a neoliberal stage set, but assertions of lost identity and radical cultural breaks with totalitarian pasts had less obvious purchase than in other parts of Europe.

This has not been through lack of trying by traditionalists. In the United Kingdom, their cause received an enormous boost with the reactionary interventions of the heir to the throne, Prince Charles. In 1984, the prince chose a celebration at Hampton Court to celebrate 150 years of the Royal Institute of British Architects to launch his all-out assault on Modernism, describing Ahrends, Burton and Koralek's proposed extension to the National Gallery in Trafalgar Square as a 'monstrous carbuncle on the face of a much-loved and elegant friend.' The scheme (admittedly, a curate's egg) was promptly scrapped. The following year, HRH set up the Prince of Wales's Institute of Architecture, now part of The Prince's Foundation, to champion traditional architecture and provide training in associated crafts. The Foundation has six teaching principles that include 'Design Using Natural Harmonics' (apparently some sort of Gaia theory-related landscape mysticism) and to 'Build Beautifully,' – a wording that has resonances which suggest that it was not used by chance. A magazine, *Perspectives on Architecture,* followed. Its first issue announced that it wanted to 'campaign for beauty.' The prince intervened again with a 1987 speech at a Mansion House dinner, channelling the late Poet Laureate John Betjeman in stating: 'You have to give this much to the Luftwaffe, when it knocked down our buildings, it did not replace them with anything more offensive than rubble.'

Charles then used the privilege of centuries of inherited wealth to put his ideas into practice with a new settlement on land he owned on the outskirts of the market town of Dorchester. Poundbury was to become the Prince's suburban *Hameau de la Roi* – a neo-Classical housing fantasia for several thousand subjects employing the leading Classicists to design it. He chose traditionalist architect Léon Krier to plan it. The results vary from odd but accurate Georgian replicas to, given its purpose as a display village for the Classical cause, some surprisingly badly proportioned buildings that fail even as convincing Classicism. Prince Charles himself designed Poundbury's absurd fire station.

One of the most discomforting aspects to this exercise is the employment of Krier himself, infamously a fan of Hitler's architect Albert Speer. In Krier's 1985 monograph on Speer, he wrote: 'Classical architecture was implicitly condemned by the Nuremberg tribunals to a heavier sentence than Speer the Reichsminister.'[19] Part of Krier's argument is that the Nazis also used Modernism. They did on occasion, but for factories and the like; not for their prestige monuments or symbolic buildings. Krier also argued that Speers's giganticist plan for remodelling Berlin as Germania – a totalitarian city set out on belligerent axes – could have been put to democratic use. No matter that Speer appropriated almost 24,000 Jewish homes to be levelled in order to create Germania or that their occupants were sent to their deaths. No matter that concentration camp prisoners were used by Speer as slave labour to quarry stone for Hitler's grandiose architectural vision. Speer's self-serving defence of himself as an apolitical technocrat has been comprehensively demolished since but still Krier remains a fan – and an architectural advisor to Britain's next king. In his 1998 book *Architecture: Choice or Fate* (dedicated, as the critic Rowan Moore has pointed out, '*a mon prince*'), Krier published two images side by side. 'True' pluralism is illustrated by three separate faces – one Black, one white, one Asiatic. 'False' pluralism is illustrated by a cubist mixed-race interweaving of the three faces. Krier has denied that it is racist.[20] At the very least, it suggests a hostility to the cosmopolitan.

Despite all this activity, traditionalist architecture remained a marginal activity in the UK. One of the few Classical public monuments in London of recent times, is, interestingly, to those who bombed Dresden. The grandiose Bomber Command Memorial erected in 2012 in London's Green Park takes the form of a Doric-columned honour temple. Built of Portland Stone, its roof is constructed using aluminium from a downed Halifax. Inside the structure, by architect Liam O'Connor, you look up at heroic statues of airmen. A Winston Churchill quote appears on one wall: 'The fighters are our salvation but the bombers alone provide the means of victory.' This is simply untrue: However brave the individual crew members, the area bombing campaign has never been convincingly shown to have made any difference to winning or shortening the conflict (with the possible, very limited exception of the oil facility bombing campaign at the end of the war). After the outcry over the Dresden firestorm, however, Churchill was silent about the role of Bomber Command to the chagrin of the surviving airmen. The squad's leader Bomber Harris only got his own statue in 1992 and in the face of much outrage. Bomber Command's problematic legacy explains why it has had no memorial previously and why the memorial initiative had to be a private endeavour with significant funding from tax exile and Conservative Party Deputy Chairman Lord Ashcroft. There is also a carved message of supposed reconciliation: 'This memorial also commemorates those of all nations who lost their lives in the bombing of 1939–1945,' neatly eliding those who died under Axis bombing with those of the Allied campaign. There is no explicit regret.

ᘓ

2.6. Bomber Command Memorial in Green Park, London, completed in 2012 by classical architect Liam O'Connor. An inscription of a Churchill quote on the structure falsely suggests that the area-bombing campaign against German civilian centres such as Dresden brought the Allies victory.

Beyond the Bomber Command Memorial bombast, the rarity of large-scale neo-Classical or traditionalist reconstruction in Britain does not mean that historicism has not been having an effect; it is just that its gains have been more recent than in Germany and are seen more in policy than in actual buildings. Although it was Thatcherism that first got the knives out for the architectural legacy of the welfare state, this continued under Tony Blair, whose first public speech on winning the 1997 general election was against the backdrop of neglected public housing on London's Aylesbury Estate 'where all that is left of the high hopes of the post-war planners is derelict concrete'.[21] In hindsight, Blair's speech was a warning – of the marginalisation of Modernist public housing and its tenants and the deregulation that led, ultimately, to the Grenfell fire.

As in Germany, culture warriors in Britain have begun taking aim directly at the very form and look of cities. The Right has a visceral hatred for Modernism because it represents democratic socialism and the post-war welfare state settlement. The assault on its architecture is both symbolic and actual. It is a desire to unmake the relatively successful cosmopolitan mosaic of British inner cities, pushing working class housing to the periphery and rebuilding city centres as privileged, segregated pleasure domes unpolluted by difference. It is a desire to erase the architectural evidence in front of our eyes that an alternative society is not just possible but was attempted, however imperfectly, in Western democracies between the 1940s and 1970s. It is an attempt to cancel a more egalitarian and pluralist future. What is at stake is the erasure of an architecture that faithfully mirrors the ambiguities, complexities, and struggles of the contemporary urban experience in the face of a coordinated attempt to obscure these societal problems and to reinstate a singularly white and European image of human progress based on a false narrative of the past.

An organisation at the heart of this agenda is the Policy Exchange think tank. In 2013 it published a report called *Building More, Building Beautiful*. One of its authors was Sir Roger Scruton, the arch-conservative philosopher with an obsession about beauty derived from Plato and Kant. From the cover onwards – a drawing of Georgian houses that gets the historical details all wrong – the first draft was an ill-informed argument for traditionalism. The oddity of Scruton's worldview drawls off the page: 'Good manners, dress codes, polite speech, clean habits – all these we adopt for aesthetic reasons, because they harmonize our conduct with that of other people.' A champion of fox hunting, Wagner, and the Church of England, Scruton was, essentially, a tweedy culture warrior for the Hard Right. He happily delivered a lecture to the Traditional Britain Group, a Far Right successor to the Western Goals Institute whose aims are a return to tradition and Christianity and to the heterosexual family as the primary social unit, as well as a resistance to immigration, multiculturalism, and the welfare state. Scruton has railed against 'alien objects' (that is, non-traditional buildings) in city centres that are aspects of 'a growing moral void.'

This poison found an ideal scapegoat in the Grenfell disaster, a twenty-three-story London tower block that went up in flames in 2017, killing more than seventy residents, about which Scruton later told an audience of architects at Central Saint Martins: 'If it hadn't been so ugly to begin with, the whole problem would never have happened,' blaming the inferno on the tower's aesthetics.[22] Its ugliness necessitated its recladding and this was the cause of the disaster rather than the neoliberal character of much recent construction procurement and approvals processes that had included the faking of building safety tests.

The Policy Exchange's 2013 report had earlier argued that 'ugly, high-rise' post-war estates encourage crime and social alienation. It called on then London mayor Boris Johnson to redevelop these multi-storey estates into traditional houses and streets – privatised, of course. The report included a spurious, weighted poll where a shoddy picture of the highly desirable apartments at the Brutalist Barbican complex in the City of London appeared to be selected to encourage immoral Modernism to be snubbed by focus groups. Horizontal windows transgress the humane, Scruton argues, and windows without Classicism's decorative mouldings were 'mere holes in the wall.' Fundamentally, he believed beauty to be a universal and eternal value that he linked to 'moral discipline' lost in the permissive 1960s. It is obvious that ideas of what is beautiful change across time, place and culture, but Scruton appears to believe that beauty's rules were laid down by God or by nature and come with columns and a pediment. Though prickly as a hedgehog, Scruton proved a remarkably influential figure in Britain and among the populist governments of Eastern Europe. He once described the UK's Neo-Nazi National Front party as an 'egalitarian … movement' and date rape as a 'supposed crime.'

Scruton's reactionary aesthetics were one prong of the anti-modern agenda. Further dismantling of planning controls was the other, and these matters took a further turn with the election of David Cameron's quietly ideological Conservative government in 2010. The present planning regime has its origins in the post-war settlement. Legislation such as the Town & Country

Planning Act 1947; the establishment of new towns, national parks, protective greenbelts around cities; and other measures were, as with the National Health Service and rail nationalisation, part of a settlement designed (within social democratic limits) to improve equity and create public goods. All anathema to the free marketeers.

In 2014, the Tory planning minister Nick Boles spoke at the right-wing and opaquely funded Legatum Institute to announce £150 million for tackling public housing estates – a renewal process in which public sector tenants are often cleansed from an area to allow private housing to be built: 'We created these huge, rather Brutalist estates in the heart of London,' Boles told his audience. 'Created a culture of crime and alienation, a sense of being separated from the rest of London.' He called for 'squares, and crescents' and for '60s monstrosities' to be 'replaced with new Pimlicos [an area of Victorian Italianate terraces] for Londoners to live in.' His audience was sympathetic: Were those '60s estates used for social control by Labour? he was asked. Are we seeing a move away from feudal Socialism? Boles answered: 'Stalinism didn't work in Russia and it didn't work in inner-city London either.'[23]

Scruton's intellectual guide was David Watkin, the author of *Morality and Architecture* (1977) and a noted reactionary in his own right, hostile to any expression of cultural modernity. Watkin's book set out to pull the rug from under Modernism's idea of itself as a style allied with social justice. While it adroitly pointed out some of Modernism's own mythmaking, this was done in bad faith and in the name of the re-imposition of traditional architecture. The book was highly influential in Trad circles and was a precursor to Scruton's 1980 philosophy book *The Aesthetics of Architecture*, with its similar arguments about the inevitability and correctness of Classicism and tradition in determining beauty and a horror of the modern world and its welfare state architecture. Modernists, Scruton implied, are 'people who never settle.'[24] Again that idea of the rootless cosmopolitan.

Unsurprisingly, Sir Roger, who has echoed anti-Semitic tropes about financier George Soros, was lauded by East European populists including the racist and authoritarian Hungarian prime minister Viktor Orbán. A year before Scruton's death in 2020, Orbán travelled to London to award the by then ailing philosopher the Order of Merit of the Republic of Hungary (Middle Cross), saying Scruton had 'foreseen the threats of illegal migration' and had recognised that freedom was based on 'nation states and Christian civilization.' Orbán has also posted a picture of himself on Facebook holding up the Hungarian edition of Douglas Murray's *The Strange Death of Europe: Immigration, Identity, Islam.*

In November 2018, Scruton was appointed chair of the Cameron government's Building Better, Building Beautiful Commission, a set up inspired by the earlier Policy Exchange work. Scruton believed Britain's chronic housing crisis was a matter of aesthetics rather than politics or economics. His Commission's argument was that nimbies will accept more housing in their backyards as long as its style would 'fit around a church, a green and a manor house.' The task was to change the planning system to encourage housing that built on 'the knowledge and tradition' of communities. Around the same time, David Cameron appointed a Housing Design Panel packed with conservatives such as the rigidly Classical architect Quinlan Terry who had built at Prince Charles's Poundbury. Thankfully, the Scruton Commission's final report, *Creating Space for Beauty,* was much watered down after timely interventions by construction experts more in touch with contemporary realities. However, his thinking is now being promulgated by successors in government. It has established a direction of travel enthusiastically taken up by Latin-spouting Boris Johnson and the culture warriors in his cabinet.

After Scruton's death, leadership of the Beauty Commission passed to fellow traveller Nicholas Boys Smith, once an advisor on tax reform and welfare to Conservative prime ministers and who was himself involved in the 2013 Policy Exchange report. Boys Smith also founded Create Streets, an organisation dedicated to New Urbanism that promotes dense, traditional streets and squares and forms of development such as terraces and perimeter blocks with public frontages and secure private back-lands. As urban design (rather than architecture), this is in many ways uncontroversial and welcome. Importantly, such design ideas didn't emerge only from New Urbanism but were steadily becoming mainstream urbanistic thinking among the grassroots from the 1960s and Jane Jacobs onwards, and were increasingly accepted by many Modernists and non-Modernists alike in recognition that traffic-driven and segregationist Modernist city planning had been an enormous mistake. However, New Urbanism and Create Streets not only pushed traditional street patterns, they also wanted traditional buildings to line those streets, buildings that could only be low-rise and, of course, 'beautiful.'

'In our first seven years,' boasts the organisation's website, 'Create Streets has already managed to have a major impact on English planning policy.'[25] The organisation describes itself as non-partisan, but that is hardly the case. Boys Smith is a former director of the free-market think tank Reform and a fellow of the Legatum Institute, and he has links to the *Conservative Home* blog. The former banker and management consultant has since been appointed a commissioner of Historic England, the quasi-government organisation that guides the national historic environment, despite him being neither an architect, a town planner, an architectural historian, nor an archaeologist. Create Streets has since partnered with the World Monuments Fund and the Victoria and Albert Museum on a post-war reconstruction event.

The culmination of these years of machinations was the Johnson government's 2020 white paper *Planning for the Future* that sought to dismantle the post-war planning system in favour of a developers' charter that would split the country into development zones and prevent individuals and groups from objecting to planning proposals as they emerge. *Planning for the Future* also proposed a 'fast-track for beauty' whereby those proposing to 'build beautifully' would automatically be permitted. Whose standard of beauty? Sir Roger's or Boys Smith's? The Royal Institute of British Architects described the proposals as 'shameful.' Housing charity Shelter predicted that social housing 'could face extinction.' One of the figures behind the white paper was Jack Airey, a special advisor appointed as part of Dominic Cummings's libertarian takeover of 10 Downing Street and co-conspirator with Scruton on his 'building beautiful' agenda.

In January 2020 Airey had written a report for the Policy Exchange that prefigured the planning proposals. *Rethinking the Planning System for the 21st Century* argued that 'Market conditions should instead determine how urban space is used.' Essentially this is a market that, as long as it meets the traditionalist's standards of beauty – preferably classical or some other way suitable to a manor house of churchyard setting – can do exactly what it likes. Later the same year, Housing Secretary Robert Jenrick announced further changes to planning's 'permitted development rights' that, he confirmed as part of a Policy Exchange panel, provide a 'big opportunity' to demolish buildings from the 1960s and 1970s.[26]

Airey was also editor of *Building Beautiful*, a 2019 Policy Exchange collection of essays with a foreword by a housing minister that aimed to influence the Beauty Commission's thinking.[27] Airey claimed in his introduction that it wanted to avoid falling into 'a trap of debating one architectural tradition over another,' but along with Scruton himself, four of its architect contributors were classicists: Robert Adam, Francis Terry, Demetri Porphyrios, and Ben Bolgar (a director at The Prince's Foundation). A fifth, Sir Terry Farrell, recently collaborated with Create Streets on an Earls Court project that was a Classically-derived alternative to that proposed by the scheme's official architects. The young Syrian architect Marwa Al-Sabouni also contributed a piece. Her much-praised but hopelessly naive 2016 book *The Battle for Home* has a foreword by Scruton and, they both, more than a little improbably, put blame on Assad's Modernist housing projects – their design rather than their community segregated inhabitants – for causing community divisions that led to the outbreak of war.[28]

The dramatic planning changes were redrafted after being stymied by shire Tories horrified at the implications for their own towns and villages. Yet the thrust of this right-wing city-shaping project remains in an updated planning bill that, at the time of writing, paused on the zoning but proposed a radical curtailment of the public's right to object to development proposals and more centralized policy making in government hands (as well as making it harder to change problematic street names). Already, policies on beauty have been incorporated into national planning guidance along with the statue preservation clause and 'retain and explain'. A National Model Design Code has been issued, informed by the work of Scruton's Commission, and an interim Office for Place was set up to enforce the plans under Boys Smith. Councils were instructed to put local design codes in place that conformed with the national rules. A mooted 'Right to Regenerate' initiative would speed up the ability to demolish Modernist housing estates and buildings.

The codes and the planning white papers are not just a free-market land grab through re-zoning; they can be seen as evidence of a long-term goal of turning back the clock to a world of tradition, of a wish for Georgian pattern books for facades, for city centres socially cleansed of poor estates and replaced with squares and crescents for the wealthy. For the moment, the national code has also been watered down after successful pushback, but the threat remains with the code a mechanism that would easily allow government to further dictate design under future iterations.

Not uncoincidentally, the Policy Exchange published its *Strong Suburbs* paper (an inevitable watercolour of a Georgian street on its cover) at the same time, authored by a former Adam Smith Institute staffer and an ally of Scruton and fronted with an endorsement by Jenrick about giving power back to the people. Not unreasonably, it proposes that low-density suburbs can become denser and thus more sustainable while creating additional housing but this is by building 'new terraces in the public's favourite style' – that is, pastiche Georgian and Victorian terraces. According to the accompanying press release, the mad mechanism set out for achieving this would be to turn a street's property owners (not tenants, mind) into developers who could award themselves planning permission following a street vote, bypassing current planning controls that operate through democratically elected councils. '...the average home-owner ... could make hundreds of thousands, and on occasion millions of pounds' by turning back the architectural clock a century or two while doubling (or more) their height of their properties. A version of these 'street votes' duly found their way into the 2022 version of the planning bill along with a continued emphasis on government defined 'beauty'.[29]

A parallel process was seen in Trump's America where a culture war push toward the Classical was also a feature. In February 2020, a draft of a proposed executive order was leaked: 'Making Federal Buildings Beautiful Again.' The order was intended to rewrite 1962 guidance on commissioning federal buildings that at that time had specifically rejected an official architectural style, arguing that designs should reflect the time in which they were built. If Donald Trump had not lost the 2020 election, his proposals would have meant that all new federal buildings would be Classical. Reactionary Southern states such as Alabama have in any case been commissioning public buildings in a pastiche Classicism for some years now – especially courthouses.

A President's Committee for the Re-Beautification of Federal Architecture was also proposed to enforce this design nation-wide. That weasel word 'beauty' again. This was (and is) all taking place in a context where white supremacist groups such as the Patriot Front can call for a 'new Caesar to revive the American dream' in its *American Fascist Manifesto*. The fall of Rome is regularly invoked and mass immigration or sexual immorality blamed for the fall. This is a long-standing narrative on the Right, back to Gibbon via Enoch Powell's 'Rivers of Blood' speech referencing the *Aeneid*. So long-standing indeed, that as far back as 1884 William Morris cautioned against the values of the Greek revivalists of his time who happily championed a chattel slavery civilization and overlooked its brutality and injustice.[30]

The Trump administration's push was promoted by a pressure group, the National Civic Art Society and its president,

Justin Shubow of the right-wing Federalist Society. He is one of two society board members appointed under Trump to the US Commission of Fine Arts that approves designs for government buildings in the District of Columbia. Shubow has railed repeatedly against the alleged elitism of the architecture profession: 'If the architects had their way, elevator music in New Orleans public housing would be screeching Stockhausen not native Louis Armstrong or Fats Domino,' he wrote in *Forbes Magazine*. 'Modernists have no room for harmony, rhythm, or soul; they are high-culture elitists, not multiculturalists who celebrate class and ethnic diversity.' Shubow's bid to claim diversity as a value of the traditionalist Right is a laughable twist on the 'Modernism as avant-garde degeneracy' narrative and a staggering hypocrisy given the Right's emphasis on the superiority of European cultural tradition.[31]

In bolstering their position, the Trads often trot out examples of individual Modernist architects with far from progressive views: Le Corbusier was once a member of a Fascist party; anti-ornamentalist Adolf Loos an undoubted racist and misogynist. All true. Their intention, however, is to undermine the general progressive thrust of the Modernist project at the same time as diverting attention from architectural traditionalism's infinitely tighter links to the authoritarian. Aware of these associations, the cultural Right is keen to mischaracterise hostility to its agenda as the reductive equation that all Classicism equals totalitarianism.

American critic Michael Sorkin was splendidly scornful of Poundbury advisor Leon Krier's use of this straw man formulation: 'Who is it that claims the Parthenon is totalitarian?' asked Sorkin. Which Modernists argue this position? None. 'The statement ... is actually a fig leaf for Krier's absolutist claim of the obverse: all modernism is totalitarian.'

Again, there is nothing intrinsically political about an architectural style, but while there are many Lefty architectural conservationists and even some traditionalists (often informed by a William Morris–inflected humanism), the fanbase of contemporary classical architecture ranges, in the main, from right-of-centre to extreme Right. This is the same Krier, after all, who defended Nazi architect Albert Speer's gross architectural machismo on the grounds that it is as absurd to blame an aeroplane for being aerodynamic as it is to condemn Speer's work for being monumental. Sorkin's pithy response: 'Or the gas chambers for being efficient?'[32]

3

The Anti-Cosmopolitans

Yes to bell towers, no to minarets.

Roberto Calderoli, former Lega Nord senator, (2009)[1]

'Tip pig's blood ... Get some bacon and sprinkle it ... Pour some alcohol on the site.' The tactics suggested on the 'Winds of Jihad' blog to frustrate the construction of a mosque in Cairns, northern Queensland, may have been vile – as well as being doctrinally futile – but they are not untypical even in a country such as Australia whose first permanent mosque is more than 130 years old. The blog's claim that 'mosques are symbols of Arab imperialism and supremacy' is clearly a nonsense but this 'minaretphobia' where 'alien' features on a skyline are seen as a threat to a city and a nation's traditional identity have been echoed in similar campaigns across the western world. In 2015, for example, they were repeated by Paul Golding, the leader of the Far Right group Britain First who suggested burying a pig's carcass on the site of a proposed mosque in Dudley in the English Midlands. In London and elsewhere, outright neo-Nazis or those that have connections to them, have organised mosque invasions and 'Christian patrols' in Muslim neighbourhoods as part of an often-violent way of controlling public space – a classic Fascist strategy.

Calls for bans on minarets are only the pointy end of a culture war Islamophobia that has also extended to the banning of burqas, head veils, and other visible manifestations of Islam. Far from being confined to the lunatic fringe, such views have become state policy in countries such as France. They are linked to the 'great replacement' conspiracy theory espoused by French author Renaud Camus that warns of a 'white genocide.' The phrase was echoed in the 2017 torchlit 'Jews will not replace us' chants by American white supremacists who gathered in Charlottesville. There's an anti-cosmopolitanism on the march that makes appeals to architectural traditionalists and which deploys myths about self-chosen cultural ghettoes and no-go areas for whites or the police in its effort to claim that cosmopolitan diversity has failed and to 'other' difference, including architectural difference. Like Germany's traditionalist reconstructions, it uses illusions and outright lies about the past to shape the present.

In my previous book *The Destruction of Memory,* this process was discussed in the context of armed conflict and its immediate aftermath where it is sharper and more readily perceivable; the war in Bosnia is one obvious example. Here, attacks on cities such as Sarajevo, where mosque, synagogue, and church had stood side by side for centuries, were also attacks on a belief in diversity itself – an act of 'urbicide' by uncomprehending monocultural outsiders against the vital social mosaic of the cosmopolitanism city. But the process is very much a peacetime phenomenon too. In the era of the war on terror, we have been seeing, once again, the architecture of fear, of walls and division. Separate living is even blamed, with little or no evidence, for causing terrorism, a position promoted far beyond the Winds of Jihad blog in parliaments and the mainstream media where it is influencing contemporary city-shaping. Well beyond any battlefield, lies about cities and ghettoes are being promulgated and truths about segregation hidden in this latest round of culture wars whose aims include enforcing an anti-cosmopolitan world view.

CR

'If you believe you are a citizen of the World, you are a citizen of nowhere,' Cameron's successor Theresa May told the Tory conference in 2016, who, she added with a populist flourish aimed at uniting a deeply divided party, 'behave as though they have more in common with international elites than with the people down the road.' Yet again the the 'rootless cosmopolitan' is blamed. As Home Secretary, it had been May who instructed government vans to drive around immigrant areas with messages on their side threatening deportation for undocumented people as part of her Hostile Environment policy.

The word 'cosmopolitan' derives from the Greek word *kosmopolitēs* ('citizen of the world' as opposed to citizen of nowhere). Its broad meaning is that all people are, or can be, included within a community in ways that challenge commonly recognized attachments such as parochially shared cultures or nation-states. It is a concept that has been attacked by politicians of every stripe.

Despite British cities being *relatively* successful cosmopolitan environments by Western standards, David Cameron, in his first speech on terrorism as British prime minister, told the 2011 Munich Security Conference that multiculturalism was to blame for extremism. While he tried to distance himself from Islamophobes in his discussions on home-grown Islamist terrorism, for example, specifically repudiating 'the banning of new mosques, as is suggested in some parts of Europe,' he took aim at Britain's cosmopolitan record: 'Under the doctrine of state multiculturalism,' he claimed,

> we have encouraged different cultures to live separate lives, apart from each other and apart from the mainstream. We've failed to provide a vision of society to which they feel they want to belong. We've even tolerated these segregated communities behaving in ways that run completely counter to our values.[2]

At the same time, he dismissed causal explanations for the supposed phenomena – discrimination, poverty, alienation, and Western foreign policy – in favour of a free floating extremism stemming from 'a question of identity' caused by individuals stuck between traditional parents and modern Britain, radicalised in those same mosques, who are unable to 'identify with Britain 'We have allowed the weakening of our collective identity,' he said. In judging Muslim organisations, argued Cameron, we must ask: 'do they encourage integration or separation?'[3]

While not downplaying the serious systematic discrimination faced by urban minorities, the pluralism of many post-war Western Europe cities has been more notably a success rather than a failure, especially in Britain, and especially where it runs deeper than multiculturalism in its superficial 'steelbands, saris and samosas' mode. However imperfect, many inner cities are made up of successfully diverse neighbourhoods with happily co-habiting cultures. When conservatives fret about minority communities living separately, what they are usually objecting to at core is diversity itself or the presence of, to their mind, too many people of colour rather than to genuine segregation. At the same time, their idea of integration is one that precludes minorities being allowed to give their presence or culture visible expression in the streets and on the skylines of our cities, beyond tokenistic motifs such as the lanterns and entrance gates found in various Chinatowns. These traditionalists do not want our cities to be genuinely cosmopolitan or to visually reflect this reality.

Cécile Laborde, professor of political theory at University College London, argues the hypocritical thinking of the likes of Cameron with his 'Big Society' strategy of neighbourhood identity and self-help actually promoted division and separation while arguing against it:

> Citizens are no longer expected to mingle and mix and work together: rather, they should set up their own little private communities catering for their own, cultivating parochial identities and priorities, white middle class, or Muslim, or evangelical, or whatever.[4]

Capitalism is here reasserting one of its oldest, indeed one of its defining features – divide and rule. Separating people by falsely created or falsely fixed constructs such as race, sexuality, and gender (all the better to exploit by class) and the disparagement of other cultures is as old as colonialism and empire. This is given physical manifestation through segregation or sometimes its opposite, enforced integration, practices with roots in empire.

Minorities are put in a no-win situation. Never mind that modern 'ghettoes' are often the result of white flight created by those that move away from difference, or by restrictions on minorities' freedom of movement and their justified fear of discrimination and violence, or that, even so, research has shown that Muslims and other minorities, far from refusing to integrate, generally prefer mixed neighbourhoods.[5] For the white establishment, there can be too little segregation – the predominant attitude over time – or too much segregation. The Right is even willing to weaponise diversity in its scapegoating, using queer safety and women's rights as a stick to beat Muslims, shaking otherness in the face of the other.

Across Europe, political leaders have similarly disavowed their former multicultural strategies. Despite her later humanitarian policy of allowing in a million refugees fleeing war in the Middle East, former German chancellor Angela Merkel had previously argued that multiculturalism 'has failed and failed utterly.' In France, praying in the street was banned for Muslims in the name of French secularism even though it was a phenomenon that was the direct consequence of the ongoing hurdles to getting enough mosques built. The ban was among a slew of laws designed to repress the visibility of Islam and its symbols in the public realm; the relationship between Islam and *laïcité* (roughly, secularism) having become the main sphere of French cultural anxiety, especially since the war on terror.

Following the Black Lives Matter protests in the summer of 2020, this rejection of Islamic visibility was joined by a defence of the colonial in the French public realm: 'I tell you very clearly: the Republic will not erase any trace or any name from its history ... She will not unbolt statues,' decreed an inflexible President Macron in the face of demands to remove the statues of Jean-Baptiste Colbert (who had drawn up the code governing the treatment of slaves in the colonies) in front of the National Assembly and of Jules Ferry who had promoted the French colonial 'civilising mission.'[6]

Macron's colleagues borrowed phraseology from the Fascist Right and from Trump's warnings of 'Far Left Fascism' in a series of speeches condemning 'Islamo-gauchism' – an improbable threat from a non-existent alliance between Islamist fundamentalism and radical Leftist thinking that has supposedly infested French universities. Despite being risible conceptually and nastily redolent of Nazi conflations of Bolshevism and Judaism, Islamo-leftism became a subject debated seriously in the media for months on end as Macron and the Right tried to supress 'woke' academia and BLM activists who were challenging the status quo. Macron's interior minister described them as 'intellectual accomplices' to terrorist acts while the French Senate adopted a bill to restrict university research funding to projects that 'align with the values of the Republic.'

In Poland, meanwhile, where history wars have been in full cry for decades led by battles over the control of cultural institutions, the ruling Law and Justice Party has, in recent years, intensified its attacks on critics of the state and on offending symbols. A 2016 law, promulgated under the jurisdiction of the politicised Institute of Political Remembrance, ordered that all street names and similar honorific commemorations linked to the Soviet era were to be replaced wholesale. Memorials to figures on the Left were systematically removed such as the plaque marking the birthplace of Rosa Luxemburg in Zamośćs. It is also now illegal to discuss Polish complicity in the Holocaust which is described as the 'the pedagogy of shame'. Similar measures have been put in place in other former Eastern Bloc nations. This is not a liberal-minded rejection of Stalinist or Putinesque totalitarian thinking but the consequence of Hard Right nationalism that has no intention of tolerating the cosmopolitan or entertaining equality be it political, racial, sexuality, or gender-based.

Of course, the use of architecture and planning to segregate and reject the cosmopolitan is not confined to racial groups.

Separation has been entirely normalised to the point of rarely provoking comment in terms of gender. The split between the domestic space of the nuclear family and the workplace over the past two centuries has atomised the experience of many women and has been compounded by design practices such as suburbanisation and transport planning decisions that favour male patterns of movement and which exclude women from full rights to the city. There has been precious little change to these spatial structures for women anywhere in the world with the physical configuration of urban environments being thought of as a natural evolution of urban life rather than the consequence of politically and economically driven design decisions.

Similarly, queer lives and spatial freedoms have, as with gendered spaces, been controlled and patrolled for centuries despite the post-war emergence of, (in retrospect) relatively short-lived, gay neighbourhoods in some major cities. Culture war reaction to these new freedoms can be intense. In Poland, Catholicism and nationalism combined led to the declaration of 'LGBT-free' zones in more than 100 towns and cities – almost a third of municipalities across the country. President Andrzej Duda called the promotion of LGBTQ rights an ideology 'even more destructive' than Communism. The Archbishop of Krakow warned of a neo-Marxist 'rainbow plague.' Queer visibility in Poland has been hampered since the 1990s as the country's neoliberal reforms meant that informal spaces available for queer bars and clubs were sold off, but the municipal campaign began in 2018 after the right-wing *Gazeta Polska* newspaper started distributing 'LGBT-free zone' stickers. Queer activists have faced prosecution including those who had produced an 'Atlas of Hate' mapping the exclusion zones and erected unofficial 'LGBT-free zone' signs at municipal boundaries to make the symbolic discrimination visible. Queer activist Małgorzata Szutowicz was arrested for draping rainbow flags over statues in Warsaw. In 2021, libel laws were used to silence academics in cases successfully brought by the Polish League Against Defamation (a Law and Justice Party front) and, encouraged by the Catholic Church, blasphemy actions were begun against queer artists and activists.

These extremist segregationist stickering tactics are now being copied in the UK by anti-trans groups. In 2022, the *Daily Mail* published a pseudonymous piece by 'Grace York' celebrating a campaign of 'adult human female' (a trans-hostile euphemism reasserting biological sex) stickering purportedly designed to 'protect single-sex spaces' but with the stickers being used with intimidatory abandon at places as various as pub toilets, gym changing rooms, post boxes, petrol pumps, on trains, and on the back of cinema seats. Their exclusory messaging in the public realm is clear.[7]

Architecture and town planning's exclusory and segregation practices take physical as well as policy form through border walls, separate settlements, cordons sanitaires, and the use of infrastructure such as railways and highways to separate groups. All are tactics with origins in the imperial colonies of the Netherlands, Spain, Britain, and France. They were often intimately wrapped up in evolving colonial trade and labour practices and evolving property law and became entangled in emerging racial theories used to justify slavery. These practices were both imported back to the imperial homelands and exported to other settler-colonial societies around the world, not least in the development of South Africa's system of Apartheid and Jim Crow in the United States.

Apart from the trading cities of imperial China, perhaps the earliest spatial arrangements based on the novel concept of skin colour arose in seventeenth-century colonial Madras (today's Chennai). The city was divided by the East India Company with a fortress-like wall into what were initially called 'Christian Town' and 'Gentue [Hindu]Town' but which, from the 1660s, and certainly by the time of Thomas Pitt's map of the city dated around 1711, became 'White Town' and 'Black Town' – in other words, Europeans and non-Europeans. White Town literally became whiter as its buildings were stuccoed with a shiny crushed shell plaster called *chunam*. The segregatory colour coding was resented by the city's Indians who also resisted attempts to get them to pay for the dividing wall.[8] The change

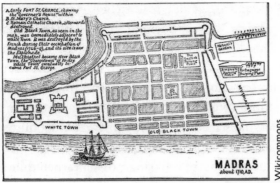

3.1 Colonial segregation practices spread around the world and were part of the emerging racialisation process used to justify the slave trade. Thomas Pitt's map of c.1711 shows the city of Madras divided by a wall into a White Town (at left) and Black Town. Local Hindus resisted attempts by the British to make them pay for the wall.

in place nomenclature from faith to racialised skin colour reflected the fact that religious categories no longer served commercial colonialists sufficiently when they were more interested in making money than the will of God. Because with the latter came the risk of unwelcome limitations on the enslavement of fellow Christians in the Americas. Likewise, notions about miasma and the proximity of diseased slums to the upper classes was a matter of fear to be legislated for, and this had spatial segregation consequences in colonial Calcutta as much as London. Class-based changes in property covenants were used in both mother countries and their overseas possessions to separate races well into the twentieth century.

This divisive pattern was put into effect in countless cantons across the subcontinent and in the building of the new Raj capital in New Delhi as well as cities across the colonial empires – from Hong Kong, Jakarta, San Francisco and Honolulu to Australia and South Africa, and back and forth between colonies and home to Europe itself where this thinking informed eugenics and, ultimately, Nazi Germany and Goebbels' ghetto 'death boxes.' In the twentieth century, the United States practiced all these mentioned methods while rolling out Jim Crow-like separation of the races not just in the South but nationwide. These colonial-era concepts continue to inform present urban policy.

Race, of course, cannot readily be separated from class and class-derived lack of opportunities to live where one chooses and class has been the ubiquitous organising principle throughout the towns and cities of recorded history. Indeed, permanent settlements (as opposed to hunter-gatherer societies) were predicated upon and enabled accumulation and the formation of hierarchies. This has, however, contributed to the present-day fiction that urban race-based separation is simply the inevitable outcome of varying purchasing power rather than deliberate discrimination that for working class minorities doubly compounds a lack of control over places of settlement.

Contrary to the accepted narrative, and with the obvious exception of the indigenous Native American population that had been systematically displaced, enslaved, or murdered as settler colonialism pushed west, nineteenth-century towns and cities in America were almost without exception highly mixed places. Here, racial separation was by no means the inevitable spatial expression of supposed defensive human territorialism and fear of the other. For many centuries, segregation was not even necessary to ensure the continuance of the US slavery economy. This despite the reluctant 'Great Emancipator' Abraham Lincoln's view, in a speech of September 1858, that there was a physical difference between the races that would forever forbid their 'living together on terms of social and political equality.'[9] The story of poor Black ghettoes, a defining and semi-carceral experience still today for around a third of urban African Americans, is one whose growth and shaping was not accidental but the consequence of a purposeful policy to limit freedoms. It is a history of racism certainly, but one entangled with class-based discrimination and factors such as industrialisation, de-industrialisation, and the growth of transport infrastructure and suburbs. In the South, for example, Jim Crow did not enforce physical residential separation entirely but instead regulated interaction between Black and whites including spatially even when they lived close by. It was purposeful measures and instruments that led to the formation of the North American urban ghetto.

After the Civil War and manumission, and until the end of the nineteenth century, the southern United States continued with its established pattern of close if unequal living following the characteristic settlement structure of most southern towns where whites lived on the avenues and Black labourers and servants in humbler side streets and alleyways off these same avenues.

The idea of the ethnic ghetto in the late nineteenth-century cities of the North was also a myth. Despite the many 'Little Italys', 'Greektowns', and the like, the vast numbers of European immigrants did not live in national groups but in multi-ethnic, pluralist neighbourhoods of immense diversity. African Americans likewise mixed and prospered and included a notable professional class. The difference between people of European origins and African Americans is that the former could, if finances allowed, move where they like and, over generations, integrate on their own terms with a wider cosmopolitan society. The Black experience became the opposite with neighbourhoods being increasingly separately defined and physically confined. 'As late as 1900,' write Massey and Denton in *American Apartheid: Segregation and the Making of the Underclass,*

> the typical black urbanite still lived in a neighbourhood that was predominantly white. The evolution of segregated, all-black neighbourhoods occurred later and was not the result of impersonal market forces. It did not reflect the desires of African Americans themselves.[10]

It was enforced, and often more intensely in northern cities than in those of the former Confederacy, especially after the First World War when the corralling of Black Americans into overcrowded slum neighbourhoods intensified. Legislation was one tool. Baltimore was the first city to officially attempt to enforce residential segregation block by block, and from the 1920s, restrictive covenants forbidding white homeowners from selling to racial groups proliferated across the US as part of a multi-pronged segregation strategy that later included an area-based racially profiled system of home loan lending and investment at the federal level and efforts by estate agents and developers to exclude non-whites from new housing.

Among these practices was red-lining on home-lending maps that supported white moves to the suburbs and denied funding, both home loans and infrastructure investment, to Black inner-city areas. So successful were these tactics that American cities of the period were more segregated, more forcibly isolated, than pre-Apartheid Johannesburg despite similar efforts there. Extreme violence including the fire-bombing of homes was the regular response for those who had the temerity to escape the ghetto and settle in whiter areas and, it has been argued, this was more important than legal measures in enforcing the ghetto. This was the period when, lamenting disunity within the mul-tiracial working class, W E B Du Bois developed his concept of the public and psychological wage of racialised white identity. Du Bois also wrote of the 'two worlds with and without the Veil,' a reference to the segregation barriers that physically pro-tected whites from seeing discrimination and Black struggle.[11]

At the same time, the myth of the self-chosen ethnic ghetto was being cemented by followers of the Chicago School of sociology, a way of thinking that had enormous influence on planners and city-makers in Europe as well as in the United States. In 1933 Ernest Burgess mapped Chicago's various German, Irish, Italian, Russian, and other immigrant ghettoes. The figures have since been shown to be bogus: 'Burgess's Irish ghetto contained only 3 percent of Chicago's Irish population, and only 50 percent of the city's Italian's lived in the "Little Italys" he identified.'[12] All these areas were diverse with dozens of different immigrant groups living side by side.

Architectural devices were also used to physically enforce US segregation. Many new residential areas built physical walls to keep African Americans out (or in, if around segregated public housing blocks) and these were implemented by both public and private agencies. In the Detroit of 1941, for example, a developer of an all-white suburb was given Federal Housing Administration mortgage guarantees only after agreeing to pay for a half-mile-long concrete wall to separate the planned suburb from the adjacent Black neighbourhood. Parts of the wall survive as evidence of the practice.[13] Less obviously racist barriers were also a tactic; for example, the Federal Housing Administration's manual recommended that highway construction could effectively separate the races to protect white property values. In the twentieth century, New York was reshaped by city official Robert Moses, who had 'low-hanging overpasses' built over the Long Island parkways leading to Jones Beach to prevent the 12-foot-high buses used mostly by the poor, and so disproportionately by Black and brown New Yorkers, from reaching the seaside.

US legal scholar Sarah Schindler has charted these architectural and town planning exclusion measures such as closing roads between Black and white areas, or refusing to provide public transport routes or even sidewalks in order to control the movement of those seen as undesirable. The difficulty of finding useable evidence of the discriminatory intent of such measures behind smokescreens of supposedly neutral rationales such as traffic reduction has, time and again, meant the courts have not upheld cases brought by those discriminated against even where the prejudicial thinking behind the moves has been obvious. 'Architectural regulation is powerful in part because it is unseen,' she writes:

> it allows governments to shape our actions without our perceiving that our experience has been deliberately shaped. This hidden power suggests that lawmakers and judges should be especially diligent in analysing the exclusionary impacts of architecture, but research demonstrates that they often give these impacts little to no consideration.[14]

Once in place, such physical measures can be very difficult to undo and the effects of such spatial exclusions are far some over. Segregative practices and divisions persist in all manner of ways. Take Minneapolis-St Paul, where covenants, freeway placements, and selective redevelopment were among the measures limiting Black settlement. The impacts can still be seen in all sorts of unexpected ways; tree cover, for example, closely maps on to places in Minneapolis that had racist residential covenants leaving African American areas suffering in shadeless streets of red-lined areas. Asthma rates and low birth weights correlate with the treeless areas of this racist base map. These are the streets on which George Floyd died.

If the twentieth-century United States is a history of enforced ghetto formation, that of post-war Europe is largely its opposite – one of ghetto myths. Compared to American cities, the operating methods of Europe's urban divisions have been generally more subtle than Jim Crow, with race-based segregation generally less stark or at least less obvious. In many European cities, wartime bombing and post-war redevelopment of blitzed and slum sites led to a complex mosaic of social and private housing where rich and poor, Black and white, might live close by even if their daily lives did not truly intersect.

It is true though that newcomers – Turkish *Gastarbeiter* in Germany or workers from the former colonies of the Maghreb coming into France and Spain, or from across the former empire into Britain – faced discrimination, and their choices in residence were restricted by more than affordability. France in particular pursued a policy of pushing non-whites to public housing on the margins. But nowhere in Europe has this amounted to the creation of mono-racial ghettoes in the American sense, still less no-go areas for indigenous whites. Not that you would know this from the media and politicians who have spent decades pursuing scare stories of dark and ungovernable enclaves threatening to overwhelm inner cities.

This has become ever more prevalent following 9/11, which generated its own architecture of fear characterised by increased surveillance, physical separation, and the control of public space. The war on terror has concentrated attention on the notion of a Muslim enemy within which is now Europe's primary focus of manufactured panic about place-based separation, of 'no-go area' myths underpinned by, and underpinning, a narrative about the failure of the cosmopolitan ideal of the post-war city.

What is especially disturbing is that such nonsense is now not the preserve only of a Fascist fringe; it has been mainstreamed and in some European countries is dictating government policies aimed at breaking up communities in the name of integration and national security.

These attitudes are summed up in the work of commentators such as the English journalist Douglas Murray. Murray, associate editor at *The Spectator* and the founder of the Centre for Social Cohesion, is part of a neo-conservative coterie of writers, think-tankers, and academics who bring with them not just a clash of civilisations ideology but a traditionalist, anti-cosmopolitan view of the built environment. Murray claims that it is not race but the creed of immigrants that concerns him; he argues that a faithless, exhausted, and 'degenerate' Europe is committing suicide, letting its liberal Christian culture be supplanted by fast-breeding, religiously confident, and illiberal Muslims. The thesis set out in books such as Murray's best-seller *The Strange Death of Europe* reads as a more polite version of great replacement theory.[15] Visual cultural differences are seen as affronts: The 'mass movement of peoples in Europe,' Murray writes, has led to 'streets in the cold and rainy northern towns of Europe filled with people dressed for the foothills of Pakistan or the sandstorms of Arabia.'[16]

His books have had a scandalously warm welcome in Britain. Government minister Michael Gove and journalists Melanie Phillips, Rod Liddle, Nick Cohen, among others, have lined up to praise his writing. In 2006, Murray, a self-declared 'atheist Christian', gave a speech to the Pim Fortuyn Memorial Conference, named for the Far Right Dutch politician, that characterised the threat from the 'thuggery' of Islam as a war where the West's defences have been undermined by cultural relativism : 'It is late in the day, but Europe still has time to turn around the demographic time-bomb which will soon see a number of our largest cities fall to Muslim majorities,' he declared. There are militants in our midst who will never like us, he argued: 'There is not an inch of ground to give on this one.'[17]

As in France, ghetto myths prevail in Britain, not just in the press but in the heart of government and even in its equality agency. In a 2005 speech, Trevor Phillips, formerly head of Equality and Human Rights Commission, warned in the aftermath of the 7/7 bombing on London that ghetto formation would lead to 'crime, no-go areas and chronic cultural conflict.' He claimed that the United Kingdom was sleepwalking toward US-style ghettos. Some districts, he said, are on the way to becoming 'literal black holes into which nobody goes without fear and trepidation and from which nobody ever escapes undamaged.'[18] Yet census figures and all other genuine evidence shows, indisputably, that, outside Northern Ireland, segregation in the UK has been declining, not increasing.

The lie that self-segregation in UK cities such as Bradford is a breeding terrorism has also been nailed in fact-based projects such as the comprehensive 2009 report 'Sleepwalking to Segregation?: Challenging Myths About Race and Migration.'[19] The report showed that in Bradford and other cities, mixed wards were increasing as white people moved back into ever more diverse areas. If separation was increasing anywhere, it was only in schools and this was the direct consequences of Conservative governments wresting control of schooling from elected local councils to the privatised academy system where increasing numbers of faith-based academies are in the actual business of segregation. Yet still these ideas have taken hold. A 2018 poll found that a third of Briton's believed such zones existed in the United Kingdom, including almost half of those who voted for Brexit.[20]

Never mind the facts, all the evidence to the contrary. In 2021, the British press renewed its scaremongering about 'no-go areas for white people' where Muslims live under 'Taliban rules'. In Bradford locals apparently fear it would become an 'apartheid city.' Laughably, another target in the *Daily Mail*'s coverage was Didsbury, one of Manchester's most hipsterfied neighbourhoods, where a church saved from demolition had become a mosque – back in 1967.[21] Weeks earlier the same newspaper had identified Didsbury as one of the nation's most desirable property hot spots.

Across mainland Europe too, the issue of a failure to integrate has become a notable component of contemporary culture wars amid urban myths about so-called Islamic no-go areas under sharia law. This is seen nowhere more intensely than in France where *laïcite* has become less about the freedom of religious practice (as it was originally conceived) and more about hostility to any religious expression in public space. In practice, this is selectively applied in petty and cruel ways to Muslim symbols such as headscarves and burkinis but not to Notre Dame or annual town hall Nativity displays. Douglas Murray complains of a visit to Paris that some metro lines are like 'taking an underground train in an African city' with the passengers on their way to low-paid service jobs 'or appear to be heading nowhere.'[22] Go to the Parisian suburb of Saint-Denis, and the square outside the basilica, he complains, 'is a souk more than a market.'

Paris still has some working-class districts clinging on in the eastern arrondissements, but the contrast with mosaic cities such as London is remarkable. Paris has seen its poor pushed steadily to it margins since at least Haussmann, a shift cemented in place by the construction of the encircling urban motorway, the Périphérique, begun in 1958 and completed in 1973, on the remaining land of the city's outer Thiers Wall. The Périphérique became a formidable fortification between the gentrifying historic city (which was never carpet bombed so rarely redeveloped for social housing) and the poor workforce beyond. The polluted road became the busiest in France, a rolling barrier of metal when not jammed to a standstill; eight lanes of tarmac (ten or twelve where there are slip roads), concrete, fences, and level changes supplemented in some areas by rail lines. Pedestrian routes across it are limited; there are not even pavements in some locations.

To dyed-in-the-wool Parisians, the land beyond is not even Paris but the *banlieue*s, literally the suburbs, but a loaded term. As France was relinquishing its North African colonies in the early 1960s – bloodily so in Algeria – immigrant workers were drafted to France for construction and menial jobs. Some 100,000 were compulsorily housed first in marginal slum hostels (*bidonvilles*) close to construction sites then, from the 1970s onwards, in the *banlieues* beyond the Périphérique where vast public housing estates known as HLMS or *cités* were set up. A phrase 'the threshold of tolerance' was coined in 1964 in connection with the Paris suburb of Nanterre that without any empirical evidence whatsoever, set a figure above which the proportion of incoming foreigners was deemed to cause tensions and conflict.

While some of the architecture is of high quality, much of it was cheap, poorly designed, and set out as enclaves that only emphasised their separation from the normal life of the capital. As the immigrant population increased, the white population declined relatively. Intense discrimination and police repression, soaring unemployment, and a lack of transport to access jobs elsewhere, together created an environment of dissent and frustration resulting in periodic rioting. Job applications from addresses here are more likely to be rejected and youth joblessness is sky high.

Forcibly confined to the margins, the inhabitants of *banlieues* with large minority populations were then told that they were failing to integrate. Immigrants kids were simultaneously too visible if in the middle of city, hanging out at Les Halles or around the Gare du Nord, and too dangerously invisible and probably up to no good at the city edge. Efforts directed at breaking up so-called French 'ghettoes' date back at least to 1991 when the weekly *Nouvel Observateur* argued for an 'Anti-Ghetto Act' that might act as a 'Marshal plan for the banlieues' and stave off the blossoming of 'Bronxes' in France. Even so, these areas remain poor but heterogeneous. They show features of segregation but are not ghettoes in the US sense.

The international perception of ghettoes and Islamic no-go areas in European cities can be traced to 2002 when US reporter David Ignatius wrote that Paris's 'North African' suburbs were no-go zones at night. The term was popularised in 2006 by Daniel Pipes, the historian and writer who established Middle East Forum and Campus Watch – an organisation that tracks students and academics critical of Israel or supportive of

Arab-world liberation struggles. Both Pipes and Murray have been billed as speakers at events by the Federalist Society, the influential right-wing organisation whose members have included six of the nine current US Supreme Court judges. Pipes himself credits the 'no-go' term to Norwegian blogger Fjordman, a pseudonym of Peder Are Nøstvold Jensen, whose posts were mentioned 111 times in the manifesto of white supremacist terrorist Andres Breivik.

Pipes reserved special credulity for his lurid accounts of French areas designated as *zones urbaines sensibles* (sensitive urban zones; SUZ), urban regeneration areas of the *banlieues* and elsewhere. To Pipes, however, this was all a euphemism and the SUZ's existence was evidence 'that the French state no longer has full control over its territory,' the homes of some 5 million people.[23] After visiting Europe in 2013, Pipes was forced to modify his views when they collided with reality: 'For a visiting American, these areas are very mild, even dull,' he confessed. 'We who know the Bronx and Detroit expect urban hell in Europe too, but there things look fine. The immigrant areas are hardly beautiful, but buildings are intact, greenery abounds, and order prevails.' Pipes, however, returned to using the term once more before settling on 'partial no-go zones.'

The idea of European no-go zones refused to die, however, and was revived, notably by Fox News, after the Charlie Hebdo attack, again using the existence of French SUZs. Paris threatened to sue. A claim made on Fox News that British cities such as Birmingham 'are totally Muslim where non-Muslims just simply don't go in' led Prime Minster David Cameron to complain and an apology was issued. This has not stopped Fox, other media outlets, and US politicians from continuing to spread the lie.

The claims continue and not only in America. In 2018, German chancellor Angela Merkel repeated statements by the chief of the German police union that there were no-go areas in their country that the state must 'do something about.' Her government declined to name any particular area she had in mind.[24]

In parallel, the narrative emerged that young Muslims out of sight in these areas were becoming radicalised, prey to terrorism's recruiters by dint of their lack of physical integration into the mainstream, and almost directly as a consequence of the alienating effects of Modernist housing estates. While often the site of riots and other disturbances, the impression being given was that the disaffected of Paris's high-rise estates – the notorious *cités* – such as those of Trappes or Aubervillier were now as likely to turn to terrorism as overturn a police car. Instead of estate rioting, we are told suicide belts were now being smuggled across the divide from this desolate other-land to the old 10th and 11th arrondissements.

Likewise, the former suburb of Molenbeek in Brussels, once the 'Little Manchester' of the Belgian capital which had suffered a dreary post-war rebuild across swathes of the commune, was dubbed 'Jihadi Central.' However, in 2015, the television news footage of the police hunting terror suspects in the Parisian suburb of Saint-Denis and in Belgian Molenbeek did not show police banging down the doors of miserable slab blocks but searching for weapons and suspects in the roof gutters and cellars of standard terraced houses in older parts of these districts. Molenbeek is little more than a mile from the tourists guzzling beer in Brussels' Grand Place, not a distant edge district beyond a wide beltway.

Miserable living conditions in these post-industrial areas where tens of thousands of jobs have been lost must inspire radicalism or hopelessness of various stripes. And it is certainly at least possible that creating a feeling of otherness might make it easier to dehumanise and attack a perceived enemy; it being easier to take an AK-47 to strangers than a neighbour. But architecture as terrorism's determinist cause is as mythical as the no-go areas themselves. A failure to address racism and race-based segregation is not being tackled at root but is instead being used to justify a surveillance state and dispersal policies.

Architecture is not destiny. We need to look well beyond the physicality of the city to find explanations for a state of mind that can shoot at café frequenters and concert-goers. Equality and justice are more powerful than elegant Hausmann boulevards in preventing violence. Some enforced divisions and alienation remain all too real though, as one angry young *ban-lieue* resident told *The New Yorker* in 2015 when asked whether the suburbs of Paris were incubators of terrorism. More to the point, he said: 'I've never seen the Mona Lisa. I want to see it before I die.'[25]

Under President Macron, however, anxieties about Muslims living separate lives have only intensified. In October 2020, Macron announced a new law against religious 'separatism' and 'foreign influences' that, he stated, had caused a crisis in French Islam. 'We have created our own separatism in some of our areas,' claimed the president (some reports of the speech included use of the term 'ghettoization').[26] 'We have concentrated populations of the same origins, the same religion.' The good cop/bad cop solution proposed included investing a few million in education about Islamic culture and civilisation and in housing for the poor, but the government also proposed placing mosques under greater state control. Organisations would have to sign up to a 'secular charter' and any found promoting ideas contrary to republican values would be dissolved. Extra funding, said the president ominously, would 'assure a republican presence in every road, every building.'[27]

All this is based on the lie, as in the United States, that urban segregation is self-chosen. Ghetto and no-go rhetoric only inflames discriminatory attitudes that intensify separation. By rejecting the cosmopolitan, and the terms on which minorities are allowed to express themselves (including, as we will see, in architectural terms), the Right is demanding total assimilation and the erasure of difference. Their thinking has no logic. It forgets that the most segregated areas in all Western countries tend to be white majority areas.

Academic Loïc Wacquant is among those who have set out in great detail the myths about self-segregation. He describes them as a moral panic and warns of the fundamental differences between the externally enforced ghettoes of the United States and the simply cosmopolitan, racially mixed, working-class but industrially gutted areas of countries such as France. Wacquant says bluntly that the use of the stigmatising word 'ghetto' in the French context is 'scientifically fraudulent and politically irresponsible.'[28] Following serious riots in the 1980s, writes Wacquant, countless mayors

> have rushed to invoke the spectre of the *"quartiers-ghettos,"* either with the aim of justifying ex-post a policy of urban redevelopment undertaken for completely unrelated reasons, or, on the contrary, to dress up falsely generous intentions in their refusal to see public housing built in their boroughs, or, finally, to clamour for the creation of a municipal police force in order to reinforce the surveillance of the populations confined to their problem *cités*.[29]

Today, the transformational measures to improve the suburbs include ambitious public transport connections between core and periphery and to turn parts of the Périphérique itself into parkland which can only be welcomed whatever the reasoning. It is also expected by some that the Olympic Games to be held in Paris in 2024 will be the saviour of the *banlieues*. Some of its infrastructure is focused on areas such as Saint-Denis. Locals remain rightly sceptical.

In some European countries there have been attempts to enforce desegregation of supposedly self-chosen ghettos in the name of integration and plurality, but which are actually attempts to supress difference. In Denmark, this rhetoric is being put into rancid practice. Under a government pressured by Far Right politicians, the country has been shaping ghetto laws whose explicit aim is to break up residential clusters of ethnic minorities on the spurious grounds that these groups are refusing to integrate. Regeneration efforts now aim to disperse ethnic communities. While the term 'ghetto' has now been dropped from the legislation, its intent remains the same – to stop too many non-western people of colour living near to each other.

The law is aimed at any neighbourhood of more than 1,000 people where more than half are 'non-Western', alongside other criteria such as levels of unemployment, income, education, and crime. Some 6 percent of Denmark's population is defined as non-Western. At the time of writing, fifteen neighbourhoods have been identified. Penalties for certain offenses in these areas will be doubled and child daycare by others made compulsory, with family allowance payments withdrawn from those who do not comply. The discrimination, against poor people of colour especially, is obvious.

Some politicians want to go further with evening curfews and tags for children. The Danish People's Party has already helped push through laws banning full face veils, and its politicians are open about wanting ethnic minorities to abandon their cultural identity. Cosmopolitan identities are seen as incompatible with the nationalist idea of the homogenous *Folkhemmet* – the 'people's home'. Astonishingly, the result of the law will be to reduce the availability of public housing by 40 percent in these already poor areas. Some 1.3 million square meters of Denmark's public housing will be demolished by 2030. Danish architecture firms are already drawing up proposals to make it so, including in the so-called ghetto neighbourhood of Røsenhoj. The ethics of this are appalling and not mitigated by proudly stated aims of upcycling prefabricated building elements into new projects where minority numbers will be limited. This is more than enforced integration but forced assimilation driven by the politics of fear and in part facilitated using the mechanism of architecture and urban design.

Importantly, it is not just *where* people live which has been weaponised in the culture wars but *how* they visibly express themselves in the city. There is a sense that it is not just Muslims and othered minorities but their symbols – from dress codes to the minarets and domes of a traditional mosque – that are alien intruders, invading the cities of the West. 'Where a mosque has become a centre of hate it should be closed and pulled down,' Charles Murray told his appreciative audience at the Pim Fortuyn Memorial Conference. 'If that means that some Muslims don't have a mosque to go to, then they'll just have to realise that they aren't owed one.'[30] Murray bemoans the decline of Western

Christian culture and the shallowness of contemporary architecture that he sets against praise for the great historic cathedrals of Europe. Murray also echoes Franco in singling out the El Escorial palace outside Madrid for particular praise. 'If it is true that the best test of a civilisation are the buildings it leaves behind,' he says, 'our descendants will take a very dim view of us.'[31]

Mosques are not only attacked regularly and face calls for their demolition if their imams step out of line, they face a tough time getting built in the first place. This is not only the result of contemporary racism but racism in architectural history including an ignorance of the cosmopolitan origins of Western architecture, not least the great cathedrals that Murray so admires. It ignores that Islam and its architecture have been a part of Europe for over a thousand years. Yet 'minaretphobia' remains a phenomenon.

In Switzerland, where Muslims make up some 5 percent of the population and Islam is a relatively new religion, the immigrant Muslim community is not untypical of much of today's Europe in having limited resources. As in the rest of Europe, newcomers' first places of worship are often former shops or redundant churches rather than purpose-built mosques. As the Muslim population in Switzerland has increased since the 1980s and the desire to create more appropriate faith buildings has grown more insistent, resistance to the architectural expression of Islam emerged. Campaigns organised in the early 2000s by the Far Right Swiss People's Party (SVP) against the construction of minarets led to a 2009 national referendum in which a ban on minaret construction was supported by 57.5 percent of participants. This at a time when only four minarets existed in the entire country. Echoing the Australian Winds of Jihad blog, the SVP argued that minarets were not so much religious architectural features as politico-religious claims to power. SVP campaign posters depicted minarets as missiles, linking Islam to terrorism. Only four out of twenty-six cantons opposed the proposed constitutional ban.

Debates on how to enforce such a law included discussions of what constitutes a minaret and what is a minaret-like tower. The

3.2 The Hard-right Swiss People's Party forced a referendum banning minarets in Switzerland. The poster, equating minarets with terrorist missiles, was used by Far-Right groups across Europe and elsewhere campaigning against mosque proposals.

same year, Frauenfeld council declined to consider a ventilation shaft to which a metal cone and crescent moon had been added to be a minaret because the structure was still, officially, a vent shaft. In another town, local Muslims were only allowed a vestigial one-metre-high minaret stuck to the front of the former supermarket being repurposed as a mosque.

In response to the Swiss initiative, Roberto Calderoli of Italy's racist Lega Nord said, 'Switzerland is sending us a clear signal: yes to bell towers, no to minarets.'[32] Other politicians followed. In neighbouring Austria where neo-Fascist politicians later formed part of a ruling national coalition, the state of Carinthia drafted a law banning 'unusual buildings.' The Freedom Party's Heinz-Christian Strache, who has campaigned to legalize Nazi symbols, was as strident about his opposition to minarets as he was about kerbside falafel stands replacing bratwurst stalls on the streets of the capital, arguing that 'Vienna must not become Istanbul.' It is almost a folkloric fear of an Ottoman enemy at the gates, an evocation of Suleiman the Magnificent's 1529 Siege of Vienna. In Italy, Calderoli cited the same battle as well as the Ottoman naval defeat at Lepanto.

This is more than simple aesthetic difference or a clinging to tradition. Along with burqa bans and measures such as the refusal to allow the call to prayer being broadcast from minarets (church bells are fine, of course), it amounts to a refusal to countenance minority visibility in public space. It is a desire to exclude the other in pursuit of ethnic and cultural purity. Opposition to particularly large 'mega-mosques' with congregations of thousands, such as those proposed in Seville and Cologne can prove especially vicious. In Cologne, protests drew in neo-Nazis from Germany and neighbouring countries. The city's archbishop, Cardinal Joachim Meisner, admitted that the mosque proposal for a former factory site not far from the cathedral gave him an 'uneasy feeling' about the 'different panorama' that would result from the proposed 55-metre-high minarets rising near the cathedral's 157-metre-high Gothic spires, the defining image of the city. Even ostensible liberals such as the German journalist Ralph Giordano, whose family survived the Holocaust, waded in against the mosque, arguing that it amounted to the creeping Islamisation of our land' and a 'declaration of war.'[33] His comments were credited in some quarters with normalising an anti-cosmopolitan Islamophobia in Germany as a threat to liberal democracy.

When the United Nations Human Rights Council narrowly condemned such Islamophobic mosque opposition, the US ambassador to the UN objected to the resolution. Right-wing politicians across Europe, meanwhile, expressed support for the Swiss ban, and the Danish People's Party proposed a similar referendum in Denmark where no minarets existed. French prime minster Nicolas Sarkozy argued, improbably, that the Swiss ban had nothing to do with religious freedom, echoing Marine Le Pen who stated that 'elites should stop denying the aspirations and fears of the European people, who, without opposing religious freedom, reject ostentatious signs that political-religious Muslim groups want to impose.'[34] Le Pen's posters also began to feature minarets refashioned as missiles. In 2010, she made an infamous speech complaining about Muslims praying in the streets in the absence of an available mosque: 'It is an occupation of territory ... Okay, there are no tanks or soldiers, but it is still an occupation.'[35] Emphasising cultural difference rather than biological racialisation was a deliberate tactic. The National Rally's 2017 manifesto called for the closure of extremist mosques and the promotion of European historical and cultural heritage.[36] The European Union became less of a target for the National

3.3 Identity Evropa poster. The US white supremacist group is one of a number of Far-Right and Neo-Nazi organisations that have used classical imagery in propaganda that claims Western civilisation is in danger from Islam.

Rally and instead was seen as a potential bastion of European Christian culture against Islam and the liberal cosmopolitanism of the elite.

Endless similar stories could be told from across the continent as well as in the United States, Australia, and elsewhere. Polish nationalists and their architectural champions today find it hard to conceive of their country as once astonishingly diverse, home to millions of ethnic Germans and Jews, and where co-existence extended to Roma, Eastern Orthodoxy, and a small Muslim Tartar community so venerable it meant that Poland had twenty-eight mosques and prayer houses by the end of the eighteenth century. (England didn't get its first purpose-built mosque until 1889.) Minaretphobia is a relatively new phenom-enon in Poland where previously mosques had been accepted as part of the patchwork of some cities' diversity. As recently as the 1980s, a church and local non-Muslims alike all helped with the building of a neighbourhood Tartar mosque in Gdan'sk.

Prejudicial post-Communist and post–9/11 nationalism of the sort peddled by Poland's Law and Justice Party make that hard to imagine today. Warsaw only achieved its first purpose-built

modern mosque in 2015 after a hostile campaign was over-
come. Here too, anti-mosque demonstrators adopted graphics
of minarets converted into terrorist missiles and argued that
mosques were contrary to European values. An unprecedented
series of attacks on established mosques spread across Poland
including, in 2014, graffiti of a pig on the walls of Kruszyniany's
seventeenth-century wooden mosque and on graves in the
adjacent Muslim cemetery.[37] A pig's head was thrown into the
recently completed Warsaw mosque.

One could equally be talking about Hungary where Victor
Orbán had claimed Hungary 'has never been multicultural'
and argued that homogeneity is a Hungarian virtue despite the
country's founder King Istávan praising the multilingual diversity within its borders a thousand years ago.[38]

The idea of minarets and mosque domes as alien architectural features of contemporary Western townscapes is, in any
case, historically illiterate. The gothic architecture of Cologne
cathedral and the Gothic more generally has, despite being a
Germanic term, an origin myth located in France and specifically Abbé Suger's twelfth-century reconstruction of Saint-Denis,
then outside Paris at the time of the Crusades. Here, Suger used
devices such as the pointed arch and Europe's first rose window.
In reality, however, the Gothic's origins are far more promiscuous and ecclesiastical features such as rose windows, pointed
arches, vaulting, and twin bell towers derive at least in part from
Middle Eastern antecedents either directly from Islamic traditions or indirectly from the Romanesque and Byzantine. The
fifth-century church of Qalb Lozeh in Syria near Aleppo with its
pair of towers flanking a rose window is one important anteced-
ent, and its westward influence may indeed have been courtesy
of returning crusaders.

Suger's pointed arches were seen first at Cairo, Amalfi, and
Monte Cassino, then at the Benedictine abbey at Cluny, which
is where Suger saw them. The secular Gothic found in Venetian
palazzos has similar influences. Sir Christopher Wren turned his
nose up at this 'Saracen style' when it came to reconstructing

old St Paul's after the Great Fire of London despite using a dome which itself has partially eastern origins – an early example of the style wars between the Gothic and Classical over which better represented English identity. It is a trajectory that has long been accepted by serious scholars and is not new knowledge.

This stylistic debt to the East was set out at length in Diana Darke's provocatively titled *Stealing from the Saracens: How Islamic Architecture Shaped Europe* that sought to dispel Euro-centric origin myths.[39] A 2020 discussion of her book in *The Guardian* was given the foolish headline 'Looted landmarks: How Notre-Dame, Big Ben and St Mark's Were Stolen from the East.'[40] The stand-first went further, suggesting these 'beacons of western civilisation' were 'plundered' as if they were cultural appropriation or architectural black face. This is not Darke's argument, despite her title. She is alive to the long history of architectural syncretism and the free flow of ideas and culture including the influence of Greco-Roman styles on Islamic and Arab Christian architecture. A similar story might be told of the onion domes of central and Eastern Europe which, despite being utilised by Russian nationalists, also have a promiscuous history. As far west as Munich, the twin towers of the Frauen-kirche have sixteenth-century domed cupolas that owe much to this cultural complexity. In the popular telling, they were inspired by the Dome of the Rock in Jerusalem on the misun-derstanding that this Islamic building was the Jewish Temple of Solomon. All this forgets in any case that Islam has been part of Europe for centuries – from Spain to the Balkans and indeed, European Istanbul itself. One path to the cosmopolitan was the centuries of Islamic rule in al-Andalus and its spectacular archi-tectural efflorescence and where, briefly, Muslim Cordoba was the biggest city on the continent. These origins have tied Spanish Islamophobes in knots ever since, from Franco to opponents of a contemporary mega mosque in Seville despite a minaret turned bell-tower – La Giralda – being the historical symbol of city that has inspired countless imitators across Europe and the United States.

Contemporary opposition to mosque proposals is not confined, however, to decrying traditional mosque forms as alien. The Cologne Central Mosque is a Postmodern confection that only nods to the dome and minaret model, while a proposal for a 'mega mosque' in East London in the early 2000s by Mangera Yvars Architects was seen off even though it adopted the swooping and angular language of architectural Deconstruction not massively dissimilar to Zaha Hadid's 2012 Olympics pool about to be built nearby. Yet still more than a quarter of a million people signed a petition against the mosque and in defence of a 'Christian England.'[41] There were traffic generation issues, but it was the scale and conspicuousness of the Mangera Yvars scheme, the presence of a Muslim 'other' made visible with the cityscape, that offended conservatives. In any case, it is unlikely to make little difference to racists if mosques are indistinguishable from churches as European Jewry found under the Third Reich. Stylistic conformity of synagogues did not prevent their symbolic presence offending the Nazis; hundreds were systematically destroyed on Kristallnacht on 9 November 1938 including Semper's Gottfried Dresden synagogue with its Romanesque exterior that deliberately expressed an architectural attachment to Germany. The Nazis had no truck with either architectural assimilation or difference.

The long and rich history of architecture's cosmopolitan evolution has been forgotten or set aside as concepts such as Europe, then Christendom, and 'the West' took root in opposition to difference and alongside the taxonomies and racialisation justifying slavery and colonialism. Irene Cheng, writing about structural racialism in architectural theory, notes its parallels with late eighteenth- and nineteenth-century racial science thinking that aligned types of design with types of people and nations and arranging them in a hierarchy that informed ideas about what it meant to be modern and even about Modernism itself.[42]

Cheng points to the extravagantly named Frenchman Antoine-Chrysostome Quatremère de Quincy, who in 1788 identified three origins for architecture: the hunter's cave (giving rise to Egyptian monolithic structures), the pastoralist tent ancestor to

Chinese timber architecture, and the settled farmer's hut which, he argued, was the basis of Greek architecture and therefore the more progressive model. A fourth type was added to the race-based classification by Edward Freeman in 1849 – the Gothic cathedral inspired by the forests of the North, whose savage grandeur led to hardy virtues. Eugène Viollet-le-Duc elaborated these racial ideas, twinning racialised physiognomy, the shape of the eyes, the slope of a forehead, and on and on, illustrated with helpful drawings, with supposed personality types – Blacks being an abject race, Semites contemplative, and so on. (The drawings of racial types could be seen as pre-figuring Leon Krier's sketched critique of Modernist design mixing described in the previous chapter.) The people of Arya with their wooden framed constructions were clearly the bravest and born to command. In Britain, architects such as George Gilbert Scott argued that the Gothic was of Germanic origin and, for England, the 'native architecture of our own race and country'. This was obviously all catnip to later Aryan supremacists. In Austria, early Modernists such as Adolf Loos borrowed from Owen Jones 1856 Grammar of Ornament when he argued that decoration was fit only for primitives, criminals, and homosexuals.

In the colonies this sort of design thinking could be used to further segregation. Hong Kong had its infamous Hill Reservation Ordinance of 1904 that reserved higher ground such as Victoria Peak for whites on the spurious grounds that Europeans were more susceptible to diseases of the climate than locals. Regulations also stipulated that houses in white areas had to be in 'conformity with the character ... of the other houses in their neighbourhood,' which had the desired effect of excluding the Chinese and Chinese architecture.[43] These suspicious stylistic arguments about character resemble contemporary minaretphobia.

The opposite approach could also be used to shape colonial territorial claims: In the imperial garden city of New Delhi, the colonial style was the Indo-Saracenic and was used to create an illusion of continuity with a princely Indian past and thus justify British rule. While architect Edwin Lutyens consciously wished to connect with India's own magnificent architectural heritage, he wasn't above bulldozing genuine historic monuments to create his new imperially appropriate ersatz versions.

Delhi is now on UNESCO's official 'tentative' list of potential World Heritage Sites. Its proposed inscription describes the relevant four precincts of the cities – Old and New – that are nominated without mentioning New Delhi's original controlling purpose. Instead, a concealing neutral language is deployed describing the building of the new city as 'addressing contemporary imperatives' and 'capturing the spirit of syncretism evident in Delhi for many centuries' – effectively confirming the original colonial justification of continuity. With such UNESCO designations, racist city-making becomes instead a narrative of beautification and architectural innovation.

Going the other way, oriental traditions were employed in the colonialist mother countries for novel and frivolous effect through design crazes such as Chinoiserie. These can be the consequence of a sincere admiration of a different way of doing things, but admiration can still mean limited acceptance of daily realities, especially the presence in Western cities of the peoples who produced such beauty. Contemporary Munich, for instance, has resisted new mosques including one proposed opposite the Catholic church of Sankt Korbinian in the working-class Untersendling district. It was blocked at every turn by the combined forces of hostile locals, the courts, and the state. Changes to the traditional appearance of the area were cited as justification. Yet the city already has the fantastical minaret-like Art Nouveau chimney of the Muffatwerk power plant that has soared above the city's river for more than a century and is a much loved landmark. This is decades older than Sankt Korbinian, which was reconstructed in 1951 in a heavy-handed neo-Baroque after bombing. Similarly, Dresden has its 1909 'Tobacco Mosque' (in reality the 1909 Yenidze cigarette factory) on the edge of the historic centre and built as an elaborate orientalist fantasy complete with dome and minaret chimneys. It was not though the fantastical Tobacco Mosque that was bombed by neo-Nazis in 2016 but the humble Fatih

Cammii mosque housed in a blandly modern two-storey structure in the Dresden suburbs, barely distinguishable from its
neighbours. No dome. No minaret.

What does it say when a western city will embrace only an
architectural fantasy of difference but attack the daily reality of
diversity? In such a context, where architectural influences are
not an exchange freely and fairly given but conducted within the
context of dominance and violence, perhaps cultural appropriation is a fair critique.

Over the border in Strasbourg in the summer of 2021, the
project for France's biggest mosque stalled once more. There
were claims it would rival the city's medieval cathedral despite
being located on a peripheral industrial estate. It became mired in
fears of an Islamic 'enemy within' funded from overseas, in this
case Turkish money. Macron said he will outlaw foreign funding
for French mosques. Denied a financial deal with Morocco, the
Muslims of Angers in western France will, meanwhile, carry on
worshipping in a redundant slaughterhouse as their forty-year
campaign for a purpose-built mosque plods on.

Despite all the calls for greater integration by minorities, it
is enforced invisibility by dominant groups hostile to the genuinely cosmopolitan that remains the persistent pattern, whether
through spatial segregation as in the United States, or the tactic
of forced dispersal as in Denmark, or through opposition to
symbolic buildings. When your architecture isn't to be tolerated
on the skyline, it is you and your community that is the deeper
target of distrust. Invisibility becomes an unknowability, an othering, expanding the space for myths and fake news to persist.
If divide-and-rule succeeds and plurality fails, pushing the poor
and disadvantaged to the margins, it will be at the hands of
the anti-cosmopolitans and their lies, not complacent pluralists.
Difference does not imply separation – it is simply difference.
And it is not difference but othering that brings ignorance and
violence, it is poverty and humiliation that brings division.

In *For the Muslims*, a book about contemporary Islamophobia in France and whose title deliberately references an 1896

article by Zola, '*Pour Les Juifs*' written amidst the Dreyfus Affair, Edwy Plenel writes:

> Fear itself becomes the argument of state power, setting society against itself in a fantasy of homogeneity and dragging it into an endless quest for scapegoats in which the Other, the different, the dissimilar, the dissonant, assumes the face of the foreigner, a foreignness both intimate and threatening. The adversary is then easily depicted as the internal enemy ... that must at all costs be supressed or excluded, even annihilated by preventative counter-violence.[44]

4

Authenticity: The Material Truth

Do not let us deceive ourselves in this important matter; it is impossible, as impossible as to raise the dead, to restore anything that has ever been great or beautiful in architecture.

John Ruskin, *The Seven Lamps of Architecture* (1849)[1]

In April 2016, Boris Johnson, then still London mayor, unveiled a curious object in the middle of Trafalgar Square. Standing there like a six-metre-high slab of stale butter was a 'replica' of the third-century Arch of Septimius Severus at Palmyra, a monument blown up by Da'esh when it overran the World Heritage Site the previous May. The triumphal arch was commissioned by the recently formed Institute for Digital Archaeology (IDA), an organisation allied to Oxford and Harvard universities and backed by Gulf money. Institute founder Roger Michel had been on the BBC promoting the stunt: 'I think that this may be the most exact reproduction of any kind of classical structure ever made.'[2]

Michel is a boosterish figure, a former criminal trial lawyer who is partial to the grand statement. He told the world that the repro arch was the product of the institute's technical ingenuity using its Million Image Database from which a precise 3D digital

Alamy

4.1 Boris Johnson as Mayor London unveiling a digital version of the triumphal arch at Palmyra blown up by Da'esh. The Institute of Digital Archaeology proposed placing the reduced scale and poorly detailed copy at the World Heritage Site in Syria.

model had been created. Except what the tourists milling in the square saw was not an exact reproduction but a vague approximation, laser-cut with a robot arm in a Tuscan quarry from a blandly uniform, bright yellow Egyptian stone that was nothing like Palmyra's pinkish-gold masonry. The million images used to ensure accuracy were actually more like hundreds, or, at most, a few thousand, of amateur shots. And it showed. The 'carved' details were all curiously flattened, the acanthus leaves of its Corinthian capitals rendered as blank stubs. All this was not assembled in a traditional manner by masons but was made of moulded sections threaded together on steel rods like an archaeological kebab so that it could head off to other venues on the next leg of an IDA promotional world tour.

Inexplicably, the whole arch was only two-thirds the scale of the original, meaning that, set against the grandeur of Trafalgar Square's classical institutions, its dignity was overwhelmed and the seriousness of its loss diminished. Intended as a symbolic statement of resistance to iconoclasm, of the will to rebuild the collective heritage of humanity, the installation was instead an alternative arch for a time of alternative facts.

Rebuilding monuments is not easy, especially after violent destruction. It raises profound questions not just about authenticity and copies but of the use we make of architectural history. Rebuilding – whether by perpetrators or their victims – can serve to mask the genuine, if unpalatable, past: erasing the gaps, the voids, the ruination that bears witness to traumatic events. It can conceal the reality of the present. It matters that our history is real. Even if well-intentioned, erecting an undersized Italian-cut, Egyptian stone arch in the middle of Syria is about as far from authentic as you can get. The repro arch would not be 'heading home' to Syria as the IDA claimed; it was never there.

When the Bamiyan Buddhas were dynamited by the Taliban in 2001, UNESCO was clear that rebuilding the statues from their pulverised rubble was not an option, that reconstruction would be unacceptable fakery even if it used tiny fragments of the original material bonded back together. Better, like Dresden's Frauenkirche when it was still a ruin, that the Buddhas' empty niches stand as a memorial to the horrors of conflict. Yet UNESCO has since funded the rebuilding of a facsimile shrine in Timbuktu destroyed by Islamists, rebuilt Mostar's shattered bridge, and proposed a similar reconstruction at Palmyra. Something is changing. And radically.

The architectural and monumental can offer powerful evidence of wrongdoing in history, whether the unreliable narratives of lying statues or the consequences of the manipulation of the built environment for oppression, ethnic cleansing, and genocide – but, crucially, only if it is genuine. Otherwise, reconstruction can be another way of erasing history. While it is questionable that the idea of a 'post-truth' world is anything new, the changing architectural attitude to the authenticity, the differentiation between the genuine and the artificial, is certainly taking place within a context where science, expertise, and objectivity are also being challenged. Verifiable facts about the past are being elided with the interpretation of those facts. This amounts to the draining away of internationally agreed foundational concepts such as authenticity – a literal historical materialism – in the face of an increasing falsification of the historic architectural record which brings with it profound dangers. It contributes to the sense of an unreliable world where we do not know whether something is true or false, whether a building is genuinely historic and therefore valuable evidence of the past or merely a clever copy. This is a gift to the totalitarian who benefits from exploiting any uncertainty over the observable facts of the world.

Authenticity has a history that long precedes its recent misuse as a marketing or pop-psychology concept. As far back as 1849 John Ruskin railed against the heavy-handed Victorian restoration of monuments to a speculative notion of their original appearance rather than the conservation of what genuinely remained of them. He described this in the *Lamp of Memory*, one of *The Seven Lamps of Architecture*, as

> ...the most total destruction which a building can suffer; a destruction out of which no remnants can be gathered: a destruction accompanied with false description of the thing destroyed. False, also, in the manner of parody, - the most loathsome manner of falsehood. Do not let us deceive ourselves in this important matter; it is impossible, as impossible as to raise the dead, to restore anything that has ever been great or beautiful in architecture.[3]

Among others, Ruskin had in mind Eugène Viollet-le Duc, the French architect who turned the castle at Carcassonne into a proto-Disney fantasy. Viollet-le Duc, who also added the tall, fanciful flèche to the roof of Notre Dame de Paris which collapsed in the fire of 2019, had erased the evidence of the French Revolution's iconoclastic secularism by reinstating the cathedral's smashed statuary. William Morris, socialist and designer, was equally horrified by the Viollet-le Duc approach and by the scraping away of additions to English cathedrals and churches to supposedly reveal purer, early forms. He founded the Society for the Protection of Ancient Buildings (SPAB) in 1877 to put a halt to the practice. The Society's Manifesto speaks of the 'feeble and lifeless forgery' of restoring buildings to an imagined original appearance. Such thinking evolved alongside the first stirrings of Modernism. It was later captured in the seminal 1931 Athens Charter on architectural conservation.

As Chandler and Pace note in their insightful academic volume, *The Production of Heritage*, Morris challenged the monumentalisation of historic buildings and championed instead, including in the SPAB Manifesto, the idea that history existed 'in the gaps', in the layers of alterations that showed human action through time.[4] (In some ways, this is analogous to Hannah Arendt's understanding of the importance of the relationship of humanity to the physical public realm.) Authenticity then, isn't just the original iteration but the meaningful historical layers.

For much of the post-war period, UNESCO, the global arbiter of good conservation practice, had its decisions guided by the 1964 Venice Charter for the Conservation and Restoration of Monuments and Sites which was the successor to the Athens document. The Venice Charter was drawn up by an interdisciplinary team of conservationists that established the International Council on Monuments and Sites (ICOMOS), the advisory body to UNESCO on heritage matters.[5] It opens by stating: 'Imbued with a message from the past, the historic monuments of generations of people remain to the present day as living witnesses of their age-old traditions.'[6] Material fabric as evidence was thus the central concept. In the spirit of the earlier Athens document, the landmark Venice Charter states that only the 'reassembling of existing but dismembered parts' (anastylosis) is allowable on sites, with inauthentic reconstruction or recreation tantamount to fakery. The messages from history that the genuine physical fabric conveyed were not to be made illegible or untrustworthy.

Though not an initial criterion, authenticity later became a defining issue when considering the designation of would-be World Heritage Sites (WHS). Yet quietly, steadily, this conservation consensus about the centrality of authenticity is being eroded. And if truth is the first casualty of war, authenticity has become a casualty of reconstruction in its peacetime aftermath.

The Old Town of Warsaw is the poster child of post-war reconstruction. The Polish capital was levelled in stages by the Nazis during the Second World War – initially as a consequence of the 1939 invasion, then under a systematic dismantling of its chief monuments and statues which was a constituent part of the genocide against Polish Slavs. Himmler identified Warsaw as the 'brain' of Poland and set about decapitating it physically at the same time as eliminating its intelligentsia. This process accelerated with the destruction of the Jewish Ghetto, then under the street-by-street leveling of the city in response to the Warsaw Uprising. By the time of Warsaw's liberation, only 34 buildings of its 957 major monuments remained. The Old Town, the New Town (dating back to the fifteenth century), and countless cubic feet of buildings had been reduced to rubble. Even sewers, trees, and tram tracks were dug up.[7]

Extraordinarily, in April 1945, amid hunger and homelessness and before the final German surrender to the Allies, the Varsovians set about rebuilding their capital as an act of resistance to the Nazis' intended erasure of Slavic culture. This was not simply about recreating war losses out of nostalgia, it was about undoing an attempted genocide where cultural genocide was intrinsic to the Nazi plan to eradicate a group's identity alongside murdering a nation bodily. Frederic Jameson may have decried the rebuilding of Warsaw as a 'Disney-related' operation, but these were very specific circumstances, quite unlike the current historicist reconstruction of German cities such as Dresden. Warsaw's rebuilding began with houses in the main square of the Old Town and spread from there over many decades, watched by an admiring world; palaces, churches (even under atheistic Stalinist direction), townhouses, museums, monuments, and statuary. The Old Town was largely complete by

1961, but its culmination, the reconstruction of the interior of the rebuilt Royal Castle had to wait until 1988.

And yet the myths around Warsaw's heroic reconstruction are many. One popular myth, that still found its way into a 2015 BBC documentary, is that the city's reconstruction was made possible only by reference to the precise topographical paintings of Bernardo Bellotto (c.1721–1780), a nephew and student of Canaletto. Bellotto arrived in Warsaw as court painter after previously depicting Dresden for the Saxon king. He stayed in Poland for sixteen years and painted twenty-six Warsaw views. These once hung in the castle's Panorama Room. The story told is that these paintings were used as a record of what had been destroyed and to guide reconstruction of the capital in every detail. Bellotto's paintings are likely to have played some limited role, but this narrative sidelines the risks taken by many architects and art historians who, under the noses of the Nazis, secretly recorded the occupied city, hiding drawings, photographs, and other material including thousands of building elements – doors, fireplaces, paneling – in stashes at the Technical University, the Piotrków Monastery, and other locations. It was these pre-war records, gathered in circumstances of tremendous personal danger, that were essential to the reconstruction programme.[8]

The Bellotto story is a relatively harmless romance, but other aspects of the reconstruction are more problematic. From the outset, Warsaw's reconstruction was essentially a political as much as an architectural project and it began in the Socialist Realism period under Stalin which looked to particular architectural traditions rather than modernity. Hence some of the rebuild was not a return to the pre-war position but, especially beyond the core of the Old Town and the Royal Route toward the castle, involved widened avenues and imposing a ponderous Stalinist Classicism rather than a truly academic rebuild of what once existed. Reconstructing the Old Town helped the Soviet-controlled regime gain legitimacy, with some completions timed to coincide with political anniversaries and parades. The regime's propaganda was that the post-war capital was even more beautiful than before the war.

Neither is the Old Town the exact facsimile suggested by the Bellotto narrative and presented to today's visitors. It is far from being a literal recreation of what the Nazis levelled. What was rebuilt depended on Stalinist perceptions of what was progressive or nineteenth-century architecture. The political aim was to provide continuity and thus legitimacy between the new Communist rulers and a specifically independent Polish past. Progressive, in this mangling of architectural history, included Renaissance or Neoclassical structures from Poland's independent period pre-1830. In this telling, the Art Nouveau and Catholic Baroque represented reactionary periods where the country was dominated by foreign powers. An edict was issued forbidding the reconstruction of any edifice built after 1850.[9] Later modifications to earlier buildings were also excised from the reconstructed interpretation of the city. Minister Wladyslaw Wolski explained in 1950: 'When choosing the historic period for reconstruction of a given monument, we should choose the best period for us from a cultural and social point of view ... we have to act boldly and avoid certain unpleasant periods.'[10]

Warsaw's Old Town as we see it today is then a fantasy – inspired by Bellotto, certainly, but nevertheless a fantasy – of the seventeenth- and eighteenth-century city. The main street of Nowy Świat, for example, was rebuilt ignoring the later nineteenth-century buildings that existed pre-war and with its building heights regularised. As Jasper Goldman notes of the fakery:

> Even the details of the individual buildings were altered ... religious elements were removed in favour of supposedly neutral decorations. On one building ... surviving statues on its façade of the Agnus Dei and St Mary were destroyed and replaced with a wild boar and the goddess Diana.[11]

Perhaps understandably, the interiors of many buildings were not recreated but designed for modern usage behind historicist facades. Other buildings were not recreated in order to reduce densities. In the process, genuine survivals such as medieval vaults and foundations under the newly built 'replicas' as well as valuable features such as wall paintings were unnecessarily erased and the genuine substituted with the fake. When the castle was finally reconstructed from 1971 after hesitation about a royalist symbol reappearing on the city's skyline, it included two towers that hadn't survived the seventeenth century. Beyond the historic core, other nineteenth-century buildings that had survived the Nazi onslaught but were deemed too capitalist were demolished – especially tenement houses where the rich lived on the main floors and the servants in the basement.

The substitution of fakes for genuine fabric was justified, in public at least, on aesthetic rather than political grounds. Hostility to nineteenth-century housing at the time was far from confined to Eastern Europe, but these houses were typical of the area used for the Jewish Ghetto and the decision not to reconstruct them may partly have been due to the pernicious political narrative across the Eastern Bloc that subsumed the specific persecution of the Jews in favour of a generalised 'victims of Fascism' position. This was promoted in war memorials and other commemorative monuments. The theme park approach thus concealed the genuine class divisions and ethnic diversity of the pre-war city in the name of state capitalism and Polish unity. 'The communist rhetoric,' notes Goldman, 'was notably more critical of the capitalists who created the pre-war form of Warsaw than it was of the Nazis who destroyed it.'[12]

Warsaw's reconstruction might be seen, despite its flaws, as an understandable and benign architectural resistance to Nazi cultural genocide. However, it also has to be seen in this wider context. The resurrection of Warsaw took place at a time when millions of ethnic Germans who had lived in East Prussia and elsewhere for centuries were ethnically cleansed and many German civilians were murdered. There was a vengeful quality to the Polish reclamation of places that had a historic German character. Given the oppression of Poles and the dismemberment of Poland over hundreds of years, this is hardly surprising but that does not make it right. The subsequent destruction and remaking of Germanic cities across Poland could not be justified as resisting cultural genocide. Poland instead went on the offensive.

The de-Germanisation of cities extended from population expulsions to architecture; stones from war-ravaged Breslau (renamed Wroclaw in Polish) were transported to Warsaw to be used in the rebuilding of the Old Town, and the German appearance of many Breslau monuments were altered to emphasise their Polish character – in a place that had not been ruled by a Pole since 1335. Polish refugees from Lwów were moved to Breslau, changing the population balance. A similar process was seen elsewhere, including, to at least some degree, the rebuilt historic core of Gdansk.[13] Poznań too was a majority German-speaking town after its founding in the thirteenth century, yet it was also seen as a hearthstone of the Polish nation that had suffered under enforced Germanisation in the nineteenth century. The Germans were expelled from Poznań by the Poles after the First World War, but the city was brutally Germanised again under the Nazis. After fierce fighting ruined much of the city, it was rebuilt after the Second World War once more in a determinedly Polish manner, with widespread use of architectural fakery.

Architectural nationalism is nothing new and takes different forms in different eras. In Central and Eastern Europe at the end of the nineteenth century, cities and nations from the Baltic to the Adriatic that were seeking self-determination often evoked these aspirations using variations on national romantic Jungendstil and folkloric architectural motifs. A literal nation-building occurred. Although Modernism could be employed, especially between the wars, to express economic and technical vitality, a constant appeal was to ancient independent cultural pasts to justify separate political futures.

The new nationalist buildings of post–First World War Eastern Europe were often monumental in scale and almost always used historic styles or archaic references. In Romania, for example, this took the form of Classical buildings that harked back to the region's ancient incarnation as the Roman province of Dacia.

In the Baltic States and elsewhere, new historicist churches, parliament chambers, and institutes were swiftly erected and entire town centres were remodelled. Nationalist architectural curating also involved the removal of 'alien' objects, just as the Russian Orthodox Alexander Nevsky Cathedral was erased from the Polish capital. Warsaw's tallest building when completed in 1912, the cathedral was seen as symbol of imperial Russia's occupation and demolished from 1924 along with almost all the city's other Orthodox churches. A proposal to turn it into a museum of Polish martyrology (a very telling use) did not save it.

After the Second World War and again today, this narrow, nationalist tendency has been resurgent. The end of the Soviet Union may have ended one tyranny but, in many countries, what has replaced it are ideologies hostile to difference and which prioritise simple, mythic pasts over messily complex presents. This time around the nationalists are not content with raising new monuments in supposedly local styles but, as in Germany, are busily disinterring edifices from the past, building fakes in denial of the intervening reality. What began as an exercise to rescue Warsaw from Nazi oblivion reappears now as chauvinistic, nationalist re-imaginings.

The promotion of Poznań's Polish architectural character, for instance, has returned with a vigour that is celebrated wildly in online traditional architecture forums. Terraces of faux Baroque townhouses have been created where once stood nineteenth and early twentieth-century commercial buildings. Today, it is Communist-era Modernism rather than Nazism that is being blamed for decades of uglification and disregard for Polish heritage. This resurrection cult has replaced statues of Marx and Lenin with appeals to faith, the traditional family, and the motherland.

In Poznań and elsewhere, castles and palaces – sites of state strength – have been one notable focus. At the royal castle of Esztergom in Hungary, the remains of a medieval structure have had a Postmodern makeover that includes building a substantial gateway that never previously existed. The same is now happening at Budapest's castle despite it being a World Heritage Site. The ducal palace in Vilnius, meanwhile, was almost entirely flattened in 1801 when Lithuania was absorbed into the Imperial Russia and only reappeared on the map a few years ago on the orders of the country's Communist-turned-social-democrat president in an assertion of national identity. The rebuilding was based on sparse documentation and without even a ruin to adapt.

These reconstructions, often created on the basis of as poor documentation as at the Vilnius ducal palace, are not rescue projects conducted in the wake of, and in the name of resistance to, wartime cultural repression, or even (solely) as an immediate response to the ending of Soviet Union's suppression of national identities in the Eastern Bloc, but are often schemes urged on by nationalist populists or by the Hard and Far Right. Authentic histories of cosmopolitan co-existence are vanishing under these architectural fantasies and authentic built fabric sometimes ruined in the process. In Eastern Europe especially, heritage projects have become another arm of the history wars, sitting alongside media censorship, the control of historical museums, politicisation of the judiciary, and attacks on human rights. Such intense focus on national identity is the perfect breeding ground for inauthenticity – for inventing traditions and imagining new communities that carefully patrol who belongs and who is othered and not welcome. In hindsight, the reconstruction of Warsaw's Old Town helped open the floodgates for less justifiable nationalist architectural fantasy projects.

There nineteenth-century architectural fakes and copies, especially following disasters such as fires and earthquakes and, compared to the manipulations above, these may, relatively speaking, be ideologically neutral even if sometimes ill-advised in terms of an authentic historical record. In his 2020 book, John Darlington of the World Monuments Fund takes us on a canter through some of these copies. He includes the reconstruction of the Venice's landmark campanile in St Mark's Square after it collapsed in 1902 during repairs (building works can be a particularly hazardous time for fragile historic structures) and the dozens of faux Eiffel Towers around the world which no one would mistake for the real thing.[14]

Similarly, re-instating a lost sash windows on an individual Georgian house will make the proportion system of its façade readable once more and is unlikely to have wider implications. But the wholesale reconstruction of a building or an historic city quarter is an entirely different matter. Even if the intention is not to deceive, deceive some of these reconstructions do, especially over decades when societies forget the reconstruction episode altogether. Crucially though, it is the *intent* behind the reconstruction that matters, which may range from straightforward aesthetic and academic reinstatement, the lure of the tourist dollar, or outright manipulation for political ends.

Attitudes to correct repair and renewal vary over time, from culture to culture, and between countries. Until recently, Britain, for example, maintained a relatively firm line on authenticity, derived from Ruskin and Morris and confirmed by Athens and Venice. Very few buildings destroyed in the Blitz were reconstructed from scratch. Projects such as the Modernist Coventry Cathedral standing amid the ruins of its medieval predecessor instead demonstrate the opposite, layered exemplar. In contrast to this standard British, and to varying degrees, the Western European approach, wooden Shinto shrines in Japan are regularly taken down and reassembled. At the Ise Jingu complex, the rebuild cycle is just twenty years. These ritual renewal ceremonies date back more than 1,000 years and are, with legitimacy, regarded as part of these sites' authenticity rather its opposite – the ritual is integral to the site's history and its protocols are consistent and understood. Today, however, even in Britain the emphasis on authenticity is now being eroded.

The nineteenth-century remodelling of St Albans Cathedral to create an imagined version of its earlier incarnation, destroying much original fabric in the process, was an architectural scandal that directly led William Morris and Philip Webb to found Society for the Protection of Ancient Buildings (SPAB) and kickstart modern conservation practice.

However, despite the justified outrage, and the construction of a faux medieval shrine for St Alban within one of England's earliest Christian sites, when it came to the cathedral's second shrine – to Saint Amphibalus – the restoration's architect Sir George Gilbert Scott simply re-assembled what remained of its stone fragments gathered in from around the cathedral. He used bricks to infill the missing sections. Old work and new work were clearly differentiated. In this way, and in a manner that anticipated later conservation charters, the tragic results of Henry VIII's iconoclasm directed at religious art and the worship of shrines that accompanied the Dissolution of the Monasteries could clearly be read many centuries later. Gilbert Scott's assemblage was not a thing of beauty, but it was intriguing and sent us messages about history. It nicely illustrated Morris's words that 'whatever history it destroyed, left history in the gap.' What was missing can be as informative as what remains.

4.2 Munich's Alte Pinakotheken was reconstructed after the war by architect Hans Döllgast. It carefully collaged the authentic ruin with clearly identifiable new work in brick reclaimed from city bomb-sites. Traditionalists have attempted to have the collage replaced with copies of the original facades.

Except all this history has now vanished under a cathedral project to reconstruct the shrine of Amphibalus once more. Completed in 2021, skilful stone masons have created an approximation of the medieval shrine, substituting new stone carvings for Scott's bricks and smoothing over the gaps between old and new stone. It now takes a practiced eye to tell the difference. The aesthetic consequences of both the birth of the Church of England and of nineteenth-century artistic battles have been erased. Information panels nearby tell visitors, falsely, that the shrine was 'not a museum piece or historical item' and confuse terms that should be used precisely such as 'restoration,' 're-creation,' and 'reconstruction.'[15]

The signs that authenticity is being undermined have been appearing elsewhere in the UK. In 2020, for example, the Scottish National Party began exploring the rebuilding of some Scottish castles, in ruins for centuries, to form parador-like luxury hotels in a toxic combination of financial exploitation and nationalism. This might have been acceptable in 1919 when, famously, Castle Eilean Donan was reimagined but it would have been an unthinkable suggestion in the post-war period until just a few years ago.

In contrast to European conservation standards, the United States of the last century, the country of Walt Disney, has played astonishingly fast and loose with many of its heritage sites even where (or perhaps especially where) they are most politically charged. The White House itself is, essentially, a fake. In June 1948, the alarm was raised when a piano leg came crashing through the ceiling of a dining room below. The 1817 building constructed after the British burned down its predecessor was falling apart after a combination of decades of neglect and ill-advised structural changes. President Truman decided a three-year rebuild was necessary.

The entire mansion was gutted to insert a new steel and concrete structure leaving only the external walls standing. A new basement and sub-basement with air-raid shelter were also added. Apart from some salvaged panelling, the interior became an entirely new re-imagination of the early 1800s incarnation of the house. The whole process began on the quiet because Truman was in the middle of an election campaign and was not keen on a collapsing White House as metaphor. In the decades following, windows were replaced for additional security and further changes made and extensions added. There is barely a square inch of historic White House fabric left.

This cavalier approach to history at the presidential mansion was nothing in comparison to the forgery surrounding Lincoln's Cabin, a simple wooden structure built at Sinking Spring Farm, Kentucky, in which Abraham Lincoln was supposedly born in 1809. The original cabin is thought to have vanished by the time of Lincoln's death, but this did not stop Alfred Ennett, an entrepreneur who bought the Lincoln farm in 1895, from passing off another cabin as Lincoln's birthplace. This was then taken on a national tour where it was exhibited alongside another cabin purporting to be the birthplace of Jefferson Davis. On the way to one showground the 'Lincoln' and 'Jefferson' logs got mixed up and the resulting melange billed as the 'Lincoln and Jefferson Cabin.'

The cabins were then taken by train back to Kentucky. En route, crowds gathered to touch the logs as if they were religious relics. The Lincoln cabin – reduced in size again after some of the extra logs it acquired were removed – was re-erected within a memorial hall built in the form of a Greek temple. Designed by John Russell Pope, the temple had fifty-six steps to symbolise each year of Lincoln's life. When it was discovered that the cabin was too large to comfortably fit in his new temple, Pope simply cut a few feet off the cabin's length and width: 'Now just twelve by seventeen feet, it fits fine,' writes James W Loewen in *Lies Across America*. 'It also fits fine with the nation's ideological needs. Americans want to believe in the "log cabin myth" and the tinier the cabin, the bigger the myth ... of the "rags to riches" story.'[16]

Lincoln's own son protested that the cabin falsely painted a picture of poverty whereas the Lincolns actually owned two farms and other nearby property. As Loewen points out, the

National Park Service that manages the site acts as if this fake, created for entirely commercial reasons (rather than any Shinto-style timber renewal ritual), is a precious artefact. Like the Turin Shroud, the Lincoln cabin remains sacred despite all the evidence to the contrary. Flash photography is banned. According to Loewen, the National Park Service now calls the exhibited cabin the 'Traditional Lincoln Birthplace Cabin,' which, he suggests, gives 'traditional' an additional definition as a 'hoax over time.' Without evidence, the National Park Service suggested that the cabin structure may incorporate some original logs. Rather than admitting that the whole place is a fiction, it talks of 'a lack of documentation' for the cabin's authentication. Today, the site's website describes the structure as the 'Symbolic Cabin' but the damage has been done.

Unfortunately, the National Parks Service and St Albans Cathedral are far from alone in being heritage guardians with a sometimes less than scientific approach to the evidence of history. More and more, the gatekeepers of heritage and conservation, who one might expect to put authenticity, facts, material certainty, and historical accuracy front and centre in their work, are increasingly side-stepping such concepts. This includes UNESCO, the global custodian and arbiter of good practice. There are many reasons for this, not least UNESCO's desire to be more inclusive of 'intangible' (non-material) aspects of threatened cultures such as music, language, and food traditions rather than focusing solely on grand monuments or magnificent designed landscapes.

In some ways this attitude derives from postmodern critiques about an unwarranted Western focus on objects and objectivity rather than how the meaning of things and places is transmitted and received. Academics at Stirling University, for example, have claimed that authenticity is not intrinsic to an object 'but rather is about how we experience "truthfulness" and the auratic qualities of our subject, based on material qualities, a sense of "pastness," and the networks of social relations it is embedded in over time.'[17] This comes close to arguing that the real and true is only what we *feel* it to be rather than what can be evidenced. However, the main push has two main drivers – the technological tools available for reconstruction and the disasters of war.

Taking technology first, an important difference between historic reconstruction and today's is that twenty-first-century tools such as laser scanning and three-dimensional printing appear to make faithful reconstruction unproblematic. This is an illusion. Richard Hughes, a conservation expert at Arup who was involved in the restoration of Aleppo's citadel prior to the outbreak of the Syrian war, has described the Institute for Digital Archaeology's Palmyra 'replica' as 'absolutely appalling in terms of authenticity.'[18] Hughes is enthused by the ability of the digital to capture large amounts of data that can tell us how a building collapsed in an earthquake, for example, and how it can be put back together. The difficulty of handling the sheer scale of data needed for accuracy remains an issue (especially in poor and war-torn regions). 'But,' he adds, 'Whether it is assisting in authenticity is debatable. There's a big difference between the mathematical and the real.'

For now at least, and perhaps perpetually, there is still something missing in machine-produced outputs:

> The craftsman as an artist can differentiate his work from a comrade of a thousand years ago – see how they dealt with weaknesses in a stone block [for instance]. There is a language there that isn't in the technological language. I want the [touch], the smell, the biological infections on the surface of the stone.[19]

He says that this is what 'gives charm, mood, spirit of place' – a response to the genuineness of the material rather than the attitudes we bring to it. Asked to think of a successful reconstruction at the scale of an entire monument using digital techniques, he can't: 'It's getting there for smaller objects in museums...but I haven't come across anything in real, whole buildings.'

Notwithstanding this, an effusive article in *The Guardian* ahead of the erection of the Institute for Digital Archaeology

Palmyra arch on Trafalgar Square reported as fact Roger Michel's claim that his printers could reproduce not just the texture and surface contour of stone but its physical makeup.

> They can extrude layers of the same sand, water and sodium bicarbonate that formed the artificial stone often used by the ancients. They can reconstitute the original dust of a ruin in situ. It is no different in concept from the French archaeologists who, in the last century, re-erected Palmyra's colonnade.[20]

Leaving aside the fact that reassembling genuine toppled stones is an entirely different thing from extruding a fake, the quality of the IDA's resulting arch showed the claims to be absurdly untrue. Even if accurate copies of buildings or monuments will soon be possible, they do not include original, authentic material. Yet this was a claim repeated in the same paper in 2021.

There are now myriad digital projects internationally to scan threatened monuments with the idea of enabling the reconstruction of those lost to disasters. Many of these ventures are overlapping and uncoordinated, wasting limited heritage resources. Some are sympathetic and useful; others appear more about building institutional reputations. These complicated issues were the subject of an installation at the 2016 Venice Architecture Biennale by the Victoria and Albert Museum called *A World of Fragile Parts*. It was an intelligent show but one that still appeared in thrall to the power of the digital to heal.

In 1867, the V&A's first director, Henry Cole, formulated the International Convention of Promoting Universally Reproductions of Works of Art for several nations to swap fine copies of important works. Copies, such as those that populate the V&A's fabulous Cast Court, were seen as spreading knowledge. By 2017, the V&A was suggesting that Cole's convention should be rewritten, in part because of these technological advances. The V&A, together with twenty other leading international museums and UNESCO, subsequently came together to launch the Reproduction of Art and Cultural Heritage (ReACH) initiative to look further at these questions. The Reach Declaration was signed in December that year as guidance for museums working with reproductions. The Declaration states that 'digital technologies can enable us to record, document and, in some instances, *recreate* works that are threatened by environmental hazards, rapid economic development, mass-tourism, thefts and other natural and human-made disasters ... or that have been lost.'

Lost? Just how lost? Can we expect a reconstruction of the Hanging Gardens of Babylon? The Summer Palace of Beijing razed by the British in the Second Opium War? Old Coventry Cathedral? The Garrison Church at Potsdam? Just because we can rebuild, superficially at least, accurately, does that mean we should? The ethical dimensions and consequences for a trusted material historic record from digital copies were noticeably left unaddressed in the Declaration. UNESCO's position on digital copies is also yet to be resolved; the organisation recently lent its logo to an exhibition in Rome of 3D-printed copies of sculptures smashed by Da'esh and supported a similar exhibition in Paris that promoted digital reconstructions.

In 1945, UNESCO was forged out of the huge cultural damage caused by the Second World War. Its founding purpose, as set out in the preamble to the organisation's constitution, states that 'wars begin in the minds of men, it is in the minds of men that the defences of peace must be constructed.' It is a belief that peace would be secured not on the basis of politics or economics but on the basis of humanity's moral and intellectual solidarity. Clearly, UNESCO and its sister body the United Nations have failed in this purpose, not least because without honestly addressing politics and economics, failure is inevitable. However, the nationalist politics of the organisation's members has repeatedly fettered its ability to do good. Worse, its response to attacks on culture in conflicts is now also having a deleterious effect on authenticity and historical truth in peacetime. At the same time, conflict-related heritage preservation efforts have themselves become militarised as we will see in the following chapter.

In 2016, I interviewed Francesco Bandarin, then UNESCO's assistant director-general for culture. Bandarin questioned the agreed international stance on issues of authenticity and particularly reconstruction after war damage: 'The Charter of Venice was written by art historians, not architects,' he argued. 'It was very strict, European stuff, a twentieth-century Italian idea. This is why it never works for architecture so we have to reinterpret it.'[21]

Bandarin's arguments here do not accord with the facts. The Venice Charter's founding committee, far from being all art historians, included many with architectural training, including its chair Piero Gazzola, as well as many leading archaeologists directly concerned with historic sites. Venice was also substantially informed by principles set out in the 1933 Charter of Athens led by Le Corbusier and fellow architects at the IV International Congress of Modern Architecture. For example, the 1933 document's *Legacy of History* section states, 'The re-use of past styles of building for new structures in historic areas under the pretext of aesthetics has disastrous consequences. The continuance or the introduction of such habits in any form should not be tolerated.' Both these charters are then architecturally informed and remain far from being arcane documents of relevance only to conservators removing layers of paint and varnish in museum workshops.

In reality, these standards have been used successfully by conservation architects around the world for generations. Among the working practices derived from the Venice Charter is the sensible measure that all new work to old buildings should, where possible, be identifiable and reversible. In 1982, UNESCO's heritage advisory body ICOMOS issued its Declaration of Dresden on the 'Reconstruction of Monuments Destroyed by War.' Item 4 noted:

> Since men have been influenced by the wartime destruction and by reconstruction work after the war to regard monuments with increasing interest, in particular as providing evidence of history, fresh emphasis has been placed on the demand to preserve the original substance of the monument.

The position was that complete reconstruction of severely damaged monuments should be an 'exceptional circumstance.'[22] Given Dresden's subsequent trajectory, the Declaration is unfortunately named.

'Deliberate destruction has created a new context,' countered Bandarin. 'At the time Bamiyan was an exceptional case.' He's referring to the March 2001 destruction of the sixth-century Buddhas of Bamiyan, two colossal statues carved into niches in an Afghan cliffside. UNESCO and governments across the Islamic world had protested the Taliban's announced plans to destroy the Buddhas. Various alternatives were offered including a Japanese offer to relocate them to Japan. But the Taliban's Mullah Omar was unmoved. He gave various unconvincing reasons for dynamiting them, saying, for instance, that he had been shocked by visiting western archaeologists offering to finance minor repairs at a time when the Afghans were suffering hunger and destitution. ('Had they come for humanitarian work, I would have never ordered the Buddha's destruction.'[23]) Omar later argued that the Taliban were smashing idols in accordance with their fundamentalist take on Islamic law. In fact, their destruction should be seen within the context of the Taliban's ethnic cleansing of a local Shia people and their cultural symbols, which included the Buddhas.[24]

Whatever the reason, their loss shocked the world. But once it was clear that they had been pulverised beyond reassembly, UNESCO was clear – however sorrowful their loss, there was no possibility of their authentic reconstruction. Subsequent attempts to reconstruct parts of the monument have provoked sometimes ugly disputes among heritage professionals, including between branches of ICOMOS.

Bamiyan was, unfortunately, far from an exceptional example of monuments deliberately targeted in conflicts. The war in the former Yugoslavia over the previous decade had been catastrophic for culture, highlighting the issue of attacks on monuments in a way not seen since the Second World War. The region's Ottoman heritage was a particular casualty. Almost every minaret (more than a thousand) and most mosques were damaged or destroyed while museums, libraries, archives, and traditional Ottoman houses were targeted for shelling or arson by Serb and Croat armies and paramilitaries. This wasn't the consequences of being on the front line but part of a deliberate pattern of cultural cleansing happening alongside a violent ethnic cleansing of towns and villages with heritage destruction weaponised alongside mass murder and mass rape.

The aim was an historical erasure to remove any proof that a community had lived in a particular territory for centuries, especially in co-existence with other cultural groups, by removing the evidence of their historic presence and ensuring that the expelled had no reason to return.[25] All twelve mosques in Foča – some very old and very beautiful – were destroyed as the town's Muslims were violently driven out and Foča renamed Srbinje – bluntly, Serbtown.

In 1994, in the wake of the offensive against Bosnian monuments such as Mostar Bridge and the Serb shelling of Dubrovnik, a panel of international heritage experts met in Nara, Japan, to hammer out the Nara Document on Authenticity, an important revision to the Venice Charter's precepts. The Nara Document has consequently been seen as a direct response to the Yugoslav conflict, rising out of concern about destruction and the entirely inauthentic and prejudicial reconstruction projects that were using the cover of war to build new and inauthentic nationalist monuments on historic sites but whose real aim was to cement ethnic cleansing.

However, the issues had deeper origins. While the concept of authenticity is long-standing, the word itself hadn't been used, at least initially, in key international texts such as the 1972 World Heritage Convention that, among other measures, established the WHS programme. So decades before Nara, arguments had raged as to whether rebuilt central Warsaw or the French citadel of Carcassonne that had been gussied up by Viollet-le-Duc were sufficiently authentic to qualify as World Heritage Sites. The arguments intensified from the late 1970s, as member states began to understand the national prestige and lucrative tourism potential that a WHS listing could bring. In particular, Japan wanted to add its temple sites to the WHS list and was worried that Western concepts of authenticity – seen as cultural imperialism in some quarters – might prove a block to inclusion because of the Shinto reconstruction practices.

Nara may have been a long time emerging, but the devastation of Bosnia was the urgent context and mood music for its agreement. As its preamble notes:

> In a world that is increasingly subject to the forces of globalization and homogenization, and in a world in which the search for cultural identity is sometimes pursued through aggressive nationalism and the suppression of the cultures of minorities, the essential contribution made by the consideration of authenticity in conservation practice is to clarify and illuminate the collective memory of humanity.[26]

At first glance, this is excellent stuff, and in part it is. But the Nara Document's expanding list of attributes determining authenticity, went beyond materiality to include intangible and nebulous ones like 'tradition,' and 'feeling.' The centrality of facts, evidence, and authentic fabric was being diluted. So in a world where scientific truths are resisted, Nara, while apparently reaffirming Venice Charter principles, has also been the springboard for worrying departures from good practice that had previously safeguarded the genuineness of material artefacts as evidence of the past by introducing loose and unscientific ideas such as 'spirit'. The Nara Document ultimately argues that a principal requirement of authenticity is that information about that place 'may be *understood* [my emphasis] as credible or truthful.'[27] 'Understood' as true is a dangerously loose concept of truth.

New practices influenced by UNESCO's own realpolitik and mythmaking are now being promulgated under Nara's broader definition of the authentic. It has helped justify decisions such as declaring Old Mostar Bridge, which had been entirely rebuilt in 2004 along with the surrounding Ottoman buildings, to be a freshly minted World Heritage Site. The Old Bridge Area of the

Old City of Mostar, rebuilt from war damage rubble, was duly inscribed by UNESCO on the WHS list the following year. This despite the guidance for selecting World Heritage Sites making authenticity an explicit requirement for inclusion.

The UNESCO documentation justifying Mostar's WHS inclusion is maddening in its evasions and wishful thinking. The targeted destruction of Mostar's Old Bridge – the Stari Most – by Croat artillery in 1993 was a defining moment of the Bosnian War. A symbol of the city, its collapse into the river below after concerted shelling marked the completion of the ethno-nationalist segregation of what had been previously one of the country's most multicultural cities. The war saw Muslims driven out of their homes in the west and centre of Mostar and the survivors confined to, essentially, the ruins of the east bank. After the 1995 Dayton Accords that divided Bosnia into ethnic cantons as the price of peace, an international effort to reconstruct the bridge commenced under UNESCO's guiding hand. While some of the destroyed bridge's stones were hauled up from the riverbed, the great majority of the masonry was too pulverised or otherwise damaged to be put back in place as per the Venice Charter. Instead, new stone was quarried and, even though it was skilfully and expertly reconstructed using traditional techniques, the inconvenient truth is that the Stari Most is not the old bridge reassembled but materially a brand-new bridge. Despite being a copy, albeit constructed using traditional methods, the relevant UNESCO text talks about 'the authenticity of the form, use of authentic materials and techniques.' It avoids referring to original materials being reassembled (which didn't really happen) but argues instead that 'remaining original material has been exposed in a museum, becoming an inseparable part of the reconstruction.' As an argument for authenticity by the planet's leading heritage body, a separate museum display of the original stones is, to use a technical term, bullshit.

The linguistic gymnastics continue with the phrase that the 'reconstruction has not been hidden at all.' While construction hardly occurred behind closed doors, this wording conceals the fact that the rebuilt bridge does not incorporate the scars of

Wikicommons

4.3 The reconstructed Mostar Bridge, the Stari Most. Traditional materials and techniques were used. Despite it being a modern recreation rather than being authentically historic, UNESCO inscribed the bridge and its rebuilt surroundings a World Heritage Site.

its past traumas. It is not a layered critical reconstruction that properly differentiates new work from old or incorporates the experience of war.

The bridge itself is not the exclusive focus of the WHS inscription. The components cited for inclusion in the WHS extended to carefully rebuilt Ottoman houses nearby, some of which had been reduced to knee high rubble in the war, as well as the archaeological remains of the early and pre-Ottoman period and the intangible value of the wider river valley landscape. The net was cast wide to sidestep too close a focus on the inauthenticity of the bridge itself. What you see today across much of the bridge area is expertly copied but it is only patchily authentic. UNESCO's assessment that the site remains 'genuine' in its key features and architectural landmarks is also wide of the mark when one takes in the giant Catholic crosses and outsize church campanili built to glower over Muslim Mostar, in the manner of segregationist Confederate statues.

A further argument made for its inclusion on the UNESCO list was that pre-war, the bridge had been a symbol of plurality and its destruction a symbol of division, so its reconstruction was a metaphorical bridging of the communities. Certainly the sixteenth-century bridge was a symbol of the city, but whether it was ever a symbol of plurality per se is another matter. Such symbols weren't really necessary until the war caused divisions, and symbolism does not, in any case, neatly map onto authenticity. Mostar's WHS inscription argues that the Old Bridge area is 'an outstanding example of a multicultural urban settlement' and states that the reconstructed bridge and old city are 'a symbol of reconciliation, international co-operation and of the coexistence of diverse cultural, ethnic and religious communities.'[28] A less than decade-old project supervised by UNESCO itself is here stretching the concepts of world heritage and authenticity to breaking point and beyond – all in the name of symbolism.

Just as important, the ability of a reconstructed bridge to bring reconciliation and co-existence to Mostar directly contradicts the facts on the ground. Mostar remains as divided as ever despite attempts to force West Mostar's Croats and the Muslims east of the Neretva river to cohabit. Overall, Croats now dominate. A reconstructed high school near the bridge remains indicative of the continuing stand-off. It has both Muslim and Croat pupils under one roof but in separate classrooms, with separate teachers and curricula. The only place the next generation of Mostarians meet is when they need to use the toilet. Pupils and their parents rarely step foot on the rebuilt bridge to cross to the 'other' community on its respective sides.[29]

As a consequence, thousands of new graduates leave the city each year to escape the situation. Professor Azra Hromadzic in her book *Citizens of an Empty Nation* argues that the cantonising Dayton Accords that assigned Bosnian Serbs their own self-governing region was a model that denies Bosnia's pre-war pluralist history where places such as the high school do not simply reflect the ethnic divisions in Bosnian society but reproduces them.[30] There are no shared spaces in the city, only ethnic spaces, observes Hromadzic. Arguably, the reconstructed bridge, while presenting an almost too easy metaphor and image of connection, is an attempt to conceal the failures of the international community to rebuild deeper, more effective connections. Even at the time of its reconstruction, leading Mostar heritage architect Amir Pasic warned: 'The bridge is not so important. Education is the key in this town.'[31] Pasic means co-education. Far from the bridge achieving reconciliation, ethno-nationalist tensions in Mostar have been worsening in recent years.

Given UNESCO's mandate for securing peace, it is not surprising that the organisation is invested in reconstruction as reconciliation. And it can feel like an obvious truth that the reconstruction of destroyed monuments brings communities back together. But there is a conspicuous lack of evidence to support this deterministic belief. In fact, partial or nationalist-tinged reconstruction efforts could just as well intensify divisions as we have seen all over Eastern Europe, in India, and in Turkey's destructive 'conservation' efforts at Armenian and Kurdish sites within its borders. Yet the reconciliation argument is one that UNESCO and its camp followers have since repeatedly used elsewhere, such as in its justification for rebuilding mud shrines in Timbuktu destroyed by Islamist insurgents in 2012 which, akin to Shinto shrines, were at least regularly resurfaced with new earth. This does not mean reconciliation has been achieved in this part of Mali. Far from it.

UNESCO's self-serving but unscientific arguments are playing fast and loose with the material evidence of damaged places as it ties itself in knots to justify inauthentic reconstruction decisions on political grounds. Whilst reconstructing monuments destroyed by aggressors in the name of ethnic cleansing and genocide – the ultimate culture wars – can have strong moral justification, these special circumstances are simultaneously eroded when the form of the reconstruction conceals the trauma of its initial destruction, denying to history the very evidence of past events, erasing object lessons in the consequences of division and war. It is right to resist genocidaires by frustrating the cultural component of genocidal efforts and reinstating the architectural artefacts that demonstrate a multicultural city was a reality in the past and the aim in the future, but one need not justify that stance with legerdemain. So while it may be justified to rebuild old Mostar and its symbolic bridge in the face of ethnic cleansers and genocidaires intent on eradicating Ottoman culture, when

UNESCO then declares the results to be an authentic World Heritage Site, it is undermining truth and the facts of history.

UNESCO has an unfortunate record on this score, notably with facsimile Warsaw, which, after a degree of hesitation, was eventually included on the WHS list in 1980. Again, the reconstruction of monuments in the face of the Nazi physical and cultural genocide of the city's Slavs and Jews has many justifications, but must this inauthentic Warsaw also be designated a World Heritage Site? And what justification is there for the inaccuracies in its inscription text that describes Warsaw's Old Town as an 'identical reconstruction' when, as have seen above and as conservation experts know full well, it is far from identical.

The arguments are becoming ever more specious: At an ICOMOS conference held in the Polish capital in the 2018, the organisation issued the Warsaw Recommendation on Recovery and Reconstruction for World Heritage Cultural Heritage. Inspired by the city in which it was meeting, it justifies the inclusion of Warsaw on the WHS list of war-destroyed places on the basis that the destruction itself adds to its heritage significance – its Outstanding Universal Value – and that designation is in the interests of social justice and reconciliation. This turns authenticity on its head and makes the consequences of the destruction of the authentic something to be valued. A similar approach took place when the Bamiyan Valley was made a WHS in 2003. The inscription here emphasizes the wider Bamiyan landscape as well as the destruction of the monumental Bamiyan Buddhas in 2001 as one of 'recurring reactions to iconic art.' The very absence of the two sculptures at its heart thus becomes an argument justifying its inclusion.

Chasing illusions in this way is becoming not just foolish but cynical. It undermines trust in the organisation's disinterested expertise and, ultimately therefore, in UNESCO's peacebuilding premise. Manipulating the concept of authenticity in this way has consequences for the maintenance of material truths worldwide, well beyond any battlefield.

The contradictions are becoming ever more obvious. In 2009,

UNESCO's World Heritage Committee decided to remove Dresden from the WHS list, the first cultural site ever to be struck off in this fashion, because of the potential damage caused to its setting by a proposed new road bridge over the Elbe Valley. Yet this same Committee, which first inscribed the city on the WHS list in 2004, was entirely sanguine about the false Frauenkirche then emerging, and the faux Baroque mummifying Dresden's heart on a daily basis. It described the city as an 'artistic whole' and the Frauenkirche as part of an authentic restoration, a correction of the city's skyline as captured in the paintings of Bernardo Bellotto and others. Which is more damaging to history and authenticity– an honestly new if poorly sited bridge, or offering top-level support to outright and politically problematic fakery? What had changed about the assessment of Dresden since it was first refused WHS status in 1989 on the grounds that it was inauthentic and its acceptance in 2004 other than the erection of ever more false history? In between these two events, Nara was adopted, UNESCO's political expediency became more pronounced, and conflict and climate crisis threats to heritage increased.

UNESCO and some of in satellite organisations such as ICOMOS continue to question the value of authenticity, some asking whether it should be abandoned altogether as a concept. While it feels wrong to kick UNESCO when it is down, founded as it was with such hope following the disasters of war and now assailed by the global Right, the organisation has lost its way as the peak gatekeeper organisation for the planet's past.

To date, UNESCO has still not created its own code of ethics about digitally generated copies, to determine when, where, how, and if they should be used. It remains to be seen if its attitude to reconstructing the Bamiyan Buddhas will change given its newly relaxed attitude to authenticity. Before the Taliban retook the country in the summer of 2021, the Afghan ministry of culture and the governor of the Bamiyan region both wanted at least one of the statues rebuilt, with an eye to future tourism. Digital technologies would certainly make this an easier task – superficially at least.

In some circumstances, copies do have their place. For instance, there is now a high-quality copy of Tutankhamun's tomb at the Valley of the Kings to visit and realistic facsimile cave paintings in artificial caverns in France and Spain to see. But these *supplement* rather than replace the originals that were being damaged by tourism. There is a world of difference between a high-quality reproduction that is clearly seen as such and one that replaces a lost original. You can, for example, choose between the excellent digital copy of Veronese's masterpiece *The Wedding Feast at Cana* that hangs once more in its original location in a Venetian refectory or the original in the Louvre that was looted by Napoleon and is now in a gallery setting for which it was never intended. Neither of these is necessarily masquerading as something it isn't.

These honest replicas still raise complications, however. In one study, tourists visiting the copy tomb of King Tut rated it more favourably than the original because their movements were less restricted. As a result, they felt that the replica was the more authentic experience than the original.[32] By contrast, other studies suggest a different response. In a test conducted by philosophers at the City University of New York, participants were told they could choose between seeing the ashes of the real Mona Lisa after it was destroyed by fire or an undetectable duplicate of the painting. Eighty percent chose the authentic ashes.[33]

Authenticity pertains not just to buildings and objects but to the spaces we inhabit. Hannah Arendt was concerned with the spatial because of the relationship between the tangible world and its inhabitants.[34] She made a distinction between created space and the natural world of the Earth, that is, the cultural intervention in the natural in order to shape it for human life. This tangible constructed world, Arendt argued, is durable, created as a collective endeavour, and is held in common and in continuity with our predecessors and successors and is part of how we create meaning in society. For continuity to provide this reliability, it needs to be authentic – otherwise, in what are we placing our trust and understanding?

Yet inauthenticity is today spreading to include the public spaces of cities. In some ways this is even more concerning because of the importance of these spaces as common grounds where people come together. This importance has been understood from the Ancient Greek *polis* (as Arendt discussed in *The Human Condition*) through to Jürgen Habermas's analysis of the public realm's emancipatory role as a third sphere between the state and the market, and subject to the power of neither when it re-emerged as part of the transition between feudalism and capitalism. Habermas was particularly focused on the decline and privatisation of the public realm in twentieth-century America with the shift to the suburb and the mall (he was commenting on an increasingly segregated country), so the rise of fake public space in the twenty-first century should give us particular pause.

'Pseudo-space' refers to privately owned and patrolled urban spaces masquerading as genuinely public realm and where free debate, especially protest, is often forbidden or restricted. It is now a notable feature of the Anglosphere property world from Sydney to Manhattan with London providing numerous examples. These restricted spaces are found in countless developments in the capital, including the extensive landscaping surrounding London's former City Hall on land owned by the sovereign wealth fund of Kuwait where journalists are refused access to report without permission. Or take Paternoster Square adjacent to St Paul's Cathedral. Once a tangle of historic streets, after wartime bombing it became a Modernist office complex before being redeveloped once more from the late 1990s by its new owner. After interventions by the Prince of Wales, it was designed in a decidedly classical character of colonnades and piazzas. There the resemblances to a genuine Renaissance public square end. When the City was a target for the Occupy movement in late 2015, attempts by protestors to use Paternoster Square were blocked by police and followed by a High Court injunction defining the square as private land (in contrast to the original planning permission that stated the opposite). At King's Cross, meanwhile, a regeneration scheme by the developer

Argent sets out streets and squares that, superficially, give all the appearance of being a normal part of the city but are in reality a privately controlled enclave that, notoriously, linked its CCTV camera network to facial recognition software.

In a time when debate and discussion happen largely online, Arendt's analysis might seem outdated, but her writing shows us what we lose when we are confined to the virtual. She makes the point that public life is not just about words but about actions in space and that there needs to be a physical, permanent world to contain these actions in order for this debate, this web of human affairs, the person-to-person connections, to truly flourish. Which is why the privatisation and fictionalisation of the public realm is so dangerous to politics and to acts of resistance. An authentic real world makes things verifiable; it is where people come together and interact as a collective rather than being isolated at a keyboard. Tangibility matters to creating a world in common where we reflect on our commonality, understand the past, and shape the future. Once gone, this slowly accumulated, complex, commonly held, and real world is immensely difficult to authentically stitch back together.

5

The Military–
Heritage Complex

All social action is situated within specific regimes of power. To
ignore the context of such interventions ... leads at best to the
depoliticization of warfare and its agents, and at worst ... to the
adoption of the rhetoric of the invader and coloniser.

Yannis Hamilakis, *The "War on Terror" and
the Military – Archaeology Complex,* (2009)[1]

The Coalition of the Willing's 2003 invasion of Iraq led to a
human and cultural catastrophe in which heritage was made
immensely more vulnerable by the collapse of civil society. The
looting of archaeological sites and museums spiked. The Iraq
Museum in Baghdad is of world importance and was near the
top of a list of eighty sites to be secured by the invading US
Army but in practice, it was left vulnerable and unguarded with
devastating consequences while the US troops protected the oil
ministry instead.

Heritage was subsequently targeted in the sectarian aftermath
of the invasion. Abu Musab al-Zarqawi, the 'Emir' of al-Qaeda
in Iraq, ruthlessly stoked sectarian outrage and intercommu-
nal violence between Shia and Sunni in part by the calculated
bombing of Iraqi mosques such as that at the al-Askari Shrine

in Samarra – one of the holiest in Shia Islam. He was killed in a US air strike in Iraq in 2006 but in the years after his death, al-Zarqawi's organization morphed into an entity known by various labels – Islamic State, the Islamic State of Iraq and Syria (ISIS), Islamic State of Iraq and the Levant (ISIL), or the more insultingly accurate Arab acronym Da'esh. Da'esh then picked up where al-Zarqawi left off, with its keen understanding of the way that destruction of cultural sites can serve many purposes; terror, propaganda, conquest, and genocide, as well as giving spatial expression to its proposed caliphate.

In the wake of the Arab Spring in 2011, these tactics spiraled out of control through Syria and Iraq, across North Africa, and south to Mali. Superficially, blowing up ancient, pre-Islamic, and often non-figurative historic monuments and sites is baffling even by the standards of Da'esh whose iconoclastic religious doctrine has its origins in Saudi Wahhabism. The destruction was, however, also political in nature, as an expression of an ideology that challenges the post-colonial settlement – the illogical, externally imposed national boundaries and the corrupt, repressive regimes backed by the West and Russia that followed.

From across the Maghreb to Pakistan and beyond, identities were being asserted that were uncompromisingly hostile to Christian churches, Shia shrines, Sufi tombs, museums, and World Heritage Sites. Scholars were shot by snipers, site custodians beheaded by militants. TV stations beamed out videos proudly uploaded by Da'esh showing its demolition unit Katayib Taswiya bulldozing ancient Nimrud and the 2,000-year-old remains of Hatra, both in Iraq. The audience for this was both its own supporters and its enemies; the message it communicated was one of disdain for the West and its so-called universal values. It is thought, for instance, that a round of shrine destruction by the Islamist Ansar Dine in Timbuktu in July 2012 was a pointed response to resolutions by UNESCO's World Heritage Committee meeting in St Petersburg. And some Da'esh videos were fakes. One notorious example is the footage of the destruction of Jonah's Tomb in Mosul in July 2014, which was reported worldwide as fact some weeks before it actually occurred.

In retrospect, it was naïve to hope that these groups might share in Western Enlightenment concepts such as world heritage when the West's political and military project has only brought them subjugation. Appalling though the horrors perpetrated by Da'esh against people and their cultures have been, the narrative being spun in the West and international bodies such as the United Nations Security Council and UNESCO seeks to focus the blame on Islamists in a way that sometimes shades into Islamophobia. But this is not the whole story.

Take Syria, for example. When civil war broke out in early 2011, it was the Assad regime fighting an uprising by its own people. Immeasurable damage was done to monuments and museums that had nothing to do with iconoclastic Islamists. Long before Da'esh emerged as a significant force in Syria, World Heritage Sites across the country and many lesser known ancient places were used as battlefields between the Syrian Armed Forces and opposition groups such as the Free Syrian Army. Conducted with cavalier disregard to the impact, tank positions were mounted in archaeological sites, shells fired at ancient structures, and thousands of barrel bombs dropped by the government on rebel-held areas of historic cities such as Aleppo and Homs.

The initial damage to Palmyra was reported in the first year of the war as the Syrian Army dug in with tanks and heavy weapons. These actions militarized the archaeological site, making Palmyra a target. Russian and Turkish forces subsequently caused damage to key heritage sites across Syria. Yet the Western media and most heritage NGOs focused almost exclusively on the cultural destruction by Da'esh. This became part of making the case for Western military intervention.

Overall, the damage caused by Da'esh, while extensive and especially heinous when a component of its crimes against humanity, is a notably minor subset of the damage caused across Syria and Iraq by all warring parties. There was an uptick in the reporting of Da'esh attacks on cultural sites in the autumn of 2014 at the same time as the United States began its airstrikes – Operation Inherent Resolve. On 22 September, a few hours before the bombing began, Secretary of State John Kerry gave a speech at the Metropolitan Museum in New York at the opening of an exhibition of Assyrian artefacts: 'Ancient treasures in Iraq and in Syria have now become the casualties of continuing warfare and looting,' he said.

> And no one group has done more to put our shared cultural heritage in the gun sights than ISIL ... the civilized world must take a stand ... those who deny the evidence or choose excuses over action are playing with fire ... we believe it is imperative that we act now.[2]

Bombing was being justified in the name of rescuing culture.

As Jessica Holland noted, Kerry's speech was a version of the same foreign policy narrative that President Barack Obama had been telling, in which atrocities by Da'esh were stripped of context. Kerry referred to these crimes as 'ugly, savage, inexplicable, valueless barbarism' and the most virulent symptom thus far of two countries that have fallen into a mess of poverty, infrastructure failure, corruption, and opportunistic power grabs: 'Bashar Al-Assad, of course, looms large in this picture,' wrote Holland,

> but Kerry sandwiched in only one mention of the Syrian president, in relation to his regime's shelling of an ancient Roman temple, into a catalog of ISIL's destruction. Assad's many other, graver crimes don't fit with the message being shaped.[3]

This omission was not simply down to the fog of war but a manipulation of the narrative. So it is of particular concern that the heritage professionals whose work is central to maintaining the objective historical record have, since the post–9/11 war on terror and the US invasion of Afghanistan and Iraq, become increasingly tangled up with armed forces in what the academic Yannis Hamilakis terms the 'military–archaeology complex' but might more widely be called the military–heritage complex, a web of archaeologists, anthropologists and other heritage workers. Their involvement has been championed as repairing, or better still preventing, the damage caused by conflicts. To their critics, working with armies means that heritage professionals' independence is lost and the ethical problems of collaborating with overseas military campaigns too easily set aside.

In the twentieth century, international frameworks were developed whose aim was to diminish damage and make war crimes of attacks on civilian centres and cultural monuments and their contents. Central to this were the Geneva Conventions and the 1954 *Hague Convention for the Protection of Cultural Property in the Event of Armed Conflict* among whose provisions are those forbidding attacks on cultural sites except when – and this is an infamous loophole – it is a military necessity.

Much important work has been done by UNESCO and its advisory bodies, including the International Council on Monuments and Sites (ICOMOS), its museum sister organisation, the International Council of Museums (ICOM), and the Blue Shield, an international organisation established under the 1954 Convention that was to be, in theory at least, a heritage protection equivalent to the Red Cross.[4] The Hague Convention has, unfortunately, also been conspicuous in its failure to protect historic places, a situation that has intensified as global power blocs have disintegrated and where conflicts might be fought between non-state actors or have a pronounced ethno-nationalist dimension. Here especially, history isn't accidentally damaged; it is the intended target.[5]

Heritage organisations had been slow in making any headway in increasing heritage protection in these circumstances but more recently there has been some movement. The armed forces of the United States and the United Kingdom, for instance, have been persuaded to set up Cultural Property Protection (CPP) units that aim to limit the damage done to historic sites during their military operations (although the US unit, at least, is not fully operational). At the same time though, the way heritage professionals are now engaging with the military is being seen as more and more problematic to the point of complicity.[6]

Yannis Hamilakis argues that there has been a 'monumental failure' of most archaeologists and other heritage professionals to articulate a political and ethical response to the 'war on terror.' In places such as Coalition-occupied Iraq, they are adopting 'uncritically the rhetoric of the invading ... power.'[7] This, he suggests even extends to the work of forensic archaeologists uncovering mass graves of Saddam's victims which, while clearly important for the families of those murdered, also needs to be considered in a context where the graves were used to support the largely fabricated case for war. Tony Blair's Foreign Secretary Jack Straw did exactly this, addressing Parliament using the words of forensic archaeologist Margaret Cox, who had been involved in Iraqi exhumations, to argue that the Baathist regime was 'propped up with the bones of the Iraqi people buried beneath its sands.'[8]

The role of heritage experts in assembling 'no-strike lists' with the coordinates of historic sites to be avoided during the Western bombing of Libya, Syria, Iraq, and Yemen has especially come under scrutiny. A charge is that in assembling these lists, independent professionals have become embedded rather than independent, like journalists in Coalition Iraq.

An obvious argument in favour of such lists is that, in theory at least, they help protect culturally important locations from being destroyed by aerial attacks, artillery shelling or other damage during military campaigns. Heritage and conflict academic Emma Cunliffe believes that such lists have proven their worth, citing the NATO strikes on Libya where Colonel Gadaffi had located moveable listening stations around the fortified Roman farm of Ras al-Mergeb in an attempt, it is said, to shield them from attack. The site's inclusion on a no-strike list supplied to NATO and the US Defense Intelligence Agency, argues Cunliffe, led to NATO modifying its approach to use multiple closer range air strikes rather than a larger single blow. This resulted in minimal damage to history while destroying the military objective.[9] Leaving aside the many occasions when so-called precision strikes have caused devastating civilian casualties, one must set the success of one precision strike in protecting a heritage site against the continuing chaos that NATO's actions unleashed in Libya, a collapse of society that is a much more formidable and ongoing threat to culture and the historic record.

At the same time, Cunliffe responsibly sets out episodes where no-strike lists have been misused by armies. She quotes the research of Richard Rhodes into preparations for US attacks on Japan in the Second World War where an archaeologist supplied a ranked list of sensitive cultural sites that led to frantic appeals not to drop an atomic bomb on historic Kyoto. Hiroshima and Nagasaki were the victims of Little Boy and Fat Man instead. It is hard to see this change of target as a victory for the process, for humanity, or for heritage. Likewise, there have been unverified claims that the recent war in Yemen has seen less damage to historic places since heritage professionals provided the Saudis with 'no-strike lists.' This has to be placed within the context of an illegal and often indiscriminate Saudi military campaign that has devastated the country, a war conducted against civilians with weapons supplied by Britain at the same time as the British Council has been providing support for the protection of Yemeni cultural heritage. One hand giveth, the other taketh away.

A further problem is that no-strike lists are normally made up only of major monuments, leaving off locally valued sites that can be most at risk – especially important where they are linked to minority identities and thus an attractive target in campaigns of cultural cleansing and genocide. In Iraq, Mesopotamian sites valued by the West as part of its own long history were included on the no-strike lists, while many other important places with less occidental resonance were ignored. Likewise, there was not a notable scramble by international heritage bodies to prepare a no-strike list for archaeologically rich Gaza when it was pounded by Israeli shells under the 2008 Operation Cast Lead and in other attacks that caused severe damage to several sites, including Gaza's only antiquities museum.

Conceivably too, these lists could actually make such places a target. After hospitals in insurgent-controlled area of Syria voluntarily shared their GPS coordinates with Russia, Assad's ally, under the UN's 'humanitarian de-confliction' system, many were then systematically bombed by Syria and Russia.

Heritage advisors to the military feel that they are damned if they do cooperate to mitigate potential cultural damage and damned if they don't, by abdicating their professional duty of care to cultural property.

Hamilakis acknowledges that many heritage professionals publicly opposed the Iraq invasion, but as he points out:

> all social action is situated within specific regimes of power. To ignore the context of such interventions and treat the efforts to rescue antiquities as an abstract act, antiquities that appeared as endangered by an equally abstract threat of "war" (as it was a "natural" disaster) leads at best to the depoliticization of warfare and its agents, and at worse ... to the adoption of the rhetoric of the invader and coloniser.[10]

American archaeological and anthropological organisations, for instance, compared the Iraqi regime unfavourably to the United States and its supposed commitment to freedom, democracy, and the rule of law.[11]

In an effort to get Western armed forces to take culture and heritage seriously, some heritage groups have emphasised that harm to cultural places could arouse local hostility to a military occupation as well as being bad international PR. They may be effective arguments, but is it the sector's role to bolster an invasion's success? Since at least the nineteenth century, peace advocates have been aware that by making war less horrific, more rule-bound, they may become enablers, promoting the idea of a war fairly fought and thus more likely to be contemplated.

Some specialists have accepted advisory and training roles to the Pentagon and the UK Ministry of Defence, often working in secrecy even as the campaigns are damaging material culture. René Teijgeler, a former Dutch army reservist (the few dozen army officers in various armies' CPP units are nearly all reservists) is now on the board of the NGO Heritage for Peace after serving as cultural advisor in Iraq and in Afghanistan. He writes that 'it is not the primary task of cultural heritage management to prevent or stop war ... politician declare war and soldiers wage war.' Archaeologist Umberto Albarella, a vocal critical of the military–heritage complex, takes Teijgeler to task on this approach: 'Factually, his statement is certainly correct, but the problem is that such preparation means to work with the governments of the countries that have generated the problem in the first instance.'[12] Albarella asks whether the same forensic archaeologists would be sent back to Iraq to uncover the bodies of those killed by Coalition bombing.

It is understandable that some would see this as an embedded relationship, especially if reducing harm to material cultural artefacts in one place comes at the price of human lives in redirected strikes. In the broadest sense, such efforts can make an attack more acceptable to the Western public by selling the idea of a good war fairly fought. Other heritage workers refuse altogether to work with armies, condemning the militarisation of their field of study and protesting invitations to army officers to speak at academic conferences. The Iraqi archaeologist Zainab Bahrani who worked early on with the Coalition Provisional Authority has said since that the process was a charade and she is among those who would refuse to work with the military again.

Professor Peter Stone, UNESCO chair in Cultural Property Protection and Peace at Newcastle University and president of the Blue Shield, is another who has been challenged by Albarella directly for his close work with the military, including assembling no-strike lists for British and NATO forces. Would Professor Stone provide the same level of cooperation with the military if the target country had been Denmark or his own hometown rather than Iraq, muses Albarella? Stone, who has done more than most to persuade armed forces to take care of culture, pushes back, arguing that the stance of Albarella and Hamilakis is a pacifist one: 'But that is a stance that leaves cultural property in an extremely vulnerable position. I'm reluctant to stand by and watch without trying to mitigate the risks during armed conflict.'

He points out that in heritage disasters where the first responders need CPP training, these personnel are often military. He rejects the idea that he and similar colleagues are embedded: '"Embedded" implies, to me at least, the inability to criticise. As the [Blue Shield] we have criticised what we perceive to be limitations in the guidelines.' He says that he would be equally happy to criticise the UK's Ministry of Defence if it doesn't deliver. There is, he stresses, 'no alternative but to try to influence those who are capable of doing significant damage, and also capable of being proactively protective.'[13]

Peacetime cultural training is one thing, however, and preparation for a specific military action another. Stone makes the point that good cultural protection 'may contribute to mission success.' This goes well beyond training troops in avoiding cultural casualties, to something perilously close to backing the aims of a particular military mission. From making heritage protection an element of a *casus belli*, to no-strike lists, to assisting with mission success, it is no wonder that the neutrality of heritage organisations is being questioned and their ability to intervene objectively is consequently faltering. Murky waters.

The waters become very murky indeed over the question of the looting of artefacts from conflict zones and calls to store historic objects in safe havens away from the fighting, issues wrapped up in wider, peacetime questions of neocolonialism and politics. UNESCO, Western governments, and heritage NGOs circulate the myth that trafficking in looted antiquities is a substantial (rather than very minor, at best) source of funding for terrorists – especially for Da'esh. This is based on little evidence. While all conflict exacerbates looting – from unsecured museums and from archaeological sites particularly – the fate of antiquities, as with immovable material culture, has become cynically weaponized. Highly suspect accounts of the importance of antiquities looting to Da'esh's income stream, where figures ranging from $36 million to hundreds of millions have been accepted at face value, are circulated in ways that support military agendas.

In May 2015, US special forces raided a Da'esh safe house near

Deir ez-Zor in Syria, killing the high ranking Da'esh officer, Abu Sayyaf, freeing an enslaved young female Yazidi, and retrieving a cache of documentation. Among them were receipt books relating to the 20 percent taxes on activities levied by the Diwan al-Rikaz, the Da'esh agency that taxed resources dug from the ground such as oil and antiquities. (Da'esh wasn't itself digging but issuing licences to looting locals.) This was trumpeted by the United States, and reported around the world, as proof positive of the systematic looting and trafficking of antiquities to finance terror. It led in 2017 to United Nations Security Council Resolution 2347 that condemns cultural destruction and the trade in looted items for financing terrorism, building on an earlier UNESCO Executive Board Decision. This was applauded as a sign that the Security Council was finally taking culture seriously.

Except what the receipts showed – and their veracity is doubted by some – is that antiquities make a miniscule contribution to Da'esh's income, amounting to perhaps $1.25 million over several months from the Deir ez-Zor governorate. According to the receipts, the vast majority of the revenue came from two unusually valuable items. Extrapolated figures suggest that antiquities income amounts to 0.5 percent of the governorate's monthly revenue – a minimal amount compared to cash from activities such as bottled water plants, petrol stations, and a cement factory that produced the same income every ten days as the antiquities' receipts suggest over more than six months. The largest proportion of Da'esh's income is likely to have come from 'taxes' that were more like gang extortion – the confiscation of houses, cars, and other individuals' possessions. Other regions may show different proportions.

It was pointed out that if Da'esh were making millions, the trade in London, New York, and elsewhere would have been in the billions after the usual markups. Someone would have noticed. Instead, many of the objects that have reached the art market have been identified as fakes. Oil and antiquities are among the few exports, however, that Da'esh's opponents could seek – and be seen – to disrupt.

What's more, some of the worst looting has been in areas that Da'esh has either never held or won control of only after the worst of the looting had already been carried out by others, including by the Syrian army and non-jihadist opposition groups such as the Free Syrian Army. A study of satellite data from almost 1,300 archaeological sites by Dartmouth College anthropology professor Jesse Casana, published in *Near Eastern Archaeology* in September 2015, came to the conclusion that looting was at its most widespread in areas where civil authorities were weakest, whoever was nominally in charge, whether Da'esh, Assad's government, the Kurdish YPG, or other rebel groups.[14] Yet only Da'esh hogged the looting headlines. Da'esh was blamed for looting at Palmyra carried out by Assad's forces and rebel groups before it even arrived there. In all, almost a quarter of heavy looting across the country has been attributed to the Syrian regime and its associates.

It is true that industrial-scale looting of archaeological sites across Iraq and Syria has caused incalculable damage, even if it is delivering items of limited value to an art market not much interested in the unprovenanced and quotidian mass of items. Most artefacts dug up are worthless or near worthless in monetary terms but are invaluable for our understanding of the past. Inflating the financial value of these items, as the international community and media has done, can, however, only encourage desperately poor locals to ruin sites in the expectation of riches. That is, it worsens the spoliation of history while making no difference at all to the financing of terrorism. UNESCO, for one, should know better. The exaggeration can be explained, at least in part, as a justification for military intervention. It serves to shift the focus away from the wider cause of the cultural catastrophe whose root causes include the legacy of colonial interference in the region and an escalating destabilisation since the war on terror began.

In April 2015, UNESCO's Executive Board highlighted the problem of cultural destruction and looting and called on UNESCO's then director-general Irina Bokova to initiate a dialogue on the possible establishment of 'protected cultural zones' in Syria 'around heritage sites of recognized and shared cultural significance.' The concept of 'protected cultural zones' in Syria was first introduced by the director-general at the high-level international conference Heritage and Cultural Diversity at Risk in Iraq and Syria held in December 2014 in Paris. It was hoped that a 'freeze' in hostilities at a key cultural site would foster dialogue between the conflict parties. That is, cultural heritage protection was being seen as a means of de-escalation and reconciliation rather than, as it has been in practice, an aspect of managing the damage caused by conflict. The Omayyad Mosque of Aleppo was suggested as a pilot.

The in-country protected zones came to nothing. What was pursued instead is the idea of international 'safe havens' for transportable cultural objects endangered by armed conflicts or terrorism at the request of the country affected. This was one of the recommendations of the landmark UN Security Council Resolution 2347. It stems from loosely termed provisions in the 1954 Hague Convention.

On the face of it, rescuing moveable cultural artefacts from war zones would seem an unalloyed good. There are precedents. During the Spanish Civil War, Spanish art treasures were eventually moved to Switzerland and in 1939, at the outbreak of the Second World War, endangered Polish works of art were sent to Canada. However, who gets to decide what is saved and who ensures the return of the saved objects raises unavoidable ethical and political questions, especially where a state has changed hands as a conflict unfolds. Those items valued by governments rather than those of minorities whose culture can be most under threat – sometimes from these same governments – benefit the most. The voices of minority groups are lost here.

Then there is the enormous problem of ensuring that these objects find their way back to new governments or new national entities. It took the post-war communist Polish government some fifteen years of wrangling to get its art treasures back from Canada. In 2009, the Netherlands 'handed back' sixty-nine looted items to Iraq. But this was only a symbolic handover; the items actually remained on display in a Dutch museum because the situation in Iraq was still deemed unsafe and adequate conditions for their protection could not be met. At the time of writing, a long-running court battle was continuing about a collection of Scythian gold objects indigenous to the Crimea and loaned to the Allard Pearson Museum in Amsterdam for an exhibition before the illegal annexation of Crimea by the Russian Federation in 2014. Russia and Ukraine wrangled about where the treasure should end up – occupied Crimea or in Kyiv? In 2021, a Dutch appeal court finally ruled in favour of Kyiv. Then came Russia's brutal invasion of wider Ukraine.

Here, too, incidentally, cultural property protection arguments were deployed by champions of Western military intervention to push NATO into direct engagement, including as part of the casus belli advanced by US president Joe Biden that evidence was mounting of a genocide underway designed to wipe out Ukrainian identity. There was the idea that Ukrainian heritage was being specifically targeted as an aspect of this aim.

Writing two months into the conflict, however, cultural sites appear, in the main, to have been damaged incidentally rather than actively amidst Putin's profound disregard for civilian life and urban fabric. There is little doubt about war crimes and crimes against humanity being committed, but intentional genocide against a Ukrainian identity group is not yet evidenced. (This might well change, especially in areas that Russia seeks to control or occupy permanently such as the Donbas and where we might expect selective cultural erasure, so patterns of cultural damage that could evidence this must be carefully monitored.)

Some of very same people arguing for artefact removal to safe havens – or even military intervention to save culture – are those who oppose restitution of looted items long held by major museums in the West. Greece, for example, is unlikely to see the British Museum as a safe haven that can better look after the Elgin Marbles, and both Greece and Egypt have raised concerns about the safe havens concept, with the Greek prime minister stating that it was a solution of last resort.

The J. Paul Getty Trust has done an enormous amount for

cultural heritage in danger around the world and its president and CEO James Cuno now calls for safe havens and military intervention under the auspices of UN Blue Helmets. But this is the same James Cuno who has strongly and repeatedly opposed the restitution of objects from Western museum collections. He argues that they are universal museums that allow comparative study and promote understanding. In support of safe havens he has claimed that distributing cultural objects around the word will ensure their survival. In a letter to the *New York Times*, he wrote of the cultural vandalism by Da'esh: 'This unconscionable destruction is an argument for why portable works of art should be distributed throughout the world and not concentrated in one place.' Referencing the colonial era practice of 'partage' where foreign archaeologists could take home a proportion of their finds, Cuno's take was: 'The world can only be grateful for the earlier regime of 'partage,' which allowed for the sharing of Assyrian antiquities with museums worldwide that could preserve them.'[15]

This entirely ignores the way partage was abused by Western archaeologists, including the subterfuge used to spirit away the famous bust of Nefertiti to Berlin, covered in dirt to hide her importance. All this is hardly encouraging for the timely return of cultural objects to their home country. And it is not clear in some safe haven regimens just who has the final say over when the time for return is right.

Whatever the good faith, empathy, and sincere views about cultural pluralism held by many individual heritage and museum professionals who see saving culture from destruction as a public service and a moral duty, their actions take place in contexts whose terrible facts need to be acknowledged if more good than harm is to be done. This includes recognising the consequences and continued impact of historical colonialism on many of the colonised societies whose culture many in the coloniser nations are now trying to protect. These same colonial powers, that are today pursuing armed interventions that bring only further war rather than peace, remain unwilling to discuss the basic truths of their own histories and resist restitution of cultural items pillaged in colonial adventures. Instead, progressives who question the dubious provenance of these collections are the target of the Right's culture wars.

Anybody working in this field needs to acknowledge these historic and lived realities before they can truly understand the outcomes of their resolutions, policies, papers, and rescue missions to save culture. Otherwise they cannot act effectively and appropriately, most especially so when this involves calls for military involvement. The Getty's James Cuno argued that cultural objects should be treated as refugee objects and given protection and shelter; new homes away from the conflict.[16] This care might be eminently reasonable if human refugees were also protected and not left destitute in camps, fenced out of refuge countries, see their children drown in the Mediterranean surf or find themselves languishing in abusive detention on Pacific islands.

In this real-world context, calls for moving Assyrian sculptural treasures to, say, the comfort of the Louvre or a villa in Malibu but not safeguarding the people whose culture produced them, makes hollow any of the professed claims to link cultural heritage and human rights now being made by UNESCO and many others in the heritage world. What does training a dozen or so reservists as cultural protection specialists in the US or British armed forces amount to in such a context? In the UK, a few hundred thousand pounds has been spent on such training, a laughable budget when 380 Tomahawk missiles, each costing more than double that, rained down on the Iraqi people and their culture in a single day of the Coalition's Shock and Aware attack on Iraq. As Hamilakis observes:

> A militarised archaeology [or heritage sector] ... does not simply lose its autonomy and independence, and thus its ability to critique military and political authority, it also provides ... academic legitimacy to military campaigns and their political projects ... The willingness of some parts of the military to make 'rescuing antiquities' part of their business, to set up an archaeological

branch in their midst, invests their operations with respectability and legitimacy [and] acts therapeutically for domestic audiences in the invading countries.[17]

Hamilakis rejects accusations that he is counselling a 'do nothing' approach to heritage protection and argues instead for initiatives working with local archaeologists in occupied countries and for cultural reparations rather than simply aid. 'In some cases,' Hamilakis acknowledges,

> archaeologists and others may of course have no option but to liaise with military authorities and nobody has suggested that this should be avoided at all costs. But such engagement should always happen openly and publicly rather than in secrecy. Moreover, any engagement should be constantly aware of its legitimising effects, and its deployment within broader regimes of truth and rule.[18]

☙

More positively, since the conflicts in the former Yugoslavia, and even more so since the actions of Da'esh, some in the international community have been inching their way toward a better understanding of the intimate connection to the fate of people and their cultural expression, whether material culture such as monuments or traditions and language. Increasingly it is recognised that the dynamiting of a mosque or library may also be an attack on the community itself. Cultural cleansing often accompanies ethnic cleansing and murder; genocide goes hand in hand with cultural genocide. The intent is to eradicate a group's identity as well as bodily. The erasure of historic sites may not only be about denying the right of a people to belong in a place but also to manipulate the material historical record to remove the evidence of their long history in that place.

International efforts to protect minorities from such harm or their culture from a related fate are still, in practice, almost always failures. In part, this is because much of the international law on the conduct of armed conflicts that aims to protect culture, is divorced from international humanitarian instruments aiming to protect people – war crimes as distinct from crimes against humanity. And neither is well equipped to address either the slow ratchet of erasure outside of a full-scale hot war or to halt the actions of non-state actors within a conflict. At the same time, human rights initiatives have become cynically co-opted by government to pursue soft power and influence overseas.

The United States has supported reconstruction projects using financial resources such as the Ambassadors Fund for Cultural Preservation (AFCP) in places ranging from Iraq to Hue in Vietnam, the ancient royal city that was ruined during the 1968 Tet Offensive and its recapture by the United States. In an academic paper (incomplete and unpublished at the time of writing), the eminently sensible US law academic and Blue Shield member Patty Gerstenblith points out that 'While one could characterize US support for reconstruction projects ... as acts of [contrition], the scope of the AFCP is considerably broader.' She quotes academics Luke and Kersel, who write:

> Because cultural heritage in many countries is extremely political, the AFCP is very much an instrument of foreign relations, steeped in Western mores of value that reify colonial notions of what represents a particular culture, who should have access to the past, and who should care for the ... remains.[19]

What is funded is increasingly likely to be that which projects soft power rather than that which would make the most local difference.

In extreme cases such as genocide, intervention of some kind is, in theory, a duty that can override sovereignty even if one cannot have much faith in interventionist powers to exercise that duty properly; we should have no illusions that these powers would fairly prosecute a humanitarian war – if there is ever such a thing. However, attacks on material objects and representative architecture can provide an early warning sign that ethnic cleansing or genocide is a looming threat as it was in 1938 on

Kristallnacht or, more recently, the heritage destruction marking the onset of campaigns against the Yazidi and Shias of Iraq, the Rohingya of Myanmar, and Uighur Muslims in Xinjiang. Viewing the protection of material culture as a component of human rights rather than simply a question of patrimony and aesthetics should help us see how they are integrated.

There is still some way to go on this, however, when even organisations such as Amnesty International can downplay the intertwining: In responding to the International Criminal Court's landmark 2016 conviction of Ahmad Al Faqi Al-Mahdi, a senior member of Ansar Dine, for the destruction of religious and historical monuments in Timbuktu, Amnesty senior legal advisor Erica Bussey acknowledged that to destroy the culture and identity of a population was a crime. But she chose the same moment to emphasise the lack of convictions for violent crimes against civilians during the same 2012 conflict as if the progress in addressing cultural heritage protection might overshadow justice for people: 'This positive development should not let us lose sight of the fact that hundreds of civilians were murdered, tortured and raped,' she said calling for further arrest warrants.[20] The reminder might be useful but the tone could suggest a hierarchy of priorities rather than an understanding that such violent and destructive acts against bodies and the cultural are not separate phenomena but are thoroughly integrated.

We should be supportive that, at long last, UNESCO is holding meetings, writing reports and passing resolutions that explicitly link the destruction of cultural heritage with humanitarianism, security, and peacebuilding. It has, for instance, offered financial and training support for those rescuing or rebuilding heritage in Iraq, including recaptured Mosul. And in November 2015, it adopted a strategy to protect culture and promote cultural pluralism in the event of armed conflict.[21] This was followed by an Action Plan to implement the strategy – although a hefty chunk of the $25 million budget went to UNESCO's own administration of the plan.[22] Yet it was not long before the international community was reneging on its promises. A 2013 UN Security Council resolution that set up a peacekeeping mission for

Mali initially included cultural protection in its remit alongside humanitarian assistance, but this duty was removed when the mandate was renewed in 2018.

Like the UN itself, a good deal of UNESCO's problems stem from the fact that it is subject to the pressure of its constituent state parties – especially those with the kind of military and financial muscle to project their demands internationally. This becomes obvious in the decisions of its constituent bodies such as the World Heritage Committee that, while they have always been politicised, have become increasingly so. Independent advice from its advisory bodies such as ICOMOS in matters such as inscribing World Heritage Sites is often set aside.

Being hostage to its member states has, along with its sclerotic bureaucracy, been UNESCO's Achilles heel since its inception. A particularly illustrative episode is the wrangling over the fate of the Khmer temple of Preah Vihear on the disputed Thai–Cambodian border. The small eleventh-century clifftop complex is immensely remote, reachable from the main temple complex at Siem Reap only by a slow two-day drive through jungle that culminates with a muddy track through a recently logged landscape and a final decanting for a truck ride up to the temple escarpment and its commanding views over neighbouring Thailand.

Yet this remote place became an international focus for heritage chicanery. The temple had been subject to on-off conflict and diplomatic disputes since the early twentieth century when the border was demarcated under French colonial influence in a ruling never accepted by Thailand. In 2008, the UNESCO World Heritage Committee's inscription of the temple as a World Heritage Site on Cambodia's nomination the previous year led to fighting breaking out once more along the border after decades of calm. Press reports gave the impression that the temple had been ravaged by the 2008 shelling but when I visited during a lull in the skirmishes, evidence of damage to the temple structures was minimal. Other temple sites along the border were captured by the opposing armies.

Writing in her insightful history of UNESCO, archaeologist Lynn Meskell explains how the process of selecting Preah Vihear as a World Heritage Site became entangled in US interests in the region. Wikileaks documents revealed cables from 2005 showing that US diplomacy was crucial to Preah Vihear's inscription on the World Heritage Site list. One cable from the US ambassador in Phnom Penh to the State Department prior to inscription sets out the US interests in linking the decision on Preah Vihear's status to its investment strategy in Cambodia by entangling it in the resolution of overlapping territorial claims between Cambodia and Thailand in the Gulf of Thailand, where US companies were trying to secure lucrative contracts for gas drilling.

Diplomatic cables flew back and forth, noting other matters such as the importance of US airbases in Thailand, US arms sales, and growing Chinese influence and investment in the region – including the logged jungle just driven through. 'An equation began to emerge: if Cambodia retained its temple, Thailand might enhance its underwater assets, and the United States might negotiate for extended contracts,' writes Meskell. The cables show that companies such as Boeing, Nike, and McDonalds were eyeing Cambodia for investment. 'The political, economic, and the cultural became inseparable,' she continues. 'And all this was being leveraged in the name of conservation, around the inscription of one site on the UNESCO World Heritage List.'[23] Chevron later got its gas concessions, at the price of a small border war that threatened the survival of an ancient temple.

This is by no means an isolated incident. Similar unedifying episodes make a nonsense of claims of consistent decision-making based on genuine heritage significance and which accord with scientific and people-centred conservation practices. In Panama, for example, UNESCO was impotent in the face of patently false claims. The Panamanian government denied that it was building a problematic elevated coastal highway alongside a World Heritage Site called Panamá Viejo and the Historic District of Panamá, despite photographs presented to UNESCO's World Heritage Committee in 2012 showing exactly that; a viaduct's massive concrete supports rising out of the sea. UNESCO's attempts to prevent further development incursions upon the WHS were rebuffed with the help of Panama's BRICS bloc allies (Brazil, Russia, India, China and South Africa) amidst corruption claims involving a Brazilian company whose executives had sat with Panama's delegation at a UNESCO meeting. Siding with Panama, South Africa's ambassador called the sixteenth-century buildings of the site, one of the oldest colonial settlements in the Americas, an 'unsightly village' and argued, supported by India, that the viaduct improved the view of the site. 'In this astonishing turn of events, the highway *becomes* the World Heritage Site …This inversion undermines the credibility of the Committee and the [World Heritage] Convention, effectively jettisoning conservation from their remit,' says Meskell.[24]

Arguably, matters are just as bad when a member state is reluctant to nominate its own sites for WHS status as Australia has been when it comes to its important Aboriginal sites which have been damaged or are still threatened by lucrative extractive industries. While notoriously, in Saudi Arabia, it is the state itself that has destroyed many historic places of worldwide significance for doctrinal and commercial reasons including much of historic Mecca and Medina. Hundreds of Ottoman-era buildings, especially places that could be the focus of idolatry including ancient sites associated with Muhammed's life have been destroyed. The house of the Prophet's first wife, Khadijah, was replaced by a public toilet. Since these are neither designated World Heritage Sites nor an open conflict situation, UNESCO maintains that it has no mandate to intervene.

Similarly, the systematic assault on Armenian monuments and architecture in Azerbaijan and the disputed Armenian enclaves of Nakhichevan and Nagorno-Karabakh carried out over decades in order to cement Azerbaijani claims to the land has seen UNESCO react at a snail's pace or not at all. The destruction has included the bombing of a cathedral and the stone-by-stone erasure of entire historic cemeteries with their thousands of elaborately carved grave markers. Armenian heritage activists have accused cash-strapped UNESCO of being more concerned with Azerbaijan's financial contributions to the organisation than cultural genocide. In 2017 *The Guardian* reported that the then UNESCO director-general Irina Bokova's husband, Kalin Mitrev, accepted a half million-dollar consulting fee from a PR firm that funnelled an estimated $3 billion into initiatives to promote the international standing of the Azerbaijani government.

Bokova's predecessor Kōichirō Matsuura also had work links with Azerbaijan and was awarded a diplomatic service medal by Baku.[25] International justice finally creaked into action in Nagorno-Karabakh in December 2021 when, sidestepping UNESCO's lassitude, the International Court of Justice ordered Azerbaijan to prevent and punish its racist acts of vandalism and desecration of Armenian heritage. Theoretically, the UN Security Council is tasked with enforcement and the judgement could prove far-reaching but, disappointingly, the IJC's provisional decision did not spell out any mechanisms to achieve protection.

Otherwise, despite the best efforts of the ICOMOS experts advising UNESCO, the entire World Heritage Site system is falling into disrepute. Attempts to apply objective tests of historical importance, authenticity, and the crucial measure of 'outstanding universal value' are mired in this national politicking, issues of gentrification and urban development, and destructive practices such as logging and mining. The system has become far more about marketing and tourism – which brings its own level of additional damage – rather than the safeguarding of the world's most important historic sites and the local people living in and around them. Instead of a focus on conserving the past, the main goal appears to be strategic development. This is the case in Mosul, where UNESCO is rushing to reconstruct the principal landmarks destroyed by Da'esh while what survives of the historic fabric of the wider city is being sacrificed to property speculators. Even the most egregious damage to a freshly minted World Heritage Site appears to elicit barely a murmur from UNESCO if the aggressor is a key ally and the target is domestic opposition.

5.1 Sur, the historic quarter of the Kurdish city of Diyarbakir in Turkey. Its fortress is a World Heritage Site. The area was devastated by the Turkish military in 2016. UNESCO was essentially silent about the episode. President Erdogan later sought to paint the area's redevelopment as a regeneration project.

In 2015 the walled city of Diyarbakir in Turkey was inscribed on the WHS list. The following year, when the World Heritage Committee was meeting in Istanbul, the Turkish army launched a ferocious assault on the Kurd-led stronghold, killing hundreds and devastating the city's historic fabric, with an estimated 800 or more structures in the ancient Sur district at Diyarbakir's core razed and the rubble subsequently bulldozed into the Tigris. Thousands more were damaged. Again, UNESCO failed to react. Turkish novelist Ömer Zülfü Livaneli resigned as a UNESCO goodwill ambassador in protest at its inaction. Local architects complained to Paris in vain. President Erdogan, unadmonished, later promised to cleanse the city of terrorists through 'urban regeneration,' expropriating most of the historic area.

Only years later did the World Heritage Committee grumble about the proper processes not being followed and call for a halt to the redevelopments that would harm Diyarbakir's heritage significance. That was, essentially, the sum of it. Sadly, UNESCO's idealised role in the popular imagination as the global protector of humanity's common legacy is profoundly misplaced.

The consequences of UNESCO's operational narrowness in working chiefly through its member states may, charitably, be said to flow in substantial part from the remit and organisational structure it was given at the outset. But as we have seen, some states are more equal than others when it comes to their freedom to act and their ability to escape censure for their own actions or inactions.

All these issues – authenticity, objectivity, politicking, unevidenced claims as to the reconciliatory role of heritage protection, and rapid reconstruction and the role of technology in that reconstruction – came together in the Syrian war at sites such as the WHS-listed, Krak des Chevaliers. Close to Homs, the crusader castle was one of the world's most complete medieval fortresses before being damaged either by the Syrian rebels holed up inside for two years or by the shelling of Assad forces in an eventually successful attempt to dislodge them.

The narrative in some heritage circles blames the rebels for destroying parts of the interior, including a medieval staircase, in order to hold off the Assad regime that has since been praised for rapidly repairing the structure with the assistance of Hungarian archaeologists after they recaptured it in 2014. Others point the finger at aerial bombardment by the Syrian Army for causing the worst damage. A few tourists now visit and events have been held such as a *son et lumière* in 2018 where, in decidedly poor taste, Syrian soldiers, part of the army that shelled the monument, re-enacted their taking of the citadel.[26] Hasty rebuilding, often in the name of normalisation and reconciliation, supporting a tourism industry or spurring on economic development can result in the obliteration of evidence showing how the damage was caused and who by, and so the responsibility for war crimes and crimes against humanity.

Protecting sites such as Krak des Chevaliers and determining responsibility is made all the harder by bodies such as UNESCO and ICOMOS engaging with the Assad regime's antiquities directorate (Syria being a UNESCO state party) but emphatically not with the armed non-state actors such as those occupying the castle and thus rendering it a military target. It would have been sensible to remind the rebels of the danger in which they were placing the castle and other heritage sites, but such an engagement is off limits. Any dissenters to this official position of dealing with state parties only are firmly warned off. This is not true impartiality and, when dealing with a government that happily barrel bombed the historic old city of Aleppo, it is not very effective either. Meanwhile, initiatives to engage with non-state actors to further the protection of civilians such as those by the neutral NGO Geneva Call has seen it accused of consorting with terrorists.

Palmyra was an even bigger tragedy than the castle. The World Heritage Site is a spectacular place, an oasis northeast of Damascus where the impressive ruins of one of the cultural centres and trading cities of the ancient world remained for over a millennium. Its ruins sprawl across the desert – great temples and public buildings, a grand axial colonnade of columns 1,100 metres-long culminating in a triumphal arch, a theatre and, close-by, an aqueduct and the necropoli with the tower mausolea and funerary sculpture of its wealthy. The central temples of Baalshamin and Bel were among the most important religious buildings of the Near East. Before the war, the major threat facing it was the encroachment of the nearby town of Tadmor.

It was the use of Palmyra during the civil war as a military base by Assad's army that had first made it a military objective and caused damage to the site. It has also been claimed that Syrian airstrikes damaged porticos and cellas as early as 2013. Then in May 2015 the archaeological site and nearby town were overrun by Da'esh. It met little resistance with the Syrian army busy targeting other opposition groups. Within months, Da'esh began destroying Palmyra's pre-Islamic monuments starting in the Valley of the Tombs and followed by the reduction of the Temple of Baalshamin (already damaged by Assad's army) and the central Temple of Bel, to rubble. Statues in the site's museum were beheaded. The iconoclastic campaign culminated in October 2015 with the toppling of the Triumphal Arch at one end of the colonnade.

Palmyra joined Bamiyan and the siege of Dubrovnik as globally condemned episodes of cultural devastation. Da'esh spectacles of thuggish horror compounded the view that this was a war on civilisation by medieval minds. It executed captured soldiers in Palmyra's amphitheatre and killed renowned Palmyra scholar Khaled al-Asaad, reportedly for refusing to disclose the location of treasures from the site's museum. He was beheaded and his body hung from a Roman column.

Boris Johnson, then London's mayor, called for air strikes against Da'esh and an exclusion zone for Palmyra. And almost immediately, commentators were calling for the reconstruction of Palmyra's destroyed monuments. Roger Michel and the Institute for Digital Archaeology began plotting its inept copy arch as a centrepiece of its reconstruction. These calls intensified the following March when Da'esh was pushed out of Palmyra following an offensive by the Syrian Army and its allies (chiefly the Russians), culminating in the recapture of the town and archaeological site at the end of March 2016. The media celebrated the rescue of Palmyra's remaining heritage.

Less emphasis was placed on the manner of the recapture. A report by the Cultural Heritage Initiative of American Society of Overseas Research (ASOR) tells a more complex story. Released shortly afterwards, it included an initial damage assessment from photographs and satellite imagery and offered a detailed account of the events leading up to its recapture.[27] The Russian aerial offensive had begun in Syria the previous September and its targets were not just Da'esh but other opposition-held areas including deadly airstrikes on civilian targets such as hospitals and residential neighbourhoods as part of the Palmyra offensive on the town of Tadmor close to the archaeological site. This was conducted in conjunction with artillery and helicopter attacks by the Syrian army.

In early March, at the beginning of the ground offensive, a local activist group called Palmyra Coordination reported via Facebook that airstrikes had destroyed at least half of Tadmor's neighbourhoods as well as medical facilities, schools, mosques, and the town's church. The Syrian Network for Human Rights claimed that strikes by the Syrian army had targeted mosques and that Russian planes had further damaged what remained of the Temple of Bel after Da'esh's ravages. After Assad's troops captured Palmyra, there were reports of army violence against, and theft from, the area's remaining residents. Russia, for its part, denied that its earlier airstrikes had struck Tadmor including its historic citadel, but during the March ground operations and continued aerial bombardment there were further reports of damage to both Tadmor and the Palmyra archaeological site 500 metres away, some corroborated by video evidence. A Russian official claimed 2,000 airstrikes in March alone. The enormous human cost and the wrecking of living Tadmor was a high price to pay for rescuing dead Palmyra.

Almost immediately Russian heritage experts arrived from Moscow along with staff from the Syrian Directorate-General of Antiquities and Museums (DGAM) to assess the damage; then, in a bizarre display at the beginning of May, the Russians flew in the Mariinsky Orchestra from St Petersburg to perform a triumphalist concert in the Roman theatre conducted by Kremlin favourite Valery Gergiev, who had backed the Russian occupation of Crimea and government campaigns against LGBTQ+ people but said the concert was a protest against barbarians. Among those also taking part in the concert was Vladimir Putin's close friend, the cellist Sergei Roldugin.

The audience included Syrian and Russian soldiers, the director of the Hermitage, representatives from China and Serbia, a UNESCO delegation, and Putin himself, who addressed the crowd via video link to celebrate the Russian humanitarian triumph against the evil of terrorism and cultural destruction. The concert was broadcast live on Russian TV interspersed with footage of its forces recapturing Palmyra. The Russian government was still opposing Security Council resolutions imposing sanctions on Assad and maintaining the lie that no Syrian civilians have been killed by Russian bombing. Despite its entanglement in the Ukraine, Russian involvement in Palmyra is unlikely to end soon – it has a military base outside Palmyra and there are tempting prospects in the extensive gas fields nearby. A matter of days after Russia's 2016 concert, the Museum of Ma'arrat al-Nu'man with its world-class collection of mosaics housed in a sixteenth-century caravanserai in an opposition-held area was struck for the second time by the Syrian air force with two rockets. This followed the dropping of barrel bombs on the museum by Syrian helicopters the previous June.

Poor taste, lies, and hypocrisy might be expected from Putin's Russia. What was more startlingly, however, was the endorsement for Russia's Palmyra campaign immediately offered by UNESCO. This served to bring the organisation's officially neutral approach into great question. On 27 March 2016, just as the Syrian regime and its allies announced their victory over Da'esh, UNESCO released a statement about a congratulatory phone call earlier that same day between Bokova and President Putin to discuss the 'liberation of Palmyra.' Putin assured Bokova of his willingness to help with the reconstruction of the cultural heritage of Syria (a heritage his and Assad's forces had helped damage). Meanwhile, Bokova also invited Maamun Abdulkarim, the director of the Syrian DGAM, to come to Paris to discuss Bokova's full support for the restoration of Palmyra, underscoring 'the critical role of cultural heritage for resilience, national unity, and peace.'

The statement suggests that Syrian national unity is in the hands of Assad and that Putin is on the side of the angels. It bolstered the image of the Syrian regime as a protector of culture and civilisation that the Assad family had been happy to exploit for decades. It also assumes that the peace was won with the recapture of Palmyra. It was certainly a turning point for the Syrian army that had been on the point of disintegration until Russia threw its weight behind Assad. Bokova repeated that Palmyra would be rehabilitated and rebuilt and said she would send a committee of UNESCO experts to Palmyra as soon as possible.

UNESCO's position outraged many in the heritage sector, and protests condemned her announcements. Salam Al Kuntar, an émigré Syrian archaeologist who was based at the University of

Pennsylvania's Museum of Archaeology and Anthropology and also worked with the Smithsonian on an initiative to safeguard Syrian and Iraqi heritage, used online community platform Avaaz to launch a scathing petition that, while acknowledging the assaults of Da'esh on people and culture, pithily accused Bokova and UNESCO of not considering the ramifications of issuing a hasty statement in the midst of an ongoing brutal war. 'The intention of UNESCO and other organizations to engage in a restoration and reconstruction process of the ancient site of Palmyra right now is both inopportune and unrealistic,' read the petition.

> It comes at great shock to us that the protection and future of Syrian heritage is discussed with and decided by Russian President Vladimir Putin, an active player in this gruesome conflict and a perpetrator of human and cultural rights violations. UNESCO has a commitment to building peace in the minds of women and men. Taking a partisan position that celebrates the Syrian regime and Russian military achievements will not help construct a lasting peace or restore Palmyra's famed cultural heritage.[28]

The petition reminded UNESCO of its duty to act neutrally and scientifically, calling for emergency works to protect the surviving ruins from deterioration and a detailed investigation of the destruction and looting at Palmyra since the start of the Syrian conflict. 'But we firmly oppose any hasty reconstruction initiated by UNESCO and carried out by parties directly involved in the Syrian tragedy.' As it was, Da'esh recaptured Palmyra six months after Putin's concert and it was to remain in its hands until March 2017. Da'esh promptly and predictably blew apart sections of the Roman theatre where the Russian concert was held. The UNESCO/Russian restoration would have to wait.

The outrage may have given UNESCO temporary pause; it did not attend a meeting on Palmyra in Damascus later that year. 'But they are still not actively engaging with opposition-held areas,'

Al Kuntar later told *Disegno* magazine. 'There's no "neutral" in this context,' she added in response to UNESCO officials putting forward this defence for only dealing with Damascus. 'It's about refusing to engage with a government that is committing war crimes and human rights abuses.'[29]

For its part, ICOMOS launched Project Anqa to document cultural heritage sites across the Middle East, using new technology such as 3D laser scanning, photogrammetry, and aerial imaging through drones as part of a campaign of recording that might allow subsequent reconstruction. It began training Syrian government archaeologists in Damascus, but only for sites under Assad's control. The UNESCO/ICOMOS prohibition on working with opposition groups means that Assad's agenda is served; the needs of monuments outside government-held areas were not seeing the same attention. 'If they [heritage experts] work with the opposition, the DGAM will simply cut ties with them,' says Al Kuntar who points out that opposition-held areas don't have access to UN funding or for visas for archaeologists and others wanting to work outside Assad's control.[30]

In the end, Bokova proved a polarising figure. A child of Bulgaria's Stalinist elite, educated in Moscow, and a regular visitor there during her tenure as director-general, she was accused of not being a neutral figure and of privileging the Assad–Russia axis. The questions intensified when she was in the running to succeed Ban Ki-moon as head of the United Nations and reports about failures of her record led to her bringing a defamation case against the *Daily Mail*. The business dealings of her businessman husband adding to the atmosphere. To others in the international heritage community, she is something of a hero for working hard to highlight the threat to heritage in conflicts. She addressed the UN Security Council in 2017 to remind it that heritage destruction is a war crime that tears societies apart when used as part of a strategy of cultural cleansing. The UN then successfully passed Resolution 2347 recognising that the protecting heritage is a security imperative inseparable from defending human lives.

'She's still regarded as a goddess by some in the heritage community,' says one heritage insider,

> but we are getting very tired of UNESCO and Bokova's approach. UNESCO wouldn't do anything that Assad wasn't happy with and that was a real problem. It has been very a top-down approach and so the local community, who you have to bring into play, becomes less invested.[31]

The report published by ASOR's Cultural Heritage Initiative points out that 'over the longer term, the greatest threat to Palmyra is mismanagement stemming from prioritizing immediate and highly visible results, ultimately grounded in larger political objectives, rather than being guided by conservation best practice, community-based heritage management, and sustainability.' The proposed immediate reconstruction of the demolished Baalshamin Temple and Temple of Bel was described as political expediency that 'not only poses an unfeasible and misguided heritage management solution, but also fails to address the greatest threats to ancient Palmyra, let alone the needs of the modern community.'[32] There has been very little discussion internationally about how to help the devastated inhabitants of Tadmor.

A similar situation faces other important heritage sites such as Aleppo's Old City, destroyed largely by Assad. Later in 2016, in its State of Conservation Report, UNESCO's World Heritage Committee recognised the communal tensions that reconstruction could cause if not handled correctly, but it continued to argue, in the midst of an ongoing war and without empirical evidence, that rebuilding efforts could promote 'the collective healing process' and 'reconciliation.' Mostar all over again. As it is, the Syrian regime is bulldozing emptied-out, former rebel-held suburbs of Damascus such as Qaboun in the name of a 'new Syria' of upmarket commercial and residential developments.

It is essential that post-war decisions involve local communities if they really are to have any hope of bringing such benefits, but an enormous problem in this is that pre-war inhabitants have often fled and been replaced by those with different traditions or nationalist agendas – as happened in Bosnia and is happening now in Syria and in Iraq where UNESCO is helping rebuild Mosul's key monuments in the absence of the city's former cosmopolitan character, including its large Christian component. Over-hasty reconstruction of symbolic places intensifies these dilemmas. UNESCO later shifted its position saying that there would be a full technical evaluation of the damage to Palmyra before final rebuilding decisions are taken but, as with Mostar Bridge, the very openness to reconstruction marks a sea change.

Syria's DGAM soon declared that the reports of damage at Palmyra were exaggerated and that 80 percent of the ruins were in good shape, but other experts are more circumspect – especially where structures have been reduced to little more than dust. Certainly, the Triumphal Arch was only partially brought down, and some reports say at least some of its original stonework can be reassembled (anastylosis) in an authentic manner. Thankfully, the swashbuckling Institute for Digital Archaeology's plasticky arch, praised by Boris Johnson as an act of defiance to 'barbarians,' might not be needed. But should Palmyra be rebuilt at all? To recreate the site as it was immediately before the recent Syrian war would be a denial of the history of the conflict and its consequences.

As it is, the arch that Da'esh toppled was the arch restored in the 1930s during the French colonial occupation when, from 1929, Palmyra underwent extensive reconstruction which saw the cavalier removal of later but important accretions to the Temple of Bel from its use as a Byzantine church and then a mosque. At Krak des Chevaliers, ancient buildings were removed in the name of restoring Crusader purity. All this took place on the heels of the Great Syrian Revolt (1925–27) against French rule. The terrible aerial bombing of Damascus by the French in suppressing the revolt destroyed its citadel, historic bazaars and palaces. The loss of this history became an international scandal while the deaths of the Syrians went largely unremarked. French archaeologists were again working with Assad's antiquities department at the same time as President

Macron, prior to the invasion of Ukraine, was calling for a rapprochement with Putin. *Plus ça change, plus c'est la même chose*. Who is regarded as the barbarian can sometimes only be a matter of timing and power.

At the same time as its role in protecting culture has become suffocated by national interests, UNESCO now appears to operate on the premise that any wartime damage should be undone. This goes well beyond the relatively small number of World Heritage Sites themselves to taint international conservation work generally, where unproven assertions that heritage is an effective tool for reconciliation are being used as justification for changes in worldwide conservation practice that are now driving misguided reconstruction and development. These shifts, together with digital techniques for copying and faking, are being applied in uncodified ways that exaggerate their accuracy and undermine the centrality of genuine, authentic historic fabric. They pick away at essential concepts such as truth in construction and erode the role of the monumental record as material evidence of the past, evidence that is essential for understanding criminal responsibility and for helping establish the facts about that past on which the future might depend.

Restoring architecture can never in itself lay to rest conflicts, but, hastily done, erecting pre-conflict perfect copies, where there is no visible, material memory of the original injustice or memory of a war, can only hinder the recognition of guilt or the expiation upon which truth and reconciliation depends. Reconstruction may, in limited circumstances, be a reasonable act of resistance to attempts to erase a people and their identity, but even then there needs to be a coherent policy framework that recognises the importance of authenticity as a guiding truth in rebuilding, even if in some rare instances it is only to consciously and carefully (and within safeguards) set it aside. We need to be wary of building unreliable worlds that disguise the truth. We cannot learn from the past in ways that avoid future conflict if we can't rely on the material evidence, the physical archive that architecture provides to history.

6

The Evidence
of History

Burning books is not the same as burning bodies, but when one
intervenes ... against mass destruction of churches and books
one arrives just in time to prevent the burning of bodies.
– Raphael Lemkin, *Letter to James Rosenberg*, (1948)[1]

Professor Eyal Weizman and his colleagues at Forensic
Architecture are hunched over laptops in their white painted
eyrie beneath the roof of Goldsmith's College in London when
I visit in the spring of 2017. Between slices of green apple and
dark chocolate, Weizman is looking at phone video clips he has
been sent from the aftermath of the 7 April chemical attack on
Douma in Syria, an event that Assad and his allies claimed was
faked. Weizman points out the hole that a chlorine gas canister
has made as it has crashed through the ceiling of a home, tearing
concrete and reinforcement bars down and inwards. Russian
TV is pushing the lie that the concrete was pecked off from
the inside.

Another clip shows a chlorine gas canister lying incongru-
ously on a bed where it has come to land. A man is standing
next to it wearing a gas mask. The frosty white surface of the
canister suggests that it is still discharging its contents. The

New York Times collaborated with Forensic Architecture to get to the truth about the incident, examining matters such as the fallen metal grid lodged beneath the canister that matched the ceiling reinforcement bars. 'That bit of ceiling is a recording device,' says Weizman. 'You can work backwards from it to see the forces that shaped it.' On such detailed evidence war crimes trials can be won or lost.[2]

Eyal Weizman was born in Haifa in Israel and became an architect and an activist, exposing how his fellow professionals were complicit in creating facts on the ground that expanded Israeli control and restricted the ability of Palestinians to build housing on occupied land – 'ethnic cleansing through architecture' he agrees.[3] 'Crimes' he notes, 'can be committed on drawing boards.' He made enemies and commissions at his architecture practice in Tel Aviv dried up. He moved to London and set up Forensic Architecture in 2011. The studio is now a group of architects, investigative journalists, and other specialists who combine architectural and digital techniques to undertake 'counter-forensics,' investigations into incidents from migrant drownings in the Mediterranean to the attempted genocide of the Yazidi people by Da'esh in Iraq.

Three-dimensional models – both physical and digital – are created that analyse the trajectories of rockets, damage to buildings, the sound of guns going off, wave and weather patterns. They examine evidence and find culprits. A bomb cloud, Weizman's given to pointing out, can be a building and its contents in gaseous form – concrete, timber, human bodies. The architectural evidence supplements witness and victim testimony. Amnesty International and Human Rights Watch are among the NGOs that have used his services.

In an age of fake news, Forensic Architecture and other organisations like it could not be more vital. Weizman agrees that the conspiratorial and populist Right are not only contesting facts but claiming that facts themselves are not verifiable and that their own baseless perspective is equally valid, whether on climate change or evolution versus creationism – that the evidence doesn't matter. It does. 'Truth is a common good,' he says, 'like water or air, even if some politicians have polluted it.' Weizman argues that every material object can be regarded as a sensor, even if sometimes an uncertain or incomplete one. Indeed, buildings might be among the best sensors of societal and political change because they are immobile, anchored in space, and in close interaction with human bodies.[4] They also act as historical documents that bear witness to the social and political reasons for their construction and destruction.

Much of Weizman's early work revolved around human rights violations against the Palestinians by the Israeli army and Israeli security state. In one case, thousands of crowd-sourced photographs and phone footage of the bomb clouds from rocket attacks on Gaza were successfully used to prove that the Israeli army's destruction was part of the 'Hannibal Directive,' where the army would rather kill one of its own soldiers than have them captured by Hamas militants. Forensic Architecture's findings changed Israeli policy.[5]

Forensic Architecture was later asked by the United Nations to investigate a pattern of US drone strikes from Somalia to Afghanistan, Yemen to Gaza, strikes that the United States sometimes denied had taken place. These often leave a distinctive small hole on the outside of structures, explains Weizman: 'Most other airborne munitions detonate upon impact, leaving most of the blast force outside the structure,' but drone missiles have a delayed fuse.

A few milliseconds delay between first impact on the roof and detonation allows a missile to break through several layers of roof, walls, and floors ... before detonating ... where a payload of hundreds of lethal streel fragments is designed to destroy flesh but leave the structure intact.[6]

The work of Weizman and partners at the Bureau of Investigative Journalism found that in Pakistan about 62 percent of strikes aimed at Islamist groups were against domestic buildings with as many as 1,614 civilian casualties in Pakistan alone by 2014.[7] Accurate detail is always crucial – not just of the

materiality of the objects being examined but also the materiality of how they are recorded and the problem of uneven access
to evidence when very often it is the state authorities under
suspicion who control the crime scene.

The work is not just conducted within conflict zones. In London,
at the behest of the local community, Forensic Architecture
undertook modelling of the June 2017 Grenfell Fire. It assembled 48,000 user-generated videos, some just a few seconds
long, to create a 3D visual testimony.

At the time of writing, police, coroner, and public inquiries
into the Grenfell Fire have been concentrating on the mechanics
of how the deadly combustible cladding came to be applied to
the exterior of the tower as well as other failed architectural
details and who was responsible for designing and specifying
these matters. Investigations have thrown up a web of bad design
and construction practices and the falsification of materials
safety data. But all this evidence needs to be read in conjunction with its contextual rationale and this context is yet to be
fully unpacked. This includes the deregulation and privatisation of the national building control system and materials safety
laboratories, the outsourcing of public housing management,
and, fundamentally, the under-investment and denigration of
the social value of public housing, especially Modernist housing.
Whatever the initial fuse, the guilty party is, at root, capitalism.

Writing about Grenfell, *Guardian* columnist Aditya
Chakrabortty correctly revived Friedrich Engels' description of
the deaths resulting from the housing and working conditions of
industrial Manchester as 'social murder.' Engels also critiqued the
class-based restructuring of Paris from 1853 by Georges-Eugene
Haussmann, arranged to benefit the bourgeoisie, property
development, and to marginalise and control the working class.
In his book *The Housing Question*, Engels describes, in terms
that would be recognisable today, how the Haussmann method
simply disguises the attempt to tackle poor housing by shifting
the problem elsewhere, hiding it behind elegant main frontages
'in such a way that the solution continually reproduces the

question anew.' Haussmannisation, incidentally, was in turn exported to the colonial cities of the Global South.

'Over 170 years later, Britain remains a country that murders its poor,' wrote Chakrabortty.

> When four separate government ministers are warned that Grenfell and other high rises are a serious fire risk, then an inferno isn't unfortunate. It is inevitable. Those dozens of Grenfell residents didn't die: they were killed. What happened last week wasn't a "terrible tragedy" or some other studio-sofa platitude: it was social murder.[8]

The pertinent architectural evidence here goes beyond the physical fabric to the way architecture is procured and regulated and its users safeguarded. 'The social violence documented by Engels wasn't aimed at a particular person and wasn't usually intentional,' continues Chakrabortty. 'These were acts licensed by those in public or private sector authority, who decided the lives of poor people mattered less than the profits of the rich.' It is also a violence resulting from concrete public housing being supposedly beautified (in Sir Roger Scruton's terms); over-clad to 'improve' the views of the tower for its wealthy neighbours.

The permanence, or more properly relative permanence, of architecture does not easily go away, but when it does it often does so with a bang – of the artillery shell or the wrecker's ball or in the rush of flames. Just like lying monuments, the resulting ruins and absences can still inform us about the truths of the past, both in the broadest ideological sense and in determining criminal responsibility: Who dropped the barrel bomb? Who sundered the bridge and destroyed mosques in the name of ethnic cleansing and genocide? Who looted the museum and smashed its artefacts? Who allowed the wrapping of high-rise housing with deadly, inflammable cladding?

What is notable about the culture warriors of the Right railing against, say, the decolonisation movement's reasonable demands that we update our understanding of imperialism and question our commemorative landscape, is that not only do they deny that the past can be shaped in the service of false testimony – whether that is Dresden's Old Town or Eastern Europe's nationalist resurrections – but that they are usually reluctant to accept any newly emerging evidence of the truth about the past.

An understanding of architecture as evidence is not entirely new – the Nazi's systematic destruction of Slavic culture was raised in a limited way at the Nuremberg Trials, for example, and more comprehensively by war crimes trials held in Poland. Over the past quarter century, however, the architectural has been sifted more and more in the search for culpability. Weizman (and this book) have been influenced by Dutch architectural historian Robert Jan van Pelt, whose work on Auschwitz-Birkenau calibrated the exact design details that demonstrate how some half a million people were murdered in the 200 square metre space of the camp's Crematoria II as well as millions more across the Nazi camp system. Van Pelt too understands how buildings and the imprint of violence upon them can be witnesses.

It is ugly that such proof is needed – yet it is. 'No holes, no Holocaust!' has been a central argument of Holocaust deniers for decades. Frenchman Robert Faurisson spent much energy on promoting the slogan, as did David Irving, the discredited historian of the Third Reich. The mantra refers to the deniers' claims that no holes have ever been found in the roofs of the gas chambers at Auschwitz-Birkenau through which the murderous Zyklon-B gas pellets were delivered. If there were no holes, then the rooms were not gas chambers and thus the camp not an extermination camp. Deniers were only able to advance this nonsense because in late 1944, with Soviet troops advancing, the Nazis first dismantled and then blew up the gas chambers and crematoria at the camp in an attempt to destroy physical evidence of the genocide. Equipment was loaded into trains and taken away. A tangle of masonry and reinforcing bars from the collapsed structures was left behind.

The 'No Holes' contention exploiting this attempted erasure of the material evidence was used by Irving in his High Court libel case against historian Deborah Lipstadt and Penguin

Books. Irving had brought the case in 1996, asserting that Lipstadt's 1993 book *Denying the Holocaust: The Growing Assault on Truth and Memory* had defamed him in its charge that he deliberately distorted historical evidence.[9] Fortunately for history, Irving lost. The court found that indeed he was a Holocaust denier, a racist, and an anti-Semite who had purposefully manipulated archival material (including documents that were forgeries) to diminish Hitler's role in the Holocaust.

At the heart of Lipstadt's defence was a meticulous 700-page report by van Pelt setting out the architectural evidence for the Holocaust. Van Pelt, who appeared in court as an expert witness, later turned his evidence into a book, *The Case for Auschwitz*.[10] As well as researching eyewitness testimony from both perpetrators and victims, van Pelt assembled a comprehensive account of the planning, construction, and operation of the gas chambers. Van Pelt's book is page after page of horrors – the bureaucratic logic of its construction, an architectural incarnation of evil. With even the smallest apparent discrepancy leapt upon by denialists, van Pelt had to be relentless in setting out every detail from every source.

When the Germans burned the camp archives in January 1945 as they fled the Red Army, they overlooked the building office some distance away whose contents included architectural drawings and paperwork.[11] Among other items, Van Pelt assembled architectural blueprints, patents for ovens, and inventory numbers matching retrieved gas-tight doors as well as the correspondence of the camp's chief architect Karl Bischoff (who was never prosecuted for his role), construction contracts, budgets requests for materials, and worksite reports. Allied aerial reconnaissance photographs were also examined at the trial where there was much debate about strange marks on some reconnaissance photographs, which Irving claimed was evidence of fakery. They turned out to be prisoners who appeared as dark dots that were the same size as a silver salt grain of the photographic film. Weizman calls this situation, where the object depicted is close to the size of the recording material, be it film crystals or digital pixels, the 'threshold of detectability.'

Crucially, there was the surviving fabric of the structures themselves. The failure of SS dynamite charges to fully destroy Crematoria II left a tent of collapsed concrete and steel. Details survived such as a gas chamber door whose hinges were repositioned so that it could open outwards to avoid the dead bodies clogging its movement. The door's glass peephole to check the progress of the mass murder was fitted with a hemispherical metal grid on the inside to prevent those being gassed from smashing the glass in their desperation. Still, the glass had been shattered on occasion and one surviving worker described how the peepholes were subsequently closed up with blocks of wood or metal and the electrical cabling and ventilation design changed after those fighting for their lives ripped out cabling and damaged equipment with their bare hands.[12] At trial, David Irving claimed that all civilian gas-tight air-raid shelters had peepholes, ignoring the custom-made nature of the doors. [13]

There was more, much more. Former prisoner Michael Kula, a mechanic who had been assigned to the camp's metal workshop, had once given testimony describing how he had helped make the internal wire columns with their nested layers of meshes into which the poison pellets lodged after being dropped through the holes in the ceilings of gas chambers.[14] Kula's witness evidence was vital given that the wire columns were a later amendment to the original design for which the working drawings (7015/IV–109/6) had been lost and because the columns themselves were removed by retreating Nazis. [15]

Other elements were retrieved from the ruins such as the zinc ventilation duct caps blown away by the explosions. These were subsequently tested and found to be covered in traces of hydrogen cyanide. All these details helped crush Irving's arguments, ensuring he lost the case. After the verdict, a further forensic study of the physical remains of the gas chambers structures was carried out by experts in 2000, and they were finally able to locate three of the four holes in the ruined roof of Crema/Gas Chamber II. Their study found 'clear signs of openings; straight cast edges [to them] in the concrete of the roof' and reinforcement bars that bent toward the holes and were cleanly cut (rather than being bent as a result the 1944 explosions). A fourth hole was partly hidden by a fold in the rubble that was created by the explosion; only the edge of it can be seen and it remained undisturbed.[16] 'What it does prove – conclusively and scientifically,' say the forensic study's authors,

> is that there were holes in the roofs of the crematoriums in Auschwitz ... This finding adds the final link to the chain of evidence that now indisputably converges in the fact that the gas chambers in Auschwitz-Birkenau were used to kill human beings with poison gas.[17]

Irving's earlier writings were also examined at the libel trial. His book *The Destruction of Dresden* (1963) made his name for the sensational figure given for the number of dead in the 1945 firestorm. In various subsequent editions of the book, Irving increased his already highly inflated figure up to a preposterous claim of 250,000 victims of the raid using, crucially, document 'TB 47' supposedly based on a police report that others believed to be a forgery. The fictitious victim count had its origin in wartime Nazi propaganda weekly *Das Reich* and was circulated by Goebbels. By any sensible measure, there were not enough destroyed buildings in Dresden to house the dead he claimed, nor the number of German refugees supposedly sleeping on the city's streets. Irving's 1996 biography on Goebbels also included falsifications provided by Holocaust denier and convicted anti-Semite Ingrid Weckert of the numbers of synagogues and Jewish businesses destroyed on Kristallnacht that served to diminish the severity of the pogrom and reduce Hitler's personal culpability.[18]

Deborah Lipstadt was correct in warning that the sidelining of empirical truth by treating any interpretation of history as permissible was enabling Holocaust denial. For Richard Evans, noted historian of Germany who took the stand for the defense, it was the very concept of historical truth that was on trial as much as the truth of the Holocaust. Other historians make a distinction between evidence used in history and evidence used in court, but Evans believes that this distinction is impossible to sustain. He was supported by figures such as the philosopher A C Grayling, who argued against the postmodern idea that historical scholarship can only result in present narratives about lost pasts, pasts that could never be satisfactorily retrieved. On the contrary, Evans argues, the construction of 'an accurate picture of what happened by the discovery of verifiable facts' was possible.[19]

Van Pelt had a similar view. He also took postmodernism to task, not least philosopher Jean-François Lyotard who in the 1970s came perilously close to lending intellectual weight to Holocaust denier Robert Faurisson in his willingness to explore postmodern language games of the sort that Faurisson himself used to argue that historical truth regarding the gas chambers at Auschwitz could never be established. Evans is derisive of the work of postmodernist historians Ellen Somekawa and Elizabeth Smith, who argue that all interpretations of history have validity and that 'rather than believe in the absolute truth of what we are writing, we must believe in the moral or political position we are taking with it.' This is a definition of history that lets the likes of Irving off the hook.

Evans repost: 'No historians really believe in the absolute truth of that they are writing, simply in its probable truth, which they have done their utmost to establish by following the usual rules of evidence.'[20]

While mistakes might be made by honest historians, deliberate manipulations and falsifications that use evidence in a partial manner are another matter entirely. Evans uses the analogy of painters painting a mountain – they may have different perspectives and painterly interpretations and may even disagree about aspects of its physical appearance but they will all be painting the same mountain. An objective historian, says Evans, is one who works within these limits.[21] 'Irving was not examining and interpreting these events,' wrote Evans, 'he was twisting the evidence to make it appear that they had not taken place. There was no debate among historians on the basic factuality of the gas chambers.'[22] If historical objectivity is less readily achieved than some would like to admit, this means that, rather than being abandoned entirely, it should be striven for more vigorously and transparently using all the evidence available including that of monuments, architecture, and the form of cities.

That evidence needs to be authentic if the architectural as testimony is not to be abused. Denialists were given unwitting potential leverage by the decision of Polish authorities after the war to reconstruct and reconfigure parts of the camp for the establishment of the Auschwitz-Birkenau State Museum, formalised in 1947. The site covers hundreds of acres including the main camp Auschwitz I and Auschwitz II (Birkenau). In an earlier book, *Auschwitz: 1270 to the Present*, van Pelt and co-author Deborah Dwork described what survives and raised important questions about what visitors actually see. They note that 'Auschwitz I, though apparently unchanged, is quite different from the camp the Soviets liberated in 1945.'[23]

It is essentially as it was in c.1940–42 with the camp as expanded in the following years omitted. This excludes soldiers' work halls and well-built barracks that survived but are now outside the camp museum. Our image of Auschwitz is thus shaped only by the miserable sheds used by the camp inmates and the crematoria rather than its vast scale of operation. The infamous *Arbeit Macht Frei* gate at the beginning of the memorial site, for example, was actually seen by very few victims of the genocide who were taken directly from trains to Birkenau because the arch was not relocated to the new edge of the camp after it was expanded. The authors argue that this altered Auschwitz arrival sequence amounts to a 'post-war obfuscation and a loss.'[24]

Far more concerning, however, was the post-war reconstruction of the Crematorium I building, complete with gas chamber, four hatched roof openings (the holes), ovens, and a chimney. All are a fake tourism exhibit. The genuine crematoria where the bulk of the systematic murder took place, including the much-examined ruins of Crematorium II, are miles away at the mostly dismantled Birkenau camp. With the real Crematorium I gone, the museum's initial curators had decided a fake

6.1 Crematoria I at Auschwitz, destroyed by the departing Nazis, was reconstructed in facsimile when Auschwitz reopened as a museum and memorial site in the immediate post war period. Its reconstruction opened the project to charges of falsification of history that Holocaust deniers exploited eagerly.

crematorium was a necessary culmination to short Auschwitz visits because visitors rarely bothered to trek the distance to the real crematoria ruins at Birkenau: 'There are no signs to explain these restitutions,' write van Pelt and Dwork, 'and the guides remained silent about it when they take visitors through this building [Crematorium I] that is presumed by the tourist to be the place where it *happened*.'[25]

The authors argue that this was not just a well-meaning exhibition design decision but part of the post-war government agenda in Poland which sought to marginalise the fate of the Jews in favour of generalised Polish victims of Fascism with a consequent focus on Auschwitz I, which was central to the story of Polish martyrdom rather than Auschwitz II/Birkenau, where mainly European Jewry were killed. The collections of victims' hair, spectacles, suitcases, and the like were moved from Birkenau to the more convenient museum environment of Auschwitz I, adding to the problems of authenticity and further confusing the real narrative.

Just as van Pelt and Dwork were preparing to publish their 1996 book, French journalist Eric Conan wrote 'Memory of Evil,' a long, angry article in the French magazine *L'Express* about his recent visit to Auschwitz to see conservation work underway. In it he details the way the site has been manipulated since the war by the Communist authorities and the failures to preserve its authenticity, including the re-assembly of the few surviving prisoner barrack blocks on top of concrete slabs rather than the bare earth prisoners had to contend with during the camp's operation, so contributing to an undermining of the awfulness of the real living conditions. As Conan warned, this inauthenticity, especially the recreated gas chamber building, was fodder for conspiracy-minded denialists, especially because earlier museum officials had refused to acknowledge the problem:

> Crematorium I was reconstructed in its supposed original state. Everything in it is false: the dimensions of the gas chamber, the locations of the doors, the openings for the pouring in of Zyklon B, the ovens ... the height of the chimney.[26]

David Irving immediately leapt on the article, writing that 'everything about it is a fake,' the gas-chambers a 'fraud.'[27]

This was followed with an article by the high-profile Holocaust denier Robert Faurisson, first published in 1998 in the French magazine *National Hebdo* with the headline 'Aveux Méritoires' (Meritorious Confessions) and then in English the following year in the denialist *Journal of Historical Review*. It is still circulating on its website.[28] Faurisson again wilfully misuses the rebuilt gas chamber as an entry point to wholesale denialism, arguing not just that the copy crematorium is inauthentic and inaccurate (which it is) but that the original was 'a very conventional crematory facility.' Crematorium I had, in fact, only been used for extermination for a short time before the industrial scale killing began at Birkenau, but a conventional crematorium it was not. Faurisson was assisted in his fiction precisely because the archaeological evidence of this important difference was destroyed by the museum's reconstructed exhibit. The inauthenticity of Crematorium I was contaminating the reputation of the genuine Crematorium II. What Faurisson does not mention is that a large part of Conan's article is taken up by detailing the scrupulous new conservation regime at Auschwitz that was finally taking the issue of authenticity seriously. Conservators were now doing their utmost to preserve original structures, materials, and artefacts – every plank, shoe, and skein of hair.

Alarmingly though, such inauthentic and misleading curation remains an issue elsewhere. Dachau is on the outskirts of Munich, the camp unnerving in its location so close to the small town of Dachau's suburban villas rather than being hidden well away from civilian eyes. The first camp of its type when it opened in March 1933, it was originally used for political enemies of the Nazi regime and later held other groups, notably Jews, clergy, gay men, Sinti and Roma. It was at Dachau that the brutal camp regime was perfected before being disseminated across the Nazi camp system. While some 41,500 were worked or beaten to death, summarily executed, experimented upon or died of hunger and disease, Dachau wasn't built as an extermination camp. What the visitor sees today, however, confuses this important fact.

You approach the camp between stands of susurrating trees growing on parts of the demolished SS facilities before you arrive at the main prisoner area. Some other important parts of Dachau including the SS interrogation areas were cleared as late as the 1980s while other buildings are still in use by the Bavarian riot police. Immediately after liberation, the camp was put to various purposes including residential use of the prisoners' barracks. These were all later demolished before some were then some reconstructed in the 1960s, along with some of the perimeter fencing when Dachau became a memorial site. The inauthentic neatness of these reconstructed blocks gives the air of particularly low-rent holiday chalets, belying the horrors of the camp. Inexplicably, an avenue of poplars has been planted between them, softening the landscape further.

From the main camp, you cross a bridge over a small river where waterweed drifts calmly to the camp crematoria set in an attractive leafy garden. Here one is confronted by curatorial decisions that, in another potential gift to denialists, mislead about the evidence of mass killing at the camp. The second Dachau crematoria known as Barrack X was built in 1943 and survives more or less intact, with sinister delousing chambers at one end (that also used Zyklon B) and ovens for burning bodies at the other. Between is a gas chamber. In the disrobing area next to the gas chamber, a modern wall plaque tells visitors: 'this was the centre of potential mass murder ... up to 150 people at a time could be suffocated.' You are invited to walk through the chamber and told by the signage that the facility was 'disguised as showers' to deceive those about to be gassed en masse.[29]

'Potential' is a weasel word here, as is the idea of hundreds being fooled into entering an ostensible shower room. Mass extermination by gas did not happen at Dachau. While the ovens were used to burn many of the camp's dead, from what we know the gas chamber may only on very few occasions have been used for experiments or the selective killing of individuals or small groups. Yet the on-site interpretation (the information displayed) gives the visitor the distinct impression that Barrack X was an integral part of the Nazi mass-extermination system.

Unlike Auschwitz, then, the problem at Dachau is not simply inauthentic reconstructions that denialists can exploit, but rather the curatorial interpretation of a genuine architectural survival. Interpretation can be as misleading as monuments themselves and must be scrupulous. Playing fast and loose with the truth and its interpretation only gives the Irvings of this world ammunition to seize upon. A guard sunning himself on a low wall outside Dachau's gas chamber is phlegmatic about the inaccurate story visitors are being told: 'Yes,' he agrees, 'it is a problem. But most visitors don't read the signs.' Which only makes the misunderstandings worse. 'We cannot change it; Historians need evidence,' he adds confusingly, turning the idea of evidence on its head.

It is not only the reconstructions and interpretation that are problematic at Dachau but who is memorialised here with honour and who is missing from the account. The Catholic Church has intruded monstrously with the building of a memorial chapel on Dachau's main camp axis (Jewish, Protestant, and Russian Orthodox chapels are shunted to the sides) and the building of a cross-shaped Carmelite nunnery (1964) behind the Catholic chapel whose entrance is, incredibly, through a repurposed guard tower. The justification for this is that many Catholic clergy died at Dachau. The vast majority of these were Poles victimised as Slavic intelligentsia and community leaders though, rather than for specifically for their faith (although that happened too).

Roma, Sinti and gay men, on the other hand, were purposely excluded from memorialisation when the site was conserved and to an unacceptable degree remain so today. Dachau and Sachsenhausen outside Berlin were the two main camps where gay men were held in their thousands. As their pink badges gave them a low rank in the camp hierarchy, survival rates were dismal, even without the agonising medical experiments performed on them

Robert Bevan

6.2 Memorial – a photo of the main memorial at the Dachau camp that excludes the triangle symbols for Roma, Sinti, and gay men.

at Dachau. At the end of the war, some inmates had to continue serving sentences handed down by the Nazis in prisons because homosexuality remained illegal and the camps weren't legal prisons. The contemporary visitor is told virtually nothing of this.

Sculptor Nandor Gild's famous 1968 international memorial at the centre of the camp illustrates the problem. It is in two parts, a metal grid of emaciated figures tangle in barbed wire with, opposite, an overscaled tangle of chains that incorporates the coloured camp badges – red for political prisoners, yellow for Jews, and so on. The pink triangle worn by gay men was purposely missed from the memorial, reflecting continued prejudice in West Germany. Also missing was the black/green badge the Roma and Sinti had to wear. When asked about a memorial at the camp post-war, Dachau's mayor Hans Zauner was disdainful of the 'homosexuals and criminals' held there: "Do you want a memorial for such people?"[30]

Outrageous though these exclusions were in 1968, the marginalisation continues today. The long Maintenance Building adjacent to the memorial is where arriving prisoners were processed and dehumanised. Today it contains a vast exhibition devised in 2003 that sets out almost every aspect of camp life comprehensively, going into great detail over matters such as how prisoners' belongings were stored, punishments meted out, and the experiences of different prisoner groups, including, to some degree, the Roma. Yet there are barely a couple of paragraphs in this enormous display that are devoted to the fate of gay men in Dachau. At its very end is a small side room where additional memorials donated by various groups over the years are stored like a commemorative lumber room. Here, among the jumble of 130 or so objects, plaques, and decaying wreaths is a small stone pink triangle commissioned by gay rights activists that, after many years of dispute, was grudgingly accepted into the collection in the early 1990s. It is decidedly an afterthought; its location disrespectful. The visitors guide (as of 2020) says the pink triangle plaque was 'donated [in] 1985,' which ignores the fact that it had to be stored for years in the Protestant chapel while the wrangling over its place in the camp continued.

Dachau describes itself in its literature as having 'a particularly important and significant role to play in international commemorative culture'. A shame then that it is not fulfilling that role adequately.

When eyewitnesses to the Holocaust (or for that matter, survivors of the chemical attacks in Syria) are no longer around to deliver their testimony in person, the material evidence must remain. When not undermined by inauthentic reconstruction, the architectural record is a reliable witness, providing evidence of a pattern of actions with a particular purpose in mind. We can use this evidence of crimes to know something beyond reasonable doubt, including the crime of genocide.

To date, genocide has been defined in strictly corporeal terms. According to the 1948 'Convention on the Prevention and Punishment of the Crime of Genocide', genocide is the killing of members of the target group or causing them bodily or mental harm, inflicting deadly living conditions, preventing births, and forcibly transferring the group's children to another group. All these are ways of attempting to destroy a group as a whole or in part. Establishing 'intent' is crucial in distinguishing genocide (the 'crime of crimes') from other episodes where culture is attacked such as war crimes and genocide's undefined cousin, ethnic cleansing. However, the Convention does not consider the erasure of identity though cultural destruction, as was seen on Kristallnacht, or in Tibet at the hands of China, or in Bosnia during the wars in the former Yugoslavia, to be a method of erasing a group.

The trials at the International Criminal Tribunal for the Former Yugoslavia (ICTY) established by the United Nations were seen as making radical progress in addressing crimes of cultural destruction in conflicts. From its establishment in 1993, courtrooms at The Hague heard more than a dozen cases addressing such cultural destruction as war crimes or as crimes against humanity, both of which forbid willful damage to cultural sites. As the ICTY heard, monuments were not just collateral damage in the path of clashing armies; they were deliberately targeted for cultural cleansing, to wipe away evidence of a community's existence in a given place. But the trials also demonstrate a continued failure since the Second World War to take the targeting of culture fully into account and, especially, to accept the concept of cultural genocide – a term not in itself recognised under international law.

The tribunals heard that monument destruction was often ineluctably bound up with the killing of people. In August 2004, for example, investigators searching the Ćehotina River in Bosnia discovered the decomposed bodies of Muslim men and women from the nearby town of Foča who had been missing for twelve years. They were buried under seven metres of rubble that had been bulldozed into the water – the debris from the Aladža Mosque, the elegant, multicoloured edifice that had been one of the most important Ottoman buildings in the former Yugoslavia. Foča, once a Muslim majority town, was one of the first to suffer what was then described as ethnic cleansing but some say should rightly be called a genocide.

The levelling of the Aladža Mosque formed part of the case against Radovan Karadžić, the former president of Republika Srpska, the Serb-dominated, self-declared republic, later recognized as a constituent part of Bosnia and Herzegovina under the Dayton Accords that ended the worst of the fighting but was seen by many as a grubby reward for successful genocide. As well as the crimes against humanity committed in places such as Foča, at the centre of the ICTY case against Karadžić were charges of genocide for the murder of more than 7,000 Bosnian men and boys at Srebrenica in 1995. There were also crimes against humanity charges for the terror campaign of shelling and sniping against the residents of Sarajevo. The fate of the Aladža Mosque was offered as an example of the wanton destruction of private property and public property including cultural monuments and sacred sites that formed part of a campaign of terror, persecution, deportation, murder, and extermination. Karadžić was found guilty and, in respect of the Srebrenica atrocities specifically, guilty of genocide. He was sentenced to forty years in prison, later increased to life.

The ICTY succeeded in establishing that persecution was committed in the context of a systematic attack against civilians and that, despite the court's statutes not specifically including attacks on cultural property as a crime against humanity, this could indeed form part of an illegal attack on the identity of a people. This approach was integral to the Kordić and Čerkez case, the political and military leaders of the vicious Croatian militia (HVO) in Bosnia who were each sentenced to twenty-five years for the savage ethnic cleansing of Muslims from the Lasva Valley. The Trial Chamber found:

> there was a pattern of destruction and plunder in all the places attacked by the HVO and that the HVO deliberately targeted mosques and other religious and educational institutions. All this was part of the common plan ... *i.e.* attacking towns and villages with the concomitant destruction and plunder, killing, injury and detention.[31]

The pattern of attacks on cultural property was thus part of the evidence demonstrating a coordinated campaign of persecution, as well as the substance of that persecution.

Crucially, however, what never occurred at the ICTY was a recognition of a specific crime termed 'cultural genocide' or the recognition of cultural genocide as an intrinsic component of genocide, the deliberate devastation of a people's culture in order to destroy their identity as a group.

The Krstić case at the ICTY, for instance, focused on the mass murder in the failed UN safe area of Srebrenica where Radislav Krstić, commander of the Drina Corps became the first person convicted of genocide at the ICTY, though the conviction was later reduced to aiding and abetting genocide. Noting the attack on Srebrenica's principal mosque, which took place alongside the extermination of thousands of Bosnian men and boys, ITCY judge Mohamed Shahabuddeen warned:

> It is established that the mere destruction of a culture of a group is not genocide ... but there is a need for care. The destruction of culture may serve evidentially to confirm an intent ... to destroy a group as such.

That is, cultural destruction can be an indicator that genocide is occurring but the shelling of a mosques is not genocide in itself, only a possible marker of it.

However, the person who was the driving force behind the 1948 Genocide Convention most definitely saw assaults on culture as directly linked to attacks on people; indeed, in some ways he saw this as his central concept. Raphael Lemkin was a Polish lawyer born in 1900 in what is now Belarus. He coined the word 'genocide' (from the Greek *genos*, tribe, and the Latin *cide*, killer) and campaigned his whole life for the incorporation of his concept into international law. His views were informed by the Armenian genocide and the British extermination of Tasmania's Aboriginal population, about which he wrote in detail. Lemkin believed that culture derived from the pre-cultural needs of a biological life. He called this 'derived needs' or 'cultural imperatives' but it was as constitutive for human group life as physical well-being. He wrote: 'It takes centuries and sometimes thousands of years to create a culture but genocide can destroy a culture instantly, like a fire can destroy a building.'

Writing in the 1930s, Lemkin directly linked barbarity – the 'premeditated destruction of national, racial, religious and social collectivities' – with vandalism, which 'meant the destruction of the cultural pattern of a group, such as the language, the traditions, the monuments, archives, libraries, churches. In brief: the shrines of the soul of a nation.'

In *Axis Rule in Occupied Europe*, Lemkin's highly influential 1944 exploration of Nazi race extermination policy and laws, he argued that genocide is a coordinated plan of different actions aiming at the destruction of essential foundations of the life of groups, with the aim of their annihilation. Objectives include the disintegration of political and social institutions, culture, language, national feelings, and religion, as well as the destruction of the personal security, liberty, health, dignity, and, of course, the lives of the individuals belonging to such groups. They are actions directed against the group as an *entity*, individuals being harmed not as individuals per se but because of their membership of a target group.[32]

For Lemkin, genocidal coercion was a two-stage process – first destruction, then the imposition of the dominant group's culture. Indeed, Lemkin discussed cultural genocide in various ways – as a first step toward killing, as a technique of genocide, but also as the essential aim of the crime – to eliminate a group's essence and identity.

The 1948 Genocide Convention was still in draft at the United Nations at the time of Nuremberg trials of 1945–46. Yet despite the vast destruction of culture in the Second World War mentioned at the trials and Lemkin's lobbying at the UN, his proposed vandalism clauses were subsequently blocked by nations with significant indigenous populations. The United States led this opposition, supported by Australia, Canada, New Zealand, and others who worried about laying themselves open to charges of cultural genocide flowing from the treatment of their own indigenous peoples and forced assimilation policies. That there is a difference in peacetime between a dominant culture gradually absorbing a more fragile one, tragic as that can be, and a campaign of coerced cultural suppression did not blunt the opposition because many of these countries had indeed been guilty of coercion.

Eleanor Roosevelt, as chairwoman of the US delegation to the convention negotiations, argued that 'minority questions did not exist on the American continent.' Her position – an assimilationist view of the melting-pot character of American society – had no place for the 'special rights' of minority groups and left little room to consider the cultural deracination still being experienced by, for example, Native Americans. Australia also voted down the cultural clauses; it was in the midst of what became known as the assimilationist Stolen Generations strategy of removing indigenous children from their families. Its White Australia immigration policy was also set in place.[33] Norway and Sweden were among the other countries voting against the vandalism clauses, worried about the potential link between cultural genocide and the forced assimilation of the Sámi.

Denmark's delegate had a different point, arguing that the concept collapsed the difference between gas chambers and 'the closing of libraries,' rejecting Communist bloc arguments that the destruction of cultural monuments could, like Kristallnacht, be a warning of a genocide to follow. However, the Pakistani delegate on the UN committee debating the draft agreed with Lemkin, arguing that cultural genocide was the aim, with physical genocide the means.

The Convention's success was its potential application in peacetime, well beyond the laws regarding the conduct of war. The price of this achievement though was the exclusion of cultural questions that could come back to bite settler colonial nations especially. Lemkin was devastated about the dropping of the cultural component of genocide: 'I defended it successfully through two drafts,' Lemkin later recalled in his autobiography, 'but realizing that realpolitik would block the vandalism clauses,' Lemkin decided 'with a heavy heart' not to press the issue further.[34]

Consequently, after 1948, culture as a component of genocide was marginalised. At the 1961 trial of Adolf Eichmann in Jerusalem, for example, Salo Baron, the respected historian and friend of Hannah Arendt, was invited to testify. He was heavily rebuked by Prime Minister Ben-Gurion for emphasizing the effect of the Holocaust on Europe's Jewish culture and the potential for cultural renewal and restitution within Europe. Israeli historian Hanna Yablonka argues that this rebuke stemmed from ideological differences between the Diaspora and Israeli Zionists intent on building the Jewish State. Baron's references to cultural genocide were excluded from the Eichmann judgment.[35]

The exclusion would have consequences elsewhere, too. Following the Chinese invasion of Tibet in 1950, for instance, there was a wholesale suppression of language and religion, the destruction of both the theocratic state's monasteries and Tibetan secular architecture (replaced with Han Chinese buildings) and the mass migration of ethnic Chinese into formerly Tibetan lands. China's actions, its determination to suppress separatism, can readily be seen as an intention to destroy the cultural identity of the Tibetan group – even in the absence of mass murder.[36] In 2008 the Dalai Lama repeated his accusation of an ongoing cultural genocide of Tibetans by China. The Tibetans survive as a people but their cultural identity – or at least its material expression – has been diminished. What remains has been clung on to at great cost.

China never faced genocide charges for its actions in Tibet – genocide is a lot harder to prove without the intent that can be demonstrated by a pattern of cultural destruction – but, with the absence of Lemkin's vandalism clauses in international law, little attention is paid to these patterns. With the actions of Da'esh in mind, however, cultural destruction came to the fore once more when UNESCO Director-General Irina Bokova appeared to echo Lemkin's words in an appeal issued in March 2012. She stated: 'Damage to the heritage of the country is damage to the soul of its people and its identity.'[37] However, the absence of culture from the Genocide Convention meant that this and her other statements defending heritage and cultural pluralism were hobbled in how they could describe the pattern of destruction and its intent. UNESCO repeatedly used the looser phrase "cultural cleansing" rather "cultural genocide" – a terminology also used in UN Security Council resolutions. Genocide was only used in relation to attacks on Yazidis in northern Iraq who, under Da'esh, endured mass murder, rape, sexual slavery – as well as the targeting of their temples. But it was the killings rather than the cultural destruction that allowed genocide to be invoked. Even though neither cultural cleansing nor cultural genocide have a formal and precise legal basis as terminology, the UN and UNESCO would appear to be avoiding using the latter term for fear of reopening debate about the Lemkin vandalism clauses.

Even when cultural crimes do get to trial, the ICTY's proceedings have shown time and again that cultural destruction and the cultural component of genocide and ethnic cleansing is sidelined in favour of a focus on attacks against the person, forgoing the proper link between heritage protection and human rights. It was a struggle, in fact, to persuade The Hague that the destruction of Mostar Bridge was not an allowable military necessity. The episode was placed by prosecutors in a separate clause of the indictment related to structures dedicated to religion and education. This was an effort, some critical observers argued, to keep the bridge marginal to the proceedings so as not to impede the question of guilt on the wider Mostar charges.

Generally, more than half the prosecutions for attacks on cultural property at the ICTY failed. According to court judgments, this was often due to a failure to gather sufficient evidence from eyewitnesses and forensic experts, so limiting the contribution patterns of destruction make to a full understanding of what happened and also why – the genocidal intent.[38]

The crucially important Karadžić case, which more than many others demonstrated the pattern of persecution, torture, concentration camps, war crimes and genocide – the vast and murderous political project – was particularly dismal in this regard. While he stood accused of terrorising the citizens of Saravejo, the single most symbolic act of destruction in that city – the shelling of Bosnia's National Library – was struck from the indictment even though the International Court of Justice found Serb forces to be responsible.

Worse, while the Srebrenica genocide prosecution was successful, the second charge of genocide against Karadžić was not. The second, failed charge held him responsible for the horrors visited on many Bosnian municipalities including Foča, Višegrad, Banja Luka, Prijedor, and Zvornik, where extensive destruction of monuments took place alongside killings. The judges said that the prosecutors had not demonstrated that, in these places, Karadžić had the necessary *intent* to destroy the Muslim and Croat populations, so the genocide charge was not proven. That outcome could have been very different if the cultural component of genocide was properly part of international law or perhaps even if the necessary evidence had simply been collected. In private, former ICTY judges, prosecutors, and expert witnesses acknowledge the many missed opportunities to prosecute and the paucity of the architectural evidence gathered – even a neglectful reluctance to prosecute cultural crimes at all with, too often, cultural destruction still seen as an unintended crime rather as part of a deliberate, if not necessarily articulated, aim. In retrospect, says one former prosecutor, the tribunal should have had cultural property experts on its staff as well as lawyers.

Failures also happened at the International Court of Justice (ISJ), the United Nation's court at The Hague. Croatia had charged Serbia with genocide and Belgrade counter-sued. Both countries' claims were thrown out mainly because Serbia had not been a signatory to the Genocide Convention when many of the crimes took place. In an incendiary dissenting opinion, prosecutor Judge Antonio Trindade argued that the ISJ was denying justice by demanding too onerous a level of evidence to prove intent to commit genocide: 'Whether one wishes to admit it or not, body and soul come together and it is utterly superficial ... to attempt to dissociate one from the other,' he said.[39]

His written opinion, almost as lengthy as the official verdict and including literary quotes and philosophical passages, set out what he regards as overlooked evidence: the consistent pattern experienced across Serb-occupied Croatia where in towns such as Vukovar, Croat-built culture was systematically targeted at the same time as Croat civilians were murdered and evicted. This provided evidence, he said (quoting Lemkin) of a desire to eradicate a people. Trindade's critics suggested that while he has moral right on his side, he was attempting to circumvent the letter of international law regarding culture and genocide. Trindade, however, hoped his opinion would help bolster legal precedent or 'persuasive authority.'

The regularly trotted out but specious argument that only an aesthete with a warped sense of priorities would put crimes against culture on a par with crimes against people surfaced again with the trial at the International Criminal Court (ICC) of

Al Faqi Al-Mahdi for the destruction in 2012 of a mosque and nine of Timbuktu's World Heritage Site-listed mud-built shrines. Al-Mahdi's trial was the first devoted solely to cultural destruction to be held in an international forum. Under the court's governing Rome Statute, he was charged with the war crime of directing attacks against historic monuments and buildings dedicated to religion. Al-Mahdi pleaded guilty and was sentenced in September 2016 to nine years in prison. The decision to prosecute provoked hostile responses, notably from Jonathan Jones, an art critic for *The Guardian,* who wrote:

> The most precious work of art in the world is still worth less than a single human life. War crimes as a category must be kept distinct ... The destruction of art is vile and offensive to many – but it is not mass murder and we should not pretend it is the same.[40]

This is a false and foolish dichotomy when it is beyond doubt that attacks on human lives and on material culture are often bound up together.

Whatever the shortcomings of the ICC in terms of its lack of resources, its failure to gather evidence on other terrible crimes and, as some commentators argue, its focus on prosecuting Africans rather than politicians and generals in the West, the Al-Mahdi trial had been an opportunity to foreground the seriousness of cultural attacks, which had been side-lined in previous cases. The prosecution is to be welcomed if it helps people properly understand the true horror and intent that can lie behind the levelling of a monument, where the loss of a work of art can also be a step toward the loss of a people and their identity. This goes well beyond a failure to abide by the rules of violent engagement. Humanitarian laws and the laws of armed conflict need to be reconciled, and Lemkin's concept of cultural genocide needs revisiting. Those who have seen their cultural edifices destroyed around them understand this. It was ordinary Malians, not aesthetes, who risked their lives by forming protective human chains around their monuments and spiriting away ancient library texts, whatever Jonathan Jones might think.

CR

Beyond the 1948 Convention, the West's own 'civilized' values continued to be flexible when this serves its political interests. The UN's Universal Declaration of Human Rights, for example, was drawn up at the same time as the Genocide Convention, and in that document too clauses guaranteeing minority cultural rights were eliminated from drafts. Australia was among the countries that voted for their excision, and its attitude is typical of settler-colonial governments. Head of the Australian mission John Hood argued that, while he did not question the wisdom of the 'free development of diversified groups' for other countries, 'Australia had adopted the principle that assimilation of all groups was in the best interest of all in the long run.'[41] Assimilation can simply be a euphemism for cultural genocide.

It is an attitude that continues into the twenty-first century. The United States, Canada, and Australia all refused to support the 2007 UN Declaration on the Rights of Indigenous Peoples, which contains loose protections against the assimilation and destruction of cultures, even though a declaration, unlike a convention, cannot bind a government to act. The European Convention on Human Rights, meanwhile, has no cultural content at all. In any case, such documents focus on the rights of individuals rather than groups that may be under threat. The conventions around looting and on establishing World Heritage Sites are also silent about indigenous rights despite these issues arising frequently.

The struggle for Indigenous rights, the intent behind colonial campaigns to suppress First Nations and their cultures, and the role of material evidence in determining the past are still very much live issues in Australia whose history wars have been continuing for decades. Their intensity ebbs and flows but they never going away entirely as the relationship between Aboriginal people and later incomers is recalibrated down the generations.

Arguably, Australia's history wars began in 1968 when anthropologist Bill Stanner coined the term 'the Great Australian

Silence' for the way in which, instead of discussing the consequences of colonialism for the Aborigines, the only stories told
were of British exploration and settlement achievement. After
Australia became independent, the military sacrifice of the
diggers in the world wars was added to this narrative. Aboriginal history was, by contrast, suppressed.

Captain Cook in particular remains commemorated at every
turn – in monuments and toponyms, from a river and entire
town to a university and an electoral constituency. The large
1879 bronze of Cook clutching a telescope in Sydney's Hyde
Park is elevated atop a tall granite pedestal for easier exultation.
It took more than ten years to get it completed after a public
subscription to fund it fell embarrassingly short. The inscription
on one side of the plinth reads 'Discovered This Territory 1770,'
reinforcing the lie of *terra nullius* – an empty land ready to be
claimed.

The narrative continues to the present. In 2019, the conservative Federal Government announced a A$6.7 million grant to
the Australian National Maritime Museum so that its replica of
Cook's ship the Endeavour could circumnavigate the country
to celebrate Cook's voyage. Prime Minister Scott Morrison
claimed this was a 're-enactment' before it was swiftly pointed
out that the Endeavour only ever sailed up Australia's east coast
in a process of erasure via mapping along the way that gave new
English names to ancient Aboriginal places. The Covid-19 pan-
demic forced the cancellation of this fantastical voyage.

The UN Permanent Forum on Indigenous Issues has described
such 'discovery' doctrines as the foundation of the violation
of human rights, doctrines first promulgated after Columbus
returned to Europe in 1493 after his 'discovery' of the Americas.
Pope Alexander VI declared that lands not ruled by Christians
kings were available for colonization.[42] All this nation-building
with its attendant monuments might be less mendacious if it had
been matched by a similar commemoration of the darker aspects
of the Australian story, including the "exterminating war" that
saw massacres of Aboriginal people along shifting frontiers as
white settlement expanded into Indigenous lands.

The memorial site to the 1838 Myall Creek Massacre in the uplands of northern New South Wales – a series of boulders along a path – which opened in 2000 is a rare exception that proves this rule. William Cox, a road builder of the early 1800s who recommended manuring the ground with the carcasses of dead Aboriginals is, by contrast, still honoured by having a river named for him. This is far from unusual.

In the decade after Stanner, more writers published works addressing this narrative marginalization, raising issues such as the frontier wars and massacres that accompanied European expansion, the suppression of culture, and whether this amounted to genocide. But the Australian history wars only became a full-scale culture war from the 1990s when conservative historian Geoffrey Blainey denigrated this historical revisionism as a doomy 'black armband' version of history that made contemporary white Australians unfairly guilty about their ancestors while downplaying the glorious history of settlement and the heroism of Anzac troops. Right-wing politicians, radio shock jocks, and a ferocious print media reinforced the pushback.

When the new National Museum of Australia opened in 2001, a massive Po-Mo collage of famous architectural devices designed by architects Ashton Raggatt McDougall, its gallery displays were immediately criticized for being too 'black armband,' and the conservative government ordered a review that called for more positive aspects of the European story to be told on its walls. The debate revolved around the question of evidence supporting land rights claims, setting Aboriginal oral traditions (seen as unreliable) against official records that were partial, and in the case of thousands of police records detailing the actions of the death squads of Queensland's Native Police Force, conspicuous by their absence. Chief among the Right's history warriors was Keith Windschuttle, historian and editor of the influential conservative journal *Quadrant,* whose 2002 book *The Fabrication of Aboriginal History* focused on the eradication of Tasmanian's Aborigines and the question of genocide which Windschuttle effectively rejected.

The latest history wars flare-up has been over a book, *Dark Emu* by Bruce Pascoe, published in 2014.[43] It became a slow-burn sensation over the following years, resulting in a version for young people and a documentary by ABC, the national broadcaster. Pascoe's book set out to nail the lie of terra nullius, using colonial explorers' diaries and letters and archaeological and architectural sources to argue that, far from being a largely empty continent with only a small and scattered population of hunter gatherers, the hundreds of Aboriginal nations occupying the continent for tens of millennia had sophisticated agriculture and settled 'towns' whose existence had been systematically ignored to justify the theft of the land by colonists.

Such has been the horror that the Australian Right at the widespread interest in Pascoe's work that, extraordinarily, he was even reported to the Australian Federal Police for supposedly making fraudulent claims to Indigenous heritage. (Pascoe does not fit the narrow physical stereotype usually assumed.) The idea that Aborigines had a sophisticated civilization enrages white nationalists who otherwise happily lap up the curated glorification of Captain Cook, because the invasion of Australia and murder and displacement of its original inhabitants was intrinsic to the white settlement project and remains the very foundation of the nation's economy today which has grown rich on agriculture and extractive industries on the stolen land.

Anonymous figures set up a blog, Dark Emu Exposed – The Myth of Aboriginal Agriculture, to take apart Pascoe's evidence line by line, footnote by footnote, including its architectural evidence essentially in the service of historical denialism. Journalist Andrew Bolt, previously found by a court to have breached the country's discrimination provisions for his racial vilification, has been at the forefront of the ugly anti-Dark Emu campaign, questioning the idea of towns, houses, seed mills, animal pens, well building, and extensive aquiculture, and suggesting Pascoe has misused colonial documents. Under the headline '"Sophisticated" Aboriginal Houses – Really?' Dark Emu Exposed notes Pascoe's reliance on architect and anthropologist Paul Memmott magisterial 2007 study of traditional Aboriginal architecture,

Gunyah, Goondie + Wurley.[44] In its attempt to denigrate the very idea of Aboriginal skill, the blog suggests that the images of woven domed huts from Memmott's book that Pascoe reused were selectively chosen for their relative sophistication.

As Memmott describes in his book and as used in evidence by the bloggers, these domed huts are not from mainland Aboriginal Australia, but are more representative of the Torres Strait islanders to the north with their Melanesian and Polynesian links. Notwithstanding that the Torres Strait islanders are also among Australia's Indigenous peoples, Memmott actually does include examples of other woven structures from various mainland rainforest areas across Australia's north including Arnhem Land and Cape York (although Pascoe does not reference these). Similarly, Memmott includes a drawing of his own 'hypothetic' reconstruction of circular stone dwellings far south at Lake Condah in Victoria – 'hypothetical' mostly in the sense that their form of vegetal roof covering remains a matter of conjecture. The drawing itself is an entirely normal archaeological-architectural exercise.

The pettifogging anonymous bloggers argue that although Pascoe uses the word 'reconstruction' when using Memmott's drawing, he doesn't use the word 'hypothetical.' It is true that in his description of these buildings' roofs, Pascoe takes Memmott's educated if necessarily tentative suggestions as certainty, but the unwarranted implication is that Pascoe is attempting to deceive. What the bloggers chose not to include in their prejudicial nitpicking is that on page 193 of his book, directly overleaf from his archaeological drawing, Memmott describes how both the culture and archaeological legacy of the Gundjitmara was radically disrupted by nineteenth-century white pastoral settlers who drained swamps and lakes, knocked over stone walls, or recycled the stone in their own buildings and field boundaries, then relocated indigenous people to a Christian mission, effectively trampling down Aboriginal culture and the evidence of it.[45]

More broadly, although his stress on Aboriginal life being more akin to that of settled farmers rather than entirely nomadic hunter-gatherers is a welcome correction to the popular picture of Aboriginal people as listless desert dwellers living in pre-fabs or going walkabout, this settled farming argument also buys into Western concepts of what counts as civilized – as Pascoe himself has acknowledged since. Although they have now been almost entirely dispossessed from the fertile vastness of the coastal hinterlands, Aborigines flourished for tens of thousands of years before the invasion, and their right to the land or the refutation of terra nullius does not rely on European standards of permanent settlement, animal husbandry, or constructing chimneys. To some extent also, the critique that Pascoe was tilting at old windmills has some justification with good faith modern historians having long accepted that Australian national narrative had neglected the Aboriginal story. Yet what is accepted by experts clearly remains something of a novelty to the wider Australian public, and it is where there is lack of knowledge that culture warriors dig in and seek to sow doubt.

While the Right's criticisms of Pascoe might be regarded as bad faith, more recently a pair of good faith academics who have long worked on Indigenous projects including supporting Aboriginal land claims have also published a critique of *Dark Emu* containing similar concerns about viewing a hunter-gatherer civilization through a Eurocentric lens. *Farmers or Hunter-Gatherers? The Dark Emu Debate* by Keryn Walshe and Peter Sutton also takes Pascoe to task for playing fast and loose with evidence.[46] They argue that while Dark Emu 'purports to be factual,' it is 'littered with unsourced material, is poorly researched, distorts and exaggerates many points, selectively emphasises evidence to suit those opinions, and ignores large bodies of information that do not support the author's opinions.' Among the disputed facts is Pascoe's use of the record of 1836 explorer Thomas Mitchell, who was astonished to come across a deserted Aboriginal town that he estimated was home to 1,000 people, a claim described as 'pure fiction' by Sutton.[47] The lesson here, as at Auschwitz-Birkenau, is that the devil is in the detail and even the slightest error or overstatement provides juicy fodder for eager denialists.

At the same time, the lack of protection for surviving Aboriginal historical places continues to be a scandal. In 2020, for example, mining giant Rio Tinto had to apologise for dynamiting a c.46,000-year-old Aboriginal heritage site at the Juukan Gorge in the remote Pilbara region of Western Australia (WA). Blasting close to the sacred site is believed to have destroyed the only partially researched gorge where artefacts discovered in 2014 included plaited hair fragments from a belt and a 28,000-year-old kangaroo bone pick – Australia's oldest bone tool artefact yet found. Some heritage commentators likened the blast to the Taliban's destruction of the Bamiyan Buddhas and the attack on Palmyra.

The episode was just the latest in decades of conflict between traditional custodians of ancient rock art and the extractive industries. Mining companies argue that they avoid heritage impacts 'where practicable'; however, permission was given in 2013 under Section 18 of the West Australian Aboriginal Heritage Act for the work at Juukan Gorge as part of the expansion of Rio Tinto's enormous Brockman 4 iron ore mine. In the last ten years, there have been more than 463 Section 18 applications to undertake mining operations that would affect Aboriginal heritage sites in the state, but the WA government repeatedly ruled out further protection or a moratorium. Other heritage sites have been simply removed from registers.

Since the 1960s, coastal WA has seen widespread damage to the world's largest collection of petroglyphs on the Burrup Peninsula (Murujuga) where among some million carvings are what may be the oldest depiction of a human face and the lean lines of a thylacine, a marsupial dog extinct for thousands of years, as well as hundreds of aligned standing stones. Areas of rock art up to 50,000 years old have been relocated to build pipelines and are fenced off from their Aboriginal custodians. Anywhere between 7.2 and 24.2 percent of the area's petroglyphs have been destroyed since 1972, a continuous chipping away at evidence of Aboriginal occupation. At the time of writing, a years-long review into a new Western Australia heritage bill is underway. Aboriginal heritage groups have already complained to the UN about its contents that they say continue to weigh in favour of the mining companies.

In 2020, the Australian government finally nominated the Murujuga cultural landscape as a tentative UNESCO World Heritage Site, but this has come after decades of delays during which industry has been allowed to expand. National heritage protection was also conspicuously delayed to allow the work to take place, and this situation is far from confined to WA. The Murujuga is only the second human-made Aboriginal site nominated by Australia which instead prioritised World Heritage Site status for the Sydney Opera House and Victorian Royal Exhibition Hall in Melbourne as well as a collection of nineteenth-century convict sites. The Melbourne Cricket Ground was likewise protected as a heritage site nationally ahead of the Burrup even though it has been almost entirely rebuilt post-war. Essentially, the country seems to maintain a White Australia policy when it comes to its uneven preservation of the evidence of European and Indigenous history. The deracination of the Aborigines goes on, and a slow, peacetime cultural genocide continues.

In writing to a colleague in 1948, Raphael Lemkin recognized that, as on Kristallnacht, attacks on a community's cultural heritage may be a warning bell for genocidal mass murder to come. 'Burning books is not the same as burning bodies,' wrote Lemkin, 'but when one intervenes ... against mass destruction of churches and books, one arrives just in time to prevent the burning of bodies.'[48] He believed that 'Physical and biological genocide are always preceded by cultural genocide.'[49] A century and a half later, there has been precious little progress in acting on Lemkin's wisdom even though various bodies including the UN have been exploring genocide early warning systems since at least 1992.

In 2004, UN Secretary-General Kofi Annan, used his keynote speech at the Stockholm International Forum on Preventing Genocide to stress the importance of this prevention work and the forum committed to developing the necessary early warning tools. The same year, the United Nation's Committee on the Elimination of Racial Discrimination (CERD) agreed on a series of warning indicators such as ID cards indicating ethnicity, segregation in schooling and housing, and the celebration of historical events that exacerbate tensions between groups of people. Other statistically based initiatives to foresee genocide followed. They have indicators and risk factors as varied as steel production (for weapons) and infant mortality. None included the fate of culture as a measure until 2014 when a UN Framework of Analysis for Atrocity Crimes gave passing mention to cultural destruction as a risk factor but effectively buried it deep in pages setting out dozens of other indicators and risk factors, some so broad as to be of stupefying vagueness.

More detail was offered in Barbara Harff and Ted Robert Gurr's empirical analysis of genocides and politicides.[50] They examined risk factors including exclusionary ideology and propaganda, trade openness (a measure of a regime's connection to international norms), and an ethnically polarized elite. Harff and Gurr's work took account of news archive items that might include, say, the destruction of houses of worship, but this information was incorporated into the model's statistical coding under the generic term 'destruction of property.' The differences between attacks on representative architecture – a mosque or an Ottoman vernacular house, for instance – and an arson attack on a contemporary block with no group identification associations have not been captured in any model. These differences could be vital as a measure of the character, the type, tone, and intent behind the violence.

Harff has also written about the accelerators, de-accelerators, and triggers (single events) that could swiftly escalate already volatile situations. One thinks of the burning of the Reichstag in 1933 that led immediately to the suppression of rights and political opponents being flung into concentration camps. Or the demolition of the sixteenth-century Babri Mosque in Ayodhya in December 1992 by Hindu extremists that led to deadly rioting in Gujarat and elsewhere. That cultural indicators are generally excluded from these warning models or downplayed and buried deep within them perhaps suggests a lingering worry that the combination of culture and genocide could implicate many nations for the treatment of their indigenous peoples. Realpolitik remains an impediment to change.

Barbara Harff's 2011 list of countries most at risk of genocide or politicide was topped by Myanmar, followed by Syria and China. It was a prescient list. While the world was awakened to the genocide of Myanmar's Rohingya Muslim minority by the mass murder and the burning of Rohingya villages in Rakhine state since late 2016, their persecution as a group is long-standing. An indication that concerted genocide was on the horizon was the communal violence in Rakhine's capital Sittwe in 2012. Hundreds of Rohingya died there at the hands of Buddhist citizens, and the rest fled but for those confined to camps or the Mingalar Ward ghetto. As part of the violence, all Sittwe's mosques were damaged or destroyed. Some remain only as ruined shells, minarets rising above the encroaching jungle. This warning was ignored.

A 2018 UN Human Rights Council report found that alongside the planned murder of men, women, and children was the burning of hundreds of villages, the systematic destruction of mosques, and other religious symbols, and a pattern of executions of Rohingya clergy, artists, and teachers – the cultural intelligentsia. New homes and facilities, almost exclusively for non-Rohingya ethnic communities, are being constructed where Rohingya homes once stood while the Rohingya were prevented from repairing damaged mosques and madrasas or building anew. Those mosques that still survive across Rakhine state following the genocide are now shuttered and often under police guard, their congregations dead or displaced.[51]

China's Uighur Muslim minority are facing similar dangers, and the pattern of repression is straight out of China's Tibetan deracination playbook in seeking to destroy a group's cultural identity without resorting, for now at least, to mass killing per se. China's sensitivity to such accusations is acute; a Mandarin translation of *The Destruction of Memory* had to be pulped after its Chinese publisher censored, without authorisation, all mention of its previous actions in Tibet. (Not long after joining ICOMOS, I was also asked by a senior member to remove mention of China and Turkey from a paper on genocide early warning systems that I had prepared for a 2012 ICOMOS conference in Istanbul after being told that it was not done to offend participating state parties. Shamefully, accepting the etiquette at face value, I complied.)

The 2006 English edition had also hinted, if only in passing, at the incipient Uighur genocide, indicated by the Chinese government having launched a campaign of cultural suppression of the Uighur language and way of life in western China and by its proposals to demolish Uighur heritage such as historic quarters of the ancient Silk Road city of Kashgar and in other towns across the Xinjiang region. That brief intimation was entirely inadequate given the scale of what was to come. In the years following, Uighur women have been forcibly sterilized, over a million people interred in 're-education' camps, and Uighur children removed from their families. First, however, the demolitions began.

6.3 The ancient Silk Road city of Kashgar has been devastated by the Chinese authorities in what amounts to an attempted cultural genocide of the Uighur people, including by the demolition of its religious and vernacular architecture and re-education camps. China has been active in UNESCO to get historic Silk Road centres inscribed as World Heritage Sites – but not Kashgar.

In 2010 journalist Joshua Hammer published an atmospheric account of his recent visit to Kashgar in *Smithsonian Magazine*.[52] He found large tracts of the fabled thousand-year-old Old City destroyed, entire labyrinthine neighbourhoods of historic mudbrick houses bulldozed.

'Now the Chinese government is doing to Kashgar's Old City what a succession of conquerors failed to accomplish: levelling it,' reported Hammer. 'Early in 2009 the Chinese government announced a $500 million "Kashgar Dangerous House Reform" program: over the next several years, China plans to knock down mosques, markets and centuries-old houses – 85 percent of the Old City.' Opponents of the programme dismiss an earthquake-proofing explanation, pointing out that no inspection of the old houses took place before demolitions and that the most conspicuous casualties of earthquakes have been structurally inflexible modern concrete housing blocks. 'In place of the ancient mud-brick houses will come modern apartment blocks and office complexes,' continued Hammer, 'some adorned with Islamic-style domes, arches and other flourishes meant to conjure up Kashgar's glory days.' The government plans to keep a small section of the Old City as a museumized version of a living culture, but much of the rebuilding is of a type indistinguishable from the Han heartlands further east.

Hammer's journalistic telling was followed in 2012 by a substantial report on the demolitions in Kashgar and elsewhere by the Washington, DC-based Uyghur Human Rights Project. The report's summary characterised the destruction as a

> targeted and highly politicized push … Uyghurs view Kashgar … as the spiritual heart of their culture, a cradle of Uyghur civilization that is fundamental to their Uyghur identity. Once seen as one of the best-preserved traditional Islamic cities in the world, Kashgar's Old City is undergoing a transformation that represents an irreplaceable loss of heritage to Uyghurs and to the international community … The destruction of Uyghur neighborhoods has resulted in the loss of both physical structures, including Uyghur homes, shops and religious sites, and patterns

of traditional Uyghur life that cannot be replicated in the new, heavily-monitored apartment blocks where many have been forcibly relocated.[53]

The pattern of demolitions has intent. A 2005 Human Rights Watch (HRW) report had already noted that the attacks on religious expression increased from 2001 when the province became more restive and the construction of new mosques was effectively banned. But the policy may date back further to 1997, following an uprising in the city of Yining. In Yili prefecture alone, local government sources record that seventy 'illegal constructions or renovations of religious sites' were subsequently demolished and dozens of imams stripped of their credentials between 1995 and 1999.[54]

Much worse was to come. In 2014 the Chinese government began its 'Strike Hard Campaign against Violent Extremism' in Xinjiang under a new Communist Party boss relocated there from Tibet where he had also had a record of clamping down on religion and of increasing surveillance. By 2018, Human Rights Watch was reporting that at least one million Muslims, out of a Turkic Muslim population of 12 million in Xinjiang, were in arbitrary detention in prisons and political education camps where forced labour and torture are recorded. Uighurs were being forced to forsake their culture and learn Mandarin Chinese in an effort at 'eradicating ideological viruses.'[55]

'It is evident that China does not foresee a significant political cost to its abusive Xinjiang campaign, partly due to its influence within the UN system,' said the HRW report. China dismissed these allegations as 'fake news.' Then in the autumn of 2020, the world's media reported an astonishing degree of cultural erasure and further camp construction based on a satellite data project and fieldwork by the Australian Strategic Policy Institute. The study found that thousands of mosques and shrines had been damaged and destroyed in the previous three years. Around two-thirds of the region's mosques had been affected and around half of all protected heritage sites, at least one dating back to the tenth century, had been damaged or destroyed. An estimated 30 percent of mosques had been demolished and a similar number had features such as domes and minarets removed. Kashgar's sixteenth-century Grand Mosque, theoretically a protected monument, had been reconstructed at half its former size.[56]

A parallel project, for which architect Alison Killing won a Pulitzer Prize in 2021, involved her closely examining satellite images for their architectural features to help identify newly established camps, looking at telling details such as cell blocks with their rows of tiny windows and translating two-dimensional images into 3D models. Architecture as evidence once more.

However, as Rachel Harris, notes in an op-ed for the US think tank the Centre for Global Policy Solutions:

> Over the past two decades, China has become a key player in the international heritage sphere, an enthusiastic partner of UNESCO's heritage initiatives, and a world leader in the number of items it has submitted to UNESCO's prestigious [WHS] heritage lists.[57]

China has taken a leading role in inscribing various Silk Road sites on UNESCO's World Heritage Site list and 'positions itself as an international heritage leader while closely aligning this heritage strategy with its economic and political goals.'[58]

Needless to say, China excluded Kashgar from consideration for World Heritage designation.

While ICOMOS has made some limited comment on the pattern of destruction, at the time of writing UNESCO has failed to condemn China's actions or name them for what they are: cultural genocide. The inaction has been the final straw for some leading heritage professionals, Francesco Bandarin, a former director of the UNESCO World Heritage Centre, Jean-Louis Luxen, the former secretary general of ICOMOS, and archaeologist Lynn Meskell were among those who founded in 2020 the group Our World Heritage to help safeguard at-risk heritage sites, establishing a 'real-time crisis centre for the public, professionals, NGOs, academics and the media to flag and track critical heritage protection situations.' In the meantime, the persecution of the Uighur continues. As one former detainee wrote of her experience: 'That was when I understood the method of the camps, the strategy being implemented: not to kill us in cold blood, but to make us slowly disappear. So slowly that no one would notice.'[59]

7

White Lies, Misunderstandings, and Well-meaning Myths

A beautiful building could reinforce our resolve to be good.
Alain de Botton, *The Architecture of Happiness*, (2006)[1]

We need more history, not less, and we need more evidence of that history if we are going to uncover and preserve the truth. Establishing the real facts about the past means not just relying on documentation that the state is willing to release but broadening our sources, gathering witness testimony, uncovering more of the countless files that governments hide in the deeper recesses of their archives, and understanding that our physical world offers vital information, whether it be the materiality of reinforcement bars blasted out of shape by a missile, or the ranks of windows in a genocidal prison camp as seen from a satellite. This includes monuments themselves, which can be evidence of past thinking as much as past acts. Such evidence can be used to prove lies and unravel bad faith narratives as well as demonstrate truths. It should not be carelessly discarded.

Benedict Anderson's concept of nationalism and national identities being forged on the basis of imagined communities is relevant here. Nation-building demands that diverse peoples and sub-groups have to imagine themselves part of a greater collective – to jointly remember a national story through the public conversation and agree about what they share culturally. To buy into this imagined national communality, they also need to forget its inconvenient or darker episodes and, to some degree, forget their differences. In this way, imagined similarities come to define the nation instead of the complex and diverse reality of the world.

Similarly, Eric Hobsbawm argued that inventing traditions is an essential part of sustaining an imagined community and its continuity with an imagined past. Singing a national anthem, honouring historic symbols, and waving flags, he says, activates this through repetition. Where no suitable glorious past exists, it is invented in ways that are then used to legitimise the present. These inventions become exploitable for nationalist, ethnic, fundamentalist, or supremacist reasons. As opposed to the temporariness of flag waving, ceremonies, or patriotic songs, the apparent permanence and stability of bricks and stone seems to lend current circumstances inevitability – as the weighty and logical outcome of history and accumulated culture to date. Which is why, when the national story is disputed, the built environment becomes a weapon in culture wars. The intentional monument, especially the figurative commemoration, has a much harder time selling an illusion of neutrality than architecture because a statue's partiality is more upfront and obvious – more didactic in what and who it demands we remember and thus hold in common. This is among the reasons that statues are often the first part of the built environment to be contested.

We are not, though, as passively accepting of these invented traditions as the builders of monuments would like to believe. Self-evidently, many people resist and don't believe the statuary

hype; monuments are not that successful in achieving their ideological aims. There can be a folly then in believing that keeping
or removing monuments will alter the world in any meaningful
way. The United Daughters of the Confederacy and their ilk
may have *intended* that the Confederate statuary help keep the
Lost Cause alive and the descendants of slavery subdued, but
that does not mean that arrangements of bronze and stone made
any substantive difference to the success of Jim Crow. Likewise,
the Cult of Colston is likely to have done little to help Bristol's
elite supress class conflict in the city. It is hard to believe that
monuments help establish, in the Gramscian sense, a particular
cultural hegemony very effectively when we barely remember
who they commemorate unless attention is drawn to them by
opposition to their presence. Statues, monuments, and architecture are inevitably relatively crude and inexact transmitters of
ideas compared to, say, the way that the media manufactures
consent, or the role played by education curricula, or the policing of the family and morality.

However, the establishment, in seeking to uphold its monumental lies, probably believes its own inventions and certainly,
it will go to extraordinary lengths to uphold fictions and avoid
change, even symbolic change, fearing the consequences of
narrative illusions shattered. Donald Trump's law and order
rhetoric in the lead-up to the presidential election in November
2020, for instance, saw federal agents not only kidnapping anti-
fascist activists off Portland's streets into unmarked vans but
armed agents sent to cities such as Chicago to preserve statues
of Christopher Columbus militarily. This does not mean that we
should share the establishment's illusions.

There is a danger that campaigners are paying too much distracting attention to the lies and manipulations of monuments
and statues as the more obvious sites of ideological distilla-
tion rather than interrogating the more concealed power of
the wider constructed environment that may, in the longer run,
prove more insidious. In the United Kingdom, for example, the
profits of slavery not only financed commemorative public artefacts and institutions but were also the financial motor for the

construction of whole streets such as London's Harley Street and entire residential quarters of the capital and of west coast ports. In Bristol, the Colston memorials are only the most obvious elements of a townscape that is dripping in the legacy of slavery. From Queen's Square, to Redcliffe, to elegant Clifton, much of the historic city was built on the brutality of the plantation system. England's oldest working theatre, Bristol's Theatre Royal of 1766, was founded by fifty patrons who included leading lobbyists for the slave trade and anti-abolitionists.[2] The French city of Nantes, likewise, was that country's main slave-trading port, doubling in size in the eighteenth century. Its built fabric is infused with the trade just as that of Antwerp and Brussels, Liverpool, Glasgow, Lisbon, Madrid, and Seville are awash with the architectural, cultural, institutional, and financial fruits of slavery and colonialism.

More than this, when the slave trade was abolished in the British Empire, the compensation paid to former slave owners by the government under the Slave Compensation Act of 1837 was invested in the burgeoning Industrial Revolution, to build factories and railways, and to build up companies well beyond the ports, among them Barclays Bank, brewer Greene King, and Lloyd's of London and others that still operate today. Modern Britain was built on the back of slavery as were the economies of other slaving nations. In concentrating on monuments as individual bad apples, we may be letting the consequences of this much broader, systematic, city- and society-wide legacy of continued discrimination off the hook. We need to make sure we are looking in the right direction.

Attempting to shift the political landscape by refashioning only the commemorative landscape may, in any case, bring limited success. With honourable exceptions, Italy has done very little to address its totalitarian legacy. This is in direct contrast to Germany where surviving Fascist monumentality is limited. It is hard to believe that either direction has had much bearing on the outcomes of each country's post-war politics, whether on the electoral fortunes of Italy's Far Right or Germany's Alternative für Deutschland despite both wielding monuments and tradition as weapons. Germany's systematic eradication of Nazi symbols, meanwhile, has not prevented neo-Nazis marching through Dresden. Likewise, the suggestion that Italy's continuous political turmoil may be the consequence of a failure to reckon with its Fascist past may indeed be reflected in the survival of its Fascist monuments, but their survival is not the cause of that failure.

It is vital to keep both the value of the material past as historical evidence and the limited power of monuments in upholding falsehoods in mind and in balance when calling for changes to our monuments and cities. The comprehensive destruction of the historical evidence that the built environment provides would be unconscionable – but so is doing nothing.

To intervene successfully, we need to address two often misunderstood things: first, the myths and misconceptions about previous twentieth-century iconoclastic waves; and second, the impact of the constructed world on our sense of self and behaviour, an impact that is far more limited than popularly supposed. There are all sorts of misunderstandings about past episodes of mass statue and symbol removal that are being cited today as justifying precedents for a new social justice-inspired iconoclasm: the comprehensive removal of Nazi commemorative statuary; the sweeping away of Soviet iconography across Eastern Europe after the Soviet Union's fall; the Iraqi people pulling down giant likenesses of Saddam. Each contains fictions and complications. Their value as precedents for radical removal campaigns is in all cases questionable.

The considerable differences between Italy and Germany's reckoning with their respective Fascist histories and their memorial legacy has often been remarked upon. In Italy, where commemoration of its nineteenth-century imperial adventures, the First World War, and the Fascist period was often elided together, the nation had the considerable advantage of being able to conceive of itself as a Nazi victim after 1943. So beyond removing likenesses of *Il Duce* (an Allied demand) and seeing street names commemorating him and Hitler renamed with

Resistance heroes, most of Italy's problem monuments remain in situ; the country has done almost nothing to address its Fascist monuments and public spaces despite the considerable influence that Mussolini-era remodelling had on some major cities.

Not least, this extends to large sections of Rome including the most recognisable surviving Fascist building on the planet, the Palazzo della Civiltà Italiana, constructed as a showpiece 'museum of civilisation' for the ideology (and completed in 1953). The palazzo's exterior with its de Chirico-like arches and Neoclassical statutory is carved with an extract from Mussolini's 1935 speech championing the Italian invasion and occupation of Ethiopia – a campaign that involved the Italian use of poison gas and the mass slaughter of civilians. Yet the Palazzo is not a site of shame but is celebrated. An extensive restoration led in 2015 to a new use for the designated national monument – as the HQ for luxury fashion house Fendi.

Germany, on the other hand, is popularly seen as having successfully vanquished its Nazi past along with its related monumental landscape as part of a voluntary post-war process of self-examination and reckoning. However, this self-reflection and the country's inventive approach to creating commemorative 'thinking sites' and Mahnmal where shame is marked, only came much, much later.

While the Allies' focus in Italy was narrowly on Mussolini memorialisation, in Germany the victors demanded systematic action. There was a comprehensive sweeping away of stone swastikas, eagles, and the like under a 1946 law passed by the occupying Allies and carried out by its armies over the next eighteen months. Far from being an element of Germany facing up to its recent past, iconoclasm was externally imposed.

In any case, the National Socialist memorial environment was surprisingly limited in most places, with an absence of colossal statues of Hitler and similar honours. Instead, the Nazis made modern and novel use of the temporary and cinematic such as lighting and banners as well as the small-scale busts and portraits of leading Nazis displayed in the interiors of offices and public buildings. On the occasions when it did invest in heavily permanent monuments and architecture, abstract symbols of power including allegorical figures were, on the whole, prioritised over the commemoration of individuals.

In addition, carpet bombing had already achieved its own vicious remaking of the Reich's city centres, obliterating much of Speer's putative Germania, for example. Where widespread Nazi monuments did survive, such as in Munich and Nuremberg, they remain today surprisingly intact. Nazi Honour Temples in Munich were demolished (again by the Allies), but, since then, there has been little attempt to undercut the axial totalitarianism of the Nazi masterplan that was driven through north of the city's centre or to tackle key Nazi monuments such as the Haus der Kunst that is, for the moment, little changed. These specific places aside, the end result was that Germany's obvious Nazi party symbolism vanished. However, Allied collusion in the status quo meant that Nazi-sympathising judges, industrialists, and local government officials often stayed in place. The iconoclasm may have helped facilitate an illusion of thoroughgoing regime change.

This situation continued with little question for the next two decades. Germany's reach for redemption via honest commemoration was, in truth, hard fought for and emerged only after some appalling initial failures. Early West German memorialisation was dominated not by the Holocaust but by concerns such as the loss of its former eastern territories and used the language of honour and fatherland. War veteran organisations were active monument builders whose patriotic commemorative sites carefully avoided recognising the Nazi war of aggression or acknowledging its victims.

In the 1950s, these building programmes had government backing. The chief architect for West Germany's war graves commission was Robert Tischler who was, at the very least, a Nazi fellow traveller and who, in the interwar period, had designed dubiously *völkisch* monuments such as Fortresses of the Dead (*Totenburgen*) and a shrine to a Hitler Youth 'martyr.'[3] Astonishingly, Wilhelm Hübotter, the designer initially commissioned by the British in 1945 to create a camp memorial at Bergen-Belsen, had previously designed an SS memorial; protests led to his removal.[4] At the same time, camp structures themselves, the evidence of atrocities, the true touchstones, were left to decay by those who wanted to forget their crimes or were actively destroyed, including by the Allies and by survivors keen to triumph over the place of their suffering. It was only following a shocking wave of anti-Semitic graffiti in 1959 that a new generation of mostly left-of-centre West Germans began to properly confront the past and record the crimes of their parent's generation as part of the famous *Vergangenheitsbewältigung* (mastering the past) period.

As with contemporary arguments over Colston and Confederates, it took protests to usher in this change, taking place from the 1960s onward amid the era of liberation struggles worldwide and the growth of the History Movement and its radical and working class history workshops that sought to counter top-down historical narratives with accounts of everyday lives. Some of the German battles over commemoration stretched out over decades. Turning the villa where the Wannsee Conference ordered the Final Solution into a museum took a quarter of a century.

It was only toward the end of the twentieth century that memorials in Germany became, according to the writer Hugo Hamilton, 'religious sites that provide a new kind of holiness and guide us towards a fair and racially tolerant society.'[5] Absolution depended on documenting the deeds of the perpetrators and repeatedly visiting these sites, he wrote. In many ways and in many places, the contested ground of Berlin especially, the German reckoning was indeed creative, influential, and sincere. In other places it is not. Munich, for example, has over 100 monuments recording aspects of the war but, rather than condemning perpetrators, almost half of them honour anti-Nazi resistance martyrs – whose impact on the Third Reich was minimal.

Of great importance to the new commemorative trajectory was the Topography of Terror, a place that, for decades, was simply an expanse of wasteland along the Berlin Wall where locust trees had self-seeded alongside the rubble mounds. The bombed Prinz-Albrecht-Straße site once housed the Gestapo headquarters, the high command and security service of the SS, and the Reich Security Main Office. Now the site is a four-hectare terrain housing a sophisticated documentation centre that interrogates both Hitler's persecution machine and the collaboration of ordinary Germans with it. Led by History Movement activists, there was a determination to challenge sanitized mainstream narratives. They were also suspicious of traditional memorials and statues.

Crucially, the Topography activists took a careful, archaeological approach to creating their 'thinking site' where consciences could be examined. From the 1980s, excavated basements and fragments of structures from the blitzed and overgrown terrain were carefully unearthed. The horrors perpetrated from

7.1 An excavated vault at the Topography of Terror in Berlin. While a site of Nazi power, the vaults were from existing buildings of the site and were not a location for Gestapo torture despite dark tourists interpreting the remains in this way.

Prinz-Albrecht-Straße were then at first explored in outdoor exhibitions, including the now open-to-the-skies vaults of the destroyed buildings which included a former hotel and a school of decorative arts put to new uses by Hitler's bureaucracy of repression. The activists wanted these dark sites to be reinterpreted rather than erased and they argued against removal of even the smallest fragments. Commemorations being created on the genuine site of events displaying authentic physical fabric began to be seen as essential even if, many decades after the event, the physical traces barely lingered. Later a documentation/exhibition centre was built.

For Ulrich Tempel, the Topography of Terror's archivist, precision and evidence is everything. However, he says, 'we don't use the word 'authenticity', we use relics and traces and they have a special function.'[6] 'We don't work with emotions,' he adds. The facts themselves should be sufficient. Yet despite all the rigour, this strategy, which aims at avoiding the spectacle, has not entirely worked. The Topography was a place where Nazi horrors were planned rather than physically perpetrated at any notable scale but, to some degree, the Topography of Terror has been co-opted into the dark tourism circuit where visitors seek out the morbid and macabre.

The complex had only a small set of underground prison cells with torture and death largely happened elsewhere in the system. Some of these cells were partially excavated in the 1980s and corroborated by the testimony of surviving former inmates before being backfilled with sand in order to preserve them. Their outline was marked on the ground. A below-ground SS canteen was also found and excavated, as were the rest of the surviving tile-lined cellar vaults that ran under the vanished buildings along the Prinz-Albrecht-Straße frontage. All this is carefully explained at the site. Tempel agrees that, despite the interpretive signage and explanatory tours available, many visitors still prefer their own fantasy that the excavated canteen and tiled hotel vaults are the gruesome remains of Gestapo torture chambers. They want gore and violence rather than the banality of evil, the paperwork at its dark heart.

In retrospect, the Topography was a high point to this period of careful commemoration. Already other German memorials were, once more becoming political battleground between progressives and traditionalists. The changes to the Neue Wache on Unter den Linden in Berlin exemplify this shifting ground. It was built in 1818 as a Prussian guardhouse by Karl Schinkel but soon became a war memorial and has undergone repeated transformations in content and meaning. Today, Käthe Kollwitz's pietà sculpture 'Mother with her Dead Son' sits under the unglazed oculus, at the centre of the structure. Often surrounded by a pool of rainwater, the sculpture in an otherwise severely empty room appears the epitome of abject sorrow, a fitting indictment of war.

The truth is more complicated. The Neue Wache has had various incarnations since being transformed into a memorial, first to the Liberation Wars against Napoleon, then the dead of the Great War, then by the Nazis, and then by the German Democratic Republic (GDR), which reopened the building in 1960 as the Memorial to the Victims of Fascism and Militarism. In 1969 a glass prism and eternal flame were placed at its centre and the remains of an unknown soldier and unnamed victim of a concentration camp interred there together with soil from camps and battlefields. Following reunification, however, the Neue Wache was rededicated by Chancellor Helmut Kohl as the Central Memorial of the Federal Republic of Germany to the Victims of War and Tyranny with the weather-battered Kollwitz sculpture now personifying, additionally, the suffering of German civilians during the Second World War.

The final decision to place the sculpture here was Kohl's and provoked outrage and opposition from the Left and memorial activists. Some objected in principle to the re-use of a Nazi and Stalinist site for a new national memorial, others to blurring the distinction between victims of German crimes and Germans who had died in the war, in the process shifting the burden of guilt. An additional plaque was eventually added listing each of the various victim groups, but the disquiet remains. Personally, I struggle between admiring its austere melancholy and worrying about its problematic messaging.

Kohl's actions were emblematic of the post-reunification shift in Germany's national story. The Chancellor presided over a period in which the narratives of the expellees from the East came to the fore once more as part of a return to the immediate post-war memorialisation of German victimhood that was designed to allow the now reunited nation to have pride in itself once more. Perversely, that pride included the way in which West Germany had made a successful reckoning with its past but this self-regard was peaking just as the country was moving away from self-examination.

A similar trend was witnessed across the former East Germany after 1989 when monuments to the victims of Fascism in town after town were rededicated to the victims of war and violent dictatorship – more vague and more slippery formulations that collapsed the particular problems of Stalinist totalitarianism into the specifics of Nazism. This monument revisionism was sometimes related to groups such as the Association of Victims of Stalinism, whose membership had links to the Hard Right. It also had other Cold War antecedents such as the 1951 'Monument to the Victims of the Berlin Airlift' near Tempelhof Airport and the CIA-funded competition launched the same year for a monument to the unknown political prisoner to be sited in Berlin in a venture fronted by London's Institute of Contemporary Art. (Reg Butler's competition-winning, forty-metre-high antennae sculpture was never built and the idea died in 1960.) By 2009, the atmosphere in Germany had changed sufficiently for a national memorial to the federal armed forces to be erected in the capital. A year later, a new memorial in Dresden's Heidefriedhof cemetery, the '*Tränenmeer*' (Sea of Tears), was laid out to commemorate the city's victimhood at the hands of Allied bombing. The Far Right attends annual wreath- laying ceremonies there.

Three decades or so of official handwringing were apparently deemed sufficient to make penance for one of the worst crimes in human history; the country is moving on.

ℭℛ

Being under the Falangist thumb well into the 1970s, Spain's reckoning with its totalitarian monuments was different again. The transition to democracy following Franco's death in 1975 was founded on the 'Pact of Forgetting,' which, far from pursuing truth and reconciliation, demanded silence and impunity for the regime's crimes in exchange for democratic stability. Falangist monuments largely stayed in place and remained so for a generation until the 2007 Historical Memory Law passed by the social-democratic PSOE government. Finally, the former dictatorship was formally condemned and mass graves were opened. Plans were made to eradicate those Franco monuments that had not been taken down on his death.

A key monument to tackle and to 'depoliticise' was the *Valle de los Caldos* (The Valley of the Fallen) outside Madrid. It was built from 1940, using the forced labour of political prisoners across thousands of mountainside acres, as a place of pilgrimage and veneration for the Falangist cause. A basilica was hollowed from the living rock beneath the thyme and pine covered slopes. It is at the scale of St Peter's in Rome and above it stands one of the tallest crosses in the world. The aggressive classical architecture was inspired, like other Francoist monumental structures, by nearby El Escorial, the menacingly austere monastery palace of autocrat and emperor Philip II. 'The stones that are to be erected,' instructed Franco, 'must have the grandeur of the monuments of old, which defy time and oblivion.'[7] The desire to create continuity with Philip's militarism was obvious in the architecture. Tens of thousands of Fascist war dead were reburied here and the complex dominated by church institutions. At its centre, under the basilica dome, was the tomb of Franco himself where religious and Far Right *nostálgicos*, some sporting Francoist insignia, continued to pay homage after his death. Many Spaniards refuse to step foot in the place. Gift shop guidebooks, meanwhile, played down the Franco connection; the official literature somehow forgetting to mention the forced labour.

The Law of Historical Memory vowed to tackle this papally approved monument to wickedness. A commission recommended that, rather than the valley being destroyed entirely, Franco should be reburied elsewhere at a normal cemetery and the valley turned into a memory and thinking site for the victims of Franco's repression – a Spanish Topography of Terror. Changes were opposed by the Right and the church every step of the way. When Franco was finally removed to his new grave in 2019, his family and supporters chanted '*¡Viva Franco!*' The Andalucían priest saying mass at the reburial service was the son of Antonio Tejero, the army officer who in 1981 stormed the Cortes Generales in a failed coup attempt against the fledgling democracy.

In the years since the passing of the law, many more Francoist street names have been changed, and busts, equestrian statues of Franco and his acolytes taken off their pedestals, and commemorative plaques levered from walls. Nonetheless, traces remain across Spain. The name of Falangist movement's founder José Antonio Primo de Rivera, for instance, remains incised in large letters across the façade of Granada's cathedral, where splashes of blood red protest paint have faded to a soft pink in the fierce sunlight. The Catholic Church was exempt from the removal measures of the 2007 law; the arm-in-arm crusade between the church and Spain's reactionaries is still far from over. And across Spain, statues of the Caudillo may have gone but, less obviously, public buildings and urban quarters still embody authoritarian Francoist values in their architecture.

With visible reminders and symbols of Franco removed, it is possible that Spain will forget and fail to remember fully and honestly. No one has yet been held to account for the many crimes of the Francoists. There has been no reckoning with how far Francoism once extended throughout Spanish society or, to some degree, still does. When Madrid-based journalist Giles Tremlett got talking to a history graduate watching the removal of an equestrian Franco in the capital, he asked her if it should stay: 'I don't like Franco,' she answered, 'but I think we should remember he existed, just so we don't make the same mistake again.'[8] Likewise, Catalan politician Jaume Bosch, who campaigned hard for change at the Valley of the Fallen, said: 'I want what was in reality something like a Nazi concentration camp to stop being a nostalgic place of pilgrimage for Francoists.' Adding however, that: ' Inevitably, whether we like it or not, it's part of our history. We don't want to pull it down.'[9]

As with the Nazis and Italian Fascist legacies, none of these Spanish monuments or their removal can reliably be said to have significantly contributed to lingering Falangism – unless, that is, one believes that the presence of monuments keeps an idea alive. There is no evidence for this. Officially, the last Franco monument was removed in 2021 from the Spanish enclave of Melilla in North Africa. Opposing the removal of this statue were the Far Right Vox party that, since 2013, has spread from its Andalucían base to become Spain's third political force. Hate-filled, misogynistic, and homophobic, Vox has called for another Reconquista to drive Muslims from Spain once more.

Franco's body may have been moved but the Right and Far Right is still deeply mired in imperial nostalgia and, in any case, has alternative symbolic gathering places such as Madrid's Plaza de Colón (Colombus) beneath a statue of the explorer.

Sometimes removals are more about making propaganda points than attempts at genuine reckoning or reconciliation. As in Allied-occupied Italy and Germany, the removal of symbols by troops was also a feature of the Coalition's occupation of Iraq. It is a myth that the erasure of Saddam's image and other Ba'athist iconography was entirely an act of joyous spontaneity by the Iraqi people. Certainly, the toppling of some Saddam statues and billboards had popular support, but it was also a cynical exercise facilitated by an illegitimate occupying force. These events are often misremembered.

Typical is a piece in *Esquire* by historian James Stout written in support of the toppling of Colston:

> I don't recall many of these objections to statue-toppling when, as a teenager, I watched the 39ft figure of Saddam Hussein ... being pulled down from its plinth by an advance unit of the US Marine Corps which stepped in ... to do the job that Iraqi hammers and fists couldn't.[10]

Stout may be correct in calling out then newspaper reporter Boris Johnson's hypocrisy for describing this toppling moment in Baghdad 'democracy' while later condemning the felling of Colston, but events aren't always what they first appear. Footage of the felling of a twelve-metre-high figure of Saddam in Firdos Square, Baghdad, was beamed around the world as the jubilant act of freed Iraqis. The moment was later revealed to have been carefully staged by US Marines and an US army psyops unit promoting the idea of liberation rather than occupation. The cordoned-off square was mostly full of American soldiers and reporters who were there to witness the staged toppling but TV images give the impression of Iraqis taking matters into their own hands. The narrative of the US Army stepping in to help the Iraqi people is wince-inducing.

Donny George, the respected director of the looted Iraq National Museum, was wary of the extent of Coalition monument erasure. "These works … are undoubtedly visually menacing," he wrote of removed statues such as the four gargantuan bronzed busts of Saddam from the roof of the Republican Palace but he opposed the US military's proposal to the remove the 1987 Victory Monument commemorating the Iran-Iraq war. The monument is made up of two triumphal arches formed by two giant pairs of crossed swords cast out of the melted rifles of dead Iraqi soldiers. The huge arms holding the swords are modelled on Saddam's own. "Monuments such as these in Baghdad and other Iraqi cities must be preserved," argued George. "Not just because of their artistic importance but also because they serve a powerful purpose as reminders of the horrors of war and Saddam Hussein's legacy. They represent good and bad aspects of Iraq's modern history and cannot simply be obliterated."[11] And while "victory" is a questionable concept for that horrific, unresolved conflict, the massive triumphal arches, complete with netfuls of Iranian soldiers' capture helmets, are indeed a genuine, if distasteful, memorial to war dead. George also pointed out that the memorial continued ancient monumental traditions in the region, traditions and symbols that Saddam himself deployed, from archaeological sites to banknotes, to invent a tradition for a nation whose borders are a modern, colonial invention and which, he hoped, could help hold its diverse people together in his authoritarian grip. The deadly fracturing of this invented nation following invasion may not have been caused by the erasure of uniting symbols and monuments but it is certainly reflected in it.

Perhaps the most misunderstood recent period of iconoclasm, however, has been the purging of Soviet-era monuments, street names, and statues across Eastern Europe since the fall of the Berlin Wall in 1989 and the dissolution of the Soviet Union in 1993. This is also repeatedly cited as a precedent for the comprehensive removal of contested sites. Again, the removals were not always as spontaneous, instantaneous, or universally popular as often thought, and the topplings have a complex history spanning three decades and the entire spectrum of political meanings attached to them – from anti-totalitarian to nationalist and neo-Fascist.

In the Soviet Union itself, Michael Gorbachev issued a 1990 decree aimed at preventing the removal or vandalism of monuments and symbols related to the history of the state. Yet the following year, in the turmoil of a failed coup attempt, a statue of Felix Dzerzhinsky, the founder of the Cheka, was officially removed from outside the central KGB building in Moscow in part to appease angry crowds. This opened the floodgates and was to be the first of many topplings.[12] Thousands of likenesses of Marx and Lenin and other Communist heroes such as Rosa Luxemburg have been removed, so many in the Ukraine that a word was coined for the practice there: the *Leninopad* (Leninfall).

One's attitude to these removals is partly dependent on one's attitude toward Marxist-Leninism and whether one believes that it inevitably led to Stalinist totalitarianism. However, the response varied from place to place: In Eastern European countries with significant Russian minorities, statues might be retained as markers of nostalgia and ethnic and linguistic identification in a febrile and uncertain present where all that was solid was melting into air. In western Ukraine, for example, statues were swiftly and comprehensively removed, while those in the eastern part of the country were occasionally retained – a difference reflected in the conflict since. Even the removal of hate figures such as Dzerzhinsky was not universally welcomed; those clinging on to the rotten ancien régime or those rightly viewing the oncoming shift from state capitalism to outright capitalism with wariness were less likely to welcome the over-throwing of the memorials. Others, a minority no doubt, viewed his presence as a necessary warning: Dario Gamboni in his book on the destruction of art quotes one woman who wanted Dzerzhinsky to stay so she'd 'be able to tell her son that this guy was a bastard.'[13]

There can be no doubt that Lenin would have shuddered at the idolatrous cult that Stalin made of his image after his death which, in some ways, acted as a substitute for the potent reli-gious icons of Russian Orthodoxy. From his body on mummified display in Red Square to the Lenin portrait in every classroom, the cult was inescapable. It faltered in the 1930s when images of Stalin began to eclipse those of Lenin only to revive from the late 1950s when Khrushchev replaced Stalin with a revived Lenin cult throughout the Eastern Bloc and beyond. It has been estimated that by the time of perestroika, there were 70,000 Lenin memorials in the Soviet Union alone. Despite the impres-sion that Russia has removed all its Lenin monuments, some 6,000 remain in place.[14]

The fate of East Berlin's Lenin Monument provoked passions on all sides. It was a multidirectional struggle between GDR diehards, those East Germans who felt that their identity was threatened by reunification, and anti-Communist ideologs of various stripes. The Lenin statue was erected in 1970, part of a process of replacing pre-war symbols such as the ruins of the Prussian royal castle. Proposals to remove the Lenin Monument intensified after reunification in 1990. The statue's defenders pointed out that after the fall of the GDR regime, the Lenin statue no longer had agency as an oppressive symbol. They arranged a banner across his chest reading '*Keine Gewalt*' (roughly, 'No

Wikicommons

7.2 East Berlin's 1970 Lenin Monument. Locals, artists and preservationists protested its removal post-reunification and various artistic transformations were proposed. A Kreuzberg arts initiative hung a sash across Lenin's chest saying 'Keine Gewalt' (ie without force/power). The statue was removed and broken into fragments which were buried.

Power'). Here too, a commentator argued that statue retention might be a warning, guarding against the return of Leninism as a doctrine.

An exhibition exploring the question of whether to preserve, modify, or destroy Lenin and other statues was held nearby. One proposal was to cover the Berlin Lenin in ivy, while another artist wanted to project on to it, turning Lenin into a shopper with a cart full of cheap electronics in pointed comment on the shift to capitalist values. In 1991 though, and over the objections of thousands of local residents in the flats surrounding the statue and Leninplatz, and the opposition of preservationists concerned with historical erasure, Berlin's Christian Democrat senator for development ordered Lenin dismantled. East Berliners were outraged that *Wessis* were dictating history, and artists called the demolition 'primitive iconoclasm' and likened it to Nazis burning books. Such was the existential threat the Lenin statue posed to the new authorities now firmly looking to the West, however, that he was cut down, chopped up, and buried in pieces on the outskirts of the capital. Leninplatz was renamed United Nations Square, but for some time afterwards, street art mourning the lost statue continued. Lenin's silhouette was stencilled across the ground alongside phrases such as 'Against Iconoclasts.'

As a response, a Berlin Senate commission was set up to examine the future of East German monuments. It recommended that works should be retained in situ while neighbourhood consultations were carried out and opportunities explored to modify, reframe, recontextualise, or otherwise comment upon the memorials where they stood before any destruction or relocation. Gamboni quotes Christine Hoh-Slodczyk, a former monuments curator in the city, who warned that removals would prevent the 'historically necessary confrontation with the object' and frustrate the turning of 'symbol of power into a symbol of impotence,' of victory into defeat, that was only possible with the passing of time.[15] The head of the Berlin Lenin was later disinterred and is now on display in the Spandau Citadel.

Throughout this period, there was an unedifying gleefulness in the West at the toppling of these communist symbols, narrated by Western governments and mainstream media as the triumph of capitalism over failed alternatives. However, as free market capitalism itself was digested over the next decades and found wanting by some in Eastern Europe, the culture and history wars began to take on new forms – as struggles between Left progressives, liberal democracy, populists who want the market but not liberal democracy, atavistic Stalinists, and outright neo-Fascists.

In Estonia, the fate of the Bronze Soldier of Tallinn, erected to commemorate the 1944 Russian liberation of the country, is an exemplar of the tensions over interpretations of history, nationalism, and ethnicity that characterise the culture wars in Eastern Europe. 'Liberate' is the contested term here; the Nazis actually left Tallinn days before the Red Army arrived, but they retreated in anticipation of the overwhelming Soviet force, leaving Estonians to briefly reclaim their capital and declare independence before being swallowed by the Soviet Union. The Soviets then instigated an influx of ethnic Russians. Estonians were ethnically cleansed from some Russified towns, and Estonian monuments were removed. Russian speakers now make up almost a third of Estonia's population and, in their turn, suffer discrimination today. When Estonia won independence once more in 1991, many Soviet-era memorials in ethnic Estonian areas came down. For a while the Bronze Soldier survived but the 'war of monuments' continued.

In 2004, a memorial to Estonians who had fought with the Nazis against the Soviets and which included Nazi iconography was unveiled by nationalists in the town of Lihula. It was taken down days later amid violent scenes and eventually removed to a private museum.[16] The episode, together with the vandalization of Soviet war memorials, has been seen by some as evidence of the rehabilitation of Fascism in Estonia. Then, in 2007, the Bronze Soldier was suddenly removed from the city centre to a cemetery. Two evenings of rioting by ethnic Russians christened the 'Bronze Nights' ensued. The statue wars continued as the country lurched rightwards. In June 2018, in the ethnic Estonian town of Mustla, a local group put up a plaque to Alfrons Rebane, an Estonian officer who had fought with the Waffen-SS. The same summer a memorial to the Jewish and Roma victims of the Holocaust at an execution site east of the capital was vandalised.[17] Blue Awakening, the Far Right identitarian youth movement, held torchlight parades through Estonian towns. The 'oppression' supposedly caused by the Lenins and their like in public spaces has been replaced by political forces that do far greater damage than lumps of bronze or stone ever could.

Examined through a lens sceptical of cause-and-effect determinism, however, statues may hardly matter at all. As Gamboni asks, echoing Musil's point about the invisibility of monuments in ordinary times: 'Were the monuments of the Communist era received as intended, or did they also prove to be in the long run "immunized against attention"?' In Soviet-controlled Prague, for instance, certain statues had to be protected by the police from regime opponents but others were entirely ignored 'apart from apparatchiks and pigeons.'[18]

The retention of totalitarian monuments or their removal, like the style wars between historical pastiche and Modernism, is not about the embodied power of monuments, but their reflection of the power and intent of their creators and destroyers. They follow ideology rather than lead it and are crude and ineffective instruments when it comes to shaping or asserting power effectively themselves.

More generally, the idea that problem monuments oppress is itself questionable. Certainly, they can provoke a strong response. In New Orleans, mayor Mitch Landrieu made a now famous speech explaining his reasons for taking down the city's Confederate monuments, asking us to imagine the situation from the perspective of an African American mother or father trying to explain to their fifth grade daughter why Robert E. Lee sat atop of the city.

> Can you do it? Can you look into the eyes of this young girl and convince her that Robert E. Lee is there to encourage her? Do you think she feels inspired and hopeful by that story? Do these monuments help her see her future with limitless potential?[19]

Yet no matter how unpleasant the intent behind these monuments and however heartfelt the reactions to them, it is not at all clear that our commemorative environment causes actual harm, a harm that may arise either from a general racialised, gendered, and heteronormative national story, or from the individual psychological response of an observer to a specific monument. It may feel commonsensical that such harm does occur, but we don't truly know. Triggering, if it is indeed caused by memorialisation, might be as much a catalyst to righteous action as a harmful threat to a person. Likewise, we do not know of any measurable effect on those who don't see themselves present in the rich male, straight, and white commemorative landscape and whether harm actually arises from being othered from it.

In Caroline Criado Perez's book *Invisible Women, Exposing Data Bias in a World Designed for Men*, she sets out how, whether it is a comfortable palm size for smart phones or how a pedestrian-unfriendly city disproportionately affects women, the world is largely made in men's image.[20] Indeed, the various effects our created environment has on anyone other than a standardized man is barely measured, never mind understood. What is and isn't measured is a political matter and this extends beyond sex to sexuality and race. Some scientists are attempting to fill the knowledge gap. Ilan Meyer, a Californian psychiatric epidemiologist, for example, developed his 'minority stress theory' to explain health disparities between sexual and gender minorities and the general population as a consequence of stigma against LGBTQ+ individuals. It is important, however, as academic and queer activist Sarah Schulman has written, to avoid victimhood and properly differentiate between conflict and abuse. Overstating harm can itself cause harm, suggests Schulman.[21]

There is the risk though that dismissing upset entirely feeds into the Right's culture war narratives of fragile 'snowflakes' unwilling to tolerate the disagreeable. In their book *Cynical Theories*, Helen Pluckrose and James Lindsay argue:

> The belief that people are fragile and that they are weakened by unpleasant or upsetting experiences is Theorized within Social Justice scholarship and activism as marginalised groups being harmed …The commitment to always trusting one's feelings, rather than trying to be objective or charitable, reflects the Social Justice focus on experiential over objective knowledge. This is also tied to identity.[22]

The authors contrast this to the previous 'dignity culture' where people were encouraged to be resilient by ignoring most slights. Furthermore, she says, the focus has shifted from 'physical harm to psychological discomfort, creating an expectation of emotional safety.'[23]

There may be some truths here, but Pluckrose and Lindsay are explicitly channelling *The Coddling of the American Mind* by Greg Lukianoff and Jonathan Haidt with its problematically centrist assumptions and whiff of self-help.[24] That book takes the position that social justice warriors are fragile in arguing that anything that doesn't kill you makes you weaker: 'Their central thesis,' Pluckrose and Lindsay note, 'is that these untruths combine to produce a psychological approach to the world that functions as a kind of reverse cognitive behavioural therapy.'[25] Either way, she argues, there is reliance on authorities to resolve conflict. Schulman makes a similar point about the dangers of such reliance.

Yet not considering the emotional response to an offensive symbol can also amount to a failure in empathy and knowledge. Bristol-based philosopher and Countering Colston activist Joanna Burch-Brown helpfully considers potential harms caused by the Colston cult within the context of transitional justice to ask whether statues of human rights abusers should be pulled down and places renamed or whether such contested heritage related to slavery and colonialism should be retained in the interests of truth telling and to support a pedagogy that aims to prevent recurrence.[26] United Nations guidance on achieving transitional justice following serious human rights abuses aims to uphold four key rights: justice, truth, reparations, and guarantees of non-recurrence. There are conceptual shortcomings to this schema, Burch-Brown acknowledges, such as the implicit (but not necessarily accurate) assumption that seeing wrongdoers held accountable helps victims – or one might add, the unproven notion that post-conflict memorials or rebuilding heritage places such as Mostar Bridge aids reconciliation. But she accepts the schema broadly if only to wonder if it is applicable to outrages conducted so many generations in the past.[27]

The UN's 2001 Durban Declaration found that the slave trade was a crime against humanity and that the descendants of ensnared and exploited Africans have a right to seek reparations. These reparations might then include the removal of iconography found offensive. But Burch-Brown is also alive to the tensions between preservation and justice: 'Different historical eras produce layers of artefacts, and these accretions create a sense of historical developments, of distance travelled and changes over time,' she writes. 'Keeping historical artefacts in place can provide new generations with a window into the past.'[28]

Her argument is one that would support authenticity, especially where the true narrative of the monument is honestly discussed and it is understood that the meaning of, say, a statue or stained glass window celebrating Edward Colston is different in today's racialised cultural context from that of the Colston cult's class-conscious instigators. Monuments may even, paradoxically, be useful focal points for discursive critique.

> If that is true, then preserving statues may potentially serve aims of accountability by keeping their figures in view of a public that has since come to view their actions critically ... It may serve aims of truth if the dissonance between contemporary values and historical ones leads people to enquire critically into the many sides of history. It may serve aims of repair if these processes help to motivate symbolic and material reparative actions.[29]

Set against this is the risk that the very act of preserving the commemorations of racist, colonialist, misogynist, or otherwise discriminatory individuals or periods is seen as being the same as legitimising the original commemoration and so upholds not just past injustices and historical lies, but also the ongoing consequences of this past as experienced in the present, including affronts to the dignity of a derogated group. 'Removing honours from human rights violators is one of the few forms of corrective justice available when a rights violator is dead,' notes Burch-Brown drily. 'The more frequently people experience attitudinal and behavioural racism in everyday life, the more likely it is that colonial iconography will be seen as reinforcing wider social messages of disregard.'[30] Which is a useful way of encapsulating the notion that we might be far less troubled by the presence of offensive contested heritage and honorific monuments in our midst if we were living in a world where minorities weren't still suffering and oppressed. In such a world, old statues would almost certainly be seen as irrelevant and powerless curiosities. Which again begs the question as to whether we are endowing monuments with too much power when we would be better expending corrective energies on material improvements rather than symbolic change.

The question of harm is, however, commonly overstated. Burch-Brown quotes Chelsey Carter, who has argued that Confederate statues add to the stress of people already enduring racial insult with consequent emotional and physical impacts, and Travis Timmerman who argues for the removal of Confederate statues on the basis that they unavoidably cause harm.

In an article for the *Museum Anthropology* journal titled 'Racist Monuments Are Killing Us,' Carter writes:

> As a black woman, every time I pass a Confederate monument I am offended. I am reminded not only of my ancestors who gave their lives fighting for my freedom, but I am insulted by the fact that the city and country that I love continue to honor a violent faction of the country that devalued my life.[31]

But Carter goes further than being offended: 'More important than how monuments provoke me affectively, the perpetual assaults are unequivocally deteriorating my health and shortening my life span.'[32] This is more than splendidly polemical – she means killing literally. It is an assertion of physical and mental harm she reiterated in a co-authored opinion piece for her local newspaper, the *St Louis Post-Dispatch*:

> These monuments are part of an urban infrastructure that is violent and deleterious to Black and brown people ... their existence does wear and tear to some bodies ... . If harm reduction and accountability are the goal, the statues should be removed immediately. This ought not be up for debate.[33]

If such commemorations are 'unequivocally' causing physical and mental harm, then we really should sit up and take notice. But we have to tread carefully because claims of actual harm are very far-reaching. Carter explains that she is talking about how race has been shown to be a key determinant of someone's 'allostatic load,' the cumulative wear and tear on a body when one is exposed to stress over a long period of time – including by discrimination through bias, systematic racism, psychological trauma, environmental stressors, neighbourhood segregation, and other factors. 'Negative imaging in the form of monuments,' continues Carter, 'are psychosocial stressors that lead to deleterious health outcomes.' She references public health specialist Arline Geronimus regarding allostatic load and the papers of other academics including Clarence Gravlee and Nancy Krieger as evidence for her harm argument. It is a parallel stream of study to Meyer's LGBTQ+ and gender-focused minority stress theory, but what Gravlee and Krieger say is somewhat different. Gravlee's paper 'How Race Becomes Biology' examines the complex relationship between biology, culture, and other factors in racialisation including environmental influences on human biology. He quotes medical research including that which appears to unequivocally demonstrate the relationship between poorer health outcomes with racial residential segregation as well as correlations between the experience of racism and poor health.[34]

Krieger – who is addressing many forms of discrimination rather than solely anti-Black racism – uses her paper to make the point that there is insufficient research or established methods to understand the ways in which discrimination harms health, including the implications of spatial factors such as living and working conditions and that this lack of enquiry is in itself discriminatory. Krieger also argues that history is not dead within us and that historical factors such as Jim Crow or the discrimination against First Nations peoples are likely to have transgenerational effects on health – not simply inherited biological characteristics (and thus related to unsubstantiated theories of epigenetic inheritance) but psychological trauma – presumably transmitted via familial dynamics. Her point, however, is that scant research resources have been dedicated to these hypotheses.[35] The notion that actual, if not easily measurable, harm is caused by monuments is important and it is powerfully attractive with, for example, harm reduction arguments being used in defence of their actions by those charged with toppling the Colston statue in Bristol. But the idea of 'unequivocal evidence' for this harm is, for now at least, a myth.

Carter's stance finds different form in the work of prominent moral philosopher Travis Timmerman, who argues for removal on the basis of morality; he argues that 'people have a moral obligation to remove most, if not all, public Confederate monuments because of the unavoidable harm they inflict on undeserving persons.'[36] He writes that those who lived through the US Civil Rights era and the millions who have read the history of Jim Crow suffering and the history of the monuments 'suffer as a result of seeing, or even simply knowing, that the Confederate monuments are still standing.'

Timmerman's only evidence for this harm appears to be the public statements of mayor Landrieu and others, yet he is certain of a 'harm-based argument' for their removal on these grounds and that there are no sufficient countervailing reasons to preserve them that are 'equally strong or stronger than the moral reasons to remove them.'

Even if Timmerman is, in the absence of any evidence, correct, this might well be specific only to Confederate monuments and their ilk, because they were set up to assist in the patrolling of Jim Crow in concretely spatial as well as abstract ideological terms. The territorial dynamics around the Colston memorialisation, for instance, were very different – at least at the outset. Does that mean a different kind of harm is caused in Bristol today, deriving from the insult to recent generations of Black and brown Bristolians who understand the history of the city's slavery-derived wealth and its insensitive monuments? Indeed, since the Windrush generation at least, the impact of Colston's cult may have shifted to embrace not just the suppression of class consciousness but to upholding Bristol's ongoing racial divisions.

It may feel instinctively true that offensive commemorations cause harm, but instinct can lead us astray. We are investing too much agency, too much belief in the power of our environment. And when we give too much agency to designed objects, we diminish ourselves as humans – the crucial political actors in any situation. The meaningful amelioration of the offense caused by statues may be better served in the long run by removing the societal cause of the offence – discrimination – rather than its inert symbols. Statues are often images of killers, but Carter has not demonstrated that monuments themselves are murderous, and neither have her sources. Likewise, the invisibility felt by women and LGBTQ+ people by their absence from the commemorative landscape may cause offense – the lack of an official memorial at Dachau to its thousands of queer victims, for instance, certainly infuriates – but this lack of representation, an absence of monumental *beaus idéal*, does not necessarily cause demonstrable harm. Do we really need to see ourselves in monuments to feel like we belong? Are statues really effective role models? Do they represent?

Seeing inanimate objects as either harmful or helpful to us treads perilously close to the crude, cause-and-effect determinism that has been a blight for generations on how we consider the influence that the built environment has on humanity and its behaviour. This needs to be thoroughly understood before deciding how to intervene in the commemorative environment. Because running through the architectural and related professions like a steel core is the belief that architecture has the power not just to respond to societal needs but, through physical changes to the environment, to *lead* the transformation of humanity, to guide us to sunlit uplands – architecture as social engineering. This belief ranges from Functionalist utopianism to the nostalgic and regressive utopianism of the new Classicists and their search for fixed, ahistorical ideas of beauty.

In this over-reaching, architecture has been its own worst enemy, undermining its claims to rationality. Determinism has even reached the study of Confederate monuments in the form of a curious 2020 statistical research paper that seeks to connect the presence of Lost Cause memorials in southern US counties (most of which have at least one) to present-day racial income inequalities, considered as a long legacy of slavery. Despite finding only weak correlations between the phenomena and an acknowledgment that no causal link had been established, the study's author still concluded that this amounts to a rationale for removing monuments. The relationship between monuments and the contemporary consequences of Jim Crow spatial tactics certainly merits further investigation, but the contention that statues *produce* inequality in any causal way remains as unproven as the notion that a statue can kill you. Again, without denying the offense they cause, this seriously overstates the power of monuments.[37]

The influence of such determinist thought cannot be over-stated. The term was coined by Maurice Broady in 1966 who was concerned about its authoritarian role. As a practice it has its origins in projects such as Jeremy Bentham's Panopticon prison, where prisoners did not know if they were being watched from a central observation point and adjusted their behaviour accordingly. It continued through the Bauhaus and through Winston Churchill's dictum that we first shape our buildings and then they shape us. Equating architectural beauty with a happier society as pop philosopher Alain de Botton has done ('a beautiful building could reinforce our resolve to be good') is foolish when you consider the horrors plotted from among the architectural pleasures of pre-war Munich or Wannsee.[38] To reiterate, we can't blame a Classical style for reaction or Fascism any more than we can blame social media for disenchantment with a venal political class. Demands for traditionalist architecture are a reflection of social forces, not a cause of them.

This determinist wrong-headedness was boosted with the rise of behavioural sciences in the twentieth century. From the 1940s onwards, architectural psychology boomed in an attempt to understand the human response to its environment. In one lab test John B Calhoun crammed rats into tiny spaces and observed the males become aggressive and the females turn into what were seen as bad mothers. Calhoun's findings and similar studies led to the simplistic view that overcrowded, dense cities were making humans behave atrociously. Such experiments and views have now been discredited.

Determinism turned too many in the architectural profession into elitist technocrats wedded to top-down attempts at reformism. Le Corbusier thought that appropriate architecture could stop revolutions happening, while the Bolshevik Constructivist Aleksei Gan believed that architecture should not simply reflect evolving society but should be an active instrument for revolutionary change. Both were guilty of substituting technocratic decisions for mass political action.

Some formulations such as Émile Durkheim and Henri Lefebvre's writings about the relationship between people and space are rich and nuanced, but they are still informed by a belief, based on little evidence, that the very form of an environment (not simply how and why it is produced) drives beliefs and behaviour and helps construct our psychology and identity.

New Urbanism, too, in its championing of traditionalist neighbourhoods and architecture, has not only been hostile to high-rises but also to twentieth-century car-based suburbia on deterministic premises. Writing in 1994, architecture critic and historian Vincent Scully described suburbs as spawning grounds for neurosis. He argued that New Urbanism's walkable developments (whose classical and vernacular buildings, it was argued elsewhere, tap into deep cultural and psychological roots) provided 'psychic protection' against such neurosis – ignoring, the reality of New Urbanism's often gated, expensive, and otherwise exclusory character.[39]

Likewise, Kevin Lynch's seminal *The Image of the City*, first published in 1960, introduced a useful urban design grammar of edges, nodes, landmarks, and the like for analysing a city's legibility. Taken as a whole, however, it was an argument that people's perceptive capacities about the city and the way they navigate it could be set out scientifically and thus manipulated. Psychological and biologically based explanations of the causal links between the built environment and behaviour and/or identity have not let up since.

In practice, this determinist theorising has taken architecture and town planning in directions that should worry those interested in social justice in the public realm. In 1985 Margaret

Thatcher's preferred urban geographer, Alice Coleman, published *Utopia on Trial: Vision and Reality in Planned Housing*.[40] She surveyed public housing and concluded that it was not poverty but Modernist design that caused social problems.

The study used matters such as litter, graffiti, dog shit as indicators, as well as measures such as the number of children taken into care. She argued that this could be laid at the door of the design of Modernist blocks that had too many floors, or too many flat doors off the same communal landings and the like. Precise problem-causing numbers were given. Why Coleman's preferred model of traditional house plus garden could suffer as many problems as an inner-city estate when on a destitute city fringe, was never explained. Argued Coleman:

> The first half of the century was dominated by the age-old system of natural selection, which left people free to secure the best accommodation they could. The second half has embraced the Utopian ideal of housing planned by a paternalistic authority, which offered hopes of improved standards but also ran the risk of trapping people in dwellings not of their own choosing.[41]

The problem then was not only Modernist design but also modern state interference in the workings of the free market. Coleman's ideas jigsawed perfectly into Thatcher's housing privatisation policy under right-to-buy that proved catastrophic for the supply of affordable housing. The methodological shortcomings of Coleman's study, such as the lack of a comparative index of socioeconomic deprivation to compare to her design variables, were roundly critiqued, yet her thinking found its way into government-funded estate remodeling experiments and, eventually, into the present Secured by Design regime in which the police have a say in matters such as housing estate layout. Nicholas Boys Smith, Sir Roger Scruton's successor, is a Coleman fan.[42]

Coleman's work was heavily informed by Oscar Newman's politically charged 'defensible space' theory of the early 1970s, which had gained new prominence under Thatcher and Reagan's neoliberalism. His 1972 book *Defensible Space* was funded by the United States National Science Foundation, a federal agency. Newman didn't believe that mixing social groups worked and suggested that cities should be redesigned into secure enclaves segregated by income, class, and ethnicity.[43] His proposals were both theoretical and, in practice, physical measures against the pluralist and cosmopolitan city. They were piloted on public housing estates in places such as Dayton, Ohio, where a series of highly controlled fenced cul-de-sacs with only one policed gate were created. There is no empirical evidence to support Newman's segregationist theories. Indeed, most serious scholarship suggests that secluded cul-de-sacs do not prevent crime and that this is better achieved by traditional street grids where there is safety in numbers and a neighbourly eye on the street.

In the United States, Newman's theories also informed the fake science of 'broken window theory' first propagated by social scientists George Kelling and James Wilson in a 1982 article in *The Atlantic* and eagerly taken up by the New York Police Department and then by Mayor Rudy Giuliani as 'zero tolerance.'[44] The theory argued that not dealing with low level problems such as graffiti, public drinking, and vandalism led to a spiral of decay and serious crime. In other words, if you don't fix one broken window, a thousand more broken windows will soon follow. It is a theory that has origins in the same Chicago School of sociology that promoted the myths of the ethnic ghetto earlier in the century. In practice, the approach has been linked to racial profiling, stop and search, and discrimination against the homeless and sexual minorities. The theory has been comprehensively refuted including by empirically based studies of street crime that have looked at other explanatory factors for drops in crime such as changes to age demographics, drugs epidemics, and unemployment rates. Major crime was also falling in US cities that had not used broken windows policing at all.[45]

To support their position, Wilson and Kelling used a 1969 experiment by psychologist Philp Zimbardo in which he abandoned two cars – one in the Bronx, New York, one in well-heeled Palo Alto, California. The car in the Bronx was swiftly broken into and wrecked while the second stood unmolested. Wilson and Kelling made a prediction of the future of the area around the Bronx car rapidly changing into 'an inhospitable and frightening jungle.' Academic Bench Ansfield is not alone in pointing out that the Zimbardo experiment and Wilson and Kelling's use of it reinforced racialised conceptions and fears of the Bronx and the idea of violent ghetto formation unless zealous policing was bought into for the most minor legal infringements. Scholar and activist Dorothy Roberts has similarly argued that, in practice, broken window-derived policing policies criminalised poor communities of colour.

The theory's usefulness to developers wanting to gentrify an area has also been noted. Notorious, has been the sanitising of Times Square in New York where social cleansing has been comprehensive. Its early targets were non-resident, queer people of colour, sex workers and the homeless. As Christina Hanhardt writes in *Policing the Planet: Why the Policing Crisis Led to Black Lives Matter*: "These projects were facilitated by popular claims about supposed new forms of disruptive, self-chosen poverty. Drawing on a colorful vocabulary and detailed descriptions, journalists and other writers generated categories of people ("bag ladies," for example) and named them as the most difficult denizens of the broader Times Square area".[46] Amidst the Aids crisis, LGBTQ+ activists also saw the threat of Ronald Reagan's proposed Family Protection Act and the attentions of the Moral Majority as linked to efforts to clean up Times Square. This is a Travis Bickle take on urban design.

Over the decades from 1984, tens of millions were spent remodelling Times Square under mayor Bloomberg, with billions more spent building commercial redevelopments on the nearby streets erected on the back of massive tax breaks. True, the public realm scheme by architecture practice Snøhetta has created a traffic free area where tourists can spend their dollars but at the expense of the city's plurality and vitality. Craig Dykers of Snøhetta stands by his efforts: "The reinvention of Times Square stands as a model for how the design of our urban landscapes can improve health and well-being of its users while providing an important stage for public gathering." [47] While certainly a place to gather, Times Square today is essentially an outdoors lobby provided by the rich for the average American to access the surrounding opportunities for corporate consumption. On public land and heavily surveilled and patrolled by private 'Public Safety Officers' (the "eyes and ears" of the NYPD) and by the force itself, the homeless, the poor and the marginalised are not among those invited to linger. Applied, of course, at the discretion of a racist police force, determinist zero tolerance theories leads to tragedies such as the police killing of Eric Garner who was arrested for selling single cigarettes on the street from untaxed packets. An NYPD held him in a prolonged choke hold with Garner's dying words "I can't breathe".

In the twenty-first century, biologically based architectural determinism has taken on fresh forms informed by neuroscience, evolutionary biology, and genetics, often championed by architects working in the lucrative health and workplace sectors and similarly founded on little evidence. The arguments become less subtle and more ludicrous as they are popularised. Psychiatrist Paul Keedwell's 2017 offering *Headspace: The Psychology of City Living* is larded with deterministic silliness based in evolutionary psychology such as the need for homes to be cavelike refuges with views so that we can see predators approaching: 'wall to ceiling windows make us feel insecure and anxious.' Research, he argues, suggests that there is an optimal window size or solid-to-void ratio; thus, the most preferred (and expensive) houses in London or Washington, DC, are Victorian terraced houses with tall windows.[48]

More sophisticated offerings include *Welcome to Your World: How the Built Environment Shapes Our Lives* by Sarah Williams Goldhagen, which looks at 'embodied cognition' and how, she argues, places nudge us to think or behave in particular ways. Certainly, Goldhagen is right when she says that people live in bodies and bodies live in space, but this leads to claims that, for example, buildings without surface-based cues (unornamented Modernism) are not 'sticky' enough to engage the body's sensory and motor system, which in turn impoverishes us. She claims that the design of a school can account for up to a quarter of a child's rate of learning. A quarter! In an interview, Goldhagen praised the work of psychologist Roger Barker, who argued that when the individual psychology of children was observed while they were undertaking tasks such as breakfast, school, chess club, and ballet, the researchers 'could tell more about kids by looking at *where* they were than by looking at *who* they were. Their individual psychology, she said, 'mattered a lot less in terms of their experience and behaviour than the environments they were in.'[49] This simply cannot be true in any empirically measurable or direct cause-and-effect way even if we accept (as we should) that we experience the built environment in an embodied way and that there is inevitably a degree of interaction between them.

Still though, architects continue to talk of their designs 'creating communities' when they can do no such thing; they can only use design to create the conditions in which communities might more readily emerge or make design decisions which would hinder the emergence of communities such as dividing walls and segregation. In the final analysis, communities are created by people and their interactions rather than structures.

And as we have seen, in the fearful post–9/11 world we now inhabit, this intractable determinism found new subjects with the idea that bad city planning and ugly architecture help cultivate terrorism as part of a determinism-inflected antipathy to Modernism. Or that monuments can stress us to the point of harming or even killing us. An identitarian response to monuments can thus bring its own form of reductive determinism.

Even without falling into the trap of determinism, however, with all the lies monuments promote, the bad history they tell, the elitist ideology they attempt but fail to enforce, why bother keeping them at all? After all, their removal could make at least *some* difference. The toppling of Colston was not only a symbol; along with the Black Lives Matter protests it vivified (at least temporarily) the national debate on racism in the United

Kingdom. Against this, there is the not inconsiderable point of the evidential role that architecture plays in understanding the past and the potential loss of the raw material of history. This alone should be reason enough for giving pause before embarking on a new iconoclastic wave.

Total removal brings other issues with it. Burch-Brown frets that, if not done correctly, removals can inflame conflict in ways that are injurious to transitional justice and she's right: 'Removals may hinder goals of reconciliation if not supported by outstanding public communication.' They may, she agrees, be interpreted as evidence that multiculturalism (or more properly the cosmopolitan) is a zero-sum game 'confirming right-wing fears that there is a movement to displace white people and white cultural heritage.'[50] The zero-sum point is well-made even though the idea of a threatened *white* cultural heritage could be seen as being far too lenient toward a racialised conspiracy theory and the manipulated history it is based upon. Conflicts over the removal of monuments have the potential to do exactly this; turning the debate toxic, a competition over whose heritage is allowed expression in the public realm. This only intensifies culture wars.

Mark Fisher's pivotal, if controversial, 2013 essay, 'Exiting the Vampire Castle' looked at solidarity and class in an age of identity politics and social media trolling, argued that class is often abandoned in favour of lenses such as race, gender, and sexuality.[51] Understandably, Fisher's objection is that these lenses have no strategy for tackling the core problem of capitalism. He goes further, however, questioning the usefulness of identity altogether: 'It is imperative to reject identitarianism, and to recognise that there are no identities only desires, interests and identifications … No-one is essentially anything.' This is a somewhat utopian approach given that, under capitalism, the personal may not be inherently political but is inescapably politicised, especially for those negotiating a world hostile to their identity (self-chosen or not).

And a radical intersectionality is certainly capable of avoiding, at one end, crude hierarchies of oppression, or, at the other, a mechanical vulgar Marxism that seeks to ignore or dissolve minority struggles and their symbols into the purely economic. Such intersectionality does seem to have been gained ground since Fisher's essay was published. That said, it is still striking how the Cult of Colston, for instance, has been critiqued, with the exception of Bristol's Radical History Group, almost entirely through the lens of race while its class role has been neglected.

Similarly, Criado-Perez's *Invisible Women* often comes close to biological essentialism and its discussion of single-sex toilets and safety in public buildings could be seen as teetering towards hostility to transgender and gender non-conforming provision.[52] Indeed, Criado-Perez pursued her point in the context of a recent culture war controversy about toilets at London's Old Vic theatre despite all the evidence pointing to transgender people being far more at risk of violence in segregated toilets than cis women.

Increased lighting and CCTV to reduce the fear of crime felt by women was also addressed in her book, a demand repeated widely after the murder the same year of Sarah Everard walking home from a south London park after dark. The risks arising out of these measures include handing further powers to the security state and simply shifting the issue elsewhere. Oversimplified, determinist responses stem from seeing the problem as one of the urban environment rather than one of male violence.

Even the language used in these debates can have its meaning re-aligned. Words such as 'material,' 'reality,' and 'truth' are now being used by trans-exclusory writers in their appeals to a reductive biological essentialism that champions both the fiction of rigid sexual dimorphism rather than the complex reality of the gender spectrum, at the same time as weaponizing social construction in a way that is determinist in the name of exclusion. Theoretical debates have real-world consequences in terms of determining those for whom physical safe spaces are made available and encouraging governments to patrol the boundaries of sex and sexuality, including legislating for where you get to pee.

ଔ

In light of all this, our current obsession with symbols might be focusing too much on the cosmetic end of identity. The idea of offence archaeology comes from the same right-wing grab-bag of dim-witted complaints that panic about cancel culture, but being concerned only with the offence caused by the pedestal honours given to historic killers rather than real world discrimination would indeed be a problem. Those engaged in producing the built environment need to understand the dangers of siting their measures of progress in identity-based culture wars rather than in material gains for our cities. These are questions not of aims but of tactics for achieving equity and for meaningfully challenging capitalism.

In her paper, Joanna Burch-Brown suggests that 'if you give the statues a shake, the structures will wobble,' referring to structural inequalities. Is this true? Former Black Panther Angela Davis, whose childhood friends died in the 1963 Ku Klux Klan bombing of the 16th Street Baptist Church in her hometown Birmingham, Alabama, is among those not convinced about the focus on symbols: 'Regardless of what people think about it,' she said of the humbling of Edward Colston, 'It's really not going to bring about change.' What matters, says Davis, is organising.[53] Elsewhere, Davis has clarified that while the demonstrations around monuments are important, we cannot simply get rid of unwanted history:

> We have to recognize the devastatingly negative role that that history has played in charting the trajectory of the United States of America. I don't think we should get rid of all of the vestiges of the past, but we need to figure out [a] context within which people can understand ... U.S. history and the role that racism and capitalism and heteropatriarchy have played in forging that history.[54]

Davis sees the assaults on statues as representing the beginnings of thinking through what needs to be done 'to bring down institutions.'[55]

Similarly, prominent civil rights movement activist Andrew Young has argued that Stone Mountain in Georgia, despite being one of the world's largest racist sculptures, created on a Klan supporter's land with Klan money, should stay where it is: 'I'm saying these are kids [of today] who grew up free...they don't realize what still enslaves them – and it's not those monuments.'[56] Comprehensive removals may even foster illusions of meaningful change. Zyhana Bryant, a student who began a petition to take down Confederate monuments including one outside Charlottesville's courthouse, observed: 'We are making the courthouse look more equitable without reckoning with the institutional racism that takes place inside.'[57] There is no direct, cause-and-effect connection between progressive monuments and social progress.

Champions of memorial removal react strongly to accusations that they are seeking to erase history. Statues, they argue, are not history and their actions are about making new history rather than changing the past. People are here confusing narratives about the past with the material facts of the past. Historian David Olusoga, who is deeply engaged with Britain's Black history, is among those who point out that many in Brexit Britain do not want to hear more about the facts of history: 'It has now got to the point where some of the statements being made are so easily refutable, so verifiably and unquestionably false, that you have to presume that the people writing them know that,' he told *The Guardian*.

> And that must lead you to another assumption, which is that they know that this is not true, but they have decided that these national myths are so important to them and their political projects, or their sense of who they are, that they don't really care about the historical truths behind them.[58]

As a summation of the place of monuments in the culture wars, this is spot on.

One would presume, then, that Olusoga would be keen to explore all the available evidence of these false narratives, whatever form that evidence takes – be it document, architecture, or monument. However, he is among a number of figures who take the view that monuments are not history at all. In a BBC interview, Olusoga said that it is 'palpable nonsense' that removing controversial statues 'somehow impoverishes history.' He added: 'It's not just that the statues we've got don't tell us our history – statues cannot tell us our history because they're acutely incapable of performing that role ... History is fluid and mobile and plastic. Statues are literally immobile – they're set in stone.'[59]

Gary Younge, sociology professor at the University of Manchester's Centre on the Dynamics of Ethnicity who helmed a report into problem monuments, also argued in *The Guardian* that the claim that statue removal erases history is 'arrant nonsense.' He writes:

> Statues are not history: They represent historical figures. They may have been set up to mark a person's historical contribution, but they are not themselves history ... to claim that statues represent history does not merely misrepresent the role of statues, it misunderstands history and their place in it.[60]

He suggested that all of them should be swept away – both those celebrating the establishment and those honouring human rights campaigners. It is a position that at least has consistency even if does not recognise that we do not only learn about history from words on a page.

Olusoga described the Colston statue as a 'mediocre piece of late-Victorian public art' (which it is) and argued that it said 'nothing truthful or of interest about Bristol.'[61] At the same time, Olusoga also stated (somewhat confusingly) that the Colston statue was never an historical artefact 'because statues on public display ... aren't artefacts, they are totems of power.' This status inexplicably changed once Colston's bronze was relocated out of its original context and into a museum:

Now I think it's the most important artefact you could select in Britain if you wanted to tell the story of Britain's tortuous relationship with its role in the Atlantic slave trade. It's now a historical artefact and it has multiple meanings and multiple layers to it. It speaks to multiple periods in its history and Bristol's history.[62]

One can only presume that he means that the object can be properly interpreted only in a museum context. There is not much logic to this position. An item can be both artefact and totem, of course, and what is history but the story of power relations?

We learn about history from many things that are not written texts, things as varied as statues, hairstyles, food, sexual mores, human-modified landscapes, and built townscapes – the list is endless. In some ways, the suspicion that artefacts are not genuine historical source material feels like a hangover from the eighteenth- and nineteenth-century stand-off between the academic historian relying solely on written records and the antiquarian interested in interpreting the physical world as a legitimate primary source. That the latter were often non-conformist or in some other way outside the university elite and circle of gentleman amateurs may have contributed to snobbish attitudes towards their work – especially paid work – but their eccentricities were also notable. For every Thomas Rickman, the Quaker architect who carefully traced the evolution of English Gothic architecture, there were many crackpot snappers-up of unconsidered trifles. But as architectural historian Rosemary Hill observes, one origin for the idea of the architectural as evidence, well before Ruskin and Morris, was the antiquarian campaign led by Richard Gough to stop architect James Wyatt destroying artefacts in his late eighteenth-century remodeling of Salisbury Cathedral because these artefacts offered insights into the ways of life, the 'men and manners of the past.[63]

It is true though, that we learn more about the contemporary values of the best of us from Colston's battered and paint splashed bronze wherever it ends up than when it was honoured on its plinth unchanged. While monuments and architecture are vital evidence of the past, this does not mean that all monuments have to remain in their current positions forever – many statues have been moved many times over the centuries. Or that monuments, buildings and cities cannot change and evolve. That would be nonsense. However, when we are dealing with evidence, we need to act with intense awareness to avoid distorting the material historical record or relying on often unreliable historical memory.

A simple lack of statues of slave owners will not necessarily mean people in the future denying the historical reality of the trade in humans. But, however tainted, these memorials confront us with the reality of how elites have seen fit to honour horrors in public – they teach us about the shameless values of the establishment and they remind us of past injustices lest we forget. It is the lies not the truths of the Colston statue and its ilk that are so revealing of the trajectory of history, as Angela Davis says. We do not have to take a statue at face value any more than we do a text. The removal of touchstones, this public history and public memory, will affect our understanding of the past, and we must acknowledge that in our decision-making. Total removal of problem monuments can only make the story less complete. Clearly, there is a tension between a historian's concern for the sanctity of evidence and justifiable distaste at the misplaced honours, but in the absence of demonstrable harm being caused we must be cautious. As Jean-François Manicom, curator of Liverpool's International Slavery Museum, has said: 'What we display is not an easy subject. It is painful but we refuse to brush it under the carpet.'[64]

One could argue then that a simple solution is to remove problem monuments to museums where painful objects do not confront us on the way to work. This may well be appropriate in some circumstances, but it can also overly depoliticise problem memorials, turning them into simply aesthetic objects without necessarily tackling them as honorific objects. At this same time, their museumification may hinder our ability to understand the intent behind the placement of these objects within the public realm. The Jefferson School African American Heritage Center in Virginia wants to go further, melting down the removed Charlottesville statue of Robert E. Lee to create a new public artwork in a programme it calls 'Swords into Plowshares.' This may be making history, but it is undeniably erasing an historical artefact at the same time. Arguably, it is destroying the evidence of a crime at the same time as removing an instrument of the commission of that crime.

It is taking an overly narrow view of the primacy of the physical world to not see that public monuments on the street, and the architectural more broadly, are just as much historical sources as a census return or court records. And we learn different things from understanding them in their street context and about the interactions between people and place, than we do from an object in a museum exhibition case. Interpretation can happen in situ as well as in a gallery.

What, for instance, was the purpose, the political message, behind erecting a bronze of Clive of India in Whitehall in 1912, centuries after his death but in the midst of unrest in imperial Bengal? Colston, Clive or Confederate, the erection of memorials decades or centuries after the subject's death is a sure sign of historical manipulation underway. But what was the intent in moving Clive only four years later in the middle of the First World War from Whitehall to a prominent place just outside the Foreign Office? To my mind, the erection and relocation of the statue demonstrates concretely the cynicism of our ruling class and its manipulation of the imperial narrative. Our offense at its prime location is, to some degree, useful – which is not an absolute argument against moving it once more. Again, a memorial can be both be a problem narrative but source of historical evidence at the same time.

Academic Macalester Bell comes at total removal from a similar angle: showing our contempt for discriminatory monuments is the correct thing to do, she argues, and warns that total removal simply absents the figure from public critique and so fails to express this contempt effectively.[65] When such complexities are considered, Travis Timmerman's claim that there are no countervailing moral reasons for preserving monuments and that 'whatever knowledge would be lost by removing the monuments could be compensated for by the creation of additional education resources' is revealed to be overly simplistic.[66]

When Timmerman writes that any information one gains from looking at a statue, or reading a plaque on a monument, 'could be found by going on Wikipedia' there is a profound philistinism operating about the historical value of the material world as well as a lack of understanding about how context is key to our reading of objects in the built environment. Evidence not only needs the material record to be authentic if it is to be credible; it also needs to be safeguarded, including from myths and misunderstandings about the benefits of wholesale iconoclastic removal.

At the same time, this does not mean that we can do nothing about offensive and lying monuments. We cannot leave it to the Right to impose bad-faith solution such as the British government's 'retain and explain' policy, which seeks to retain all and explain nothing. It is the heritage equivalent of greenwashing. Another approach entirely is necessary.

8

Subversive Transformation

No one has the right to obey.

Hannah Arendt, radio interview (1964)[1]

Hannes Obermair and I are in Bolzano-Bozen in front of the cinema screen vastness of Hans Piffrader's Mussolini frieze. With the Monument to Victory successfully tagged as a criminal by the circular digital signage clamped around one leg of its arch, attention did indeed turn to the frieze. One of Europe's largest Fascist artworks is still there but, today, standing proud of the stonework and running in front of the bas-relief, are letters, each just over a foot high, that illuminate as the daylight fades, letters that will soon reflect their LED glow in the summer puddles. They spell out: 'No-One Has the Right to Obey'.

The wording in three languages (German, Italian, and the local Ladin) is from a radio interview where Hannah Arendt was paraphrasing Kant while discussing her book about the Eichmann trial. The choice of words for Bolzano is a clever, layered commentary on the Fascist slogan BELIEVE, OBEY, FIGHT, carved into the frieze which, along with the rest of the entire artwork, remains visible beneath the new, lucid letters. The monument is preserved but its meaning has been changed

8.1 Bolzano-Bozen's Fascist frieze gained a new layer following an arts competition. 'No One Has the Right to Obey' is Hannah Arendt paraphrasing Kant. The illuminated lettering turns the frieze from site of honour to a *Mahnmal* – a site of admonishment or warning – without removing the evidence of history.

by the addition of the condemnatory phrase. Arendt is reminding us that we have an ethical duty to resist, that there is always a choice, including whether we properly act to address contested heritage in ways that serve both justice and history. Truths are being told. An Ehrenmal has become a Mahnmal, a site of honour is now a site of shame.

Instead of the erasure of evidence, we have another layer of history that intelligently comments on its predecessor. It is a subversive transformation that risks neither denial or forgetting nor leaves a repugnant commemoration unchallenged. The frieze now invites people to reflect on this history and its complex layers. 'It is deliberately tricky and questioning,' says Hannes of the chosen quotation. 'And is by far the most intelligent response. It humiliates the frieze.' Humour, he notes, is not something totalitarians are very good at, which is why humiliation is such a useful oppositional tool. Even so, the letters do not stand alone and unexplained; there is a linear plaque in the square, many metres long, that explains the full facts of the monument and the changes made to it. This is what genuine, good faith 'retain and explain' looks like.

Rather than accepting, unquestioningly, a new iconoclastic wave, intelligent transformations can tell truths about history without destroying the authentic evidence of that history, and places such as Bolzano show the way. Such an approach demands substantive interventions at scale. Adding a small plaque with mealy mouthed wording that one must stoop to read as installed at Oriel College does nothing to undercut the great honour given to Cecil Rhodes by his statue's position. His commanding figure still crowns the substantial stone college building named for him. Better, perhaps, that his statue is turned so he faces his niche, shamed in the full view of the city's High Street shoppers – or some other intervention found. New layers for commemorations that challenge their record and provide a form of contestation are best when they do not entirely obliterate the original but instead allow it to be simultaneously understood and undermined. These additive transformations have the capacity to change meaning in ways entire removal cannot achieve; to create thinking sites where consciences are examined. They separate out reverence from remembrance. They allow us to accumulate the material of history rather than diminish it.

It is an approach akin to 'critical reconstruction' in architecture where post-war ruins were restored in ways that incorporate the scars of past conflict in line with the Venice Charter and the Society for the Protection of Ancient Buildings manifesto. These make a substantial difference to truth in the townscape. In Munich, for example, the post-war reconstruction of the Alte Pinakothek does not seek to hide the ravages of war but to incorporate them. Instead of installing new decorative stonework to recreate the half-destroyed building exactly as it was, architect Hans Döllgast designed an elegant collage of brickwork, much of it retrieved from Munich bombsites, to substitute in the gaps. It is beautifully done, an architectural *kintsugi* – the cracks in Japanese ceramics repaired in gold – which completes the composition without disrupting it. It is also truthful. Döllgast had to campaign hard for years to ensure this honest approach, and traditionalists have since repeatedly pushed to undo his critical reconstruction approach and reinstate the gallery's original pre-war facades. The best architects, however, have been taking note of Döllgast's critical reconstruction. David Chipperfield and conservation architect Julian Harrap's hugely successful col-laged reworking of the once ruined Neues Museum in Berlin is a case in point – even extending it with a new wing and a Mod-ernist colonnade inspired by, but not aping, the Classical orders. Astonishingly, by contrast, the Bauhaus Museum in Weimar that opened in 2019 might be clearly a contemporary building, but its architect Heike Hanada thought it fine to quote the lines and form of the Gauforum, the Nazi parade ground opposite, in the new museum's monumental façade.

Chipperfield has now been appointed to remodel Munich's Haus der Kunst, the city's leading contemporary art gallery, but one housed in a columned Nazi temple commissioned by Hitler. It escaped bombing and remains intact with its Brobdingnagian doorways and a portico complete with swastika mosaics in its soffit. This is where the infamous, anti-Modernist degenerate art exhibition was held in 1937. It is a fraught process for Munich. Chipperfield had suggested early on that part of an honest reck-oning with the building might include chopping down the row of trees seemingly planted to hide the embarrassing edifice from the city. The suggestion provoked vocal opposition, not for the loss of the trees per se but for what might be revealed. Chipper-field is asking if the building can be forgiven or whether it will always be tarnished. 'Architecture is not a medium of irony,' Chipperfield observes drily. 'It is not very subtle. It is difficult to put notes on it.'[2]

Institutions and governments have begun using the term 'recontextualization' as a proposed solution to a problem monument, but this usually is limited to changes to curatorial 'interpretation' such as better explanatory texts nearby and plaques – putting notes on it – rather than fundamental physical changes to a monument that would change its role in a street or square at a matching scale to the monument and thus turn a commemorative honour into a site of shame. Explanatory plaques are normally insufficient and, as we saw at Dachau and on Colston's plinth, they can themselves distort truth and lie by omission. Compared to interventions of scale and conviction, it is inadequate to place a small notice or plaque next to a large monument in order to demand exoneration for the offending item while keeping it in place. Underpowered responses cannot smooth the path to successful outcomes; they can inflame. As academic Derek Alderman has written:

> The politics of commemoration is not simply about convincing people to remember the past in different ways. Rather, it also requires finding suitable locations in which to do this remembering and merging heritage with place identity in progressive and positive ways.[3]

There has to be retain and transform rather than retain and explain if retention is to be justified.

There is a long history of unsanctioned guerrilla memorialisations and counter-memorialisations that we can draw on. Among them is the recent trolling of the Soviet war memorial in Sofia where the liberating/occupying military figures were transformed through bright paint into a jokey Superman, Ronald McDonald, and Santa Claus figures. The Russians were not happy and it is true that disrespecting the role the Soviet Union played in liberating the continent from Fascism could be reflecting reactionary nationalism as much as critiquing totalitarianism. But these considered guerrilla actions are rarely the quotidian and inarticulate vandalism that their critics claim.

The contested legacy of nineteenth-century British prime minister William Gladstone has also been the subject of persistent guerrilla action over decades. As a newly elected MP, Gladstone used his maiden speech in the House of Commons to support his father's interests in plantation slavery and argue against its immediate abolition. When slavery was abolished, the Gladstone family accrued a fortune in compensation for their freed slaves. This record, and thus the many Gladstonian sites of honour up and down the land, received increased attention after the death

8.2 The 1954 Monument to the Soviet Army in Sofia. While commemorating the liberation of the city from the Axis powers, it also marks Bulgaria's occupation by the Soviet Union – a complex legacy. In 2011, a base relief at its foot was repainted secretly by artists calling themselves Destructive Creation to feature figures from American popular culture in what has been seen as a comment on Western capitalism. Russia protested. The paint was removed days later.

of George Floyd, and in at least one instance, Gladstone's name was removed from a building – at Liverpool University.

Gladstone was also a ruling class culture warrior who voted against the Factory Acts that regulated the hours of work for children. Outside Bow Church in the working class East End of London is a statue of the man on a substantial pedestal above the traffic whose outstretched hand is painted a bloody red. The figure was erected in 1882 – within Gladstone's lifetime – by the owners of the nearby Bryant & May matchstick factory as thanks for Gladstone dropping a proposed tax on matches. Gladstone sat for the likeness and its unveiling was a highly political occasion. Urban myth has it that Gladstone's mysteriously painted red hand (sometimes hands) appeared soon after as a protest arising from the fury of Bryant & May matchgirls being forced to contribute to the cost of the statue from their meagre wages. The blood on the factory owners' hands representing the deadly working conditions.

In truth, the matchgirls wages did not pay for the statue (or not directly), but from at least the late 1980s the red hand has appeared and reappeared, some think to mark the centenary of the successful London Matchgirl Strike of 1888 led by Eleanor Marx and Annie Besant. The strike was a crucial episode for trade unionism and activism among working class women. His red hand may also have come to commemorate the plantation blood on the Gladstone family's hands; for some observers that may already be the dominant message. Gladstone's hands are still periodically cleaned of paint but, overnight, the 'blood' is back. The red hand retained, together with a matching statue of Besant and Marx set up close by, might form an intersectional challenge to Gladstone, a comment on race and class, well into the future.

Across the Atlantic, New York saw the considered guerilla reworking by gender-non-conforming activists in 2015 of the bronze Stonewall National Monument in Christopher Park. Erected in 1992 to commemorate the 1969 Stonewall Riots, the symbolic birth of the gay rights movement, the monument's sculptor George Segal took his signature approach of painting his bronze human forms white to resemble their original moulds. It was not the best aesthetic decision given the decades of argument within the LGBTQ+ community about the marginalisation, the whitewashing actually, of the central role played by Black and Latinx trans women and homeless youth in the Stonewall Riots.

The activists repainted the statues' faces and hands brown and dressed them in wigs, bras, and scarves: 'What we did was rectification, not vandalism,' said one of the activists even as some gay publications called it exactly that.

Those statues are bronze (brown) underneath the layer of white paint – the symbolism behind that is infuriating. I know that some people are going to be angry, but I'm not concerned with preserving bullshit art. I'm angry about the whitewashing of LGBTQ history.[4]

Unofficial, artist-led happenings have the benefit of creating events and drawing critical attention. However, they are not a sustained challenge unless made permanent and by their nature are more likely to be of less enduring materials than the object they are commenting upon. They are also generally carried out by those without the deep pockets to pay for a permanent statue, or the power to steer their proposals through the bureaucracy demanded to erect one. Rachel Reid's unofficial 'Royal Slavery' interventions in two London squares placed faux metal slave branding irons in the hands of statues of James II and Charles II, two monarchs both deeply implicated in the slave trade via the Royal Africa Company, but the branding iron in the hand of James II lasted just a few hours before being removed while those in Charles II's grip lasted only days before being anonymously replaced with a plastic rosary.

Subversion is also occasionally commissioned or sneaked into an official work, especially temporary installations. In 1985, Krzysztof Wodiczko projected a nuclear missile onto Nelson's Column in London, making a sly if short-lived commentary on the sculptural militarisation of Trafalgar Square. Angered by Thatcher's support of the Apartheid regime in South Africa, Wodiczko then swung one of his projectors onto the façade of South African House facing the square and for two hours projected an image of a swastika onto its pediment.

In 2012, artist Sophie Ernst attached a loudhailer to a statue of Queen Victoria in the city of Wakefield, West Yorkshire, as part of an official art intervention for the Yorkshire Sculpture Park. From the speaker emanated a queenly voice reading extracts from the journals and letters of Queen Victoria and from British prime ministers including Churchill, Gladstone, Blair, and Cameron. Some of these extracts referred to the evils of colonialism, including starvation and oppression in India. The statue 'spoke' for thirty minutes before the local council, which had given permission for the work but had not known its full content, asked for the installation to come down, apparently more concerned about offending royalty than the truths about famine or massacre. As Hammad Nassar of the Paul Mellon

Centre for Studies in British Art said with some understatement: 'This was unfortunate. We need our statues to speak uncomfortable truths. In functioning democracies, the cultural sphere should be a profoundly unsafe space for sacred cows.'[5]

Permanence begins to address the long-standing power imbalances that characterise guerrilla actions, be it the elegant minimalism at Bolzano or Carlos Colombino's intense, almost literal-minded reuse of parts of a monumental figure of the deposed Paraguayan dictator Alfredo Stroessner that once stood at the highest point of the capital Asunción. Following a debate on the future of the memorial erected to a man responsible for widespread torture and death, Colombino displayed Stroessner's steel body parts between two concrete blocks, crushed and

8.3 Gladstone's red hand. The 1882 statue of William Gladstone at Bow Church, East London, funded by factory owner Theodore Bryant, usually sports a painted right hand. The guerrilla intervention was for decades seen as commemorating the 1888 matchgirl's strike led by Annie Besant at the nearby Bryant and May factory. There is a story that at the statue's unveiling the factory workers protested, complaining that their poverty wages had paid for the likeness. More recently, the red hand has been seen associated with protest against Gladstone's defence of plantation slavery.

8.4 The massive statue of General Stroessner in Asunción, Paraguay was taken down following his fall in from power in 1989 and legislation requiring the removal of public honours to the dictator. Artist Carlos Colombino, used elements of the original statue sandwiched between two concrete blocks to create a new artwork commemorating Stroessner's victims.

reconfigured but still recognizable. The new monument, placed in the Square of the Disappeared, was dedicated to the regime's victims.

Stealth tactics have worked in permanent artworks, too: In 2005, Badtjala artist Fiona Foley installed a sculpture called 'Witnessing to Silence' outside Brisbane's magistrates court that takes the form of bronze lotus flowers and columns of ashes and water. Only after the state-sponsored piece was unveiled did Foley reveal that it was a memorial to ninety-four sites where Aborigines had been massacred by colonial settlers and that the ash and water represented the disposal by burning or submerging of their bodies: 'There is a psychological denial,' Foley explained. 'I knew people would find it difficult to accept the truth.'[6]

Permanent new layers of the Bolzano type that subversively transform are, however, remarkably rare. Too often they remain in the realm of ideas. Those proposals that do come forward can be insensitive in the wrong hands. Historic England held an ideas competition for new memorial layers to contested monuments as part of its 2018 'Immortalised' season. Among the winners was MSMR Architects' proposal which would have left Colston in place but surrounded him with a representation in the paving of the infamous Brooks slave ship diagram with its hundreds of bodies squeezed below deck. Many visitors would certainly find this intervention powerful, notes Burch-Brown:

> However, for others the symbolism would be problematic. Colston's figure is lifelike, whereas the unnamed African figures are depicted in outline ... They are passive, without agency. Allowing passers-by to walk across the enslaved figures as depicted ... could be seen as insulting rather than generating respect.[7]

Ideas can be valuable, though. Banksy's proposal following the Colston toppling was far more intriguing. In a sketch he proposed restoring the battered and graffitied figure to its pedestal and commissioning some life-sized bronze statues of Black Lives Matter protestors to accompany it, engaged in pulling on a rope around Colston's neck so that the June day of his fall could be eternally celebrated – history being made by the people and history being revised without total erasure.

8.5 Bristol artist Banksy suggested that instead of removing the Colston statue, figures of protestors pulling him down should be added. In this way his toppling would be celebrated well into the future.

Another perennial recontextualising idea is to take a statue off its plinth so that its honoured and elevated status is reduced. You can then look at your opponent on an equal footing and squarely in the eye (presuming a life-sized rather than colossal figure). This too has been suggested for Colston as well as for Soviet-era monuments. In his submission for a 1993 exhibition on transformations, 'Monumental Propaganda,' held in Moscow and New York, cartoonist Art Spiegelman went one further: He took a photograph of Moscow's gigantic Socialist-Realist figures of the 'Worker and Kolkhoznitza Woman' originally created by Vera Mukhina for the 1937 World's Fair in Paris and manipulated it, shrinking the pedestal so that instead of striding into a Socialist future, the stainless steel pair were stepping off their pedestal into space like Wile E Coyote running out of solid ground on a cliff top.[8]

Another contributor suggested statues dangling from cranes, suspended in the act of placement and/or removal. John Murray proposed burying huge statues up to their neck while creating an underground viewing platform for those wishing to see their feet. (Humiliation is a common theme here.) As it happens, far from being humiliated, in Putin's Russia Mukhina's restored statue has been placed on a new plinth that increases its overall height from 34.5 metres to 60 metres, somewhat closer to its World's Fair placement height.

As we have seen, to be effective, interpretation or re-contextualisation needs to be not only sincere but of a matching presence to do its job. Civil rights activist Andrew Young's suggestion of hanging a 'freedom bell', referencing Martin Luther King Jr's famous speech, on Georgia's Stone Mountain seems hopelessly inadequate given the cliff face-sized Confederate artwork it is responding to. Before the 2017 Unite the Right rally made nuanced responses more difficult, Daniel Bluestone, director of Preservation Studies and professor of History of Art and Architecture at Boston University, had mused upon potential responses to gargantuan Confederate memorials, notably those of Charlottesville and Richmond, Virginia. An anti-racist/slavery monument of similar scale would be needed to counter the large equestrian figure of General Robert E Lee or, failing that, suggested Bluestone, provide an encircling and screening hedge that demands a viewer makes a purposeful effort to see the statue while shielding it from other park users who do not wish to interact with it and to inhibit its attempts to patrol space or form a focal point for gatherings.[9]

Counter-memorials (also called dialogic memorials, or in German, *Gegendenkmal*, for their proximate pairings with existing memorials) are where a new work is set up in relationship to an existing contested monument to comment upon it. These can be another effective tactic – although sometimes not if they are deemed to be a substitute for necessary changes to the contested monument itself. In Baltimore, artist Pablo Machioli set up his 'Madre Luz' figure in 2015 as a pregnant African American maternal figure with a raised fist confronting a military monument to Stonewall Jackson and Robert E Lee – a monument erected at the astonishingly late date of 1948 when white supremacists in the city were actively resisting de-segregation. The Lee–Jackson monument was among four spirited away on a truck by the city council overnight in 2017 after the Unite the Right rally in Charlottesville. Vandals then attacked the papier mâché Madre Luz, scrawling 'honour history' on the steps to the plinth where the statues stood.

After repairs, she was placed, at least temporarily, atop the empty plinth itself, replacing the soldier figures. But with their total removal, her confrontational stance and purpose in pointing out that the Confederate generals should be primarily understood for their armed defence of slavery proved fleeting; her rebuking poignancy vanished. The opportunity for artistic commentary, a counterpoint between the strong but conciliatory present and the belligerent and bigoted past, was over once the flatbed trucks had removed the generals. Both the original and the counter-memorial need to be permanent for the critique to be maintained.

CR

Removing monuments from honoured city centre locations to more marginal outdoor statue parks is an alternative response. One of the earliest cemeteries for dead statues was Delhi's Coronation Park where, after independence, figures of former kings and Raj officials from across the city were exiled to specially built plinths in a shabby corner that was once the site of imperial durbars. This is better than outright destruction, but their absence from the urban fray means that they are not a readily visible part of a reckoning with India's colonised past. One wonders about the purpose of the under-visited park. The decontextualization, the exiling of a figure to the urban margins, may in the long term marginalise the debate itself. Out of sight becomes out of mind.

Other statue parks are more visible such as the Communist-era relics in Budapest's Memento Park (Szoborpark), which contains dozens of statues relocated from elsewhere in the Hungarian capital. The space was laid out by architect Ákos Eleöd, who said that the park is about freedom of thought: 'Because it can be talked about, described, built, this park is about democracy. After all, only democracy is able to give the opportunity to let us think freely about dictatorship.'[10] The fragile state of Hungarian democracy since suggests limited didactic success for this venture. The site is now more associated with populist anti-communist rhetoric than a serious analysis of Stalinism and has become a theme park geared to tourists with a Trabant on display to pose with and a communist kitsch trinket market. The serious engagement with a monumental legacy has been eroded.

Isn't it better to be reminded in our city centres, as the Arendt artwork at Bolzano does, that Fascism remains a threat and that we don't have the right to obey our rulers? Moving a monument doesn't have to mean exile – changing a context can shift meaning. One could, for example, return the likeness of Edward Jenner, the pioneer of vaccination, to Trafalgar Square from Hyde Park, swapping him out for one of the generals who supplanted him after Prince Albert's death. At a stroke the militarisation and imperial character of Britain's main ceremonial space would be usefully diluted while honouring one of the great contributors to world health.

Perhaps there would be less demand for the removal of the many lying statues if more of the authentic historical artefacts that provide evidence of the past remained or if monuments commemorating wrongdoing were erected as a check on the lies. As New Orleans mayor Mitch Landrieu asks: 'Why are there no slave ship monuments, no prominent markers on public land to remember the lynchings or the slave blocks; nothing to remember this long chapter of our lives of the pain, of sacrifice, of shame.' He points out that many defenders of history and monuments 'are eerily silent on what amounts to historical malfeasance, a lie by omission.'[11]

The omissions are many. It is not only the lack of sites of conscience to bear witness to history's crimes, but an absence of sites that positively honour Black achievement or those of women, or which reveal the experience of queer lives or working class struggle. The meaning of a nation, concludes Stuart Hall in his celebrated 1999 speech 'Whose Heritage?' is known through the objects and artefacts that have been erected and have survived to symbolise its essential values, to mirror a collective social memory: 'Its Trafalgars, Dunkirks and Mafekings, its Nelsons, its Churchills, its Elgars and its Benjamin Brittens: It follows that those who cannot see themselves reflected in the ... mirror cannot properly "belong".'[12] Finding a place for these alternative narratives in the public realm has become an ever more vocal demand, and it remains an important way of rebalancing the commemorative landscape to better reflect the world. The invisibility of queer lives continues, for example, even in the relatively liberal British Isles. With the exception of some funerary monuments, until recently there were no memorials to openly LGBTQ figures that mentioned their sexuality rather than their achievements in other aspects of their lives – the plaque to Edward Carpenter at Brunswick Square, Hove, or that to Radclyffe Hall in Kensington, for instance, mention only their writing, not the agenda-setting aspects of their personal lives. Discreet veils are drawn.

'A Conversation with Oscar Wilde,' Maggi Hambling's bronze and green granite coffin/bench just off the Strand, was the first public monument to Wilde in England. It was installed in 1998 after a campaign led by actors and writers. His downfall is perhaps alluded to in the inscription – the line from Lady Windemere's Fan: 'We are all in the gutter but some of us are looking at the stars.' Wilde is still able to court controversy with some townsfolk in Worthing demanding the Blue Plaque there be removed because of Wilde's alleged pursuit of local teenagers while he lived there in 1894.

Well-meaning corrections to invisibility can bring their own issues: A plaque in York to Anne Lister, whose extensive early nineteenth-century diaries and exploits have led to her being described as 'the first modern lesbian,' referred to her instead as 'gender non-conforming,' thus erasing her lesbian identity. A revised plaque now describes her as 'Lesbian and Diarist.' On reflection, this could be seen as an exchange between trans-inclusive and trans-exclusory activists conducted through the medium of commemoration.

Figures of Martin Luther King Jr have proved equally problematic, not least because of mainstream history's preferred image of him as an unthreatening moderate rather than a man who successfully led a fiercely fought civil rights struggle to its next stage. A figure more than nine metres tall, emerging from a granite with arms crossed, selected for a four-acre memorial to King on the National Mall's Tidal Basin in Washington, was deemed too confrontational by some DC commissioners. King's pose wasn't conciliatory, he wasn't leaning in enough, it seems; was just too commanding a presence. The compromise was to give King the ghost of a smile.[13] But it was the Black majority town of Rocky Mount, North Carolina, that voted to remove their King memorial because of its 'arrogance' and because, it 'looked like a white man painted black.'[14] After spending tens of thousands of dollars exploring an alternative, the statue was eventually re-erected.

◌

The present period is not just about removals, though; a new statue mania is upon us, reminiscent of that of the late nineteenth century. In her book *Memorial Mania: Public Feeling in America*, Erica Doss sets out America's current obsession with memorialisation. She cites surveys of unexceptional towns such as Lowell, Massachusetts, where 65 out of its 252 memorials were erected in the 1980s and 1990s. From school shootings to car accidents, natural disasters to the Columbia shuttle explosion, memorials are legion in the form of plaques, cairns, quilts, statues, sacred trees, and entire museums.

Only rarely is this statue mania about correcting wrongs or representing the marginalised in the public realm. More usually, when they not being simply mawkish, these memorials are about a need to be seen – individual ego stroking. While many jurisdictions have rules forbidding commemorative memorials until ten or more years after an individual's death, these rules are often set aside for individuals or interest groups with influence, even to the point of memorialising still living people.

The dangers of over-hasty memorials were illustrated by the honours given to prolific paedophile, TV presenter, and charity fundraiser Sir Jimmy Savile. Plaques were erected and places named in his honour, even during his lifetime. They were rapidly removed and renamed when his crimes came to light following his death in 2011. The elaborate headstone of his own grave in Scarborough inscribed with the phrase 'It Was Good While It Lasted' was sent to landfill.

Little has been learned from this and similar episodes. Statues to the not only recently dead but still living celebrities are proliferating. Sporting stars are notably represented in this new mania, but celebrities of any kind will do. At Liverpool's Lime Street Station, passengers are greeted by a figure of tax-dodging local comedian Ken Dodd, complete with his signature 'tickling stick.' The likeness was commissioned while he was still alive and annoying, with 'Doddy' himself posing for photos alongside his bronze doppelgänger. The overall impression is one of triviality, vested interests, and atrocious artistic standards that, unintentionally, undermine the very concept of public honour.

Even well-meaning campaigns have been caught up. In Bristol, there has been a push to reoccupy Colston's plinth with a figure of Paul Stephenson who led a successful 1963 boycott of the city bus company for its racist employment practices and whose activism led the way toward the passing of the 1965 Race Relations Act. Then, very briefly in the summer of 2020, the Colston plinth was occupied by a figure of local BLM activist Jen Reid by artist Marc Quinn, raised there as a guerrilla action. While Stephenson and Reid might both be very worthy individuals, the fact that they are alive should automatically disqualify them from occupying a plinth as it should have done for Doddy.

Perhaps we should forget commemorating individuals altogether as it only appears to bring trouble with it either immediately or in the long term as time passes and values change, even where a memorial was erected with the best of intentions. The 1876 Emancipation Memorial in Washington, DC, for instance, features a standing Abraham Lincoln and a kneeling, grateful ex-slave thanking his liberator sculpted by Thomas Ball. It may have been paid for by freed slaves giving genuine thanks to the man, but both the memorial's iconography and Lincoln's own record on slavery are not unproblematic and were recognised as such even at the time. Frederick Douglass, speaking at the memorial's dedication ceremony, was forthright about the downsides even as he supported the initiative: 'Truth compels me to admit, even here in the presence of the monument we have erected to his memory. Abraham Lincoln was not, in the fullest sense of the word, either our man or our model.'[15]

Douglas pointed out that Lincoln had said that if he could have held the country together without ending slavery, he would have done so. Yet, argued Douglass: 'It was enough for us that Abraham Lincoln was at the head of a great movement, and was in living and earnest sympathy with that movement.'[16] 'For the first time in history,' Douglass announced to the crowd at the dedication, Black people had unveiled and 'set apart a monument of enduring bronze, every feature of which the men of after-coming generations may read something of the … great works of Abraham Lincoln.'[17] Douglass was also ambivalent about the paternalistic form of the memorial as well as about the man: 'The negro here, though rising, is still on his knees and nude,' he later wrote in a recently uncovered letter. 'What I want to see before I die is a monument representing the negro, not couchant on his knees like a four-footed animal, but erect on his feet like a man.'[18]

Insightful as ever, he said that the monument was not telling the whole truth but that Lincoln Park was large enough for further, less undignified monuments: 'Admirable as is the monument by Mr. Ball in Lincoln Park,' he wrote, 'it does not, as it seems to me, tell the whole truth, and perhaps no one monument could be made to tell the whole truth of any subject which it might be designed to illustrate.'[19]

Beginning in June 2020, serious efforts began to remove the Emancipation Memorial, undoubtedly an object of great historical and aesthetic interest, from its park. A copy of the same Emancipation Memorial in a square in Boston has already been removed and its future is not known at the time of writing. The monument's imagery is obnoxious without a doubt – and evidently from Douglass's reaction not just to modern eyes – but even in its problematic state this memorial tells us something valuable about the times in which it was erected, including the critical reaction to it. Surely an artist would be capable of reinterpreting it, adding a new layer of meaning and commenting on the old, or of taking up Douglass's suggestion of adding to the park group – a counter-memorial avant la lettre – by way of commentary.

It is striking, incidentally, how rarely aesthetic value is discussed when considering the complexity of problem monuments although, in the past, some have been saved from destruction on art historical grounds even amidst revolutions. Following the October 1917 revolution, for example, many royalist statues were removed from St Petersburg but Falconet's 1776–78 equestrian Peter the Great commissioned by Catherine the Great was retained and, in fact, became a model of monumental sculpture for later traditionalists after Stalin crushed the avant-garde. There is certainly a great difference in aesthetic and art historical interest between the massive equestrian Confederate monuments in places such as Charlottesville or Richmond and your average mass-produced 'Silent Sam'. And while both are officially regarded as historic monuments, John Cassidy's late Victorian bronze of Colston is a relatively workaday affair compared to, say, Pieter Scheemakers the Younger's idiosyncratic 1734 figure of Sir Thomas Guy that a history commission recently recommended should be relocated to a less prominent location at the hospital.

While there are various campaigns today to redress the invisibility of women, Black, brown and LGBTQ+ people, and those with disabilities by commissioning more public commemorations consistent with identity-based demands, class-based commemorations – both people and events – still struggle to find space in the public realm. The emergence of radical history groups in the 1970s and related initiatives such as London's Mural Movement began to challenge the lack of class representation, but, in retrospect, proved a relatively brief efflorescence.

Manchester is, though, a city that is proud of its radical traditions and is attempting address the situation. Until recently, the city's own outdoor memorials more often commemorated the likes of free traders John Bright and Richard Cobden than Chartists or suffragettes. It is appropriate, then, that Manchester, early industrial capitalism's dark heart (and in suitably dialectical fashion, a seedbed of resistance to it), is a place where stories of the working classes and those who have achieved fame in opposition to the state are beginning to be marked in the public realm.

In 2017 artist Phil Collins, who was fascinated by Eastern Europe's iconoclasm, ceremoniously trucked a damaged and discarded 1970s concrete statue of Friedrich Engels that he found toppled and abandoned in the Ukraine to Manchester where Engels was greeted by a celebrating crowd as part of the Manchester International Festival. For Engels it was something of a homecoming. He had lived in Manchester, based *The Condition of the Working Class in England* on the horrors of its mills and slums, and developed his concept of 'social murder' in the city. Yet there had been no memorial to him in his adopted home. Collins told *The Guardian* that as well as being the birthplace of capitalism, the factory system, and the 'magic of surplus value,' the city was also a site of resistance 'of the Chartists and the 1842 general strike, and the suffragettes and the Vegetarian Society.'[20]

For Collins, a problem for today's struggling Mancunians is that governmental 'concealed language' is used to hide the grimness of their lives, just as Engels himself showed how their deadly living conditions were intentionally concealed by the bourgeoise behind glittering new facades. Collins dismissed critics who said that with Engels he was celebrating the Gulag by pointing out the crimes carried out in the name of Jesus Christ. Additionally, the following year, Manchester finally got its monument to the Peterloo Massacre having only had to wait two centuries.

Manchester is not unusual in its past failure to commemorate challenges to the state. Attempts to honour the suffragettes outside Parliament were repeatedly obstructed by government figures before Emmeline and Christabel Pankhurst were eventually memorialized in Victoria Tower Gardens immediately to the west of the Palace of Westminster. Sylvia, the third and most radical of the Pankhursts, remained beyond the pale and was excluded from the monument.

Until very recently, there were still no statues to women among the many in Parliament Square in front of the Palace of Westminster, England's most honoured plot for political immortals. To commemorate the centenary of the Representation of the People Act 2018, moves were made to change this all-male situation. The summer of 2017 saw three planning applications lodged with Westminster City Council – for statues of Margaret Thatcher, Emmeline Pankhurst, and suffragist Millicent Fawcett in Parliament Square. Without an existing statue being removed from the current arrangement of plinths, there was not room in the layout for all three: Westminster City Council's self-declared central London 'saturation zone' was, in any case, essentially a 'no vacancies' sign forbidding new memorials – a policy it was happy to ignore to celebrate Bomber Command's wartime devastation of German civilian centres. The idea that some of the male politicians might have to make way for a woman seems not to have been contemplated. What is also clear from these applications is that it costs about £600,000 to erect and endow a bronze of seven to ten feet tall – an effective financial barrier to the further commemoration of marginalized groups alongside the bureaucratic one.

It was Fawcett who, after having to fend off a push from Thatcher's backers, managed to claim the coveted spot. She had been part of the first petition for female suffrage back in 1866 and in 1897 became president of the National Union of Women's Suffrage Societies. Gillian Wearing's bronze of Fawcett called 'Courage Calls to Courage Everywhere' was unveiled in 2018. Fawcett's words in the title are written on the placard Fawcett is brandishing.

The planning application for the statue placed great emphasis on siting Fawcett between Nelson Mandela and Gandhi – arguing that they are a trio of non-violent campaigners. Echoing efforts to tame Martin Luther King's radicalism, this is simply untrue of Mandela's African National Congress, whatever one thinks of the reasonableness of the organisation's violent actions. Emphasising Fawcett's 'non-militant' nature – as a by the book suffragist rather than a street-fighting suffragette seems designed to avoid alarming commemorative gatekeepers 100 years on.[21]

As well as place-specific counter-memorials where a new work addresses an individual pre-existing contested work, a necessary re-balancing would need to happen citywide across its commemorative landscape, with new commemorations set up to those whose stories and presence has until now been hidden from history and the public realm. New York's Mayoral Advisory Commission on City Art, Monuments, and Markers, for example, set itself five years to commission new monuments across the city 'for groups of people that have been left out, displaced, or erased from public histories and public spaces, beginning with a large-scale monument to Indigenous peoples …'[22] Other cities including London are now following a similar course.

In theory at least, some planned colonial capitals have been trying to create a more balanced and more diverse commemorative landscape for some time now. In Washington, DC, the National Capital Planning Commission is the federal agency that governs planning matters. In the past twenty years or so, the Commission has authorised twenty-one new memorials, and there are now close to 160 memorials on public land within the capital. It also produced a 2018 report, *Memorial Trends & Practice in Washington DC,* that examines patterns of memorialisation. Unsurprisingly, it found that figures tend to be male and military (57 percent of memorials in 1910, 37 percent by 2012). Of 113 memorials, approximately 6 percent 'prominently feature women.' Only two US women had been individually commemorated: open spaces campaigner Sarah Rittenhouse and Black educator and civil rights activist Mary McCleod Bethune.[23]

It's a top-down, directive regime that would likely be balked at in other cities, but it has the benefit at least of making transparent the exercise of power in relation to memorials and allows national priorities to be set. Ultimately, however, memorial sponsors have to justify the national significance of their subject to lawmakers, and it is up to Congress to 'directly address questions of under-representation in Washington's memorial landscape.'[24] Unsurprisingly, then, most of the new monuments erected in the capital over the past two decades have also been military, part of a worldwide proliferation of monuments to conflict. Among the recent Washington additions is the 'Victims of Communism Memorial' promoted by the Hard-Right Heritage Foundation.

Ottawa's Strategic Plan explicitly categorises monuments by theme in order that the 'full range of Canadian ideas and endeavours' are expressed and that the degree of balance of 'stories' can be monitored. Four underrepresented priority themes are identified – Aboriginal peoples, women, the environment, and 'ethno-cultural communities.' The plan identified sites for new memorials that are highly visible but might be away from the core commemoration area.

In Australia, these balancing efforts go back even further. A National Memorials Ordinance of 1928 established the Canberra National Memorials Committee chaired by the prime minister. Zones for military and non-military commemoration near Parliament either side of Lake Burley Griffin were established. In 2002 guidelines were published that aimed to 'encourage' a broad range of Australian 'cultural narratives.' However, it takes a strict view of what is relevant in Australia. One successful application was for a plaque celebrating 100 years of the Australian aged pension system but monuments to Gandhi and the Great Irish Potato Famine were rejected as not sufficiently Australian, as have been any monuments devoted to natural disasters. But its ten-year delay on any event memorialisation was set aside when it came to the victims of the 2002 Bali bombings. This says as much about Australia's ideological involvement in the war on terror as it does about grief.

At the heart of empire in London, the decision-making imperium on monuments is extravagantly multi-layered. The system has a byzantine complexity that it takes knowledge, connections, time, and money to negotiate: central government; London Boroughs and the City Corporation (who together control the first line planning laws in much of the capital's centre); the Mayor of London, who has direct responsibility for some statues such as those in Parliament Square and Trafalgar Square; Historic England, the national heritage gatekeeper that reports to central government; the powerful Royal Parks that rules much of the capital's central green space; and, not least, the great landowners including the Crown Estate, the Church of England, and individuals such as the Duke of Westminster. Other gatekeepers include the military and developers who might make space available for public art on their land; and then there are the art world's public art commissioning structures. Highways Acts and Public Health Acts are also brought into play. The housing and communities secretary, Robert Jenrick, can deal in inflammatory rhetoric about 'town hall militants' and 'woke worthies' having street names and monuments in their sights, but it is the establishment that has the levers to defend its monumental lies, to support the killers on every corner, and continue its othering of the greater part of London's population.

The first formalisation of memorialisation control in London was the Public Statues Act (Metropolis) of 1854 that demanded that all those wanting to erect figurative monuments within the Metropolitan police district (that is, inner London) had to consult and have the approval of the Government's Office of Works and its successor, the relevant secretary of state. The 1854 Act was finally abolished by the Enterprise and Regulatory Reform Act 2013 as part of the Tory's free-market unravelling of the planning system, a time, only a few years ago, when a culture war took second place to neoliberal economics. The Tories have no doubt regretted since the loss of extra grip that the 1854 Act would have given them.

Only rarely is any one of these gatekeeping levers out of the hands of the elite with the occasional exception of the mayoralty of London. So only on a very few occasions is room made for anyone other than a cis, white, elite male. There is still, for example, no proper memorial to the victims of the transatlantic slave trade in either Bristol or London. A national monument to the trade was designed years ago, gained planning permission and has had a site allocated in Hyde Park, but the funding has never been found to build the project. (This may be about to change.)

Successive Conservative governments refused to offer any money for it but instead pledged tens of millions to the proposed UK Holocaust Memorial directly adjacent to Parliament despite legitimate concerns about the suitability of its location. It would have, until the proposal was blocked, temporarily at least, by the High Court on planning grounds in 2022, swallowed much of a small, historic garden next to Parliament, side-lining the Pankhurst memorial located there, as well as the Buxton Memorial Fountain which commemorates the abolition of slavery. The fountain had already been demoted there from its earlier Parliament Square position as part of remodelling of the square after the Second World War. The whole episode demonstrates the risks of worthy monument campaigns setting interest groups in competition.

In New York, very few contested monuments have been removed since its Commission was established in 2018 and it began its review of what mayor Bill de Blasio called 'symbols of hate.' The Commission rejected calls for the removal of the 1892 rostral column bearing a statue of Columbus at Columbus Circle and instead proposed an 'additive approach' that focused on new monuments across the city and programs that historically contextualize the Columbus monument. The decision was complicated because Christopher Columbus has very different meanings to different groups. Descendants of the nineteenth-century Italian American community who suffered discrimination on their arrival successfully sought to incorporate Columbus into the founding mythology of the United States to cement their own belonging and standing.

The 1892 column at Columbus Circle was promoted by the Italian community and created by Italian sculptor Gaetano Russo as part of this invented tradition. At the statue's inauguration, Carlo Barsotti, president of the Committee of Italian Societies, argued that it was 'sacred to the memory of that great Italian who gave America the light of civilization.'[25] It has been argued that the Columbus story was an essential part of Italian immigrants ensuring that they were racialised as white (as were, eventually, Jewish and Irish immigrants). The Columbus myth was competing with others such as the Aryan foundation myth around the Viking Leif Erikson, a statue of whom had been unveiled in Boston five years previously, as well as a series of monuments to the Puritans set up after the Civil War. Some American Hispanics, meanwhile, consider the present condemnation of Columbus as a genocidaire by First Nations peoples and progressives as simply the latest instalment of the 'Black Legend,' the centuries-long effort to demonize Spain and its empire. Puritan and Erikson commemorations obviously carry the risk of reinforcing white nationalism, but then so does Columbus.

The Commission has stuck to this decision despite increased pressure from campaigners for full removal and a name change at the Circle in the charged atmosphere following the death of George Floyd. It remains to be seen whether the Commission's proposed additions, essentially counter-memorials rather than a transformation of the main column and statue, will be sufficiently dramatic, of appropriate scale, and politically astute in ways that will properly counter Columbus himself and address his genocide and his place in settler-colonial myths.

Much of the Commission's work has been about new art works that fill gaps for those whose communities and individual achievements have been overlooked but it has managed to offend various sections of different communities in the process. Catholic groups were angered at the omission of the first US saint, 'Mother' Francis Xavier Cabrini (who eventually got her statue) while there were those who pointed out that a proposed monument to women's suffrage didn't include any Black campaigners. A sculpture of the first African American congresswoman, Shirley Chisholm, meanwhile, was designed for a prominent site but one deemed to be in the wrong Brooklyn neighbourhood. Part of the issue has been the opacity about who had the final say in such matters. Mother Cabrini had topped the poll of women to be honoured, but the decisions of the panel of commissioning judges were then revealed to be strictly advisory only.

With so many problems arising out of traditional commemoration, some artists have turned to alternative methods – to projections and performance, to ritual and conceptual installations that reject the language of traditional monuments and explore voids and abstraction, the absent or fleeting. These appear to offer ways of intervening in the memorial world that don't entirely abandon the field of play to the traditionalists but also try to avoid getting caught up in their hierarchical honour games. Anti-monuments (sometimes also called, confusingly, 'counter-memorials') also make claims to holding peoples' attention better than a traditional memorial whose tropes such as durability, prominence, and permanence don't prevent them from becoming invisible eventually. Temporary memorials might also be anti-monuments when they revel in their ephemeral nature and reject attempts at permanence.

Among these anti-monuments is the work of German artist Jochen Gerz. In the Harburg borough of Hamburg, Gerz, together with Esther Shalev-Gerz, set up their 'Monument Against Fascism' in 1986. Over the following seven years, this twelve-metre-high column sheathed in lead was steadily sunk into the earth, covered in graffiti scratched into its surface; today only its cap is visible. Another Gerz work, '2146 Stones – Monument against Racism' (1993) at Saarbrücken, saw him work with teams of art students who, at night, stealthily removed the cobblestones on the approach to the town castle that the Nazis had used as a regional centre. They carved the names of Jewish cemeteries into the stones' underside and replaced them back in their holes, the inscription hidden. The castle square is now called Square of the Invisible Monument. A similar project that began covertly were Gunter Demnig's *Stolpersteine* (stumbling stones), small plaques set in the pavement next to the former homes of Holocaust victims, each giving their personal details. There are now more than 30,000 Stolpersteine across Germany.

Gerz comments that 'people not monuments, are the places of memory.'[26] It is people, he says, rather than monuments, that stand up to injustice. The Harburg monument didn't aim to console but to provoke, to demand interaction, to draw attention to the passage of time rather than make appeals to eternity, and, ultimately, ensure that the ethical duty to remember remains with people rather than this responsibility being left attached to a monument instead. Indeed, the more ambiguous a monument, the more it may be available as a potential 'thinking site' (*Denk-Stätte*), inviting a deeper discussion rather than instruction.

The commemorative use of a void in the city to stand in for an absence isn't entirely new – the negative space created by Dresden's collapsed Frauenkirche served such a purpose – but it is a trend that appeared to accelerate following Gerz and fellow artist Horst Hoheisel's much admired subversion of monumental traditions such as Hoheisel' inverted fountain outside Kassel town hall. One could also include sculptor Rachel Whiteread's work here such as her Holocaust memorial in Vienna, where the bookshelf castings are present but the original library, the accumulated learning in the heads of the city's Jews, is absent. Or Micha Ullman's empty sunken library at Bebelplatz in Berlin marking a Nazi book-burning ceremony. (Heinrich Heine's famous line, a variation of Lemkin's, is included on its plaque: where they burn books, they will ultimately burn people as well.) As with other anti-monuments, the relationship between the viewer and the object is less distant and deferential.

Horst Hoheisel's 1994 proposal for the Memorial to the Murdered Jews of Europe competition in Berlin took the void to an extreme and was designed to prick at Germany's state-funded worthiness and at the risk of co-option by gatekeepers steadily narrowing the aperture of commemorative acceptability. His entry proposed blowing up the Brandenburg Gate, grinding it to dust, and scattering this over the competition site. As James E. Young observes, this would 'mark one destruction with another destruction' rather than attempting to fill the empty space left by the murdered with another object. 'Of course, such a memorial undoing will never be sanctioned by the German government,' writes Young, 'and this too, is part of the artist's point ... its radicalism precludes the possibility of its execution.'[27]

Even within the limits allowed by conventional gatekeepers, in theory at least, honest monuments could be useful irritants by making demands on us to remember. But that's if people remember them properly at all. In an essay on Confederate monuments, legal scholar Sanford Levison recalls Robert Lowell's 1964 poem, *For the Union Dead,* about Boston's memorial to the Black Unionist soldiers of the Civil War: 'Their monument sticks like a fishbone in the city's throat,' writes Lowell.[28] It reminds the city of their sacrifice and the role African Americans played in liberating themselves.

Its sculptor, Augustus Saint-Gaudens, spent years on his creation, using African American live models for his bronze to ensure he was depicting the soldiers as individuals rather than the usual generic Black men. Officially called the Memorial to Robert Gould Shaw and the Massachusetts Fifty-Fourth Regiment, it was funded in part by emancipated Black people. The memorial is the first stop on Boston's Black Heritage Trail and the story of the Massachusetts Fifty-Fourth was told in the 1989 film *Glory*. Yet the bronze relief on its stone base has been repeatedly defaced including, somewhat bewilderingly, during the George Floyd protests of 2020 when phrases including 'Black Lives Matter,' 'No Justice, No Peace,' and 'Police are Pigs' were graffitied on to it. As a war memorial, it may have been seen as a generic militaristic enemy without anybody looking too closely at who is being commemorated. But its story is clearly easily forgotten. This underlines the fragility of attaching public memory to places and expecting it to remain there unchanged.

Just how and even if collective memory attaches to particular places, meaningfully and for any length of time, is an open question. It has been suggested that collective memory is useful for thinking about the space between individual memory and history. But given the inaccuracies in personal recollections and the cynical manipulation of places and traces, we need to be extremely wary of the idea that collective memory can play such a role (and in this I am revising some of the ideas set out in my 2006 book *The Destruction of Memory*). Collective memory is, after all, simply a metaphor rather than a psychological reality, and the fashionable blurring of the line between history and memory, between narrative interpretation of the past and the facts about the past, should not be encouraged – quite the opposite.

In France, Pierre Nora's multi-volume celebration of national collective memory published from 1984 as '*lieux de memoire* (sites of memory) – the places, symbols, and concepts from the Panthéon to gastronomy, the tricolour to forests – literally edits the canon of what it means to identify as French. Perry Anderson describes the elegiac exercise as 'one of the most patently ideological programmes in post-war historiography, anywhere in the world' in its quest to compile an integrated but partial vision of the nation.[29]

As Anderson points out, Nora edits from his *lieux* the entire oppressive imperial history of France, from Napoleonic conquests to the plunder of Algeria and the seizing of Indochina. 'Nora's volumes reduce all these fateful exertions to an exhibition of tropical knickknacks in Vincennes.'[30] Nora seeks to detach his *lieux* from the demands of reality, from history and politics – memory using history only when it suits.

Given the myriad problems that monuments and commemoration generate, one might be forgiven for thinking that the ideal solution would be to do away with the idea of memorials altogether, these inert objects that project their mute narratives so crudely, so imprecisely. Especially those erected to identifiable people, embodying as they often do the problematic concept of individual genius or heroism. If so, one would need to apply that ruling retrospectively if the imbalance between those visible and those excluded from the commemorative environment isn't to be perpetuated indefinitely.

There is also a robust academic argument that monuments only hasten our forgetting by reifying memories, no matter how hard they try to avoid this by using unexpected, kinetic, and evolving forms. Because once erected, memorials are easily and swiftly ignored and slowly forgotten. One erected, we walk away from them feeling that our task as citizens in remembering has been completed. Michel de Certeau argued that memory inevitably starts to decay when it is attached to things and places. Others wonder if collective memory (as opposed to the historical evidence they provide) attaches to objects at all in any reliable, accurate, or sustained way. This may help explain why statues and other monuments so easily become invisible. Hoheisel's Brandenburg Gate pulverising memorial didn't just goad the gatekeepers, as James E Young cannily observed in the *Harvard Design Magazine*, it also suggested that the best way to remember the Holocaust might be a permanently unfinished memorialisation process: 'Better a thousand years of Holocaust memorial competitions in Germany than any single "final solution" to Germany's memorial problem.'[31]

Instead of building ever more monuments, from the supposedly vital to the obviously trivial, maybe, just maybe, we should
be building far less of them or even comprehensively ridding
ourselves of what we have, Gary Younge suggests. Do we need
monuments nurturing enduring grudges, centuries after the
fact? Might we be better off abandoning these sites of invented
tradition, stop probing at historical wounds that feed rancour
and fear, and instead forget rather more of the past in the name
of forgiveness and peaceful co-existence? They only set up
demands for further oppositional narratives and the maintenance of another round of related touchstones.

While not giving much attention to memorials directly, writer
David Rieff ruminates on whether it might be better to consign
more to oblivion in his long and thoughtful essay 'In Praise of
Forgetting,' citing Edna Longley's amusing recommendation that
the next historical monument raised in her grievance-clutching
Northern Ireland should be dedicated to Amnesia and then its
location quickly forgotten.[32]

Rieff points to UNESCO's Memory of the World project as
evidence of the shady triumph of memory above all else. Ostensibly and quite properly, the Memory of the World project was
begun to protect documents and oral histories from being lost
or destroyed but has since expanded into an all-encompassing
concern for collective memory and intangible heritage. Rieff
calls the project nonsense:

> Quite simply, the world does not have memories; nor do nations;
> nor do groups of people. Individuals remember, full stop. Yet in
> the early 21st century, collective memory is often spoken of as if
> it were indeed on a par with individual, which is to say genuine,
> memory, and not infrequently, though almost never explicitly, as
> if it morally outranked it.[33]

Memory serves the takeover of history by politics, Rieff
agrees. Hence culture wars. Timothy Garton-Ash has written
that forging collective memories almost inevitably does 'extreme
violence to historical truth,' an idea that Rieff runs with: 'We do

not have to deny the value of memory to insist that the historical record (the verifiable one, not the mythopoeic one) does not justify the moral free pass that remembrance is usually accorded today.'[34] This is absolutely correct.

Rieff goes on to rubbish George Santayana's phrase, 'Those who cannot remember the past are condemned to repeat it' as a 'demonstrably false injunction' which has become conventional wisdom and that memory, as a species of morality 'now stands as one of the more unassailable pieties of our age.'[35] This takes Santayana's point about remembering too narrowly and about repetition too literally, but Rieff is making an important point about the dangers of sanctifying memory.

Yet while there are many valid attractions in these argument for forgetting, in real life the luxury of forgetting may not be available to us until truth and justice are in place. Until then, Santayana's phrase still has vital resonance. And this duty of remembrance extends far beyond its core use in relation to the Holocaust and Jewish thought. Rieff acknowledges this too, quoting historian Yosef Yerushalmi's statement that the 'antonym of "forgetting" is not "remembering" but "justice".'[36] Considering Spain's Law of Historical Memory in this light makes its effectiveness questionable to say the least. Remembrance is surely not aided by entirely removing all Francoist memorials; better to transform at least some of them into sites of shame. Total removal can be seen as a continuation of the *pacto del olvidio* in another form.

True reconciliation does not consist of merely forgetting the past.[37] Commemorations have been demanded on a number of occasions in the recommendations of truth and reconciliation processes internationally. Yet in any reconciliation process the differences between memory and history are vital. The duty of remembrance may have societal value in the sense of maintaining an alertness to radical evil, but this can also be perilous without the accurate facts of history and may even work against good history in the absence of evidential facts. The narratives promoted by monuments may also have the effect of making history simplistic. Truth and history should always take primacy over memory.

UN Special Rapporteur Farida Shaheed wrote an often-insightful report to the UN General Assembly on memorialisation set within the context of transitional justice.[38] In it, she argued that such recommendations 'often limit the choice of action by a Government, which might be otherwise tempted to destroy places of suffering and, in so doing, erase the memories attached to it.'[39] While rather over-optimistic about the positive role of commemorative monuments in post-conflict situations for achieving reconciliation – especially as compared to more pragmatic measures for fostering co-existence – Shaheed's findings also include notes of caution: 'One difficulty,' she writes, is when museums (and monuments for that matter) 'emphasise trauma as a perspective on world events ... The haze of emotionality through which individual stories are filtered makes it difficult to understand the larger political context.'[40] This is an important insight.

War memorials can be especially problematic with their often exclusory and politicised narratives that have little to do with peace or common humanity. Globally, the UN is being advised to be more careful in its promotion of top-down commemoration as part of reconciliation and reparations processes in favour of grassroots approaches to memorialization that, in the right circumstances, might better contribute to reconciliation. It is also essential to resist deterministic estimates of the power of commemorations or post-war heritage reconstruction to heal.

If monuments are vital to the maintenance of the last few centuries of nation-state capitalism, its self-pride and commensurate exclusory values and hypervigilance in controlling its boundaries, then society has paid a high price for this cult of remembrance. That is, in itself, an excellent reason for ridding ourselves of them and putting them out of mind.

Even if transformed into a Mahnmal, the danger is that, unless their mnemonic capacities are sustained in some manner (ritual being the most obvious and traditional process – perhaps rolling the increasingly battered figure of Colston into Bristol's harbour annually until it finally falls apart), one must admit that these sites of shame will also be forgotten eventually – as if the contested matters have been dealt with.

Yet the removal of an abhorrent monument unarguably entails a degree of memory loss as well as the historical loss and this has to be recognised even if it is agreed that removal is the correct approach in certain circumstances. In the long term, it may be antithetical critical layering, subversive transformation as at Bolzano, that will hold society to account for longer (if not forever) and which will be more effectively dialectical in its conversation with history.

9

What Is to Be Done?
The Monumental
and Its Limits

> The problem is then how to locate radical difference; how to
> jumpstart the sense of history so that it begins again to trans-
> mit feeble signals of time, of otherness, of change, of Utopia.
> The problem to be solved is that of breaking out of the windless
> present of the postmodern back into real historical time, and a
> history made by human beings.
>
> Frederic Jameson, *Future City*, (2003)[1]

Bolzano-Bozen did not arrive at its subversive transformations
without a protracted struggle. Some locals wanted the Fascist
frieze removed and destroyed. Perhaps surprisingly, German-
speaking Rightists were particularly keen on its demolition in
order to emphatically distance themselves from the Fascist/Nazi
period. Italian speakers, however, were more likely to want no
change at all, seeing the frieze as simply Italian history rather
than Fascist messaging. The provincial governor said that the
frieze needed removing to a store or archive 'putting it in a cage'
as if it were a wild animal. Some felt the problem frieze should

remain in place but be curtained from view, hiding it behind a screen of opaque glass. Local Fascist leader Andrea Bonazza of Casapound announced grandiosely: 'We are ready to take action to save the bas-relief.'[2]

The impasse between the disputing parties fractured only in 2011 when Silvio Berlusconi's national government (whose finance ministry occupies the former Fascist HQ) needed votes in the region for an upcoming election. Berlusconi's culture minister Sandro Bondi, infamous in Italy for admitting 'I just don't get modern art,' sent a letter to the town assenting to the idea of changes at a number of Fascist monuments. A week later, the Bolzano-Bolzen council launched a competition open to artists, architects, and historians to 'defuse' and 'contextualise' the frieze. A key lesson in achieving change, recalls Hannes Obermair, who received hate mail in the process at that time, was establishing the facts about the past: 'We wanted to tell the whole story including the darkness.' A judging commission was set up to review the 486 entries and shortlist five from which the local council could choose a winner.

At this point the council tried to cancel the results because it actually wanted a winning scheme that covered the frieze up entirely and that was not what it got. Following an outcry, though, local artists Arnold Holzknecht and Michele Bernardi were eventually announced as the outright winners. They had met the brief's demand that the frieze be transformed in a way that did not allow it to be read uninterrupted but also allowed it to be 'accessed thoughtfully.' The minimalism of the intervention, the artists say, is in pointed contrast to the grandiloquence of Fascist aesthetics. Some tweaks were demanded – for example, the letters were to be hung from the canopy above instead of drilling directly into the frieze – but it went ahead.

When the project was finally unveiled in 2017, various critics in the Berlusconi press weighed in about the erasure of history even though nothing had been taken away. Referencing the ancient Egyptian and Roman practice of rulers erasing the memory of their predecessors from statues, coins, and texts, celebrity art historian Philippe Daverio said: 'when *damnatio memoriae* occurs immediately, it's understandable, but 75 years later it seems strange.'[3] Casapound's Bonazza described the proposal as a 'Taliban act against art and the Italian community.'[4] But again, Holzknecht and Bernardi have erased nothing with their new layer– that's its whole point. Indeed, the entire frieze was cleaned, polished, and repaired in the process. (Daverio, incidentally appears to be counting his 75 years from 1942 rather than the frieze's true completion date.) There were no large street demonstrations against Arendt's words apart from the inevitable bellyaching by Casapound. And while it was debated intensively in the communal chamber, there was no discussion of it in the provincial parliament. This is a double-edged outcome in that clearly many people respected the new critical layering, but others appeared disengaged from the whole process.

Former Green Party councillor Hans Heiss thinks the relatively smooth transformation process for the frieze was partly down to it being in a less central location in the city as a whole and to fortunate timing. Economically, observes Heiss, the prosperous town had escaped the worst of the 2008 financial crisis, a context that helped keep a lid on inter-communal tensions. Two Casapound councillors lost their seats shortly after my 2020 visit. 'It doesn't mean that their power has vanished,' warns Heiss, pointing out that the group is still active and that the Far Right has a notable presence with the increasingly nationalistic and bigoted Lega and a frightening jump in support nationally for the neo-Fascist Brothers of Italy. 'It's hard to say if [changes to] the monuments had any impact,' he ponders, but adds that the torments of Italian politics could indeed derive from the fact that there has never been a deep confrontation with this totalitarian legacy and sites such as the arch and the frieze. 'Ultimately, though, there was the will to find consensus.'[5] There is, says Heiss, now less segregation and more contact between the language groups.

Giorgio Mezzalira, one of the competition judges, thinks the changes at the Monument to Victory and to the frieze at the Casa del Fascio have been more than symbolic; they have 'defused

the last weapons in the hands of the agitators of ethnic conflict, those who have forced history for political ends,' changing
places of conflict between Italians and Germans into places of
understanding. 'Even the most radical Italian and German right-
wingers [such as] Casapound and the Südtiroler Freiheit seem
to be confined to a corner and no longer able to make a strong
cultural and political impact,' he asserts.[6] Not for the moment,
at least.

> The important thing is to have understood that the passions of
> identity cannot be governed by making them slowly subside, but
> instead by showing oneself capable of facing them and interven-
> ing with cultural choices that generate positive symbols, sincere
> democratic passions, and civil and peaceful coexistence. Another
> thing I hope we have learned is that, when one finds oneself in a
> context of multiple identities and symbols, it is always better to
> "add" rather than "remove."

The failure to adequately address the politicised architectural
fabric and meaning of Bolzano more widely – beyond its principal problem monuments – is something that now exercises Hans
Heiss: 'The arch and the frieze are only fragments,' he reflects.
Transforming these monuments should have been just the first
step to dealing with the fascist and nationalist legacy of the area.
He worries about the lack of 'systematic activity' today on these
issues. The flurry of thinking and debate and change over the
last decade has now subsided.

Directly opposite the Fascist frieze, Axum-style imperial
obelisks and the inscription 'Pro Italico Imperio' celebrating
Mussolini's brutal empire still decorate the Tribunale building
where death sentences were passed on anti-Fascist partisans.
The entire neighbourhood, in fact, is a well-preserved Fascist
workers' quarter with little explanation as to why it looks as it
does. Mezzalira agrees that all across Bolzano there are 'buildings that were once symbols of a dictatorial regime that denied
freedom and democracy, oppressed linguistic minorities and celebrated the superiority of one people over the others, and which

were not removed in the immediate post-war period.' Mezzalira suggests that these buildings have 'lent themselves to easy
political exploitation and the political use of history ... fuelling
permanent contrasts between linguistic groups and reinforcing
the perception of having a past that is difficult to reconcile.'
The possibility of peaceful coexistence is made more fragile, he
believes, by identity-based spaces of belonging.

For all these drawbacks, we can learn much from Bolzano. A
problematic site of honour has been turned into a site of conscious reflection. It provides object lessons in how history can be
updated without being erased and within a good faith rather than
bad faith 'retain and explain' framework. It shows us that something can be done to counter the lies and manipulations of the
constructed world around us, even if only about monuments as
the most obvious sites of deceit. We can learn much from a town
where one freely crosses and re-crosses a river taking in tamed
monuments between Germanic gothic arches and Mussolini-era
classical arcades, choosing between *imbissen* stalls and gelato
shops, and where the citizens appear to be becoming ever more
at ease with their modern polyglot European identity.

It is questionable though whether memorialisation as a practice can ever be truly rescued from the mire of lies and spin, or
whether we should instead stop altogether peppering our cities
with stone and bronze images of those deemed important. There
are alternatives to the jeweled noose of memory (to paraphrase
poet Orlando Ricardo Menes).

To ensure there were no perpetual symbols of enmity between
Greeks, we are told via Polybius and by Plutarch, who praised
the practice, that the ancient Hellenistic custom was to erect
battlefield trophies in timber rather than stone so that they would
decay over a generation – a guard against hubris in victory also.[7]
Renewing or repairing victory trophies was not allowed, just as
tearing down monuments to defeat was also forbidden (a courtesy only extended to fellow Greek combatants).

And ironically given the personality cults that came later,
the Bolsheviks were also mindful, initially at least, of the

perpetuation of the cult of monuments and their tendency to fix ideas in time rather than allow their evolution. Albert Boime argues that Lenin, in the famous 'Monumental Propaganda' 1918 decree, proposed only temporary monuments in timber and plaster that would never exist long enough to outlast their topical, propagandist significance to the new society being born.[8] Whether the ephemeral materials policy was wholly far-sighted or partly the pragmatic logic of civil war resource shortages is not entirely clear.

There have been other prominent opponents too: 'Away with the monuments!' said Nietzsche, in a critique of Germany's historicism and history's 'monumental mode' tendency to falsify the past with temples and idols that promote conservativism and illusions of immortality among those not able to endure the mortal truth – a position influenced by ancient Greek thought.[9] Similarly, urban historian Lewis Mumford believed that modern architecture should reject the deceptive illusion of permanence advanced by monuments, arguing that they were incompatible with Modernism's belief in dynamic renewal. A disposability less easy to justify in a climate emergency on a finite planet.[10]

Perhaps though, we should be allowing our monuments to fall into ruin, let them fade from history in their own time. Monuments are, after all, just the nails sticking up from a wider city fabric that attract threads of attention from time to time. 'It is the very normality and ordinariness of our built surroundings that disguises other possibilities', writes feminist architecture academic Jos Boys, before going on to quote anthropologist David Braeber's comment that 'the ultimate hidden truth of the world is that it is something that we make, and could just as easily make differently.'[11] Perhaps there is an analogy here with individual statues representing personal bigotry and the wider urban fabric embodying systemic and institutionalised oppression; monumental bad apples versus the whole rotten state apparatus that capitalist cities embody.

Yet although monuments may not be particularly articulate at conveying meaning and are hopeless at acting as inclusive role models, and might even be a distraction ideologically, their mute testimony, their evidentiary role remains important. The risks of not preserving evidence are clear. Soon, with the final eyewitnesses to Auschwitz-Birkenau dead, the genuine material traces of the place will take on an even more important function for the truthful testimony they offer.

Still, some think it is time to let even Auschwitz's built fabric slowly disintegrate. 'Let us leave this cursed place to rot,' said historian James Young, suggesting that while some artefacts should remain, others should be allowed to slowly age so that visitors could see both what the camp was and the passage of time since.[12] Robert Jan van der Pelt, who did so much to trounce Holocaust deniers with his architectural evidence at the Irving trial, is also able to contemplate the managed decay of Auschwitz-Birkenau and its authentic traces. He once proposed creating a memorial of the site that emphasises its empty enormity, a memorial of desolation. 'Future generations may [then] walk through Birkenau but, not being of it, they will be constrained to walk over it. It will be their lot to pass over that terrain, unable to grasp the events of the killing fields.'[13] More recently he has gone further, suggesting that Auschwitz should eventually be forgotten:

> It might be that we will agree that the best way to honour those who were murdered in the camp and those who survived is by sealing it from the world, allowing grass, roots and brambles to cover, undermine and finally efface that most unnatural creation of Man. At that future date, may the slowly crumbling debris of decay suggest the final erasure of memory.[14]

German art historian Detlef Hoffmann disagrees, arguing that the idea of a triumphal return to nature and time healing all is unimaginable here: 'The ruins must be preserved.'[15] Others go further, arguing for reconstruction to ensure continued understanding. But the dangers of that approach are obvious: 'We cannot take the risk of provoking new accusations of falsification,' said David Cesarini, the late director of the Wiener Library in London. 'On the other hand, we cannot allow the ravages of time to destroy the site.'[16]

A similar balance is (in theory) being sought at perpetrator sites such as the Nazi Party rally grounds and zeppelin field at Nuremberg where Hitler declaimed to his massed supporters and Leni Riefenstahl filmed her 1935 documentary *Triumph of the Will*. US troops occupying it in 1945 blew up the crowning golden swastika; then in the 1960s the city council blew up the grandstand's double row of pillars, causing severe damage to the rest of the building before the grounds were declared an historical site in 1973.

But entropy is relentless, the concrete is still corroding, the mighty edifice crumbling. Some plead for the whole thing to be bulldozed. The city council says that would 'sweep history under the carpet.' It also resisted a strategy of managed decay and is instead now spending tens of millions of euros to conserve what survives: 'We won't rebuild, we won't restore, but we will conserve,' said Julia Lehner, Nuremberg's chief culture official. 'It is an important witness to an era – it allows us to see how dictatorial regimes stage-manage themselves. That has educational value today.'[17] These fine words have been undermined by a 2021 decision to use the intimidatingly massive Congress Hall at the rally grounds as a concert hall and cultural centre. 'Do you want to dress up a building such as this as a fancy cultural center?' asks Florian Dierl, director of the Documentation Center Nazi Party Rally Grounds who said the proposal should not be allowed to dilute the function of the memorial site.[18]

It would indeed seem strange to let the sites of victimhood vanish but see perpetrator sites such as Nuremberg's survive conserved, especially in a political climate in which the Far Right is doubling down on its anti-cosmopolitan culture wars.

In 2021, as Boris Johnson and his government were ramping up plans to hand out longer prison sentences for damaging a statue than for rape, historical pastiches were continuing apace across Germany where remade city centres are denying the truth of history. Alternative für Deutschland representatives in the

Bundestag launched a National Action Plan on Cultural Identity that decried the disintegration of the country's culture, threatened, it warned, by mass immigration, multiculturalism, decolonialism, and 'special rights' for minorities: 'Without history and tradition ... there is no cultural memory as a prerequisite for a sense of belonging together,' the AfD fretted, calling for the protection of a specifically German culture.[19]

'The successful reconstruction projects in Dresden, Frankfurt/Main, or Berlin show that there is a basic need for cultural identity,' they continued, citing Leon Krier in rejecting the 'man-hating ugliness' of Modernism. With some nerve, the document turns facts on their head, arguing that post-colonial scholarship has created a 'grotesque image' of Europe's past that is 'full of fake history.' In the wake of BLM protests, the AfD resolution also called for increased security measures to protect monuments and the reconstruction of buildings destroyed in the war using federal funds.

The resolution also quotes writer Cora Stephan, who has compared the destroyers of monuments to Mao's Red Guards: 'When historical memory is to be erased, everything becomes present, rootless and connectionless: The generational connection is erased. The ancient solidarity between man and woman crumbles under shrill feminist attacks.'[20] Not quite 'blood and soil' but not far off. The language demonstrates neatly how the language of collective memory and identity can be deployed by the Far Right as well as the Left intelligentsia.

The same month in Modi's India, another historic mosque in Uttar Pradesh, not that far from the historic flash point in Ayodhya, was destroyed by the BJP administration, its rubble bulldozed into a river while local Muslim leaders went into hiding. Around the same time, Israel ratcheted up its offensive in segregated East Jerusalem where the seizure of Palestinian homes by Jewish settlers and incursions onto Temple Mount led to renewed devastation in Gaza. In Denmark, the government dropped the word 'ghetto' from its segregation legislation but announced further crackdowns on the number of 'non-Western' residents allowed to live in certain disadvantaged neighbourhoods. In May 2021, as the British government demanded that the 'metropolitan bubble' lose control of cultural institutions and museum trustees who resisted the 'retain and explain' diktat were replaced, minister Robert Jenrick floated proposals to revise national building regulations to enforce separate toilets for each gender and ban gender-neutral facilities in new public buildings, offices, shops, hospitals, and entertainment venues, echoing the many 'bathroom bills' in US states. A few months later, Prince Charles announced a second Classical new town with thousands of neo-Georgian homes – this time on 131ha of land he owns at Faversham in Kent.

We can usefully characterise today's culture war arguments as a 'crisis of hegemony: the decay of the dominant forms of bourgeois rule,' where the neoliberal order is crumbling but its opposition is not yet powerful enough to provide an alternative vision that captures the imagination of the mass of people. It is here that the Far Right steps in to exploit the dysfunction and uncertainty, especially in its use of Islamophobia, transphobia, and appeals to heritage nostalgia and a mythologised but more certain past.[21] In this, the Far Right resembles historic anti-Semitic, misogynist, and homophobic Fascism (although it differs in other important ways) whose ideas are being absorbed by an increasingly authoritarian mainstream Right of the type found in governments the world over today. Unless we descend fully into barbarism, however, these regimes will lose the culture wars. They will find themselves on the wrong side of history, of cultural and social progress, but no one should underestimate the viciousness of their last stand.

The struggle over monuments, architecture, and the city, however, is also illustrative of a typically too narrow Gramscian framing that sees counter-hegemonic efforts as not so much about wars of position over ideas and class consciousness but a distracting scrabble over cultural products that are of various degrees of marginality. In such a framing, gentrification, for instance, is discussed not as displacement of the spaces and homes of the racialised working class, of women, and of sexual minorities, but instead becomes a lifestyle issue of hipsterism. Gramsci saw spontaneous rebellions as important in forming consciousness and the successful toppling of the Colston statue is an example of this, but using contested monuments as proxy weapons could, in the long run, prove far more useful to the Right in that it is the establishment that ultimately has the resources and gatekeeping positions to control the fate of the commemorative landscape. It can use this control to effect divide and rule, sometimes consciously deploying Gramscian arguments from a right-wing perspective.

It can sometimes feel then as if we are trapped in an eternal cycling through disaster where, as Fredric Jameson says, it is easier to imagine the end of the world than to imagine the end of capitalism. What is necessary, Jameson urges, is a 'breaking out of the windless present of the postmodern back into real historical time, and a history made by human beings.'[22] This is not about seeing the built environment as neutral or irrelevant – quite the opposite – it is about a better understanding of the inter-relationship between people and their environment and the primacy of human rather than built interventions.

For those working with the constructed past, whether monuments, historic buildings or all long-standing public places and spaces, this means understanding how the politicised built environment attempts to convey narratives and how best to intervene to ensure that truths rather than lies are being told in these places. It means understanding the methods by which an Ehrenmal can be transformed into a Mahnmal and how this is preferable to comprehensive iconoclasm. It means an ethical approach to the public realm, resisting both forced segregation or forced integration and seeking ways of overcoming invisibility and marginalisation in the cityscape. It means being aware of the illusion that beauty is innate or eternal rather than being mutable and culturally located.

We need to ensure that our physical surroundings accurately reflect the lives of all, not just of the chosen few and to not let totalitarians gull us into a dangerous nonchalance regarding the difference between the real and the ersatz. We must distinguish between irrelevant symbolism and genuinely damaging ideology, between positive real-world change and misguided architectural determinism. Importantly, achieving honest and explanatory new layers in our city through critical reconstruction and subversive transformation requires that we first tackle the gatekeepers who too often have the same class and other sectional interests as those who erected monuments in the first place and who can be as problematic as the objects they police.

We should defend organisations such as the UK's National Trust from the Right's culture warriors when they produce reports pointing out the connections between their collections and colonialism, even while acknowledging that, if not carefully located in the just allocation of resources, this can amount to empty virtue signalling: The Trust's *Colonial Countryside* report that enraged the British government and saw threats to its charitable status was published only weeks after the Trust had announced around 1,200 job losses in a 'reset' that would ravage its education services, abandoning its work with schools' curricula and especially its programmes with city schools. As objectors to the changes pointed out, this would affect poorer children the most and so, disproportionally, children of colour for whom the countryside, colonial or not, would be increasingly out of reach and unexplained. As one education volunteer put it: 'We'll go back to that sterile 20th-century experience of going round a country house – it's going to be white, middle-class elderly people going there to have cream teas and stare at the tapestries.'[23] No amount of righteous reports will undo that damage.

Perhaps this is precisely the Right's culture war tactic – to starve culture of resources and force hard choices so it can weaponise these episodes to argue that it is either decolonialism or cream teas – that we can't have both, and where an honest reckoning with the past is presented as a zero-sum approach to history and heritage. Bristol history professor and Countering Colston activist Madge Dresser astutely commented that the Tory government's actions and the imposition of the 'retain and explain policy' amounted to a power grab: 'It is a bid to control history and to bring these vital local decisions under the over-centralised and partisan grip of the Tory party.'[24]

In resisting a post-truth world, it is essential that an authentic built environment is re-asserted in the face of denial, that the facts of the world are primary and that the material evidence of the past is safeguarded so that the reliability of the world is restored. The perils of the inauthentic, of sanctifying myths and collective memories rather than the fragile truth, are clear at historic sites across the world, especially where these are sites of conscience. We need to bear this in mind when considering the digital copy or a pastiche façade or when making alterations that lessen our understanding of why a building or place is like it is and how it has changed over time. It matters supremely when we are considering how the material trace can be evidence of past crimes against humanity.

Robert Bevan

9.1 The Neues Museum in Berlin, whose wartime ruin was re-imagined by David Chipperfield and conservation architect Julian Harrap, is an object lesson in layered critical reconstruction that learns from Munich's Alte Pinakotheken. It is part of Chipperfield's ongoing reinterpretation of the Museum Island complex and the antithesis of the Humboldt Forum nearby.

We cannot carelessly give a point of entry to the liars and deniers of the mortal cost of colonialism or the Holocaust. There is a need, more than ever, for a coherent policy framework that reasserts the centrality of authenticity in guiding truth in reconstruction – even if in some cases it is only to consciously and carefully set it aside. The Charter of Venice needs updating, including to take into account the rise of the digital, but, fundamentally, it needs reaffirming. To achieve this rescue of objective material history from partial heritage means championing critical reconstruction where the fragments and layers of history and its traumas are incorporated into the fabric of a building, just as a layered subversive transformation of monumental sites and statues can ensure that their narrative is interrogated without excising the historical record. It means using the architectural and monumental for discursive rather than censorious purposes. And even before considering critical reconstruction, we need to remember that "we shall rebuild" is not always the successful prophylactic against iconoclastic destruction that it is thought to be and, in downplaying the cultural consequences of conflict, may even make conflict more likely in the long run.

Only an entirely different order of international politics can provide sustainable answers to such questions, but there is much more that could be done today. UNESCO and others are now, falteringly, attempting to make the humanitarian link between the fate of heritage in conflicts and the living people it belongs to with, for instance, a memorandum of understanding between UNESCO and the Red Cross. But for the moment these are largely paper exercises except, tellingly, where they are linked to military operations by the West. Related NGOs such as Blue Shield, the scantily resourced heritage equivalent to the Red Cross, is making some limited real-world difference around the edges but again without fully articulating a methodology for achieving this neutrally and transparently in a way that is seen to be conscious of the ethical quicksand of the military-heritage complex – and then avoiding it.

Despite being said in bad faith, the Bamiyan Buddha-destroying Taliban scholar Mullah Omar was in some ways correct in his criticism that until the West can demonstrate that it understands that the fate of struggling peoples is as important their material cultures there will be no resolution to the ongoing attacks on both.

Incorporating cultural destruction into the definition of genocide is essential to making this happen. At the very least more resources need to be dedicated to gathering the architectural evidence of war crimes and crimes against humanity and understanding heritage destruction as a vital early warning indicator of genocide and ethnic cleansing rather than it being a vague afterthought.

Among the chief reasons why these vital changes will not take place is that their application in times of war would see demands for their application in times of peace – as absolutely should be the case. Truly linking the fate of minority groups such as First Nations peoples to the fate of their culture and asserting their cultural rights in the face of settler-colonial societies would amplify the voices calling for social justice, restitution, and reparations on the path to truth and reconciliation.

There are small glimpses of hope despite the inability of UNESCO to provide leadership. For instance, a recent film by ICORP – the ICOMOS International Scientific Committee on Risk Preparedness – explores the way two different faith communities on either side of the India/Pakistan border have cared for each other's forcibly abandoned religious buildings since Partition. For the first time since 1947, a safe corridor now exists for Sikhs in India to visit one of these sites – a shrine at Muslim Kartarpur now in Pakistan.[25] Despite the many reconciliation myths surrounding it, heritage, if wisely used, can indeed help people see themselves in the mirror of belonging.

However, it can just as easily, be used to resist progress. Cornelius Holtorf, the UNESCO Chair on Heritage Futures at Linnaeus University in Sweden, questions assumptions of 'culturalism' that have long infused disciplines such as archaeology and heritage. Culturalism, he argues, assumes that individuals 'are determined by their unambiguously distinct cultures' that must be preserved 'and can only be realised within their respective cultures.' (In some ways this was Lemkin's thinking with its emphasis on protecting the cultural expression of national genius.) Holtorf notes that this idea is present on the Right and Left but is 'dangerous because it challenges civil liberties and human rights in the name of a profoundly essentializing notion of cultural diversity' within narrow, protected 'cultural cages' that downplay individual diversity and freedom within culture.[26] This is a variation on the critique that bureaucratic multiculturalism is not truly cosmopolitan because it overemphasises cultural allegiance and can, in reality, work against human rights.

'Heritage and history are very much implicated in this debate,' writes Holtorf, 'because they make differences between people a seemingly natural outcome of the past which ultimately governs who belongs where.' This has its origins in the Enlightenment and was elaborated in the Romantic Nationalism of nineteenth-century European nation formation. He quotes Norwegian anthropologist Thomas Hylland Eriksen who argued that in an age when conflicts often have an ethno-cultural dimension, UNESCO is naively fuelling identity politics, which set groups at loggerheads. Groups rights are protected ahead of the equal rights of the highly diverse and mobile individuals of today's globalised world. Holtorf suggests a de-territorialisation of culture that does not idealise tribal communities, that looks to transcend purportedly distinct human cultures, and which recognises that people have multiple, hybrid, partial, and overlapping identities and porous boundaries.

> Today, it can no longer be taken for granted that the vast majority of people living in any one area do (or would want to) share the same cultural identity, a common history and a joint sense of belong ... We all have multiple collective identities and very many of them are not anchored in the collective past.[27]

This approach has many legitimate attractions, and it is echoed in the work of writers such as Amartya Sen, who also questions multiculturalism as opposed to allowing people a multiplicity of affiliations.[28] 'Historical change is not the time for sentimentality about what is at risk of being lost but for learning, creativity and reinvention,' continues Holtorf. We should lessen our psychosocial dependency on the past especially where self-esteem is rooted in victimhood. Holtorf also questions whether the value of heritage resides in its tangible fabric but instead in what it does in society. Accepting loss of the past is, he suggests, a better way forward for sustainable peace and understanding than supposed reconciliation through mutual cultural appreciation – UNESCO's founding logic. 'Peace and understanding should not be based on who our ancestors were or may have been, and their legacies but rather who we or our children are or aspire to be.'[29]

All this is fantastic stuff as a defence of the cosmopolitan in abstract but, perhaps, too easily said if you are not being oppressed: Within the context of not just culture wars intent on rolling back progress on equality, or ethnic cleansers and genocidaires ravaging communities and destroying their material culture, Holtorf's arguments are theoretically astute but can read as the heritage equivalent of ultra-Left utopianism in practice. Certainly, we can embrace multiple affinities in the interests of a genuine intersectionality and resist nationalist ones that seek to collapse differences. But given that identity emerges in relation to place and has a complex interaction with it, we cannot abandon identity altogether when re-shaping the constructed world for the better or leave its reshaping to bad faith actors. We cannot yet let go entirely of identity as a useful concept while, being alive to its drawbacks as a tactic for challenging the fundamentals of capitalism.

At the same time, we must understand the limits of the architectural to effect change. There is a difference between creating spaces for potentiality and expecting the architectural itself to lead to social change. Social cohesion can be hindered by poor design – blocks arranged so that neighbours don't easily meet one another, locations segregated from the life of the city that reinforce isolation and that contribute to 'othering.' But this is a two-way relationship, not one where people are simply subject to the design of cities. We need to stop seeing people as essentially passive responders to their physical surroundings and unquestioning worshippers of oppressive monuments.

Attempts by 'insurgent' architects and insurgent architecture to challenge the dominant order, often by working with communities, can negotiate cracks in the façade of capitalist urbanisation and construction but, as with buildings and symbols themselves, these strategies can never entirely transcend the system. Nevertheless, they are important. Reclaiming heritage for the Left is part of this, including recognising that, whatever the intentions of conservative ideologues, the genuinely historic, human-scale traditional environment that we have inherited can be a vital bulwark against rapacious development. There is no need to be doctrinaire – we can recognise that dense terraces and mansion blocks make better and more sustainable cities without needing to shape them with deceptive Regency or Edwardian drag.

Most often though, the answers to questions of life and death are simply not architectural; design should not be substituted for human action in other spheres of life. We should take a leaf from the book of French architects Lacaton & Vassal, who once refused to alter a public space on the grounds that it was fine as it was and the public money could be spent more wisely elsewhere. Their motto, partly informed by sustainability, is 'never demolish, never remove – always add, transform and re-use.'

Architecture and city-making may be highly politicised, but no building, however radical its aesthetic or programmatically utopian, can itself change society or forge progress ahead of the human agency that creates the conditions of the time. Architecture is always the expression of existing social relations even where it makes concrete a vision of a possible alternative future. Academic Neal Leach agrees that political content does not reside in architectural form; that the built environment is politicised, a screen reflecting values back to us rather than being innately political: 'An aesthetic "revolution" which challenges the values and norms of the world,' he writes, 'should be distinguished from a social revolution which challenges the existing power structure within a broader political context.'[30] It is a crucial distinction but one which activist Modernism often confused in its hopes of being emancipatory. However, the Modernist design project was also at its best when in concert with the political, for example, in its provision of space for the Welfare State. Design can facilitate progress and we must defend this from the depredations of politicians and architectural traditionalists.

Imagination and subtlety are needed. We should embrace complexity. Sometimes it is exactly the ambivalences and contradictions that are the most interesting and revealing. New layers to monuments and additions to buildings can enrich meanings and, to use Frederic Jameson's term, resist 'historical deafness.' The iconoclastic banishing of problem monuments, the diminishment of history's accumulation of material only adds to a knowledge-lite affectlessness and depthlessness – and this in a climate that already questions authentic materiality while revelling in the surface and the copy.

For now at least, we do not have the luxury of forgetting the past altogether or of refusing to fight our side of the culture war. We have to defend groups such as Countering Colston and Rhodes Must Fall even while questioning whether comprehensive removal rather than reworking is the best tactic if we want to create thinking sites that shame rather than honour. In Britain, where even the Labour Party has sought to wrap itself in the Union Jack and to distance itself from groups such as Black Lives Matter, a defence of the cosmopolitan is unlikely to come from within Parliament.

However, while recognising that monuments matter, if we want a movement to achieve genuine change in the built environment, rather than focusing on the symbolic change provided by toppling statues, we might do better to focus the bulk of our energies on progressive demands such as resisting segregation (including through gentrification), fighting for affordable housing, and ensuring that the gatekeepers and professionals shaping this environment are more representative and inclusive.

Reparations and the correcting of past wrongs is not dependent on having more representative monuments – or at most this is a marginal component of such an achievement. At the very least we should reconsider whether we should be valorising individuals any further with memorials, a practice whose utility is at best doubtful.

It also demands that even if objectivity can never be entirely achieved, we have a duty to attempt to get as close to it as possible. Instead of postmodernism's rejection of totality and universal reality, we need to restore the primacy of truth and fact, of evidence and the material trace, of history over memory. This is about establishing the sound empirical footings on which to push past the culture wars in the name of achieving material progressive change. Architecture is not destiny, and it alone cannot create diverse communities; it can't end racism, sexism, or homophobia, or affect global politics through the arrangement of bricks and mortar.

A new cultural turn is needed in architecture and city-making that retains its interest in meaning but not at the expense of objective truth and which re-integrates cultural questions within the socioeconomic. Yes, we need to better understand the potentially malignant power of architecture and to call out chicanery, but we also need to let go of deterministic architectural myths and find a way out of defeatism to reclaim the optimism of Modernism and the utopian without fetishizing its aesthetic.

Yet while recognising that culture wars are manufactured and that progressives would rather be focusing on material change in society, these wars are having a real-world effect that we cannot ignore. President Trump may have gone (for now) but Trumpism has captured the Republican Party; according to some polls up to a third of Republicans believe patriots need to resort to violence to save the nation. A 2021 report in the *Washington Post* traced this back not simply to Trump but to culture wars architect Pat Buchanan's decades long narrative of the country being under threat from cultural liberalism.[31] This has not gone away. At the same time, peoples' understanding of the facts of history is diminishing. Almost half Americans under age forty could not name a single concentration camp or ghetto established during the Holocaust. Just under a third of Britons of all ages couldn't either.[32]

In an era of anxiety about fake news and fading memories, it is more important than ever to have an honest monumental record surrounding us and to understand how the built environment constructs consent. Tolerating uncomfortable evidence becomes easier not just with an honest reckoning but when real change is made in the world rather than simply to its symbols. We have to move beyond the truths and lies embodied in monuments, or evident in the targets of wartime destruction and the choices made in post-conflict rebuilds, to questions of authenticity in our wider peacetime environment where slower, more insidious practices of collusion and manipulation are more easily concealed than in the sharpness of war. Crucial, is an understanding of the intent behind acts of construction and destruction in peacetime as well as wartime and the placing of human rights at the centre of this task.

We need to be able to trust the tangible world around us and to trust that change comes through the agency of people, not things. And we need to follow the advice of Hannah Arendt and worldly Bolzano-Bozen: 'No one has the right to obey.'

Acknowledgements

Thanks are due to my always positive editor and insightful Leo Hollis plus no end of other helpful people.

Among them: Umberto Albarella, Jane Bevan, John Bold, Roger Bowdler, Joanna Burch-Brown, David Chipperfield, David Crowley, Emma Cunliffe, Madge Dresser, Joseph Galliano, Patty Gerstenblith, Antonio Gonzalez Zarandona, Cornelius Holtorf, Ursula Friedrich (they know who they are), Jeremy Gould, Neil Heathcote, Hans Heiss, Richard Hughes, Jenny Kingston, Moritz Kinzel, Stephen Larin, Peter Larkham, Sandra Lawrence, Keith Lowe, Simon Maghakyan, Piotr Majewski, Giorgio Mezzalira, Luke Moffett, Winfried Nerdinger, Silke Neumann, Hannes Obermair, András Riedlmayer, Roberto Rosso, Andreas Ruby, Neil Shasore, Tim Slade, Claire Smith, Bart Staszewski, Peter Stone, Karen Storey, Ulrich Tempel, Stephan Trüby, Sassa Trülzsch, Robert Jan van Pelt, Dacia Viejo Rose, Susanne Vees-Gulani, Helen Walasek, Loïc Wacquant, Mathias Wasik, Claire Zimmerman

Notes

Introduction

1   Hannah Arendt, *The Origins of Totalitarianism,* New York: Harcourt, Brace and Co., 1951, 474.

2   Hannah Arendt, *The Human Condition,* New York: Doubleday Anchor, 1958, 95–96.

3   Eric J Hobsbawm and Terence O Ranger, *The Invention of Tradition,* Cambridge: Cambridge University Press, 1983; Benedict Anderson, *Imagined Communities,* London: Verso, 2006.

4   F F J Schouten, 'Heritage as Historical Reality,' in David T. Herbert, ed., *Heritage, Tourism and Society,* London: Mansell, 1995, 21.

5   David Lowenthal, *The Past Is a Foreign Country,* Cambridge: Cambridge University Press, 1985. Robert Hewison, *The Heritage Industry: Britain in a Climate of Decline,* London: Methuen, 1987.

6   Pat Buchanan, '1992 Republican National Convention Speech,' 17 August 1992, buchanan.org/blog.

7   The Newsroom, 'Where Are the Statues of Scots Women?' *The Scotman* [online], 23 January 2016, scotsman.com/news. See the Discover Artworks database at Art UK, artuk.org.

8   See Antonio Gramsci, *Prison Notebooks, Vol. 3,* trans. J A Buttigieg, New York: Columbia University Press, 2007.

9   Quoted in Guy Puzey and Laura Kostanski, eds, *Names and Naming: People, Places, Perceptions and Power,* Bristol: Multilingual Matters, 2016, 258.

10 Michelle Alexander, *The New Jim Crow: Mass Incarceration in the Age of Colorblindness,* New York: The New Press, 2010.

11 Lee McIntyre, *Post-Truth*, Cambridge, MA: MIT Press, 2018.

12 George Orwell, *1984*, New York: Harcourt, Brace & World, 1949.

13 McIntyre, *Post-Truth*, 13.

14 Hannah Arendt, *The Origins of Totalitarianism*, New York: Harcourt, Brace, 1951, xx.

15 Timothy Snyder, 'The American Abyss,' *New York Times*, 9 January 2021.

16 Philip K Dick, Mark Hurst, and Paul Williams, *I Hope I Shall Arrive Soon*, New York: Doubleday, 1985.

17 Robert Bevan, *The Destruction of Memory: Architecture at War*, London: Reaktion, 2006.

18 "What Is Proletarian Culture, and Is It Possible?," in Leon Trotsky, *Literature and Revolution*, trans. Rose Strunsky (New York: International Publishers, 1925), 187.

19 Winston Churchill, House of Commons Rebuilding, London, 28 October 1943. See 'Churchill and the Commons Chamber', parliament.uk.

20 Kenan Malik, 'Beware the Politics of Identity,' *The Observer*, 23 February 2020.

1. Killers on Every Corner

1 Charles Gilmour, 'Cecil Rhodes Protest: On Whitehall's "Murder Mile," the Empire's Heroes Are Steeped in Innocent Blood,' *The Independent*, 12 February 2016.

2 Robert Musil, 'Denkmale' (1957) in *Gesammelte Werke*, quoted in Hans-Ernst Mittig, 'Das Denkmal,' in *Eine Geschichte der Kunst im Wondel ihrer Funktionen*, vol. II, Munich: Funkkolleg Kunst, 1987, 532.

3 See Frank Edwards, Hedwig Lee, and Michael Esposito, 'Risk of Being Killed by Police Use of Force in the United States by Age, Race–Ethnicity, and Sex,' *Proceedings of the National Academy of Sciences*, 116: 34, 2019, pnas.org.

4 Pierre Bourdieu, quoted in Derek Alderman, 'Place Naming and the Interpretation of Cultural Landscapes,' in Brian Graham and Peter Howard, eds, *The Ashgate Research Companion to Heritage and Identity*, Farnham, UK: Ashgate, 2006.

5 Bridgett Cherry and Nikolaus Pevsner, *London 2: South*, Buildings of England Series, London: Penguin Books, 1983. The statutory listing description says it was erected 1714, but this might be the date of a later plaque. Alternatively, the earliest immortalisation of a named commoner may be a 1712 statue of

John Pierrepont, a London vintner, by John Nost attached to the façade of Lucton School, near Leominster, Herefordshire.

6   From the database of the Public Monuments and Sculpture Association, National Recording Project, retrieved May 2017.

7   See 'Banking – Clayton & Morris Papers,' bonhams.com.

8   Cited in J Empson, 'Little Honoured in His Own Country: Statues in Recognition of Edward Jenner MD FRS,' *Journal of the Royal Society of Medicine* 89, 1996, 514–18.

9   Charles Gilmour, 'Cecil Rhodes Protest: On Whitehall's "Murder Mile," the Empire's Heroes Are Steeped in Innocent Blood,' *The Independent*, 12 February 2016.

10   Dario Gamboni, *The Destruction of Art: Iconoclasm and Vandalism since the French Revolution*, London: Reaktion Books, 2007, 224.

11   Gamboni, *The Destruction of Art*, 226.

12   Caroline Criado-Perez, 'I Sorted the UK's Statues by Gender – a Mere 2.7 Per Cent Are of Historical, Non-Royal Women,' *The New Statesman*, 26 March 2016.

13   Judith M Bennet, 'Remembering Elizabeth Etchingham and Agnes Oxenbridge,' in Noreen Giffney, Michelle M. Sauer, and Diane Watt, eds, *The Lesbian Premodern*, New York: Palgrave, 2011.

14   Gamboni, *The Destruction of Art*, 154.

15   See Rollin Gustav Osterweis, *The Myth of the Lost Cause 1865– 1900*, Hamden, CT: Archon Books, 1973.

16   See David W Blight, *Race and Reunion: The Civil War in American Memory*, Cambridge, MA: Belknap Press of Harvard University Press, 2001.

17   Michelle Alexander, *The New Jim Crow: Mass Incarceration in the Age of Colorblindness*, New York: The New Press, 2010, 29.

18   Catherine Clinton, ed., *Confederate Statues and Memorialization*, Athens: The University of Georgia Press, 2019, 112–16.

19   Clinton, ed., *Confederate Statues and Memorialization*.

20   Kirk Savage, *Standing Soldiers, Kneeling Slaves: Race, War, and Monument in Nineteenth-Century America*, Princeton: Princeton University Press, 2017.

21   Lorraine Boissoneault, 'What Will Happen to Stone Mountain, America's Largest Confederate Memorial?' *Smithsonian Magazine*, 22 August 2017, smithsonianmag.com. See also David B Freeman, *Carved in Stone: The History of Stone Mountain*, Macon, GA: Mercer University Press, 1997.

22   Blight, *Race and Reunion*, 97.

23   Madge Dresser, 'Squares of Distinction, Webs of Interest:

Gentility, Urban Development and the Slave Trade in Bristol c.1673–1820,' *Slavery & Abolition* 21: 3, 2000, 21–47.

24 Roger Ball, 'Myths Within Myths ... Edward Colston and That Statue,' Bristol Radical History Group, 2020, brh.org.uk.

25 See N Finney and K Lymperopoulou, *Local Ethnic Inequalities: Ethnic Differences in Education, Employment, Health and Housing in Districts of England and Wales, 2001–2011*, published by Centre on Dynamics of Ethnicity and Runnymede Trust, 2014.

26 Paul Maylam, *The Cult of Rhodes: Remembering an Imperialist in Africa*, Cape Town: David Philip, 2005, 159.

27 See Timothy Ryback, *Contested Histories in Public Spaces: Principles, Processes, Best Practices,* International Bar Association, 2021, 74, ibanet.org.

28 See 'Rhodes Must Fall in Oxford', at rmfoxford.wordpress.com.

29 Tim Sculthorpe and Eleanor Harding, 'Oxford University students who want to ban Cecil Rhodes from the campus should take their education somewhere else, Lord Patten insists in defiance of campaign' *Daily Mail*, 12 January 2016.

30 BBC News, 'Cecil Rhodes Statue to Be Kept by Oxford University College,' 29 January 2016.

31 BBC News, 'Cecil Rhodes Statue.'

32 Lizzie Dearden, 'How the UK's Far-right Is Trying to Capitalise on the Statues Row,' *The Independent*, 12 June 2020.

33 See 'Who Are We and What Do We Stand For,' Save Our Statues, saveourstatues.net.

34 See 'Why Douglas Murray Doesn't Trust People Who Say Britain Is a Racist Country', posted to Joe, 31 August 2020, m.facebook.com/www.JOE.co.uk.

35 David Smith, 'US under Siege from "Far-left Fascism", Says Trump in Mount Rushmore Speech,' *The Guardian*, 4 July 2020.

36 Christopher Knaus and agencies, '"No Pride in Genocide": Vandals Deface Captain Cook Statue in Sydney's Hyde Park,' *The Guardian*, 26 August 2017.

37 Peter Walker, Alexandra Topping and Steven Morris 'Boris Johnson says removing statues is 'to lie about our history',' *The Guardian*, 12 June 2020.

38 Report of a Commission of Inquiry Established by Oriel College, Oxford into Issues Associated with Memorials to Cecil Rhodes, April 2021.

39 See Oliver Dowen, 'HM Government Position on Contested Heritage', DCMS, 22 September 2020, assets.publishing.service.gov.uk.

40 Robert Jenrick, 'We Will Save Britain's Statues from the Woke

Militants Who Want to Censor Our Past,' *The Telegraph*, 16 January 2021.

41 Stephan Delahunty, 'Controversy as Culture Secretary Looks to Warn Charities against "Rewriting" British History,' *Third Sector*, 15 February 2021.

42 Written Ministerial Statement to the House of Commons, 18 January 2021. See 'Planning and Heritage Update; Statement made on 18 January 2021; Statement UIN HLWS709', questions-statements.parliament.uk.

43 Written Ministerial Statement, 18 January 2021.

44 July 21 National Planning Policy Framework.

45 Caitlin McFall, 'Trump Blasts Attempts to Remove Historic Statues as "Censorship",' Fox News, 20 June 2020.

46 Jessica Murray, 'Politicians Should Not "Weaponise" UK History, Says Colonialism Researcher,' *The Guardian*, 22 February 2021.

47 Commission on Race and Ethnic Disparities Report (The Sewell Report), March 2021, assets.publishing.service.gov.uk.

48 Gareth Harris, 'City of London U-turn on Historic Statues Means Slave Trader Sculptures Will Stay in Place,' *The Art Newspaper*, 8 October 2021.

49 Ian Cobain, *The History Thieves: Secrets, Lies and the Shaping of a Modern Nation*, London: Granta Books, 2016, 101–35.

50 Cobain, *The History Thieves*, 142.

51 Robert J Evans, 'Rewritten History,' *London Review of Books* 43: 23, 2 December 2021.

2. Style Wars/Culture Wars

1 Prince Charles, *Charles: The Private Man, the Public Role*, broadcast 29 June 1994 on ITV.

2 Ursula Friedrich is a pseudonym. The interviewee subsequently requested anonymity.

3 Stephan Trüby, *Rechte Räume: Politische Essays und Gespräche (Bauwelt Fundamente, 169)* (German Edition), Basel: Birkhäuser, 2020.

4 See, for example, Gavriel D Rosenfeld, *Munich and Memory: Architecture, Monuments, and the Legacy of the Third Reich*, Berkeley: University of California Press, 2000.

5 Facebook traditional architecture group, accessed 20 October 2020.

6 See Joe Matheson and Tim Veerlan, 'The Far Right's Obsession with Modern Architecture,' Failed Architecture, n.d., failedarchitecture.com. October 2020.

7   Hettie O'Brien, 'How Classical Architecture Became a Weapon for the Far-right,' *New Statesman*, 21 November 2018.

8   Dieter Bartetzko, 'Mut zum Traum,' *Frankfurter Allgemeine Zeitung*, 11 April 2015.

9   Stephan Trüby, 'Wir haben das Haus am rechten Fleck,' *Frankfurter Allgemeine Sonntagszeitung*, 8 April 2018.

10 Robert Bevan, *The Destruction of Memory: Architecture at War*, London: Reaktion, 2006, 187.

11 Philipp Oswalt, 'How Germany's Far-Right Is Gaslighting Architectural History: The Case of Potsdam's Garrison Church,' *Frieze*, 27 August 2019.

12 Oswalt, 'How Germany's Far-Right Is Gaslighting Architectural History.'

13 Marlene Militz, 'Der Turmbau zu Potsdam,' *Taz*, 9 June 2020, taz.de

14 Brian Hanson and Lucien Steil, *The Potsdam Project of The Prince of Wales's Urban Design Task Force 1996*, Prince of Wales's Institute of Architecture, 1998, luciensteil.tripod.com.

15 Bevan, *The Destruction of Memory*, 193–94.

16 Bevan, *The Destruction of Memory*, 195, quoting Michael Z Wise, *Capital Dilemma: Germany's Search for a New Architecture of Democracy*, New York: Princeton Architectural Press, 1998, 115.

17 News, 'Cross Causes Controversy Atop Reconstructed Berlin Palace,' *Deutsche Welle*, 29 May 2020, dw.com.

18 See Jason James, 'Undoing Trauma: Reconstructing the Church of Our Lady in Dresden,' *Ethos* 34: 2, 2006, 244–72.

19 Leon Krier, *Albert Speer: Architecture 1932–1942*, New York: Monacelli Press, 2013.

20 Rowan Moore, 'Is Far-right Ideology Twisting the Concept of "Heritage" in German Architecture?' *The Guardian*, 6 October 2018.

21 See 'The Aylesbury Estate, Southwark: "all that is left of the high hopes of the post-war planners is derelict concrete"', Municipal Dreams blog, 7 January 2014, municipaldreams.wordpress.com.

22 Panel discussion, Fundamentals lecture series: *Beauty*, held at Central Saint Martins, UAL on 24 January 2019, arts.ac.uk/colleges/central-saint-martins.

23 *Architecture of Prosperity: The Built Environment and Creative Capacity with Nick Boles*, Legatum Institute, 24 April 2014, youtube.com.

24 Roger Scruton, *The Classical Vernacular: Architectural Principles in an Age of Nihilism*, Manchester: Carcanet Press, 1994.

25 Create Streets, 'Our Story,' createstreets.com.

26 Will Ing, 'Jenrick Says Permitted Development Provides 'Big Opportunity' to Bulldoze Buildings,' *Architects Journal*, 8 October 2020.

27 Jack Airey, ed., *Building Beautiful*, 2019, policyexchange.org.uk.

28 Marwa Al-Sabouni, *The Battle for Home: The Vision of a Young Architect in Syria*, London: Thames & Hudson, 2016.

29 Samuel Hughes and Ben Southwood *Strong Suburbs: Enabling Streets to Control Their Own Development*, Policy Exchange, 2021, policyexchange.org.uk.

30 As noted in Alan Chandler and Michela Pace, *The Production of Heritage: The Politicisation of Architectural Conservation*, London: Routledge, 2020, 175.

31 Justin Shubow, 'Architecture Continues to Implode: More Insiders Admit the Profession Is Failing,' *Forbes*, 6 January 2015.

32 Michael Sorkin, 'Hitler's Classical Architect,' *The Nation*, 21 May 2013.

3. The Anti-Cosmopolitans

1 Charlemagne, 'The Swiss Minaret Ban,' *The Economist*, 30 November 2009.

2 David Cameron. Speech at Munich Security Conference, 5 February 2011, gov.uk.

3 Ibid

4 Cecile Laborde, 'Which "Multiculturalism" Has Failed, David Cameron' Opendemocracy.net, 14 February 2011.

5 *Muslims in Europe: A Report on 11 EU Cities*, 2d ed., Open Society Institute, 2010, opensocietyfoundation.org.

6 'Have Ferry, Bugeaud and Colbert Become Unshakeable after Macron's Speech?' web24news, 15 June 2020.

7 Grace Jones, 'Why I joined feminism's undercover fightback...' *Daily Mail*, 20 March 2022.

8 Carl Husemoller Nightingale, *Segregation: A Global History of Divided Cities*, Chicago: University of Chicago Press, 2012.

9 Nightingale, *Segregation,* 311.

10 Douglas S Massey and Nancy A Denton, *American Apartheid: Segregation and the Making of the Underclass*, ACLS Humanities E-Book, Cambridge, MA: Harvard University Press, 1993.

11 W E B Du Bois, *The Souls of Black Folk,* Chicago: A C McClurg & Co., 1903.

12 Massey and Denton, *American Apartheid,* 33.

13 Chat Travieso, 'A Nation of Walls: The Overlooked History of

Race Barriers in the United States,' Places Journal, September 2020, placesjournal.org.

14 Sarah Schindler, 'Architectural Exclusion: Discrimination and Segregation Through Physical Design of the Built Environment,' *Yale Law Journal* 124: 6, 2015.

15 Douglas Murray, *The Strange Death of Europe: Immigration, Identity, Islam,* London: Bloomsbury Continuum, 2018.

16 Murray, *The Strange Death of Europe,* 2.

17 Douglas Murray, 'What Are We to Do About Islam? A Speech to the Pim Fortuyn Memorial Conference on Europe and Islam,' The Hague, 3 March 2006.

18 Staff and Agencies, 'Britain "Sleepwalking to Segregation",' *The Guardian,* 29 September 2005.

19 Ludi Simpson and Nissa Finney, *'Sleepwalking to Segregation'? Challenging Myths About Race and Migration,* Bristol, England: Policy Press, 2009.

20 Cited in Bridge Initiative Team, 'Factsheet: No-go Zone Conspiracy Theory,' 22 May 2020, bridge.georgetown.edu.

21 MailOnline report, 'Among the Mosques: Author's Study of Muslim Britain Reveals a No-go Area for White People, Children "Attacked for Being White," Parents Making Families Live under Taliban-like Rules and Women Who Can't Leave Home Without Permission,' MailOnline, 4 June 2021, dailymail.co.uk

22 Murray, 'What Are We to Do About Islam?' 110–11.

23 See Daniel Pipes, 'The 751 No-go Zones of France,' 15 November 2006, updated 17 January 2015, danielpipes.org/blog/.

24 See 'Merkel Says Germany Has "No-go Areas;" Gov't Won't Say Where,' Associated Press, 28 February 2018, apnews.com.

25 George Packer, 'The Other France,' *The New Yorker,* 24 August 2015.

26 See for instance France 24, 'Macron Outlines Plan to Fight "Islamist Separatism" in France,' 2 October 2020, france24.com.

27 Kim Willsher, 'Macron Outlines New Law to Prevent "Islamist Separatism" in France,' *The Guardian,* 2 October 2020.

28 Loïc Wacquant, *Urban Outcasts: A Comparative Sociology of Advanced Marginality,* Cambridge, MA: Polity, 2008, 162.

29 Wacquant, *Urban Outcasts,* 143.

30 Murray, 'What Are We to Do About Islam?'

31 Murray, *The Strange Death of Europe,* 263.

32 Charlemagne, 'The Swiss Minaret Ban.'

33 Emily Harris, 'Two Mosques, Two Different Reactions in Germany,' National Public Radio, 11 October 2007.

34 'European Politicians React to Swiss Minaret Ban,' Dw-world.de, 30 November 2009.

35 Marine Le Pen, public meeting, Lyon, France, 10 December 2010, cited in Catherine Fieschi, 'Report: Muslims and the Secular City: How Right-wing Populists Shape the French Debate Over Islam,' Brookings, 28 February 2020, Brookings.edu.

36 Fieschi, 'Report.'

37 Kasia Narkowicz and Konrad Pedziwiatr, 'From Unproblematic to Contentious: Mosques in Poland,' *Journal of Ethnic and Migration Studies* 43: 3, 2017, 441–57.

38 Annabel Tremlett and Vera Messing, 'Hungary's Future: Anti-immigration, Anti-multiculturalism and Anti-Roma?' Open Democracy, 4 August 2015, opendemocracy.net.

39 Diana Darke, *Stealing from the Saracens: How Islamic Architecture Shaped Europe,* London: Hurst, 2020.

40 Oliver Wainwright, 'Looted Landmarks: How Notre-Dame, Big Ben and St Mark's Were Stolen from the East,' *The Guardian*, 13 August 2020.

41 Oliver Wainwright, 'The "Mega-mosque" and the "Mega-church": The Battle over London's Sacred Sites,' *The Guardian*, 29 October 2015.

42 Irene Cheng, Charles L Davis II, and Mabel O Wilson, eds, *Race and Modern Architecture: A Critical History from the Enlightenment to the Present*, Pittsburgh: University of Pittsburgh Press, 2020, 134–52.

43 Quoted in Nightingale, *Segregation*. Nigel Cameron, *An Illustrated History of Hong Kong*, Oxford: Oxford University Press, 1991.

44 Edwy Plenel, *For the Muslims: Islamophobia in France*, London: Verso, 2016, 38.

4. Authenticity: The Material Truth

1 John Ruskin, *The Seven Lamps of Architecture*, London: Smith, Elder, and Co., 1849, 79, in chapter VI, 'The Lamp of Memory'.

2 Roger Michel, 'Interview with the BBC World Service,' 19 April 2016, quoted in 'IDA Palmyra Arch Copy', factumfoundation. org.

3 John Ruskin, *The Seven Lamps of Architecture*, London: Smith, Elder, and Co., 1849, 79, in chapter VI, 'The Lamp of Memory'.

4 Chandler and Pace (2020)

5 The author is a member of ICOMOS and ICORP, the International Scientific Committee on Risk Preparedness, the ICOMOS committee on risk preparedness.

6 *The Venice Charter.* 2nd International Congress of Architects and

Technicians of Historic Monuments, Venice, (1964). Adopted by ICOMOS 1965.

7 For a longer discussion of Warsaw's destruction see: Robert Bevan, *The Destruction of Memory: Architecture at War*, London: Reaktion, 2006, 94–98, 181–84.

8 Bevan, *The Destruction of Memory,* 181–84.

9 Jasper Goldman, 'Warsaw: Reconstruction as Propaganda,' in Lawrence J Vale and Thomas J Campanella, eds, *The Resilient City: How Modern Cities Recover from Disaster*, Oxford: Oxford University Press, 2005, 135–58.

10 Goldman, 'Warsaw,' 142.

11 Goldman, 'Warsaw,' 142.

12 Goldman, 'Warsaw,' xx.

13 B Rymaszewski, 'Motywacje polityczne i narodowe zwiazane z zabytkami,' in A Tomaszewski, ed., *Badania i ochrona zabytków w Polsce w XX wieku* [Research on and Protection of Monuments in 20th Century Poland], Warsaw: Towarzystwo Opieki nad Zabytkami, 2000.

14 John Darlington, *Fake Heritage: Why We Rebuild Monuments,* Princeton: Yale University Press, 2020.

15 Visit to the cathedral by the author in May 2021.

16 James W Loewen, *Lies Across America,* New York: Simon & Schuster, 2000, citing Dwight Pitcaithley, 'A Splendid Hoax: The Strange Case of Lincoln's Birthplace Cabin: The Making of an American Icon,' Washington, DC: National Museum of American History Colloquium, typescript, n.d.

17 Sally Foster and Siân Jones, *New Futures for Replicas. Principles and Guidance for Museums and Heritage,* 2020, University of Stirling, replicas.stir.ac.uk/principles-and-guidance/.

18 Robert Bevan, 'Ruin or Rebuild? Conserving Heritage in an Age of Terrorism,' *The Art Newspaper*, 2017, 286.

19 Interview with the author for *The Art Newspaper*, 2016.

20 Simon Jenkins, 'After Palmyra, the Message to ISIS: What You Destroy, We Will Rebuild,' *The Guardian*, 29 March 2016.

21 Author's interview, 13 October 2016.

22 Declaration of Dresden on the 'Reconstruction of Monuments Destroyed by War,' 1982, ICMOS.org.

23 Mohammad Shehzad, 'The Rediff Interview/Mullah Omar,' Rediff.com, 12 April 2004.

24 See Bevan, *The Destruction of Memory.*

25 See Bevan, *The Destruction of Memory;* Helen Walasek, *Bosnia and the Destruction of Cultural Heritage,* Milton Park, UK: Routledge, 2015.

26 For the text of the Nara Document, see International Council

on Monuments and Sites, 'The Nara Document on Authenticity (1994),' icomos.org/charters/nara-e.pdf. See also Christina Cameron and Nobuko Inaba, 'The Making of the Nara Document on Authenticity,' *The Journal of Preservation Technology* 46: 4, 2015, 30–37.

27 For an account of this episode, see Tom Brigden, *Value in the View: Conserving Historic Urban Views,* London: RIBA Publishing, 2018.

28 Inscription available at whc.unesco.org/en/list/946.

29 Gordana Knezevic, 'Mostar, Bosnia's Most Divided City', Radio Free Europe/Radio Liberty, 8 August, 2017, rferl.org.

30 Azra Hromadzic, *Citizens of an Empty Nation: Youth and State-Making in Post-war Bosnia Herzegovina* (The Ethnography of Political Violence), Philadelphia: University of Pennsylvania Press, 2015.

31 Ian Traynor, 'Bridge Opens but Mostar Remains a Divided City, *The Guardian,* 23 July 2004.

32 Gülen Sarial-Abi, Ezgi Merdin-Uygur, and Zeynep Gürhan-Canli, 'Responses to Replica (vs. Genuine) Touristic Experiences,' *Annals of Tourism Research* 83, 2020.

33 Jesse Prinz, 'How Wonder Works,' Aeon, 21 June 2013, aeon.co.

34 Hannah Arendt, *The Human Condition,* New York: Doubleday Anchor, 1958.

5. The Military-Heritage Complex

1 Yannis Hamilakis, 'The "War on Terror" and the Military–Archaeology Complex: Iraq, Ethics, and Neo-colonialism,' *Archaeologies: Journal of the World Archaeological Congress* 5, 2009, 39–65.

2 Jessica Holland, 'In War Against ISIL, a Fine Line Between Facts and Artifacts,' Aljazeera America, 22 October 2014, america. aljazeera.com.

3 Holland, 'In War Against ISIL."

4 The author is a member of the UK Committee of the Blue Shield and ICOMOS-ICORP.

5 See Robert Bevan, *The Destruction of Memory: Architecture at War,* London: Reaktion Books (2007).

6 Bevan, *The Destruction of Memory.*

7 Yannis Hamilakis, 'The "War on Terror" and the Military–Archaeology Complex: Iraq, Ethics, and Neo-colonialism,' *Archaeologies: Journal of the World Archaeological Congress* 5, 2009, 39–65.

8 Umberto Albarella, 'Archaeologists in Conflict: Empathizing with Which Victims?' *Heritage Management* 2: 1, 2009, 105–14, sheffield.ac.uk.

9 Emma Cunliffe, 'No Strike Lists – From Use to Abuse?' Heritage in War, n.d., heritageinwar.com.

10 Hamilakis, 'The "War on Terror",'

11 Hamilakis, 'The "War on Terror".'

12 Albarella, 'Archaeologists in Conflict.'

13 Interview with the author, November 2019.

14 Jesse Casana, 'Satellite Imagery-Based Analysis of Archaeological Looting in Syria,' *Near Eastern Archaeology* 78: 3, 2015, 142–52.

15 James Cuno, Letters to the Editor, *New York Times*, 11 March 2015.

16 See 'As ISIS Destroys Artifacts, Could Some Antiquities Have Been Saved?' NPR Broadcast, 5 September 2015, npr.org.

17 Hamilakis, 'The "War on Terror".'

18 Hamilakis, 'The "War on Terror".'

19 Morag M. Kersel and Christina Luke, 'Civil Societies? Heritage Diplomacy and Neo-imperialism,' in Lynn Meskell, ed., *Global Heritage: A Reader*, West Sussex, UK: John Wiley & Sons, 2015, 70, 84. Quoted, with thanks, from a draft paper by Patty Gerstenblith 'Toward a Human Rights-Based Approach as an Element in Post-Conflict Cultural Heritage Reconstruction' (forthcoming, subject to change).

20 See press release, 'Landmark ICC Verdict against Al-Mahdi Must Be First Step to Broader Justice in Mali Conflict', 27 September 2016, amnesty.org.

21 Strategy for the reinforcement of the Organization's actions for the protection of culture and the promotion of cultural pluralism in the event of armed conflict (38/C48). Adopted November 2015 at the 38th General Conference of UNESCO.

22 'For the Protection of Culture and the Promotion of Cultural Pluralism in the Event of Armed Conflict,' adopted October 2016 by UNESCO Executive Board.

23 Lynn Meskell, *A Future in Ruins: UNESCO, World Heritage and the Dream of Peace*, Oxford: Oxford University Press, 2018. p120-121

24 Meskell, *A Future in Ruins,* 106.

25 Luke Harding, Caelainn Barr, and Dina Nagapetyants, 'UK at Centre of Secret $3 Bn Azerbaijani Money Laundering and Lobbying Scheme,' *The Guardian*, 4 September 2017. Dorian Batycka, 'Armenian Monuments in Line of Fire in Nagorno-Karabakh Conflict,' *The Art Newspaper*, 26 October 2020.

26 Tom Wescott, 'Inside the Medieval Castle That Survived a 21st Century War,' Middleasteye.net, 11 April 2019.
27 Allison Cuneo, Susan Penacho, Michael Danti, Marina Gabriel, and Jamie O'Connell, 'Special Report: The Recapture of Palmyra,' ASOR, March 2016, asor.org.
28 April 2016 petition, 'UNESCO: To Act as a Neutral Organization and Stop the Palmyra Reconstruction Plans,' secure.avaaz.org.
29 Lemma Shehadi, 'The Battle for Palmyra,' *Disegno*, no. 16, 11 January 2018, medium.com.
30 Shehadi, 'The Battle for Palmyra.'
31 Interview with the author, December 2020.
32 Cuneo et al., 'Special Report.'

6. The Evidence of History

1 Raphael Lemkin (1948) 'Letter to James Rosenberg', September 21, 1948
2 Robert Bevan, 'Turner Prize-shortlisted Forensic Architecture's Eyal Weizman: "I Want to Win Cases –not Prizes",' *Evening Standard,* 3 July 2018. For the use of architecture, archaeology, and heritage in the Israel/Palestinian conflict, see also Robert Bevan, *The Destruction of Memory: Architecture at War*, London: Reaktion, 2006.
3 Weizman: 'I Want to Win Cases – not Prizes.'
4 Eyal Weizman, *Forensic Architecture: Violence at the Threshold of Detectability*, New York: Zone Books, 2017, 52.
5 Weizman, *Forensic Architecture.*
6 Weizman, *Forensic Architecture*, 23.
7 Weizman, *Forensic Architecture*, 24.
8 Aditya Chakrabortty, 'Over 170 Years After Engels, Britain Is Still a Country That Murders Its Poor,' *The Guardian*, 20 June 2017.
9 Deborah Lipstadt, *Denying the Holocaust: The Growing Assault on Truth and Memory,* New York: The Free Press, 1993.
10 Robert Jan van Pelt, *The Case for Auschwitz: Evidence from the Irving Trial,* Bloomington: Indiana University Press, 2002, 400. See also the website Holocaust Denial on Trial, hdot.org.
11 Jan van Pelt, *The Case for Auschwitz,* 207.
12 Jan van Pelt, *The Case for Auschwitz,* 191.
13 Jan van Pelt, *The Case for Auschwitz,* 448.
14 Jan van Pelt, *The Case for Auschwitz,* 207.
15 Jan van Pelt, *The Case for Auschwitz,* 370.
16 Daniel Keren, Jamie McCarthy, and Harry W Mazal, 'The Ruins of the Gas Chambers: A Forensic Investigation of Crematoriums

at Auschwitz I and Auschwitz-Birkenau,' *Holocaust and Genocide Studies* 18: 1, 2004, 68–103.

17 Keren et al., 'The Ruins of the Gas Chambers.'

18 Richard J Evans, *Lying About Hitler: History, Holocaust and the David Irving Trial*, New York: Basic Books, 2003.

19 Evans, *Lying About Hitler,* 187.

20 Evans, *Lying About Hitler,* xx.

21 Evans, *Lying About Hitler,* 250.

22 Evans, *Lying About Hitler,* 253.

23 Deborah Dwork and Robert Jan van Pelt, *Auschwitz: 1270 to the Present*, New York: Norton, 1996, 259.

24 Dwork and Jan van Pelt, *Auschwitz,* 363.

25 Dwork and Jan van Pelt, *Auschwitz,* 364.

26 Eric Conan, 'La Mémoire du Mal,' *L'Express,* 19 January 1995 (author's translation).

27 Jan van Pelt, *The Case for Auschwitz,* 58.

28 Robert Faurisson, 'The "Gas Chamber" of Aschwitz I,' Institute for Historical Review, ihr.org.

29 Author's visit, September 2020.

30 Chris Bryant, *The Glamour Boys*, London: Bloomsbury, 2021, 145

31 Press Release: Judgement of Trial Chamber III in the Kordic and Cerkez Case, United Nations International Criminal Tribunal for the Former Yugoslavia, 26 February 2001, icty.org.

32 Raphael Lemkin, *Axis Rule in Occupied Europe: Laws of Occupation, Analysis of Government, Proposals for Redress*, Washington, DC: Carnegie Endowment for International Peace, Division of International Law, 1994.

33 Donald Bloxham and A Dirk Moses, eds, *The Oxford Handbook of Genocide Studies*, Oxford: Oxford University Press, 2010.

34 Bloxham and Moses, eds, *The Oxford Handbook of Genocide Studies.*

35 Leora Bilsky and Rachel Klagsbrun, 'The Return of Cultural Genocide?' *European Journal of International Law* 29: 2, 2018, 373–96.

36 Bevan, *The Destruction of Memory.*

37 'Director-General of UNESCO Appeals for Protection of Syria's Cultural Heritage,' UNESCO World Heritage Convention, 30 March 2012, whc.Unesco.org.

38 Serge Brammertz, Kevin C Hughes, Alison Kipp, and William B Tomljanovich, 'Attacks Against Cultural Heritage as a Weapon of War: Prosecutions at the ICTY,' *Journal of International Criminal Justice* 14: 5, 2016, 1143–74.

39 Judge Antônio A. Cançado Trindade, *The Construction of a*

Humanized International Law, Leiden; Boston: Brill Nijhoff, 2015, p. 197.

40 Jonathan Jones, 'Destroying Priceless Art Is Vile and Offensive – but It Is Not a War Crime,' *The Guardian*, 22 August 2016.

41 Damien Short, 'Reconciliation, Assimilation, and the Indigenous Peoples of Australia,' *International Political Science Review* 24: 4, 2003, 491–513.

42 Tonya Gonnella Frichner, 'Preliminary Study of the Impact on Indigenous Peoples of the International Legal Construct Known as the Doctrine of Discovery,' E/C.19/2010/13. Presented at the Permanent Forum on Indigenous Issues, Ninth Session, United Nations Economic and Social Council, New York, 27 April 2010.

43 Bruce Pascoe, *Dark Emu: Aboriginal Australia and the Birth of Agriculture*, London: Scribe, 2014.

44 Dark Emu Exposed – The Myth of Aboriginal Agriculture, dark-emu-exposed.org/ home/2016/2/9/bisecting-your-loft. Paul Memmott, *Gunyah Goondie + Wurley: The Aboriginal Architecture of Australia*, Brisbane: University of Queensland Press, 2007.

45 Memmott, *Gunyah Goondie + Wurley*, 193.

46 Keryn Walshe and Peter Sutton, *Farmers or Hunter-Gatherers? The Dark Emu Debate*, Melbourne: Melbourne University Press, 2021.

47 Stuart Rintoul, 'Debunking Dark Emu: Did the Publishing Phenomenon Get It Wrong?' *Sydney Morning Herald*, 12 June 2021.

48 Raphael Lemkin, 'Letter to James Rosenberg, September 21, 1948,' American Jewish Historical Society, *Raphael Lemkin Collection*, call P154, Box 1, Folder 19, 'Correspondence 1984.' Quoted in Donna-Lee Frieze, 'The Destruction of Sarajevo's Vijecnica: A Case of Genocidal Cultural Destruction' in Adam Jones, ed., *New Directions in Genocide Research*, Oxford: Routledge, 2012.

49 A Dirk Moses, 'Raphael Lemkin, Culture, and the Concept of Genocide,' in Donald Bloxham and A Dirk Moses, eds., *The Oxford Handbook on Genocide Studies*, Oxford: Oxford University Press, 2010, 19–41.

50 Barbara Harff, 'No Lessons Learned from the Holocaust? Assessing Risks of Genocide and Political Mass Murder since 1955,' *The American Political Science Review* 97: 1, 2003, 57–73.

51 See UNHRC's 'Myanmar: UN Fact-Finding Mission Releases Its Full Account of Massive Violations by Military in Rakhine, Kachin and Shan States,' United Nations Human Rights Commission, September 2018, ohchr.org.

52 Joshua Hammer, 'Demolishing Kashgar's History,' *Smithsonian Magazine*, March 2010.

53 See 'Living on the Margins: The Chinese State's Demolition of Uyghur Communities,' Uyghur Human Rights Project, March 2012, docs.uyghuramerican.org.

54 See Human Rights Watch, 'Devastating Blows: Religious Repression of the Uighurs in Xinjiang,' *Human Right Watch* 17: 2, 2005.

55 'China: Massive Crackdown in Muslim Region: Mass Arbitrary Detention, Religious Repression, Surveillance in Xinjiang,' Human Rights Watch, 9 September 2018, hrw.org.

56 Nathan Ruser, James Leibold, Kelsey Munro, and Tilla Hoja, 'Cultural Erasure: Tracing the Destruction of Uyghur and Islamic Spaces in Xinjiang,' Australian Strategic Policy Institute, 24 September 2020, aspi.org.au.

57 Rachel Harris, 'Uygur Heritage and the Charge of Cultural Genocide in Xinjang,' 2020, globalpolicysolutions.org.

58 Harris, 'Uygur Heritage.'

59 Gulbahar Haitiwaji with Rozen Morgat, 'Our Souls Are Dead: How I Survived a Chinese Re-education Camp for Uighurs,' *The Guardian*, 12 January 2021.

7. White Lies, Misunderstandings, and Well-meaning Myths

1 De Botton, A. (2006). *The Architecture of Happiness*. Toronto, McClelland & Stewart.

2 Madge Dresser, 'Squares of Distinction, Webs of Interest: Gentility, Urban Development and the Slave Trade in Bristol c.1673–1820,' *Slavery & Abolition* 21: 3, 2000, 21–47.

3 Jenny Wüstenberg, *Civil Society and Memory in Postwar Germany*, Cambridge: Cambridge University Press, 2018, 42–49.

4 Wüstenberg, *Civil Society and Memory in Postwar Germany*, 84.

5 Hugo Hamilton, 'The Loneliness of Being German,' *The Guardian*, 7 September 2004.

6 Interview with the author, July 2020.

7 See BOE [Official State Gazette], 2 April 1940. Bulletin 93, 2240.

8 Giles Tremlett, *Ghosts of Spain*, London: Faber & Faber, 2007, 42.

9 David Sharrock, 'Spain Reclaims Franco's Shrine,' *Sunday Times*, 2 November 2004.

10 James Stout, 'Toppling Statues Has Always Been Democracy In Its Purest Form', *Esquire*, 10th June, 2020.

11 TAN. *Saddam's statues should not be destroyed* DONNY GEORGE 1st March 2008 00:00 GMT

12 Dario Gamboni, *The Destruction of Art: Iconoclasm and Vandalism Since the French Revolution*, London: Reaktion Books, 2007, 51–90.

13 Gamboni, *The Destruction of Art*, 64.

14 Available at leninstatues.ru.

15 Gamboni, *The Destruction of Art*, 73.

16 Timothy Ryback, *Contested Histories in Public Spaces: Principles, Processes, Best Practices*, International Bar Association, 2021, 152–53, ibanet.org/contested-histories.

17 Ryback, *Contested Histories in Public Spaces*, 162.

18 Gamboni, *The Destruction of Art*, 58.

19 Mitch Landrieu's speech at the Gallier Hall, New Orleans, 'On the Removal of Four Confederate Monuments in New Orleans,' 19 May 2017, americanrhetoric.com.

20 Caroline Criado-Perez, *Invisible Women: Exposing Data Bias in a World Designed for Men*, New York: Abrams Press, 2019.

21 Sarah Schulman, *Conflict Is not Abuse: Overstating Harm, Community Responsibility and the Duty of Repair*, Vancouver: Arsenal Pulp Press, 2020.

22 Helen Pluckrose and James Lindsay, *Cynical Theories: How Universities Made Everything about Race, Gender, and Identity – And Why This Harms Everybody*, Durham, NC: Pitchford, 2020.

23 Pluckrose and Lindsay, *Cynical Theories*, 227.

24 Greg Lukianoff and Jonathan Haidt, *The Coddling of the American Mind: How Good Intentions and Bad Ideas Are Setting up a Generation for Failure*, New York: Penguin: 2018.

25 Pluckrose and Lindsay, *Cynical Theories*, 227.

26 Joanna Burch-Brown, 'Should Slavery's Statues Be Preserved? On Transitional Justice and Contested Heritage,' *Journal of Applied Philosophy* 20, 2020.

27 Burch-Brown, 'Should Slavery's Statues Be Preserved?' 3.

28 Burch-Brown, 'Should Slavery's Statues Be Preserved?' 5.

29 Burch-Brown, 'Should Slavery's Statues Be Preserved?' 5.

30 Burch-Brown, 'Should Slavery's Statues Be Preserved?' 6.

31 Chelsey Carter, "Racist Monuments Are Killing Us,' *Museum Anthropology* 41: 2, 2018, 139–41.

32 Carter, 'Racist Monuments Are Killing Us.' 139–41.

33 Chelsey Carter and Allison Mickel, 'Statues Memorialize Everything in a Person's History, Including Torture,' *St Louis Post-Dispatch*, 10 September 2020.

34 Clarence C Gravlee, 'How Race Becomes Biology: Embodiment of Social Inequality,' *American Journal of Physical Anthropology* 139: 1, 2009, 47–57.

35 Nancy Krieger, 'Methods for the Scientific Study of Discrimination and Health: An Ecosocial Approach,' *American Journal of Public Health* 102: 5, 2012, 936–44.

36 Tim Timmerman, 'A Case for Removing Confederate Monuments,'

in Bob Fischer, ed., *Ethics, Left and Right: The Moral Issues that Divide Us*, New York: Oxford University Press, 2020, 513–22.

37 Heather A O'Connell, 'Monuments Outlive History: Confederate Monuments, the Legacy of Slavery, and Black-White Inequality,' *Ethnic and Racial Studies* 43: 3, 2020, 460–78.

38 Alain de Botton, *The Architecture of Happiness*, Toronto: McClelland & Stewart, 2006.

39 Simon Richards, *Architect Knows Best: Environmental Determinism in Architecture Culture from 1956 to the Present*, London: Routledge, 2016, 45.

40 Alice Coleman, *Utopia on Trial: Vision and Reality in Planned Housing*, London: Hilary Shipman, 1985.

41 Coleman, *Utopia on Trial*, 6.

42 Interview with Alice Coleman, 'Alice in Wonderland,' Create Streets Blog, 2014, createstreets.com.

43 Richards, *Architect Knows Best*, 134.

44 George Kelling and James Wilson, 'Broken Windows,' *The Atlantic*, March 1982.

45 See, for instance, Bernard E Harcourt and Jens Ludwig, 'Broken Windows: New Evidence from New York City and a Five-City Social Experiment,' *The University of Chicago Law Review* 73: 1, 2006, 271–320.

46 Christina B. Hanhardt in *Policing the Planet: Why the Policing Crisis Led to Black Lives Matter* **edited by** Jordan T. Camp **and** Christina Heatherton (2016) London: Verso.

47 Ibid

48 Paul Keedwell, *Headspace: The Psychology of City Living*, London: Aurum Press, 2017, 30.

49 Amanda Kolson Hurley, 'This Is Your Brain on Architecture,' Bloomberg City Lab, 14 July 2017, bloomberg.com/news.

50 Burch-Brown, 'Should Slavery's Statues Be Preserved?' 9.

51 Mark Fisher, 'Exiting the Vampire Castle,' *The North Star*, 22 November 2013.

52 Criado-Perez, *Invisible Women*.

53 Lanre Bakare, 'Angela Davis: "We Knew That the Role of the Police Was to Protect White Supremacy",' *The Guardian*, 15 June 2020.

54 Interview with Angela Davis on Democracy Now! 12 June 2020, democracynow.org.

55 Interview with Angela Davis on Democracy Now!

56 Ailsa Chang, 'Civil Rights Activist Argues to Keep Confederate Monuments,' National Public Radio, 23 August 2017, npr.org.

57 Erin L Thompson, 'The South's Monuments Will Rise Again,' *Washington Post*, 5 March 2021.

58 Aamna Mohdin, 'David Olusoga on Race and Reality: "My Job Is to Be a Historian. It's Not to Make People Feel Good",' *The Guardian*, 7 June 2021.

59 Sean **Coughlan**, 'TV Historian Rejects "Nonsense" Over Keeping Statues,' BBC News, 2 February 2021.

60 Gary Younge, 'Why Every Single Statue Should Come Down,' *The Guardian*, 1 June 2021.

61 Damien Gayle, '"A Potent Historical Artefact": The Statue of Edward Colston's New Role,' *The Guardian*, 4 June 2021.

62 Ibid.

63 Rosemary Hill, *Time's Witness: History in the Age of Romanticism*, London: Allen Lane. 2021, 54-55.

64 Jean-François Manicom, 'Museum Gets to Grips with Painful Legacy of Slavery,' *The Times*, 10 June 2020.

65 Burch-Brown, 'Should Slavery's Statues Be Preserved?' 8.

66 Timmerman, 'A Case for Removing Confederate Monuments.'

8. Subversive Transformation

1 Interview with Arendt by Joachim C. Fest, 9 November, 1964. basrelief-bolzano.com.

2 Interview with the author, November 2020.

3 Derek Alderman, 'Place Naming and the Interpretation of Cultural Landscapes,' in Brian Graham and Peter Howard, eds, *The Ashgate Research Companion to Heritage and Identity*, Farnham, UK: Ashgate, 2006.

4 Bil Browning, 'Vandals Paint Stonewall Statues to Protest "Whitewashing",' *The Advocate*, 19 August 2015.

5 Hammad Nassar, 'In Order to Be British We Must Acknowledge Our "Indianness",' 15 September 2017, tate.org.uk.

6 Jack Latimore, 'There Are Few Memorials to Australia's Bloody History but That's Changing,' *The Guardian*, 4 March 2019.

7 Joanna Burch-Brown, 'Should Slavery's Statues Be Preserved? On Transitional Justice and Contested Heritage,' *Journal of Applied Philosophy* 20, 2020, 8.

8 Albert Boime, 'Perestroika and the Destablization of Soviet Monuments,' *Ars II-III*, 1993, 211–16.

9 Lecture by Professor Bluestone at the Soane Museum, London, 9 March 2017.

10 See 'Sights,' Memento Park, mementopark.hu/en.

11 Mitch Landrieu's speech at the Gallier Hall, New Orleans, 'On the Removal of Four Confederate Monuments in New Orleans,' 19 May 2017, americanrhetoric.com.

12 Lecture available as Stuart Hall, 'Whose Heritage: Un-settling "The Heritage," Re-imagining the Post-nation,' *Third Text* 13: 49, 1999, 3–13, tandfonline.com.

13 Erica Doss, *Memorial Mania: Public Feeling in America*, Chicago: University of Chicago Press, 2010, 319.

14 Doss, *Memorial Mania,* 310.

15 Oration by Frederick Douglass, delivered on the occasion of the unveiling of the Freedmen's Monument in Memory of Abraham Lincoln, in Lincoln Park, Washington, DC, 14 April 1876, loc. gov/item/12006733/.

16 Oration by Frederick Douglass.

17 Harold Holzer, 'Lincoln, Monuments and Memory in Confederate Statues and Memorialisation,' in Catherine Clinton, *Confederate Statues and Memorialization*, Athens: The University of Georgia Press, 2019.

18 Jonathan W White and Scott Sandage, 'What Frederick Douglass Had to Say About Monuments,' *Smithsonian Magazine*, 30 June 2020, smithsonianmag.com.

19 White and Sandage, 'What Frederick Douglass Had to Say.'

20 Charlotte Higgins, 'Phil Collins: Why I Took a Soviet Statue of Engels across Europe to Manchester,' *The Guardian*, 30 June 2017.

21 From the Design & Access Statement supporting the application to Westminster City Council for planning permission for the Fawcett statue.

22 The author is a member of the Mayor of London's Commission on Diversity in the Public Realm.

23 National Capital Planning Commission, *Memorials Trends & Practice in Washington, DC*, November 2013, ncpc.gov.

24 National Capital Planning Commission, *Memorials Trends & Practice in Washington, DC.*

25 Chiara Grilli, 'A Cubist Portrait of Christopher Columbus: Studying Monuments as Transcultural Works,' in Laura A Macaluso, *Monument Culture: International Perspectives on the Future of Monuments in a Changing World*, Lanham, MD: Rowman & Littlefield, 2019, 146.

26 Jochen Gerz in Achim Könneke, ed., *Jochen Gerz / Esther Shalev-Gerz: Das Harburger Mahnmal gegen Faschismus* [Monument against Fascism], Ostfildern: Hatje Cantz, 1994.

27 James E Young, 'The End of the Monument in Germany,' *Harvard Design Magazine,* no. 9, 1999.

28 Cited in Sanford Levison, *Written in Stone*, Durham, NC: Duke University Press, 1998.

29 Perry Anderson, 'Union Sucrée,' *London Review of Books* 26: 18, 23 September 2004.

30 Anderson, 'Union Sucrée.'
31 Young, 'The End of the Monument in Germany.'
32 David Rieff, *In Praise of Forgetting*, New Haven: Yale University Press, 2016.
33 Rieff, *In Praise of Forgetting*, 54–55.
34 Rieff, *In Praise of Forgetting*, 36.
35 Rieff, *In Praise of Forgetting*, 58-59.
36 Rieff, *In Praise of Forgetting*, 99.
37 Nelson Mandela, Statement of the National Executive Committee of the ANC on the Occasion of the 84th Anniversary of the African National Congress, 8 January 1996.
38 UN General Assembly, Report of the Special Rapporteur in the Field of Cultural Rights, Farida Shaheed, 'Memorialisation Processes,' Human Rights Council, 25th session, 3–28 March 2014. Agenda item 3, digitallibrary.un.org.
39 UN General Assembly, Report of the Special Rapporteur.
40 UN General Assembly, Report of the Special Rapporteur.

9. What Is to Be Done? The Monumental and Its Limits

1 Jameson, F. (2003), 'Future City', *New Left Review*, May/June.
2 Sergio Rame, 'Un led per coprire Mussolini. Polemica a Bolzano: "Atto talebano",' *IlGiornale*, 5 February 2017.
3 Rame, 'Un led per coprire Mussolini.'
4 Rame, 'Un led per coprire Mussolini.'
5 Interview with the author, 21 February 2021
6 Email interview with the author, February 2021.
7 Cian O'Driscoll, *Victory: The Triumph and Tragedy of Just War*, Oxford: Oxford University Press, 2019, 51.
8 Albert Boime, 'Perestroika and the Destabilization of Soviet Monuments,' *Ars II-III*, 1993, 211–16.
9 Scott Jenkins, 'Nietzsche's Use of Monumental History,' *Journal of Nietzsche Studies* 45: 2, 2014, 169–81, citing Friedrich Nietzsche's essay 'On the Advantage and Disadvantage of History for Life' (in the original German, 'Vom Nutzen und Nachteil der Historie für das Leben'), written in 1874 as part of his second 'Untimely Meditation,'
10 James E. Young, 'The End of the Monument in Germany,' *Harvard Design Magazine*, no. 9, 1999.
11 Jos Boys, 'Can a Building Be Sexist?' *Financial Times*, 15 May 2021.
12 Young, *'The End of the Monument in Germany'*.

13 Deborah Dwork and Robert Jan van Pelt, *Auschwitz: 1270 to the Present*, New York: Norton, 1996, 378.

14 'Cash Crisis Threat to Auschwitz,' BBC News, 26 January 2009.

15 Canon

16 Canon

17 Catherine Hickley, 'Nazi Site in Nuremberg to Be Preserved but Not Restored,' *The Art Newspaper*, 20 May 2019.

18 'Former Nazi Rally Building to Serve as Opera House,' Deutsche Welle, 15 December 2021, dw.com.

19 Alternative for Germany National Action Plan on Cultural Identity, Bundestag paper 19/28794, 21 April 2021.

20 Ibid

21 See for instance: Alex Callinicos, 'Neoliberal Capitalism Implodes: Global Catastrophe and the Far-right Today,' *International Socialism* 170, April 2021.

22 Frederic Jameson, 'Future City,' *New Left Review*, May/June 2003.

23 Patrick Barkham, 'National Trust Sacking Education Officers "Will Hit Worst Off Children",' *The Guardian*, 29 August 2020.

24 Tom Wall, 'Keep Out of Bristol's Slaver Street Names Debate, Ministers Are Told,' *The Observer*, 21 February 2021.

25 International Scientific Committee on Risk Preparedness, 'On the Road, Episode 5: Kartarpur Corridor – Collective Memories, Connected Histories,' 14 February 2021, youtube.com.

26 Cornelius Holtorf, 'What's Wrong With Cultural Diversity in World Archaeology?' *Claroscuro* 16: 16, 2017, 1–14.

27 Cornelius Holtorf, 'Embracing Change: How Cultural Resilience Is Increased Through Cultural Heritage,' *World Archaeology* 50: 4, 2018, 639–50.

28 Amartya Sen, *Identity & Violence: The Illusion of Destiny*, London: Penguin, 2007.

29 Holtorf, 'Embracing Change.'

30 See Neil Leach, 'Architecture or Revolution,' 2009, neilleach. files.wordpress.com.

31 Joseph Lowndes, 'Far-right Extremism Dominates the GOP. It Didn't Start – and Won't End – With Trump,' *Washington Post*, 8 November 2021.

32 Aamna Mohdin and Rachel Hall, 'Half of Britons Do not Know 6m Jews Were Murdered in Holocaust,' *The Guardian*, 10 November 2021.

Index